FIRES WERE **STARTED**

FIRES WERE **STARTED**

British Cinema and Thatcherism

second edition

edited by Lester Friedman

 WALLFLOWER PRESS LONDON & NEW YORK

First edition published by University of Minnesota Press in 1993

First edition published in Great Britain by UCL Press in 1993

This second, revised and updated edition published in Great Britain in 2006
Wallflower Press
6a Middleton Place, Langham Street, London W1W 7TE
www.wallflowerpress.co.uk

Copyright © Lester D. Friedman 2006

The moral right of Lester D. Friedman to be identified as the editor of this work has been asserted
in accordance with the Copyright, Designs and Patents Act of 1988.

All rights reserved; no part of this publication may be reproduced, stored in a retrieval system,
or transported in any form or by any means, electronic, mechanical, photocopying, recording
or otherwise, without the prior permission of both the copyright owners and the above
publisher of this book.

A catalogue record for this book is available from the British Library.

ISBN 1-904764-71-1 (pbk)
ISBN 1-904764-72-X (hbk)

Book design by Elsa Mathern

Printed by Replika Press Pvt Ltd., India

CONTENTS

LIST OF CONTRIBUTORS

Susan Torrey Barber is Associate Professor of Film in the School of Film and Television at Loyola Marymount University. She has published a variety of articles in *Film Quarterly* and *The Spectator* and is the recipient of the Mary Pickford Scholarship. Her academic specialities include Australian, British and Irish cinema, as well as melodrama, the western and the road picture in American cinema. Currently, she is completing a book on Australian Cinema from 1970 to the present.

Mary Desjardins is Associate Professor of Film and Television Studies at Dartmouth College. She has published widely in journals and anthologies on film and television history, feminist filmmaking and stardom. She has two books forthcoming: *Recycled Stars: The Female Star in the Age of Television and Video* and a critical anthology on Marlene Dietrich (co-edited with Gerd Gemunden).

Manthia Diawara is Professor of Comparative Literature and Africana Studies at New York University. He is the author of several highly acclaimed books, including *African Cinema: Politics and Culture* (1992), *Black American Cinema* (1993), *In Search of Africa* (1998) and *We Won't Budge: An African Exile in the World* (2003). In addition, he is the editor-in-chief of *Black Renaissance/Renaissance Noire,* as well as a filmmaker whose areas of specialisation include Africa, the United States and the Black Diaspora in Europe. His film credits include *Sembene Ousmane: The Making of African Cinema* (1993), *Rouch in Reverse* (1995), *In Search of Africa* (1999), *Diaspora Conversation* (2000) and *Bamako Sigi Kan* (2002).

Thomas Elsaesser is Professor in the Department of Media and Culture and Director of Research Film and Television at the University of Amsterdam. Among his publications are *Fassbinder's Germany: History, Identity, Subject* (1996), *Cinema Futures: Cain, Abel or Cable?* (1998), *The BFI Companion to German Cinema* (1999), *Weimar Cinema and After* (2000), *Studying Contemporary American Film* (2002, with Warren Buckland), *European Cinema: Face to Face with Hollywood* (2003) and *The Last Great American Picture Show: Hollywood Films in the 1970s* (2004).

James F. English is Professor and Chair of the English Department at the University of Pennsylvania, where he has also served as an interim Director of the Film Studies Program. He is the author of *Comic Transactions: Literature, Humor, and the Politics* of *Community in 20th-Century Britain* (1994) and *The Economy of Prestige: Prizes, Awards, and the Circulation of Cultural Value* (2005), as well as editor of the *Concise Companion to Contemporary British Fiction* (2005). He is a founding member of the Editorial Board and a current editor of *Postmodern Culture*, the first all-digital, peer-reviewed journal in the humanities. He is at present working on a study of cultural trade between the UK and the US, focusing on the different discourses of race and the challenges of intralingual translation within global English.

Lester D. Friedman is Senior Scholar-in-Residence at Hobart and William Smith Colleges. His writing revolves around issues of multiculturalism, America-Jewish identity, media and medicine, and post-World War Two American cinema. His recent publications include *Bonnie and Clyde* (2000), *Cultural Studies: Essays in Medicine and Media* (2003), and *Citizen Spielberg* (2006), and a forthcoming volume entitled *America of the 1970s*.

Paul Giles is Reader in American Literature and Director of the Rothermere American Institute at the University of Oxford. Among his publications are *American Catholic Arts and Fictions: Culture, Ideology, Aesthetics* (1992), *Transatlantic Insurrections: British Culture and the Formation of American Literature, 1730–1860* (2001) and *Virtual Americas: Transnational Fictions and the Transatlantic Imaginary* (2002).

Barry Keith Grant is Professor of Film Studies and Popular Culture at Brock University, Ontario. He is the author, co-author or editor of numerous publications, including *The Dread of Difference: Gender and the Horror Film* (1986), *Voyages of Discover: The Cinema of Frederick Wiseman* (1992), *The Film Studies Dictionary* (with Steve Blandford and Jim Hillier, 2001), *Film Genre Reader III* (2003). His work has appeared in numerous journals and anthologies, and he serves as editor of the Contemporary Film and Television Series for Wayne State University Press.

Andrew Higson is Professor of Film Studies at the University of East Anglia and Head of the School of Film and Television Studies. He has written widely on British cinema, from the silent period to the present, and on the concept of national cinema. His publications include *Waving The Flag: Constructing a National Cinema in Britain* (1995), *'Film Europe' and 'Film America': Cinema, Commerce and Cultural Exchange, 1920–1939* (1999, co-edited with Richard Maltby), *British Cinema, Past and Present* (2000, co-edited with Justine Ashby), *Young and Innocent? The Cinema in Britain, 1896–1930* (2002) and *English Heritage, English Cinema:Costume Drama since 1980* (2003).

Guy Johnson studied at the University of Southern California School of Cinema-Television, and now lives in England.

Antonia Lant is founding director of the Program in Moving Image Archiving and Preservation at New York University, and teaches there in the Department of Cinema Studies. She is author of *Blackout: Reinventing Women for Wartime British Cinema* (1991) and editor of *The Red Velvet Seat: Women's Writings on the Cinema, the First Fifty years* (2005).

Jim Leach is Professor of Film, Popular Culture and Communications at Brock University, Ontario. He is the author of *A Possible Cinema: The Films of Alain Tanner* (1984), *Claude Jutra Filmmaker* (1999) and *British Film* (2004),and is currently writing a book on Canadian cinema.

Chris Lippard is Assistant Professor of Film Studies at the University of Utah. He is the editor of *By Angels Driven: The Films of Derek Jarman* (1996), and has published articles on Dennis Potter and, forthcoming, on Jorge Sanjines. In addition to British cinema, his research interests are in Iranian and South American cinema. He is chair of the Utah Film and Video Center, a local resource for production and exhibition.

Brian McIlroy is Professor of Film Studies in the Department of Theatre, Film and Creative Writing at the University of British Columbia. His most recent book is *Shooting to Kill: Filmmaking and the 'Troubles' in Northern Ireland* (2001). He has guest edited a special issue on Irish Cinema in the *Canadian Journal of Irish Studies* (2003), and he is currently at work on a Social Sciences and Humanities Research Council of Canada-supported project entitled 'Irish Genres: Cinema and Society 1981–2006'.

Sean O'Sullivan is Assistant Professor of English at Ohio State University. He is the author of a volume on Mike Leigh, forthcoming from the University of Illinois Press series on Contemporary Film Directors. His work addresses British cinema and television, serial fiction across media, and narrative connections between the visual and verbal arts. His next project is *The Portrait and the Plot*, a study of Jacques-Louis David, Charles Dickens and Alfred Hitchcock.

Leonard Quart is Professor Emeritus of Cinema Studies at the College of Staten Island and at the CUNY Graduate Center. He is a long-time Editor and Contributing Editor of *Cineaste*, writes a bi-weekly column on urban life and politics for the *Berkshire Eagle*, and has written essays and reviews for *Dissent, Film Quarterly, London Magazine*, and *New York Newsday*. He has most recently co-authored, with Ray Carney, *The Films of Mike Leigh: Embracing the World* (2000) and, with Al Auster, the third edition of *American Film and Society Since 1945* (2001).

David Sterritt is film critic of *The Christian Science Monitor*, Professor of Theater and Film at Long Island University, and a member of the Film Studies Faculty at Columbia University. He is also chair of the National Society of Film Critics and co-chair of the Columbia University Seminar on Cinema and Interdisciplinary Interpretation. His essays and articles have appeared in such periodicals as *Cineaste, Film Comment*, the *Journal of Aesthetics and Art Criticism* and the *New York Times*. His books include *The Films of Alfred Hitchcock* (1993), *Mad to Be Saved: The Beats, the '50s, and Film* (1998), *The Films of Jean-Luc Godard: Seeing the Invisible* (1999), *Screening the Beats: Media Culture and the Beat Sensibility* (2004) and *Guiltless Pleasures: A David Sterritt Film Reader* (2005).

Deborah Tudor is Chair of the Department of Cinema and Photography at Southern Illinois University at Carbondale. She is also Treasurer of the Union for Democratic

Communication. Her articles and essays have appeared in *Jump Cut, Cineaction*, and *Afterimage*, and she is the author of *Hollywood's Vision of Team Sports* (1997). Her research interests include British and Australian cinemas, documentary, do-it-yourself media, digital cinema and war films.

Michael Walsh is Chair of Cinema at the University of Hartford. His articles on British films of the 1980s have appeared in *American Imago* and *British Cinema: Past and Present* (2000, edited by Justine Ashby and Andrew Higson). He has published widely on film, literature and theory; his most recent essays are on Chris Marker and on the new wave of motion picture art in galleries and museums, and is working on a book entitled *Thatcher and After: British Film 1979–1992*.

Tony Williams is Professor and Area Head of Film Studies in the Department of English, Southern Illinois University at Carbondale. His articles have appeared in *Cinema Journal, Wide Angle, Jack London Journal, Paradoxa* and *Asian Cinema*. Recent publications include *Structures of Desire: British Cinema 1939–1955* (2000), *The Cinema of George A. Romero: Knight of the Living Dead* (2003) and *Body and Soul: The Cinematic Vision of Robert Aldrich* (2004). He is also the co-editor, with Steven Jay Schneider, of a forthcoming volume entitled *International Horrors*.

Peter Wollen is Distinguished Professor in the Critical Studies Program at UCLA. As a scholar and filmmaker, he writes widely about visual arts and culture. His book, *Signs and Meaning in the Cinema* (1997, third edition), and his work as editor of *Screen* magazine, helped refocus the discipline of film studies. Professor Wollen co-wrote *The Passenger* (1975) and co-directed (with Laura Mulvey) films such as *Riddles of the Sphinx* (1977) and *Crystal Gazing* (1982). His most recent feature was *Friendship's Death* (1987), a science fiction movie. Among his other books are *Raiding the Icebox: Reflections on Twentieth Century Culture* (1993), *Singin' In the Rain* (1993), *Howard Hawks: American Master* (1997) and *Paris Manhattan: Writings on Art* (2004).

PREFACE TO THE FIRST EDITION

Like many film teachers in their mid-forties, I have little formal training in cinema studies. Instead, I came to film via Saturday matinees and double features, combining a love of movies with graduate studies in literary history, theory and criticism. My academic concentration was on the British Romantic Era, and though I wanted to write my doctoral dissertation on film and literature, my adviser sagely warned me that such a topic would squash my chances for a job in any reputable English department. That was 'popular culture', he said dismissively, adding that it might draw students to English classes but was clearly not suitable for serious and rigorous study. So, accepting his advice, I wrote on the works of Milton and Shelley, a choice designed to set me firmly on the traditional academic path of literary studies. But I was not quite through with film. I taught it via crossover electives with titles like 'Literature and Film' or 'The Novel and the Film'. I even published an article on *Frankenstein* in a collection about film adaptations of English novels, combining my knowledge of the nineteenth century and of film. With a sympathetic colleague, I contemplated an anthology about film and literature, one tentatively titled to mimic the phrase uttered so repetitively by our students: 'No, but I saw the movie.'

British films, in particular, filled my need for a wide variety of literary adaptations that my English department colleagues might consider acceptable. After all, such movies were based on serious works of literature, and those cultured British accents were highly valued in academic enclaves. But how disappointing most of these films really were, neither matching the power of their sources nor working as a pure cinematic experience. Their slow and ponderous pace, as well as stodgy fidelity to detail, proved no match for their American counterparts: the frenetic pacing of *Bonnie and Clyde* (1967), the bawdy humour of *The Graduate* (1969) or the cynical heroism of *The Wild Bunch* (1969). Seeing Olivier in *Henry V* (1944) or *Hamlet* (1948) proved of little interest to my students, and David Lean's meticulous *mise-en-scène* provided small recompense for having to slog through Dickens. Even the more modern films left them cold, say *Look Back in Anger* (1958) or *The Loneliness of the Long Distance Runner* (1962). They did respond a bit better to *Tom Jones* (1963), though I always suspected that the cleavage, not the cinematic style, engaged them. So, after a few years of struggling to connect literature and cinema, of teaching first-rate films of second-rate novels or second-rate films of first-rate literature, I simply gave up and taught them as essentially separate entities, each with its own unique assets and limitations. I rarely included British movies in my film classes; I'd had enough of that restrained solemnity and sedentary camera work to last me a lifetime.

I recite this brief history of my academic life to recount how many of us now teaching film first encountered British cinema and to understand, perhaps, one reason it has excited so little scholarly and commercial interest over the years. Except for the brief flurry of attention during the late 1950s and early 1960s, the so-called Free Cinema movement, and an even briefer fixation with the 'Swinging London' of the later 1960s, both audiences and academics basically ignored British cinema. Such, however, was not the case with British film during the Thatcher era. On the commercial level, both *Chariots of Fire* (1981) and *Gandhi* (1983) swept the Oscar competition, prompting verification of scriptwriter Collin Welland's exuberant declaration: 'The British are coming!' Such a cry found equal validation in the government-backed declaration of 1985 as the 'Year of the British Film', a self-promotional gimmick that drew further attention to British movies. Yet beneath all the hype was some real, some significant, substance. British filmmakers from all segments of the industry turned out picture after picture that demanded attention. They struggled with the social and economic upheavals that characterised the Thatcher years, creating a cinema that made the world take notice.

THATCHERISM

'Mrs Thatcher has resigned from No. 10. Thank God!' So read the scrawled message that greeted harried commuters at the Bethnal Green underground station in the East End, a working-class section of London. Yet to her staunch allies, Margaret Thatcher's precipitous fall from power was, as one newspaper reported, a case where 'the termites have finally felled the oak'. Clearly, few in her own country, in Europe, or for that matter around the world, took a neutral position about Great Britain's first woman prime minister, the so-called Iron Lady who won three election victories and dominated British politics for a turbulent eleven-year reign (1979–90). During this period, Thatcher often turned events in her favour, from the brief but successful war with Argentina over the Falkland Islands (April 1982), to the rancorous victory over the National Union of Mineworkers (March 1984), to the narrow escape from an IRA bombing (October 1984). Starting on 11 February 1975, when she defeated Edward Heath to gain the leadership of the (then in opposition) Conservative Party, until 22 November 1990, when she resigned after failing to gain enough votes to continue her leadership of that same party, Margaret Thatcher radically changed the face of Great Britain, offering the citizens of her country a combination of economic, political, social and ideological principles that completely broke with the post-World War Two consensus and totally restructured British daily life. After all, how many other prime ministers became an -ism during their own lifetimes?

The most prominent component of Thatcherism remains its economic policies. She deplored what she contemptuously labelled 'the Nanny State' and consistently sought ways to eliminate what she deemed as governmental 'interference' within the economic sphere. 'We should not expect the state,' she told the electorate in 1980, 'to appear in the guise of an extravagant good fairy at every christening, a loquacious companion at every stage of life's journey, the unknown mourner at every funeral' (*Newsweek*, 3 December 1990). To accomplish this, Thatcher set up programmes that favoured the individual over the collective state: promoting thrift, eliminating Keynesian deficit financing, curtailing subsidies to ailing industries, selling council houses to sitting tenants, ignoring union demands, defending 'sound' fiscal policies, privatising $57billion worth of state-owned industries, lifting foreign-exchange controls, encouraging free-market economics (Biddiss 1987: 2; Finer 1987: 129). Using such slogans as 'Roll Back the Frontiers of the State' and 'Set the People Free', the Thatcher-led Conservatives united the disgruntled middle and upper classes against the working and lower classes to assault and ultimately dismantle the institutional and governmental policies that dominated postwar Britain. As Rudolf Klein characterises it, 'for the first time since 1945 Britain actually had a Government which took pride in stressing how little it could do, instead of emphasising how much it would do' (quoted in Biddiss 1987: 7).

Socially, Thatcher defined her philosophy as incorporating decidedly 'Victorian' values. The daughter of a smalltown greengrocer from Grantham, Thatcher's personal beliefs spring from her traditional background: self-reliance, family discipline, self-control, patriotism, individual duty (see Gould & Anderson 1987: 42). 'She has presented herself as the champion of those keenest to exercise personal responsibility, to exhibit self-reliance and initiative, to maintain the traditional structure and role of the family, and to recognise the demands of duty as well as the allure of entitlements' (Biddiss 1987: 2). This form of 'competitive self-interest' was enthusiastically welcomed by the economic community, a segment of British society well suited to her particular brand of Social Darwinism. From the Left, however, her positions were characterised far less as gentility but as patriarchalism, racism and imperialist nostalgia (Hall & Jacques 1983: 11). Such beliefs also underline the two major political blunders that finally ended her career: (i) the hated Poll Tax, which reduced the tax burden on large property owners and placed it on lower- and middle-class citizens, and (ii) her stubborn refusal to bring Great Britain harmoniously into European Community (EC) integration.

In North America, Thatcher captured the public imagination as has no British politician since Winston Churchill. Much of this stems from her close personal relationship and political affinity with the popular Ronald Reagan, a man with whom she shared a commitment to curbing the role of government and establishing the power of free enterprise. His first state dinner, for example, was for her, as was his last. At home, Labour Party members often criticised Thatcher for her obsession with America, charging that she should seek closer ties with the European Community rather than with the United States; yet she never wavered from her position as America's staunchest ally throughout her entire time in office. In his book *Reagan and Thatcher* (1991), Geoffrey Smith talks about how much these two leaders had in common, from their modest upbringing in archetypal small towns, to their initial status as political outsiders viewed as ideological extremists, to their similar economic, domestic and foreign policy philosophies. Reagan, of course, fully supported Thatcher during the Falklands War, providing much-needed military and political support; she vigorously defended his attack of Libya, allowing US bombers to refuel on British air bases before taking their revenge on Colonel Qaddafi. Her deep bond with America lasted beyond Reagan's term in office: one of her last official acts as Prime Minister was to deploy 14,000 British troops to Saudi Arabia.

How, then, to capture Thatcherism in a few brief catchphrases? David Marquand spells out four basic dimensions: (i) Thatcherism is a sort of British Gaullism that grew out of a pervading sense of despair and national decline; (ii) Thatcherism rests upon an economic foundation that rejects Keynesian theory and supports a free-market economy; (iii) Thatcherism embodies a conservative Toryism that stresses patriotism and British traditions; (iv) Thatcherism is style as well as substance, a charismatic populism where 'the leader knows instinctively what the populace feel and want' (1988: 160–6). Year after year during the 1980s, movies from Great Britain engaged the attention of the world, a diverse series of pictures proving an intimate, often quite uncomfortable, look into the modern British consciousness moulded by Thatcher and her policies. Many of these films directly attacked the Thatcher government, seeing her free-market philosophy as a callous disregard for everyone but the entrepreneurial buccaneers who plundered the economy; others portrayed the strains of living in a society torn apart by racial hatred and domestic poverty. Some rejected the constraints of formal narrative structures to explore the intricacies of form and shape, of time and space. Yet all these texts, in one form or another, spring from a distinct period in British history, one dominated by the powerful rhetoric, decisive actions and pervasive ideology of Margaret Thatcher.

METHODOLOGICAL ASSUMPTIONS ABOUT AUTHORSHIP

This anthology attempts to situate a group of texts within a stream of cultural, historical and ideological factors. But to write about directors as we do will no doubt strike some as naive, since filmmaking is obviously a collaborative effort that depends on many people, technologies, situations and conditions beyond the conscious control of so-called auteurs. Yet those involved in filmmaking know that almost all production crews function via a hierarchy, one in which anyone may contribute but where one person (often the director) must ultimately decide what is and what is not included in the final work. Within the scholarly community, some will immediately dismiss this approach as ignoring the main thrust of contemporary film theory. We live in a world dominated by post-structuralist thought, one in which Roland Barthes declares the death of the author and Jacques Derrida rejects individual consciousness as the source of meaning. Deconstruction, reader-response criticism, Marxism, reception theory, semiotics, structuralism, psychoanalytic theory, phenomenology, negative hermeneutics and other contemporary modes of critical thought either downgrade or totally eliminate the traditionally dominant role of the author in the making and meaning of a text. As Bill Nichols summarises the writings of post-structuralist thinkers, the author basically 'becomes a fictitious unity masking the patterns of regulation and control that characterise the systems or codes of which the subject is only an expression' (1985: 8). Here any idea of the author as self-expressive personality free from social and aesthetic restraints virtually disappears, because one can think and communicate only through various culture-bound systems and codes. Obliterating the person, the text, in effect, creates the author's identity.

Clearly, elements of post-structuralist thought are quite liberating, particularly in regard to some basic authorial and critical issues. Conceiving of the text as composed of unlimited, even contradictory, 'meanings', rather than restricting it to one or two master themes officially sanctioned by critical consensus, opens works to a healthy abundance of diverse approaches. By thus freeing readers from the impossible task of searching for what the author 'truly means', modern theorists encourage a range of possible responses, thereby fostering a play of irreconcilable differences that rub against the grain of any particular text. Such a process exposes the cracks and fissures in texts previously seen as unified. 'The object of the critic,' argues Catherine Belsey, 'is to seek not the unity of the work, but the multiplicity and diversity of its possible meanings' (1980:104). Insistence on the inherent ideological position of all criticism forces reconsideration of previous judgements as accepted absolutes, understanding them instead as subjective points of view about a particular artwork rather than objective truths. Thus, modern theorists force us to recognise that every critic's evaluations rest on a partly conscious, partly unconscious system of particular beliefs and values about human beings and artistry.

These post-structuralist positions necessarily force authors to relinquish their traditional authority over the text, since their interpretations stand as no more 'correct' than those of other readers. Once the work is completed, therefore, the author becomes simply another commentator about its meaning. We need not feel constrained by the boundaries of an artist's personal understanding, or to cite D. H. Lawrence's famous dictum: 'Never trust the artist. Trust the tale.' A clear-cut example here would be Shakespeare; obviously, he never studied Freud, yet his works possess powerful psychological insights that make them relevant to our own time. To limit ourselves to discussing only what a sixteenth-century, bourgeois Englishman meant his plays to be about (assuming we could discover what that was) would drastically simplify the dramas, perhaps confining their value to historical artifact. But by analysing Shakespeare's plays via a terminology, a belief system if you will, that the author could never know, modern critics make the works more understandable, more meaningful, to a generation obsessed with psychoanalysis. Thus, every age 'discovers' what elements in a work of art relate most to its own needs and desires. Such is the case in the cinema, as well as in the other arts, so we should not be surprised to find filmmakers shocked by interpretations of their own movies.

But post-structuralist theories must still account for something constructed by someone, even if that someone was determined and constrained by certain systems and codes. Authors are, indeed, social constructions; they must be understood as existing with specific elements of time, style, attitude, form and meaning. But even shifting an author's voice from dominant to equal among other readers of the text should not totally eliminate him or her from the ensuing discourse. John Caughie suggests that discussions about authorship serve to tie a piece to outside social and historical forces by examining how the author's 'place within a particular social history is written into the text' (1981: 2–3). Paul Giles goes even further when he warns us that 'a critic in the 1980s should not neglect Shakespeare's modes and institutions of production, but ... not treat Shakespeare's plays as being equivalent to those of Thomas Kyd, for whom the modes of production are very similar' (1991: 2). For Pam Cook, the modern assault on the artist as sole creator has transformed, not destroyed, auteurism, 'from a way of accounting for the whole of cinema into a critical methodology which poses questions for film study and cultural practices in general' (1985: 114). Thus, a notion of authorship helps to establish a text's cultural, social and historical context, but does not limit its relevance to a particular time and place. By analysing these films produced by British directors during a distinct period, the writers in this anthology situate these texts into an amalgam of cultural, social, institutional and historical conditions.

CONSTRUCTION AND ORGANISATION

This anthology is divided into two major sections. Part One, 'Cultural Contexts and Cinematic Constructions', establishes the background for the films made during the Thatcher era that will be discussed subsequently. It makes readers dig into the soil that nourishes these movies. So, for example, Leonard Quart's essay explores the politics of Margaret Thatcher, analysing her policies and elaborating on the films that responded to her philosophy. Peter Wollen, concerned more with cinematic than political history, compares the films made during the 1980s with those made during the Free Cinema period, paying particular attention to how modernism shaped the films of Derek Jarman and Peter Greenaway. Turning his attention to the British image culture, Thomas Elsaesser scrutinises the relationships between a 'social imaginary' of Britain and the projection of a 'national imaginary' – the relation of Britishness to a national cinema. Paying more attention to the interconnections between television and film during the 1980s, Paul Giles probes Channel 4's contribution to British filmmaking during the decade, specifically how television affected the aesthetics of British films during this era.

One particular area that consistently attracted the attention of directors and screenwriters during the Thatcher years was the continued violence in Northern Ireland; Brian McIlroy contextualises a series of these films, demonstrating how mainstream filmmakers became more assertive and aggressive in their presentation of these 'problems' over the course of the decade. Like Thomas Elsaesser, Andrew Higson sees British films as commodities for consumption in the international image market, though here he focuses on the cycle of quality costume dramas called 'heritage films'. For him, these pictures depict an ambivalence of nostalgia, one that ostensibly criticises but emotionally embraces the past. The last essay in this section, Mary Desjardins' discussion of motherhood during the Thatcher era, shows how the positioning of mothers within specific narratives represents the British culture coming to terms with feminism, particularly during a time when both their monarch and their Prime Minister were women. Taken as a whole, then, the essays in this first section provide an industrial, psychological, political, social and ideological context for this era of dramatic and dynamic changes in British life.

The essays in Part Two, 'Filmmakers during the Thatcher Era', elaborate upon the works of a representative sample of directors during this period, ranging from works by established artists to new filmmakers who came to prominence in this decade. So, for example, Manthia Diawara and Antonia Lant investigate two types of collectives, each one defined by a particular ideological agenda: films made by black collectives (Ceddo, Black Audio, Sankofa) and women's independent collectives (Leeds Animation Workshop) during the 1980s. Both demonstrate how the contours of independent British film production in the 1980s, which appeared rather narrow from the vantage point of the United States, were actually aesthetically varied and thematically diverse. Next, Barry Keith Grant and Jim Leach investigate the 1980s work of two directors prominent before the Thatcher era, Ken Russell and Nicolas Roeg.

Each writer finds new and interesting changes during this time. For Grant, Russell's films during this period aptly demonstrate both the values of British tradition and a disdain for them that mirrors the tensions inherent in Thatcherism itself. Leach, using Roeg's films to explore the homogenising effect of American cultural power during the 1980s, places Roeg's British perspective on American culture within the context of the ideology of Thatcherism.

Susan Torrey Barber, too, looks at a director whose career began before Thatcher became prime minister, but whose reputation rose dramatically during her reign: Stephen Frears. She positions his films as reactions to and critiques of the dynamics of Thatcherism – specifically with respect to race, class and gender – as she charts Frears' increasing disillusionment with the Thatcher administration. Tony Williams also sees the work of a far different type of director, Terence Davies, as challenging the hegemony of Thatcherism, this time the officially sanctioned family institution. Williams charts Davies's pictorialisation of how this reactionary authoritarianism has caused misery for those outside the family norm. In a similar manner, Michael Walsh elaborates on Peter Greenaway's productions during the 1980s, seeing him as an allegorist whose features comment indirectly but decisively on the post-imperial Britain of Margaret Thatcher. Finally, Chris Lippard and Guy Johnson examine how issues of health and illness, which have long preoccupied British filmmakers, become metaphors for contagion during the 1980s; in particular, the films of Derek Jarman use sickness as a position of power from which to dissolve narrative and threaten established power relations.

Taken as a whole, then, this collection of essays establishes the unique relationship between the era of Margaret Thatcher and the diverse group of filmmakers who invigorated the British cinema during her time of power. Perhaps the only common element connecting these directors is their revulsion, to one degree or another, for the ideology of Thatcherism, though their methods of expressing that distaste cover the spectrum of aesthetic options. Some of the most potent political opposition to the Thatcher government, therefore, appeared in movie theatres rather than in the House of Commons. Ironically, of course, one might argue that a less commanding and infuriating figure than Margaret Thatcher, even one proposing similar policies, would have failed to rouse the ire of Britain's filmmakers to such a fever pitch. So, in a truly paradoxical manner, the intense and unwavering hatred of Thatcher provided the spark necessary to force Britain's best visual artists to new creative heights and, in so doing, to ignite a moribund industry. More importantly for those not intimately connected to the British culture, these pictures bear little resemblance to the tastefully tedious adaptations that so many of us associate with the British cinema. They forcefully demonstrate how filmmakers, though perhaps not legislators of the world, can at least offer a viable alternative to officially-sanctioned versions of the truth, while at the same time creating bold and serious works that reach far beyond the confines of geography and petty politics.

WORKS CITED

Belsey, Catherine (1980) *Critical Practice*. London: Methuen.

Biddiss, Michael (1987) 'Thatcherism: Concept and Interpretations', in Kenneth Minogue and Michael Biddiss (eds) *Thatcherism: Personality and Politics*. New York: St. Martin's Press, 1–20.

Caughie, John (ed.) (1981) *Theories in Authorship: A Reader*. London: Routledge and Kegan Paul.

Cook, Pam (ed.) (1985) *The Cinema Book*. New York: Pantheon.

Finer, S. E. (1987) 'Thatcherism and British Political Historian', in Kenneth Minogue and Michael Biddiss (eds) *Thatcherism: Personality and Politics*. New York: St. Martin's Press, 127–40.

Giles, Paul (1991) 'The Cinema of Catholicism: John Ford and Robert Altman', in Lester D. Friedman (ed.) *Unspeakable Images: Ethnicity in American Cinema*. Champaign: University of Illinois Press, 140–66.

Gould, Julius and Digby Anderson (1987) 'Thatcherism and British Society', in Kenneth Minogue and Michael Biddiss (eds) *Thatcherism: Personality and Politics*. New York: St. Martin's Press, 38–54.

Hall, Stuart and Martin Jacques (eds) (1983) *The Politics of Thatcherism*. London: Lawrence and Wishart.

Marquand, David (1988) 'The Paradoxes of Thatcherism', in Robert Skidelsky (ed.) *Thatcherism*. London: Basil Blackwell, 159–72.

Minogue, Kenneth and Michael Biddiss (eds) (1987) *Thatcherism: Personality and Politics*. New York: St. Martin's Press.

Nichols, Bill (ed.) (1985) *Movies and Methods: An Anthology*. Berkeley: University of California Press.

Skidelsky, Robert (ed.) (1988) *Thatcherism*. London: Basil Blackwell.

Smith, Geoffrey (1991) *Reagan and Thatcher*. New York: Norton.

PREFACE TO THE SECOND EDITION

After Wallflower Press invited me to bring forth a second edition of *Fires Were Started*, I contacted the contributors to the first edition and asked if they wanted to add anything to their original pieces. Almost everyone did, but I was particularly struck by an email from Michael Walsh; he related his recent conversation with a prominent English film scholar who, in Michael's words, 'scoffed at the very idea of Thatcherism and cinema'. Indeed, a similar position characterises many of the reviews that greeted the first edition of this book, as well as the only subsequent academic exploration of the cinema during the Thatcher era, John Hill's *British Cinema in the 1980s* (1999). Hill specifically contends that some of the contributors to *Fires Were Started* interpret 'the most unlikely of "British" films in relation to Thatcherism' (1999: 29) and that 'not all British films are linked to Thatcherism and not all can be seen as straightforwardly critical of the Thatcher regime' (ibid.). He then proceeds to examine the reasons why 'it is much easier to identify an anti-Thatcherite cinema during this period of British history than a pro-Thatcherite one' (ibid.), a tactic which seems to undermine the very position he just articulated.

Comments like those above both startle and confuse me. After all, most film scholars readily accept the concept that all films present ideologically balanced positions, even when they ostensibly address subjects that seem to have little direct connection to overtly political positions: thus, a lavish Astaire and Rogers musical is as loaded with representations of and reactions to its era as is Michael Moore's *Fahrenheit 9/11* (2004) to its time. Though the former may unconsciously depict these positions and the latter purposely foreground them, they remain embedded in both productions, inherently evident in both form and content. Furthermore, the linking of cinema culture with a specific era in a country's history is not a particularly radical perspective. Take, for example, a representative sample of the books that splice the American cinema of the 1980s to Thatcher's doctrinaire soulmate, Ronald Reagan: *The Politics of Popular Representation: Reagan, Thatcher, AIDS, and the Movies* (Kenneth MacKinnon, 1992), *No Surprises, Please!: Movies in the Reagan Decade* (Steve Vineberg, 1993), *Ronald Reagan in Hollywood: Movies and Politics* (Stephen Vaughn, 1994), *Flatlining on the Field of Dreams: Cultural Narratives in the Films of President Reagan's America* (Alan Nadel, 1997) and *American Films and Politics from Reagan to Bush Jr.* (Philip John Davies & Paul Wells, 2002). Given that British directors often confront politics more blatantly than do their counterparts in

Hollywood, and that many working during Thatcher's reign specifically referenced her government in interviews and within their films themselves, I find it surprising when British academics like Hill accuse the writers in *Fires Were Started* of being too quick to 'homogenise the films concerned and to attribute a political significance to them' (ibid.). Of course the films of the 1980s are not 'only' about the politics of Thatcherism, but virtually all of them, to one degree or another, cannot help but be influenced by the Iron Lady and her policies, either internally as part of their style and subject matter or externally by the state of the British cinema industry.

While I find Hill's basic position untenable, and with over a decade of hindsight, I do agree with some of the criticism that greeted *Fires Were Started*'s initial publication. In particular, the cogent critiques of Matthew Bernstein (1993), Paul Coates (1993), Wheeler Winston Dixon (1993) and Jane Sillars (1994) struck some responsive cords that I have addressed in this second edition. Admittedly, no book can possibly cover every issue on such a labyrinthine topic, but I hope this new edition will stimulate other scholars to follow the suggestions these critics offered, such as to explore the role that writers (Ian McEwan, Philip Ridley, Alan Bennett and Hanif Kureishi) played in the cinema of the Thatcher era, to evaluate the work of important directors such as Neil Jordan, Alex Cox and Julien Temple, not included here, and to contemplate the complex topics of spectatorship and audience as they relate to these movies. Other points they cite, however, are taken up in this new volume, including an expanded discussion of television, the addition of more women directors, deeper deliberations about the concept of 'Britishness', and essays on Mike Leigh and Ken Loach.

Questions raised by these and other reviewers demand more space than I have at my disposal here, but let me briefly respond to those who invoked the tangled issue of whether the British cinema of the 1980s reflects or critiques the Thatcher era; as Sillars puts it, do these films 'act as commentary or in opposition to this powerful political philosophy?' (1994: 102). In an amalgam of both overt and subtle ways, the cinema of this decade does both, depending on which films one cites as most characteristic of the times. On the international scene, the so-called 'heritage films' clearly reached larger audiences – particularly in the United States – than the more socially topical movies, which were often confined to distribution outlets in larger cities. Since these lush dramas visually embrace the empire nostalgia (as Higson writes) that underpinned Thatcherite ideology, they formed a cinema of wish-fulfillment that pictorialised some of the fundamental values held most dear by the Conservative government, even if based upon literary works that often satirised the very notion of Britain's greatness. On the other hand, the social critiques of film-makers such as Frears, Loach and Leigh directly attacked the financial, industrial and moral values espoused by the Thatcher government, showing how its policies had severely damaged various segments of British society. They replaced the rolling English countryside with the harsh squalor of urban life, and the gentility of the upper-classes' trivialities with the desperation of the oppressed underclass.

As I read over some of the responses to the first volume, some fires still seem to be burning, particularly among British academics who resent that an American edited this volume and that the contributors were not all British. Coates observes that almost all the British writers in the first edition were émigrés, mostly to schools in the United States, which he cites as 'poignant' evidence of Thatcher's university policies (1993: 180). The result, he claims, is that the anthology contains a distinct 'mismatch between American and British perspectives on these films' (1993: 182). More stridently, Andy Medhurst's review in *Sight and Sound* encapsulates some prevailing positions about who has the legitimate right to publish about a country's national cinema. I find most disturbing his characterisation of the original edition as a 'demonstration of American academic imperialism rather than a contribution to the study of British cinema' (1993: 45). Such an insular attack ignores the fact that the majority of those essayists were British. More crucially, if those of us outside British culture who admire and write about its cinema can be charged with imperialism, perhaps Ed Buscombe should be forbidden from writing about westerns, or Robin Wood about Hollywood horror movies, or Peter Wollen about Orson Welles. Indeed, Medhurst himself has written about issues in American cinema and culture, specifi-cally Hollywood sex comedies. His critique reveals a kind of obtuse nativism that ghettoises British cinema behind a wall of nationalistic insiderism, a stance likely to lessen rather than broaden its impact beyond its shores.

My goals in this second edition of *Fires Were Started* remain the same as those which initially motivated me to edit a book about this era of filmmaking: to examine a fascinating period that reconfigured the British cinematic landscape, a series of provocative films that wove a tapestry of powerful alternatives to officially-sanctioned versions of the truth. For me, it was a wonderful experience to revisit those initial essays and, more importantly, to fill in some holes I felt were present in the first edition. To that end, I have included four new pieces. Two, those by James English and David Sterritt, cover important directors missing from the first edition, Ken Loach and Mike Leigh, demonstrating how both men provided significant contributions to the discussions about Thatcherism swirling around them. Deborah Tudor writes on four important women directors during the 1980s: Ngozi Onwurah, Pratibha Parmar, Sally Potter and Beeban Kidron. Her essay demonstrates how writings about femi-nist issues, Mrs Thatcher's stance on herself as a woman, and the rhetoric prevalent during the Falklands crisis strongly influenced these artists. Finally, Sean O'Sullivan discusses two of the most important television productions during the Thatcher era, *Boys from the Blackstuff* (1982) and *Threads* (1984). He demonstrates how the North/South economic divide, the legacy of British documentary, the collapse of the Industrial Revolution and the fear of atomic annihilation posed issues for a nation divided and a society on the brink of chaos. I sincerely hope this new edition will encourage future scholars to dig even deeper into this exhilarating and turbulent time of creative and engaged filmmaking.

WORKS CITED

Bernstein, Matthew (1993) 'Review of *Fires Were Started*', *Film Comment*, 41, 1, 49–50.

Coates, Paul (1993) 'Review of *Fires Were Started*', *Discourse Social/Social Discourse*, 5, 3/4, 179–82.

Davies, Philip John and Paul Wells (2002) *American Film and Politics from Reagan to Bush Jr.* Manchester: Manchester University Press.

Dixon, Wheeler Winston (1993) 'Review of *Fires Were Started*', *Cineaste*, 20, 1, 51.

Hill, John (1999) *British Cinema in the 1980s*. Oxford: Oxford University Press.

MacKinnon, Kenneth (1992) *The Politics of Popular Representation: Reagan, Thatcher, AIDS, and the Movies*. Madison, NJ: Farleigh Dickinson University Press.

Medhurst, Andy (1993) 'Spaced Out: Review of *Fires Were Started*', *Sight and Sound*, 3, 6, 45.

Nadel, Alan (1997) *Flatlining on the Field of Dreams: Cultural Narratives in the Films of President Reagan's America*. New Brunswick: Rutgers University Press.

Sillars, Jane (1994) 'Review of *Fires Were Started*', *Screen*, 35, 1, 100–3.

Vaughn, Stephen (1994) *Ronald Reagan in Hollywood: Movies and Politics*. Cambridge: Cambridge University Press.

Vineberg, Steve (1993) *No Surprises, Please!: Movies in the Reagan Decade*. New York: Schirmer Books.

ACKNOWLEDGMENTS

Anthologies are curious hybrids: not quite total collaborations, they nonetheless represent the shared intellectual and emotional energy between editor and contributor. Along with their knowledge and enthusiasm, the writers in this volume also brought their receptive attitudes, wry wits and patient understanding to this project. Never did I suffer from the slings of annoyance or the arrows of outrageous egos. One of the most pleasant side benefits of working on this project was how contributors previously known only to me through their writing became friends whose voices I immediately recognised. It was lovely to reconnect with them, and my telephone bill reflects long conversations which ranged well beyond their particular essay or my specific editorial comments. I thank all the contributors to this anthology for their unflagging enthusiasm, dedication, and commitment to examining and then re-examining, British cinema during the Thatcher era; they made this potentially difficult and draining process into an enjoyable and rewarding experience.

The first edition of *Fires Were Started* was completed during my time in Syracuse University. There, at the SUNY Health Science Center, I had the assistance of Donald Goodman, our Dean and Provost, and of Sharon Osika-Michaels, our departmental secretary. At Syracuse during this same time period, I continually benefited from the intellectual stimulation of my colleague and friend, Owen Shapiro, and from the expert research skills of Denise Stevens at the E. S. Bird Library. Janaki Bakhle, acquisitions editor at University of Minnesota Press, originally commissioned this project; she also provided critical insight and support from its conception until its initial publication, ably assisted by Robert Mosimann. The people at Wallflower Press – particularly editorial director Yoram Allon and his editorial assistant Jacqueline Downs – have been exceptionally kind and creative partners in bringing forth this second edition. It has truly been a pleasure working with such dedicated professionals at both presses.

One person deserves special mention for helping me complete the first edition of the book: Michael Nelson, my graduate student in the Art Media Studies Department at Syracuse University. Michael was an integral part of this project from start to finish. He read and commented on all the early drafts, gave valuable structural suggestions and performed necessary research tasks. Every teacher should be fortunate enough to find such a student. Michael was taken from us much too soon and is greatly missed.

Finally, I want to thank the following sources for supplying the stills in this book: United Artists, Miramax, The Academy of Motion Picture Arts and Sciences, Orion, Jerry Ohlingher's Movie Material Store, the Samuel Goldwyn Company, the British Film Institute, Warner Bros., the Leeds Animation Workshop, Canon Releasing Corporation, Hemdale and *Cineaste*.

INTRODUCTION – THE EMPIRE STRIKES OUT: AN AMERICAN PERSPECTIVE ON THE BRITISH FILM INDUSTRY

Lester D. Friedman

A typical nineteenth-century *Punch* cartoon would show two people sitting at a table, with up to eight lines of dialogue under the drawing. Cartoons nowadays have quite a different emphasis and consequently more impact. Much of what is described as British cinema is still in the Victorian cartoon age.
> – Simon Perry, producer

The British cinema industry has both benefited and suffered from sharing an ostensibly common language with its powerful American competitor. Over the years, the government made sporadic attempts to support its fledgling film industry: the first Cinematograph Films Act (1927), which outlawed block booking and imposed a compulsory quota of British films; the new Films Act (1938), which upped the quotas and regulated labour conditions; the National Film Finance Corporation (1949), which supported independent productions; and the Eady Levy (1950), which added a tax to ticket sales and used the revenues to subsidise production costs. In spite of these and other measures to spur British productions, American films dominated the British film market from the early days of the cinema until the present time. Many English filmmakers found America's post-World War Two position of overwhelming box-office superiority particularly galling, claiming that Hollywood 'exploited wartime disruptions to establish an unfair advantage' (Murphy 1986: 47). In addition, the Hollywood tradition of block booking, a practice that gave foreign distributors first-rate films only if they also agreed to purchase lesser productions, left little room for homegrown products in British theatres. Finally, American studios routinely established joint projects with British production companies, thereby avoiding the government sanctions imposed on foreign films. As Alan Sapper, general secretary of the Association of Cinematograph, Television and Allied Technicians, noted:

> British film production levels rely mainly on American finance and on its ability to service national and international and cable operations. No reliance can be put on this boom period continuing for more than a year or so – if the dollar/pound exchange rate deteriorates, as far as America is concerned, so will our film production level. (Quoted in Roddick 1985: 16)

Hollywood, then, effectively colonised Britain's native markets and, except for some relatively brief periods, the British failed to mount any effective challenge to this foreign domination of their film industry.

In addition to circumventing government policies and dominating movie houses, the American film industry also damaged its British counterpart by enticing the best on- and off-screen talent to work in the United States. Thus, the rich coffers and worldwide distribution networks of Hollywood's sprawling studios eventually lured performers such as Charlie Chaplin, Richard Burton, Sean Connery, David Niven, Robert Donat, Daniel Day Lewis, Michael Caine, Jeremy Irons, Vanessa Redgrave, Malcolm McDowell, Julie Christie, Cary Grant, Albert Finney, Alec Guinness, Dirk Bogarde, Laurence Olivier, Peter O'Toole, Rex Harrison, Leslie Howard, Charles Laughton, Vivian Leigh, James Mason and Peter Sellers to work in sunny California. Similarly, world-class directors such as Alfred Hitchcock, Richard Attenborough, Clive Donner, Stephen Frears, Alan Parker, Ridley Scott, Alexander Korda, Michael Caton-Jones, Michael Apted, Terry Gilliam, Ronald Neame, Carol Reed, Victor Saville, John Schlesinger, Peter Yates, Michael Winner, Neil Jordan, Hugh Hudson, Ken Russell, John Boorman and Tony Scott all vacated Great Britain for the technical expertise, larger budgets and stronger world presence of the Hollywood feature-film business. Some nationalists castigated these performers and filmmakers for deserting their homeland and thus impoverishing their native cinema. Yet can we really blame them for seeking a niche within the American industry that regularly churned out products, rather than banking their careers on the fitful bursts of the British industry?

The rich coffers and worldwide distribution networks of the Hollywood system inevitably lure the best British actors, such as Jeremy Irons (shown above, in *Reversal of Fortune*, 1990) and Peter O'Toole (opposite, in *My Favorite Year*, 1982) to work in American movies

The British movie business also suffers from attacks by native scholars and commentators, a process Charles Barr labels 'cultural self-laceration':

> This critical work has had a consistently greater prestige internationally than British cinema itself, and the very prestige of this tradition has, with a certain irony, helped to keep the prestige of British films at a low level, as a result of the consistent way in which the most progressive and interesting elements in this criticism have – at least until recently – been actively hostile, or at best indifferent, to the work of a commercial mainstream of the British cinema. (1986: 7)

British critics who penned influential books or essays usually drew upon American rather than British films, using American not British directors to support their theories. So, for example, when Peter Wollen writes his groundbreaking *Signs and Mean-*

ing in the Cinema, he focuses on John Ford and Orson Welles and Sergei Eisenstein; when Robin Wood investigates the cinema in a series of significant books, he explores the works of Arthur Penn and Howard Hawks and Ingmar Bergman; when Laura Mulvey expounds on her influential theory of pleasure and spectatorship, she cites examples from the American films of Hitchcock and von Sternberg. Wood seemingly spoke for a generation of British critics when, in 1974, he said, 'My own reluctance to confront the British cinema is simply attributable to my sense that its achievement is so limited and so much less interesting than that of other countries' (quoted in Barr 1986: 3). By emphasising American rather than British products, these writers drew attention away from their native cinema and made Hollywood films even more dominant.

One can imagine how participants in a moviemaking industry competing directly with American products quickly understand the process described above as a perversely circular entrapment: American movies are financed better so they draw international talent, therefore they are distributed more widely, therefore they fill more local theatres and squeeze out native productions, therefore they are reviewed more often, therefore more people hear about them, therefore more people go to see them, therefore they make more money, therefore American films are better funded... Putting it more simply, producer Leon Clore once remarked, 'If the United States spoke Spanish, we would have a film industry' (quoted in Roddick 1985: 5). Of course, others propose a far simpler reason to account for Hollywood's defeat of Britain's film industry: British films are simply not very good. François Truffaut summed up this attitude most succinctly when he claimed, in his 1969 book about Hitchcock, that there was 'a certain incompatibility between the terms "cinema" and "Britain"'. Satyajit Ray expanded on this concept, claiming:

> I do not think the British are temperamentally equipped to make the best use of the movie camera. The camera forces one to face facts, to probe, to reveal, to get close to people and things; while the British nature inclines to the opposite; to stay aloof, to cloak harsh truths with innuendoes. You cannot make great films if you suffer from constricting habits of this sort. What is more, the placidity and monotony of habit patterns that mark the British way of life are the exact opposite of what constitutes the real meat for the cinema. (Quoted in Barr 1986: 9)

As previously noted, British critics never effectively countered these types of assertions. In fact, by using their talents and insights to illuminate mainly American films, while basically ignoring the products of their own culture, they implicitly concurred with statements like those made by Truffaut and Ray.

We have already seen that the British film industry suffers because its actors and directors blend in so easily with their American counterparts. In Hollywood, few British directors need an interpreter on the set, and cultured British accents endow performers with an aura of stylish sophistication. In addition, British television programmes as diverse as *The Benny Hill Show*, *EastEnders* and *Masterpiece Theatre* remain a staple of public and cable television networks, retaining a reasonably large and loyal American viewership. Finally, the oft-cited 'special' relationship between Great Britain and the United States – evidenced in England's important role in American history, the popularity of British rock music and fashion, and most recently the close connection between Margaret Thatcher and Ronald Reagan – does much to erase the natural proclivity of most Americans to distrust anything 'foreign'. Looking at these factors from the British film community's perspective, we might naturally assume that the absence of any language barriers, which allows this effortless access to American productions, would provide some positive trade-offs that compensate for the considerable damage it causes. In other words, how does a common language benefit the British movie business? For example, a similar language should allow British films to penetrate far deeper into American markets than do other non-US productions. So, we might assume, British films could find audiences beyond the usual urban areas designed for foreign film distribution; they could reach viewers in less sophisticated locales, those sites traditionally inhospitable to movie subtitles, dubbed dialogue and foreign environments.

Such has not been the case. While American film-goers welcome British directors and performers, British films rarely achieve popular acclaim and monetary rewards. Only a small percentage of British films, such as *The Private Life of Henry VIII* (1933) and *Chariots of Fire* (1981), ever match the financial levels attained by even moderately successful American pictures in the United States. The few times British companies did challenge the Americans on their home turf, notably Alexander Korda during the 1930s and J. Arthur Rank following World War Two, they put few dents in the domestic market. Other than the occasional British blockbuster, typically a co-production between local companies and American backers/studios, British films in America fared most successfully on the so-called art-house circuit, which catered to 'a small but increasingly important middle-class audience which looked askance at the commercial vulgarity of Hollywood' (Murphy 1986: 62). When we rightfully ignore essentialist statements like those of Truffaut and Ray that locate the problem of British films inherently within native character, and instead peer within the rigidly structured British society and film history, we quickly discover an interesting paradox: the same components that buttress the British cinema simultaneously hinder its widespread acceptance among American audiences. These fundamental ingredients include the British literary history, theatrical tradition, preoccupation with class issues and emphasis on the documentary.

The magisterial tradition of literary excellence represents the brightest jewel in Great Britain's cultural crown. Surely no American college or university, no matter how committed to critical theory or contemporary voices, would dare eliminate classes in Shakespeare or Milton or Shelley. Certainly no high-school student would graduate without at least some cursory exposure to a Brontë novel, a Shaw play or a Browning poem. Most Americans initially encounter these literary works within an academic environment of enthusiastic teachers insistent on communicating the beauty of Wordsworth's verse or the bleakness of Hardy's vision. Often, therefore, we associate British literary works with serious contemplation, solemn veneration and portentous meanings. Of course, teachers desperately trying to reach their students often incorporate film adaptations of classic British works into their curricula, hoping to capture the imagination of a generation weaned on MTV and far more attuned to cinematic rather than literary stimuli. Yet the inclusion of such 'Trojan horses' designed to lure students into appreciating great examples of British literature reduces these films to just another dreary homework assignment and eliminates the pleasures associated with an evening at the flicks. Such reverence and weightiness, in fact, strikes most students as stuffy, as far removed from the scent of buttered popcorn and taste of stale Kit-Kats.

The number of literary adaptations, particularly novels, within the British film industry's yearly output ranges from about 5 per cent to about 26 per cent (McFarlane 1986: 121). Yet, at least in part because of potential educational markets, film adaptations of literary works represent the greatest proportion of British films exported to the United States for residual rental purposes. Relatively few of these traditionally 'tasteful' adaptations display any sense of intellectual boldness or cinematic creativity. (Exceptions that spring to mind are the works of Alfred Hitchcock, Michael Powell and Emeric Pressburger, and Ken Russell, adaptations that rarely find their way into literature classrooms.) Instead, they genuflect reverently to the original source material, rarely daring to venture very far beyond the most stolid of approaches:

> British adaptations have exhibited a decorous, dogged fidelity to their sources, content to render through careful attention to their *mise-en-scène* the social values and emotional insight of those sources rather than subjecting them to critical scrutiny or, indeed, to robust exploitation ... The standard British film version of the novel has been a prime example of those pervasive qualities of 'good taste, characterised by restraint, understatement and sophistication' which Alan Lovell identified as the British cinema's 'negative reactions' to the more dangerous and flamboyant and vigorous aspects of Hollywood. (McFarlane 1986: 120–1)

Though American cinema, too, often cannibalises literary works, most American filmmakers view their source material simply as a blueprint, usually feeling quite free to invent or eliminate characters, drastically alter locales and totally transform endings – all done in the name of making elements 'cinematic'. Such mutations, when successful, delight mainstream audiences who care little about fidelity to literary materials. So while the British literary legacy provided its film industry with a seemingly limitless source of subjects and stories, the obsession with faithfully recreating the written work on the screen fostered a tentative cinema, one concerned more with accuracy than with audaciousness.

Like its literary heritage, the British theatrical tradition also shackled its film industry. In America during the cinema's so-called Golden Age, the respective centres for movies and plays remained a continent apart from each other: film production occurred predominately in California, and theatre, in New York City. In Great Britain, however, performers working in the theatrical centre of London could easily and quickly reach nearby studios like Ealing, Denham, Shepperton and Elstree, so they frequently made movies during the day and appeared in plays during the evening. In addition, British films drew upon established playwrights from Shakespeare to Shaw, from John Osborne to Joe Orton, as source material, usually treating them as reverentially as they did British literature:

> One senses ... signs of retreat, to the cinema as a transcription system for significant stage productions; to theatrical films as prestige cultural packages, precisely aimed at British art-house and selected foreign markets (particularly in America) ... theatrical material became something to lean on, not something to mould for a specific cinematic purpose. (Brown 1986: 162, 159)

Perhaps even more important, as Julian Petley aptly observes, 'British acting has been dominated by the theatrical tradition, yielding performances that, by comparison with Hollywood, are wordy and stagey' (1985: 111). A common denominator among the newest crop of British actors – such as Jonathan Pryce, Ben Kingsley and Bob Hoskins – remains their theatrical backgrounds. Petley, like many other critics, bemoans this tendency as 'an important aspect of the persistence of the primarily *literary* tradition of British culture, one which tends to result, in terms of cinema, in an excess of theatrical or literary adaptations or, in the case of original screenplays, scriptwriter's films' (1985: 121). So while the British theatrical tradition, which afforded a wealth of source material, also provided a steady flow of well-trained performers, their histrionic style and allegiance to the theatre inhibited, perhaps even intimidated, British filmmakers, encouraging them to concentrate on the word rather than on the image.

As the British film industry remained tethered to these literary and theatrical traditions, so it never shook free from a preoccupation with class consciousness, positioning this issue as informing all aspects of public and private daily life. This hierarchical stratification of British life reaches into every niche of society and creates a caste system far beyond the understanding of most Americans. Listen, for instance, to Hanif Kureishi, a Pakistani novelist and the screenwriter of *My Beautiful Laundrette* (1985) and *Sammy and Rosie Get Laid* (1987), as he delineates its intimate connection with racism:

> Racism goes hand-in-hand with class inequality. Among other things, racism is a kind of snobbery, a desire to see oneself as superior culturally and economically, and a desire to actively experience and enjoy that superiority by hostility or violence. And when that superiority of class and culture is unsure or is not acknowledged by the Other … but is in doubt, as with the British working class and the Pakistanis in England, then it has to be demonstrated physically. Everyone knows where they stand then – the class inequality is displayed, just as any other snob demonstrates superiority by exhibiting wealth or learning or ancestry. (1986: 29)

Such a class-bound conception finds little resonance in the cultural consciousness of the United States. Instead, our daily lives and artistic texts constantly reverberate, either overtly or covertly, with issues revolving about race.

But, for the most part, America prides itself precisely on being classless; indeed, our cherished national myths enshrine what one can do, not who you are or where you came from before that moment. The archetypal American hero remains the rugged loner who fights for personal rights and individual freedoms, not the union organiser who battles for a better hourly wage or the factory worker who struggles against the bosses. So in American society, to speak quite generally and perhaps naively, people define themselves more by race, or religion, or even ethnic groupings than by long-standing class stratifications, as they so often do in Britain. Not surprisingly, our films reflect these classless ideals and individual initiatives: the musical rewards the talented; the detective film highlights the cynical seeker of truth; the western mythologises the solitary defender of law and order; the gangster film rewards (and then destroys) the cunning criminal; the horror movie fears and pities the deformed monster. The point, however, is to defeat evil individuals, not to question, reform or destroy the basic system that spawned them. In essence, then, traditional American films see evil-doers as an aberration of a basically healthy society. They remain outside that society, intrinsically different from the mainstream and rarely signifying some internal social flaw that must be altered by fact or deed. Once they are dispatched, life returns to normal.

As opposed to this American vision of the one versus the many, British cinema depicts a persistent vision of irreconcilable binary opposites: of working class and management, of capitalism and socialism, of the lower and upper classes engaged in a ceaseless war against each other. These stark class-bound juxtapositions set off far too many internal alarms for most American viewers and, of course, the foregrounding of economic issues risks raising the biggest bogeyman of them all: the spectre of communism. Ironically, the working-class American finds little that is more threatening than communism, seeing its economic tenets as fundamentally anti-American. British films that attack the capitalistic system, seeing class issues as embedded within economic inequities, strike many American viewers as strident and offensive. Yet even British directors committed to the American film industry explore class issues within movies ostensibly about far different matters. Take, for example, Ridley Scott's surprisingly powerful summer bombshell, *Thelma and Louise* (1991). Most American directors could never equal Scott's sensitivity to the social position of these two women, seeing them as fatally constrained by their class in society as well as by their gender. Yet most American viewers ignore the class issues and focus solely on the feminist concerns, willing to challenge long-held gender stereotypes but not deeply-felt social beliefs. So while issues of class provided British moviemakers with a master theme, such concerns tended to characterise their films as mainly localised and essentially parochial.

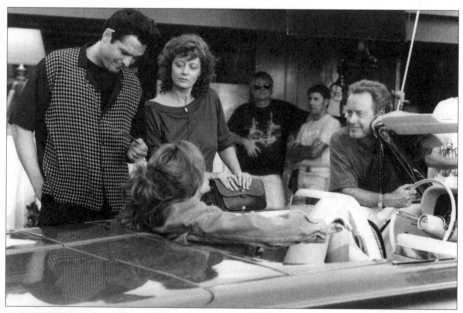

Director Ridley Scott, working mainly in the American film industry, incorporates a decidedly British sense of class-consciousness and social constraints in an unlikely vehicle, *Thelma and Louise* (1991)

American viewers uncomfortable with, or simply uninterested in, this continual emphasis on class distinctions also have little experience of the mode of filmmaking that profoundly shaped the British film industry: documentary. When was the last time you saw a non-fiction film in a movie theatre? How many times a week do you curl up on the couch to watch a documentary on television? Americans simply do not watch documentaries. In fact, only a handful have been released commercially over the years: *Harlan County, U.S.A.* (1970), *Hearts and Minds* (1974), *Roger & Me* (1989), *Truth or Dare* (1991). Probably few reading this have seen all four of these works. Even the scholarly establishment takes relatively little notice of documentaries, other than an occasional paper about Frederick Wiseman or the Maysles Brothers. With the exception of works about pioneering director Robert Flaherty, American film historians take equally sparse notice of documentary filmmaking. Take, for instance, Gerald Mast's classic study of world cinema, *A Short History of the Movies* (1986). Out of some 565 pages, Mast devotes 37 (including two about Flaherty and two about the role of documentary in English cinema) to examples of documentaries throughout the evolution of film, a number equal to the time he spends on French director Jean Renoir alone and less than half the space he allots to D. W. Griffith. One could easily imagine that a habitual American filmgoer, say one who averages a film every other week or so, would never have seen a documentary film outside of high-school health class.[1] This type of filmmaking, however, received far wider distribution and critical attention in Britain than in the United States, particularly during World War Two. Even more significantly, as Alan Lovell claims, 'the importance of the documentary movement lies not in the quality of individual films, but in the impact it had in general on British cinema' (quoted in Higson 1986: 72). That impact was aesthetic, thematic and stylistic. So, for example, the British film industry's commitment to realism as opposed to fantasy (even British fantasy films seem somehow realistic) springs from this source, as does its concern during the 1960s with exploring the lives of working-class men and its preference for black-and-white cinematography. John Grierson, a seminal figure in the development of British cinema, envisioned film as having primarily a social responsibility, unlike Hollywood movies, which functioned essentially as entertainment. Thus at the heart of the documentary idea is a powerful differentiation between 'realism' and 'escapism', between a serious, committed, engaged cinema, and mass entertainment. Further, this logic posits the 'realist' cinema, with its foundations in the documentary film movement, as the key point of reference in the call for an indigenous 'British' cinema (Higson 1986: 74).

Finally, of course, this documentary tradition found an institutionalised form in British television, as John Reith (the British television industry's equivalent to Grierson) incorporated the dogma of public service broadcasting into the consciousness of the British public. '"Actuality" and "documentary" are terms as synonymous with Britain', says Paul Swann, 'as neorealism is with Italy and the New Wave with France. Interestingly, all these were attempts to respond to the colonial control of the American film in their respective countries' (1989: 1). No British director could possibly escape the influence of Britain's documentary-realist tradition, a powerful ideological and aesthetic force that shaped directors' visions of the role and the responsibility of both the filmmaker and his or her film. So while the British documentary movement provided the commercial cinema with a particular form and focus, its aesthetics often rendered such films drably pedestrian and unable to compete with their flashy American counterparts.

The films of the Thatcher era covered in this anthology come out of these forceful traditions of a literary and theatrical heritage, of a class consciousness and documentary aesthetic that dominate the evolution of British cinema. Yet they deal with these legacies in some strikingly unique ways. Stephen Frears, for example, forges a new compromise with his literary sources, remaining faithful to the essential ideals of a piece but clearly adding his own vision to the work. Terence Davies makes excellent use of the documentary heritage, while simultaneously subverting the patriarchal oppressiveness of British society. Peter Greenaway and Derek Jarman bring a painter's eye to the modern British cinema, valuing visual details over narrative traditions. The independent collectives of blacks and of women shed increasing light on the connections between a class-bound society and the infusion of racism and sexism. But we should not see works by such directors as implicitly rejecting the strengths of previous eras. Rather, they manage to incorporate a decidedly British vision of the world without sinking into parochial specificity:

Our job in the UK is to set about defining 'British' pictures in the broadest possible terms. Our cinema can and must reflect a genuine *creative* perspective. It must reflect the desire to see Britain and the world through British eyes and attitudes, and to *communicate* what we see in an entertaining and comprehensive manner to our audiences around the world. (David Puttnam, quoted in Roddick 1985: 49)

Producer David Puttnam's quote argues for a vital British film industry that vigorously competes in the international market. Other insiders during the Thatcher era clearly understood that, rather than a lasting renaissance, this period should best be regarded, in director Christopher Petit's phrase, as 'a brief revival in production' (quoted in Roddick 1985: 22).

Whether part of a profound renaissance or a brief production revival, these pictures, often fuelled by their creators' disgust with the current state of British life, rank with the best movies made during the 1980s in any country in the world. British films of this period could not help being political (in the broadest sense of that word), as they charted the inexorably downward spiral of their homeland; but the best of them saw far beyond the passing concerns of partisan politics. Surely many of Margaret Thatcher's policies made these filmmakers' worst fears flesh. She attacked their deepest beliefs and laid waste their industry. As creators of movies, their weapon was the camera, not the rifle, and their bunker became the editing room. Though driven by their hatred of the present government, these visual artists still managed to tease the permanent out of the momentary. They instinctively understood that Mrs Thatcher's ideology, her creation and re-creation of past and present history, must be matched by an alternative vision that offered a different version of this era. Such a vision need not even be overtly political. It simply needed to observe with care and caution. To do that, these filmmakers reconfigured the British cinematic tradition. The resulting series of unique and significant films found a receptive international audience more concerned with cinematic style and thematic insights than with parochial politics. Yet, even from this close historical vantage point, we can recognise the power of their images and appreciate the depth of their imagination. Their pictures defined a turbulent era, revived the moribund British cinema, and froze a crucial moment in British culture.

NOTE

1 Documentaries are now far more popular whan when I originally wrote this piece in 1991. Works such as *Spellbound* (2002), *Capturing the Friedmans* (2003), *Inconvenient Truths* (2006) and, particularly, *Fahrenheit 9/11* (2004) have attracted far larger audiences than in the past. Both the advent of cable television, which provides fertile ground for a wide spectrum of documentary films, and the profusion of so-called 'reality programmes', which offer at least faux documentary approaches to entertainment, have contributed to the greater mainstream acceptance of non-fiction filmmaking.

WORKS CITED

Auty, Marty and Nick Roddick (eds) (1985) *British Cinema Now*. London: British Film Institute.

Barr, Charles (1986) 'Introduction: Amnesia and Schizophrenia', in Charles Barr (ed.) *All Our Yesterdays: 90 Years of British Cinema*. London: British Film Institute, 1–29.

Brown, Geoff (1986) '"Sister of the Stage": British Film and British Theatre', in Charles Barr (ed.) *All Our Yesterdays: 90 Years of British Cinema*. London: British Film Institute, 143–67.

Higson, Andrew (1986) 'Britain's Outstanding Contribution to the Film: The Documentary-Realist Tradition', in Charles Barr (ed.) (1986) *All Our Yesterdays: 90 Years of British Cinema*. London: British Film Institute, 72–97.

Hill, John (1986) *Sex, Class and Realism: British Cinema, 1956–1963*. London: British Film Institute.

Kureishi, Hanif (1986) *My Beautiful Laundrette and The Rainbow Sign*. London: Faber and Faber.

Mast, Gerald (1986) *A Short History of the Movies*, fourth edition. New York: Macmillan.

McFarlane, Brian (1986) 'A Literary Cinema? British Films and British Novels', in Charles Barr (ed.) *All Our Yesterdays: 90 Years of British Cinema*. London: British Film Institute, 120–42.

Murphy, Robert (1986) 'Under the Shadow of Hollywood', in Charles Barr (ed.) *All Our Yesterdays: 90 Years of British Cinema*. London: British Film Institute, 47–71.

Petley, Julian (1985) 'Reaching for the Stars', in Marty Auty and Nick Roddick (eds) *British Cinema Now*. London: British Film Institute, 111–22.

Roddick, Nick (1985) 'If the United States Spoke Spanish, We Would Have a Film Industry', in Marty Auty and Nick Roddick (eds) *British Cinema Now*. London: British Film Institute, 3–18.

Swann, Paul (1989) *The British Documentary Movement, 1926–1946*. Cambridge: Cambridge University Press.

Truffaut, François(1969) *Hitchcock*. London: Panther.

Wollen, Peter (1997) *Signs and Meaning in the Cinema*, third edition. London: British Film Institute.

PART ONE
CULTURAL CONTEXTS AND CINEMATIC CONSTRUCTIONS

1. THE RELIGION OF THE MARKET: THATCHERITE POLITICS AND THE BRITISH FILM OF THE 1980s

Leonard Quart

In the late 1950s and early 1960s, films like Karel Reisz's *Saturday Night and Sunday Morning* (1960), Tony Richardson's *The Loneliness of the Long Distance Runner* (1962) and Lindsay Anderson's *This Sporting Life* (1963) ushered in a 'New Wave' in British cinema that resurrected, in a more psychological and less socially-oriented form, the realistic tradition of John Grierson and Humphrey Jennings. This film revival paralleled a literary one – the revolt of the so-called Angry Young Men. Writers like John Braine, John Osborne and Colin Wilson wrote novels, plays and essays with working-class characters at their centre, creating a literature that noisily thumbed its nose at conventional class snobbery and the genteel values of polite, restrained behaviour. These writings, though much more politically conservative than they first appeared, attacked the philistinism and materialism of British society rather than the oppressiveness and inequity of its social institutions. The films, in turn, also focused on working-class characters, locales and concerns, a rarity in British cinema of the time, using psychological rather than documentary realism as a formal strategy. In fact, the films explored the consciousness and desires of their working-class protagonists and their ambivalent feelings about their own community, rather than the social texture and structure of that community itself. Films like *This Sporting Life* never expressed a hint of commitment to any specific political agenda or ideology (though Anderson and Reisz leaned to the left). Instead, they projected a broad social awareness and general sense of political responsibility conveyed, most incisively by Anderson's attack on traditional British cinema as 'snobbish, anti-intelligent, emotionally inhibited, wilfully blind to the conditions and problems of the present, dedicated to an out-of-date national ideal' (McFarlane 1986: 137).

These realist films appeared during a boom period of full employment and increased productivity, a time when Britain perceived itself to be an affluent society where unequal income distribution was beginning to disappear as a social problem and issue. Despite the growing prosperity, however, income and class inequalities continued to exist, but the political debates of the period usually avoided dealing with these unpleasant social and economic facts. The Tories had controlled the government since 1951, espousing economic policies in the late 1950s that differed little from those of Labour Party leader Hugh Gaitskill. Both parties shared a political commitment to welfare capitalism and Cold War ideology. In turn, the New Wave films expressed a social vision, more a moral and cultural critique than an overtly political one. The films' protagonists, like factory worker Arthur Seaton (Albert Finney) in *Saturday Night and Sunday Morning*, instinctively rebelled against the tedium and constraints of domestic life and work, his philosophy tersely summed up in a line like 'don't let the bastards grind you down'. Seaton, however, neither contemplated nor embraced any alternative political or social ideology. He valued sexuality and spontaneity, defied convention, and remained as alienated from his own working-class community as he was from the larger political and social system. Thus the emphasis of the New Wave films remained firmly on the autonomy and integrity of the individual versus social forces: the unseeing borstal staff in *The Loneliness of the Long Distance Runner*, the manipulative, callous rugby team owners in *This Sporting Life*; the insidious, stultifying consumer and television culture that threatened the spirit and soul running through almost all the films.

As invigorating and exciting as it was, the New Wave failed to sustain a renaissance in British cinema. Directors like Karel Reisz, Tony Richardson and John Schlesinger (*A Kind of Loving*, 1962) went on to careers in Hollywood, each directing only a couple more films in Britain; to this date, Lindsay Anderson has directed only five feature films in his home country. The next two decades saw formally imaginative, socially illuminating and psychologically penetrating films by directors like Nicolas Roeg, Ken Loach, Tony Garnett and Joseph Losey, but the vast body of British cinema remained mired in uninspired mediocrity and predictability. It was not until the Thatcher era, 1979–90, that genuine signs of a British film resurgence could again be seen. Margaret Thatcher took power during a time of profound economic trouble, government impotence and declining national prestige. In dealing with these problems, she helped construct a much different social and political world than the one promoted in the 1950s by the centrist consensual politics of Prime Minister Harold Macmillan. The accompanying film renaissance stands as one of the more positive by-products of the Thatcher ethos, though in an almost totally oppositional and critical manner.

Margaret Thatcher's father shaped her political personality. Alfred Roberts, a petit-bourgeois Methodist grocer and self-made man turned smalltown politician, lived by such values as self-help, moral virtue and public duty. In her own way, his daughter closely adhered to these values during her years as Prime Minister. Given this background, she was strongly attracted to the monetarist economic theories (an imposition of stringent controls of the money supply) of American New Right economist Milton Friedman. Though strict monetarism was abandoned during her first term, she continually displayed an almost religious commitment to the idea of the market playing the central role in the society; in a sense, she extended the economic values of the grocery store to the society at large. Thatcher vowed to reduce the regulatory role of government and bureaucracy, attacking welfare state dependency by reducing social spending, services (transportation, education and health) and taxes. She also aided the wealthy by easing the capital gains tax and cutting the top tax rate on earned income from 83 per cent to 40 per cent. She privatised public companies like British Airways, vehemently criticised socialism, espoused an ethic of individual self-sufficiency, and promoted the avaricious pursuit of personal profit as a moral virtue. Her social perspective helped purge traditional British guilt feelings about material gain, 'which inflicted alike egalitarian socialists who had no money and paternalist conservatives born with plenty of it' (Young 1989: 256).

Thatcher was an extremely overbearing, vindictive and energetic politician who acted out of a sense of moral rectitude and certitude; she never exhibited a tinge of self-doubt about her political principles and moral ends. For eleven years (as the longest-serving Prime Minister in the twentieth century) and through three victorious elections, she totally dominated and radically transformed the political and social life of Great Britain. Many of the changes Thatcher wrought in British political life remain deeply set in the country's cultural matrix. She operated as an ideological, autocratic politician who polarised opponents and tolerated no dissent from her cabinet colleagues, invoking both hostility and devotion from members of her own party, rather than seeking to mute conflict and create a political consensus. Though never really liked by the British public because of her abrasive and unsympathetic personality, she did gain their grudging respect.

Thatcher recreated the Tory party by taking power out of the hands of the squirearchy and aristocracy – cautious, paternalistic, socially concerned politicians like the Carringtons, the Pyms and the Whitelaws – who stood for moderation and compromise. Primarily men of the upper class whose politics were shaped under the aegis of Macmillan, they were committed to government spending and Keynesian economics. Their policies remained dedicated to the idea of 'one nation' rather than to Thatcher's neo-Darwinian notion of the social good being derived from the conflict of self-interested groups. After the first few difficult years, with unemployment rising to three million and the collapse of industrial production, she constructed an inclusive, populist version of the Tory Party. Furthermore, she guided the Tories as their appeal extended to the rising lower-middle class, the skilled working class, and even manual labourers – deeply encroaching on traditional Labour Party loyalty by leading the nation to a jingoistic, flag-waving 'victory' in the Falklands and by promoting the expansion of share ownership and the sale of council-owned properties to tenants (turning one million families into homeowners). Thatcher envisioned people's social class position more as a situation to be changed and overcome rather than as a historically-fixed state. She was, however, no egalitarian; for example, she opposed redistributive programmes, seeing little need to soften the gap between the wealthy and the impoverished or to cushion the social and economic pain of those who faded in the painful struggle for economic success. At the same time, she opposed any class, racial or ethnic constraints on economic mobility. Advocating the creation of a mythic meritocracy, she garnered her greatest political support from members of the self-made middle class. And though class still continues to play a prime role in British life, Thatcher did leave a legacy of a less calcified, more fluid class system.

Thatcher found her prime political villains in the trade unions, whose commitment to collective rights and blanket protections stood in direct conflict with her belief in the unrestricted play of free markets. Because of their inflationary wage claims and their destructive strikes during the Callaghan years (the late 1970s), they provided Thatcher with an unpopular enemy, one she treated in a contemptuous manner matched by no other postwar Prime Minister. Building upon her election mandate, she succeeded in passing a series of anti-union laws: the ending of the closed shop, the banning of political strikes and secondary and mass picketing, and the use of the secret ballot for the election of union leaders and the approval of strikes. With the bloody collapse of the ill-conceived coal miners' strike of 1984–85, Thatcher won the nation's admiration for the strength she demonstrated in defeating her perfect foil – left-wing, rhetoric-spouting, uncompromising miners' union leader Arthur Scargill. Her defeat of the miners led to growing worker disenchantment with unions and, coupled with a rise in unemployment in the declining manufacturing industries, to a loss of about a quarter of the country's union membership. Thus, Thatcher profoundly reduced the power of unions. Strikes became rare and when attempted were usually unsuccessful.

She did not face much stronger opposition from either the Labour Party or the centrist Liberal-SDP (Social Democratic Party) Alliance. In fact, both opposition parties stumbled about in confusion, unable to define a political course that would strike a popular spark. The Labour Party, especially, was beset with factionalism and a penchant for self-destructive politics. The party leadership had to deal with continual political onslaughts from its far left. It also carried the burden of a seemingly outmoded ideological legacy that granted Thatcher a great deal of political immunity during her time in office. This immunity allowed Thatcher, despite her anti-statist position on issues involving economic regulation, to strengthen the central government at the expense of local government. She abolished the left-wing Greater London Council, reduced local council power over education and housing, and placed stricter controls over all local expenditure. Government intrusion upon freedom of the press (and other media) also greatly increased, since she viewed national security as superseding the right to publish and broadcast. Clearly inherent in the Thatcher ethos was a strongly authoritarian, anti-libertarian strain that viewed freedom as primarily economic rather than political in nature.

During Thatcher's last term in office, she began to lose her instinct for gauging the popular mood. Her political support rapidly diminished, and she lagged behind the Labour Party in the polls. By 1990 the boom of the 1980s had ended in a trade deficit, double-digit inflation and continuing unemployment. Similarly, she presided over declining manufacturing output, labour productivity and business investment. Thatcher compounded these unfavourable economic statistics by passing an extremely unpopular poll tax. This regressive head tax fell equally on all adults between the ages of 18 to 65. Introduced in Scotland on 1 April 1989, it went into effect in England and Wales in 1990. The poll tax replaced the somewhat more progressive local property tax ('the rates') and was supposed to spread the cost of local government services like roads, policing and schools to everybody who lived in an area – council-flat tenants as well as property owners. Thatcher viewed the tax as the 'flagship' of her third term, but the law aroused the rage of both rural and inner-city inhabitants, who saw the tax as totally inequitable. Millions of people refused to pay. A massive London protest demonstration was organised, ultimately turning into one of the most violent Central London riots in decades. Freed by this dramatic shift in public mood, her own party, fearing the loss of seats, forced her unwilling resignation in November 1990. She was replaced by a very different sort of politician – her own handpicked successor, the more pragmatic and centrist, less ideological and abrasive John Major. Since leaving office, Thatcher has been a politically disruptive force for the Tories, continually sniping at Major's actions. In fact, she became sufficiently alienated from the party to announce her unwillingness to seek a parliamentary seat in the next election.

Still, despite her abrupt fall from grace and the ephemeral quality of her economic revolution, Thatcher left an indelible mark on British politics and society. She cut the economic power of the state while expanding the political power of the central government. She helped create a Britain where the rich got richer while the poor became more impoverished (with 20 per cent of the people living under the poverty line), reversing a 40-year pattern where incomes were gradually growing more equal. By 1988 the best-off 10 per cent of the population enjoyed nearly nine times more income than the worst-off 10 per cent, though real wages did go up for the majority of those who worked.

Thatcher promoted an individualist ethos and an entrepreneurial culture where the acquisition of wealth and the consumption of goods became the prime values, while the ethic of social responsibility and mutual aid began to unravel. It was now more stylish 'to consume rather than care' (Young 1989: 537). England became a more morally callous country of striking social contrasts: a decaying industrial North where mining villages and steel towns (Labour Party bastions) began to wither away, and a booming South dominated by immense office and residential construction projects (such as London's Canary Wharf) and high-tech and financial industries. The Labour Party had almost no seats in the South, except for the inner London area, while Scotland and the North returned vast Labour majorities. Amid the rising standard of living, an embittered, visible underclass began to develop; the number of homeless rose to one million (150,000 under the age of 25); burglary, car thievery and vandalism greatly increased; and the country held the dubious distinction of having the highest per capita prison population within the European Community. Still the yuppification of southern England bloomed. Building cranes, glass office buildings, bistros, boutiques and smartly-dressed investment bankers shared the London streets with scabrous homeless men living in cardboard villages and doorways on the Strand. Computer executives strolled past adolescent runaways (the weekly welfare benefits for the under-25 unemployed were severely cut) begging dolefully outside tube stations and on the steps of the National Theatre.

Thatcher entered office attacking the permissive society and trumpeting traditional bourgeois values like respectability, family and nation – and a strain of Thatcherism promoted a repressive agenda on law and order, abortion and homosexuality. But despite Thatcher's ritualistic deference to the prime significance of the family, her economic policies subverted many of those same values. In the Britain of the 1980s, acquisitive individualism and aggressive self-interest thrived, not Victorian domestic virtues. This belief in unlimited economic growth superseded the preservation of the past. However, Thatcherite entrepreneurial adventurousness and risk-taking produced some positive effects, turning Britain into an economically competitive force in Europe. Thatcher revived an almost congenitally sick and sluggish economy by promoting the development of modern business methods and technologies, attracting foreign investment, weeding out failing businesses and ending factory overmanning (Anon. 1990). Until the economic recession in 1990–91, the Thatcher years saw the growth of a more efficient and productive economy, which in 1988 was 'still growing at 4 per cent after seven years' continuous expansion' (Young 1989: 532). British society became Americanised: much more efficient, hedonistic, cash-obsessed and competitive. It was now dominated by a driven New Class, one utterly removed from the more moribund, communally-oriented working class and the complacently paternalistic upper-class cultures that traditionally dominated British life.

Thatcher's success changed the parameters of political debate and tactics. It forced Labour to transform itself into a centrist, European-style Social Democratic party, so that it could become politically competitive again. Under the leadership of Neil Kinnock, who replaced Michael Foot after the 1983 election debacle, the party modernised itself. Kinnock, an intellectually uninspired but politically adept Welshman, made the party more media- and public relations-conscious. With the help of Shadow Cabinet members like Roy Hattersley, Gerald Kaufman, Bryan Gould and John Smith, he forced Labour to re-evaluate many of its past political positions. Faced with a diminishing industrial working class, the party expanded its electoral appeal to a wider range of social interest groups, including small business people, consumers and environmentalists. It began this process by moving away from its anachronistic commitment to public ownership – repudiating clause four of the party's constitution (which calls for nationalisation of the basic industries) and pushing the left wing to the periphery of the party. Ultimately, Labour purged the Trotskyist Militant Tendency altogether, muting the power of grass-roots activists and militantly class-conscious union leaders. Party leadership now rests firmly in the hands of pragmatic members of the House of Commons, whose politics revolve around what is socially possible rather than ideologically pure.

Because Labour's union base no longer carries the same political weight, the party now advocates greater collaboration between government and industry. It also grants managements the freedom to strengthen their companies. Labour has even moved toward an ideological acceptance of the free market, except that it seeks to make it work more efficiently and with greater responsiveness to social needs and the public interest. It essentially accepts privatisation of industry, but wants to reverse some of the destructive consequences of Thatcher's policy of business deregulation; for example, strengthening the system of environmental regulation and establishing compulsory licensing in the construction industry. Almost magically, the traditional class-based Labour antagonism to business and management has begun to disappear. The party has dropped a number of other articles of its faith, including unilateralism and opposition to the European Community. It went so far as to support the Gulf War – quieting, even politically strong-arming in the name of a unified party, Labour MPs with deep reservations about the Allied military intervention. Labour is also more concerned about issues involving individual rights, and consumer and feminist concerns, than in the past. It understands that it must appeal to a greater variety of social interest groups, and that individuals are often members of more than one interest group – their political commitments being more fluid now than when class loyalty was the primary way of defining one's politics.

Thatcher (with the unplanned help of events in Eastern Europe and the former Soviet Union) probably killed off socialism as a viable political alternative in Britain, but she never destroyed the British public's support for the National Health Service (NHS) and other prime institutions of the welfare state. People may have supported Thatcher at the voting booth, but they never embraced all the ideological baggage she aggressively carried with her. After eleven years of Thatcher, a majority still desire a government that demonstrates social concern. In polls taken after Thatcher's third victory, six out of ten voters supported maintaining health care as an entirely public service, 55 per cent favoured collectivism instead of self-reliance in welfare policy, and 79 per cent desired a society that valued social concern more than the creation of wealth (Young 1989: 529). Labour responded to the public's desires by staking its political future on being able to deliver social services more efficiently (for example, improvement of adult education and worker retraining programmes and stronger management of the NHS) and to sustain fuller employment. Chastened by and sensitive to the historic political changes that took place at home and abroad during the previous decade, Labour also projected a more limited idea of what the central government can achieve. It envisioned a future state that 'will be more decentralised, more regulator and facilitator than provider and director' (Leadbeater 1990: 16). The vision is mundane, safe and unromantic, more politically reactive to Thatcher's ethos than a genuinely imaginative alternative, but probably the only politically sensible one at this historical juncture.

Thatcher's relationship with the opposition Labour Party was by necessity an antagonistic one, but her relationship with intellectuals and artists was even more embattled. Thatcher never pretended to be an intellectual. She directed her mind toward solving concrete problems rather than speculating about abstract political ideas. But nobody could deny that she was extremely sharp and capable of complete mastery of political and economic detail and policy. She also utilised a number of well-known intellectual advisers and supporters, like philosopher Anthony Quinton, ageing 'Angry Young Man' Kingsley Amis, and historians A. L. Rouse, Robert Conquest and Hugh Thomas, among others. The die, however, was cast when after first taking office, she cut deeply into university funding and eliminated 3,000 university jobs. In 1985 a government green paper, 'Higher Education into the 1990s', called for the universities 'to serve the national economy more effectively' (Young 1989: 414). The disinterested and non-utilitarian quest for knowledge now found itself subject to Thatcherite cost-benefit analysis. The universities took their rage out on Thatcher in the only way they could, Oxford bestowing the unusual rebuff of refusing to grant her an honorary degree.

The arts establishment displayed a similar revulsion, attacking her as much for what they viewed as her persona – voice, clothes and personal tastes – as for her cutting state support to arts institutions and her overall political agenda. Though Thatcher never exhibited any particular interest in the arts beyond a poem by Kipling or a Frederick Forsyth thriller, she was no more of a philistine than Labour Prime Ministers like Wilson and Callaghan. Still, institutions like the Royal Shakespeare Company or the Royal Opera House 'that depended on the public purse started at a disadvantage in the Thatcherite scale of priorities [and] had to justify their existence against ever stiffer presumptions of guilt' (Young 1989: 413). Consequently, Thatcher treated the arts, and the film business – notwithstanding her personal preferences (she disliked film) – no differently than any other business. For example, the Thatcher government passed a new Films Bill in 1984–85, one that applied market principles to the movie industry. The bill abolished the 1950 Eady Levy, a law that had distributed a per centage of box-office receipts to British-made films, and provided no replacement for these lost revenues. It also abolished a 25 per cent tax break for investment in film production and privatised the National Film Finance Corporation (NFFC), thus eliminating the 'only direct form of government involvement in the field of commercial film production in Britain' (Roddick 1985: 14).

The Thatcher government's denial of aid for British film production merely compounded the long-term problems of a historically sick industry whose audience continued to decline: the average Briton attends the cinema on an average of once a year. In contrast with the generous subsidy policies of Western European countries like Sweden, even British governments committed to state intervention rarely gave much economic support to film production. The British film industry, of course, never freed itself of Hollywood domination. This colonisation holds both for the pre-eminence of American films in British movie theatres and on television, and for Hollywood's success at weaning away many of Britain's top directors (for example, Alan Parker, Ridley Scott, Stephen Frears) to work in a secure, well-financed industry and achieve more lucrative careers. Film in Britain also confronted the generally pro-theatre, anti-cinematic bias of the arts establishment, and faced competition for an audience with some very striking and original television programming (such as Dennis Potter's *The Singing Detective*) and home video – Britain having one of the highest ownership and rental rates in the world. In contrast with the film industry, television remains a heavily subsidised business in which most film people, including directors like Ken Loach, Michael Apted and Stephen Frears, among others, have done a great deal of creative work. Another difficulty that the industry faces is that two major chains, Rank and EMI, and two smaller ones, Cannon-Classic and the Star Group, dominate national film distribution. All of these chains primarily show Hollywood films, making it difficult for independent, intellectually difficult and stylistically experimental British films to receive nationwide exposure.

Despite, however, the industry's economic precariousness and limited resources, the 1980s saw an exciting renaissance of British film. The revival, brought on by renewed American interest in British film because of *Chariots of Fire*'s (1981) success, was fuelled by America's expanded cable television market. More important for the development of a low-budget, intellectually (though rarely formally) adventurous cinema was Channel 4. This adventurous British television channel exhibited an interest in subsidising film production and commissioned films from independent producers. During the 1980s, a number of out-of-the-mainstream, commercially risky films like *The Draughtsman's Contract* (1982), *The Ploughman's Lunch* (1983), *Another Time, Another Place* (1983) and *My Beautiful Laundrette* (1985) received most of their funding from Channel 4, which allocated the greater part of its drama budget to producing feature films. These films were first released in movie theatres and subsequently shown on television. In addition, despite the Thatcher government's unwillingness to aid the film industry, it did establish a general mood that encouraged economic risk-taking and experimentation with new and more innovative business practices (for example, Channel 4).

Thatcher's prime contribution to British filmmaking was not the business climate she created, but the subject matter her policies and the culture she helped create provided British directors. The majority of British films of the 1980s never engaged in open critiques of Thatcherism, but the ethos she created seemed to become the implicit or explicit subject of many of the period's best films. Of course, many films, like John Boorman's visually striking *Excalibur* (1981), John Irvin's intimate *Turtle Diary* (1985) and Bruce Robinson's rite-of-passage *Withnail and I* (1986) seem untouched by Thatcherism. But from Ken Loach's spare, documentary-style film about drifting, unemployed youth in Sheffield, *Looks and Smiles* (1981), to Peter Greenaway's stylised allegory of Thatcherite greed and vulgarity, *The Cook, the Thief, His Wife and Her Lover* (1989), a large number of British films responded to Thatcherism.

The film that began the renaissance and helped grant British directors the confidence to confront British subjects was Hugh Hudson's Oscar-winning *Chariots of Fire*. A favourite of President Reagan, the film offered a conventional, inflated paean to a triumphant, 1924-Olympics-winning Great Britain, one skilfully evoked by the use of a booming soundtrack, a great many slow-motion shots of handsome young men running on the beach, rich period detail and romantic superimpositions. Shrewdly, this film uses the victory of anti-establishment characters, at odds with the insidious bigotry and genteel snobbery and hypocrisy of the English establishment, to exult in nationalistic feeling and implicitly endorse the Thatcherite ethos.

Heroes of the 1924 Olympics, Eric Liddell (Ian Charleson) and Harold Abrahams (Ben Cross), in *Chariots of Fire* (1981), the movie that began the British film renaissance

The film's driven central figure, Harold Abrahams (Ben Cross), a Jewish immigrant financier's son who rejects his Cambridge University masters' idea of gentlemanly values, hires a professional coach to train him for the Olympics. Abrahams and his Italian-Arab coach, Sam Mussabini (Ian Holm), are seen by the Cambridge masters as both ethnic outsiders and aggressive arrivistes – both their class and nationality are held against them. However, Abrahams wins the Olympic 100-yard dash and becomes the 'model Englishman' of the Gilbert and Sullivan song, one fully assimilating into the Establishment he always hungered to enter, ultimately being buried in an Anglican church service accompanied by a choir singing Blake's traditional hymn 'Jerusalem'.

Chariots of Fire remains overtly critical of a Britain built on rigid class demarcations and aristocratic hauteur, but in its stead it implicitly endorses the Thatcherite ethos of a nation based on a meritocracy of the ambitious, the diligent and the gifted. In the film's vision, the Establishment's values begin to shift, becoming more tolerant of individual difference and comprehending that the future no longer rests solely within their control. But the film's idea of a more dynamic, diverse nation, one where a man like Abrahams has the chance to succeed, is depicted with as much uncritical sentimentality as the Cambridge masters treat their own hierarchical and racist vision of Britain. It is a fitting message for a Thatcher-ruled Britain where the traditional class lines give way to individual achievement, usually defined in terms of wealth and status.

Other, less exportable 1980s films with British subjects deal with contemporary Britain rather than some luminous historical moment. For example, Lindsay Anderson's mordant and angry film, *Britannia Hospital* (1982), stands devoid of even one sympathetic character. Its bitter, heavy-handed satire caricatures all segments of British society – megalomaniacal scientists; resentful and indolent workers; morally unconscious, drug-stupified television people; absurd aristocrats; and ranting, violent leftist demonstrators. Anderson permeates his Britain with strikes, terrorist attacks and riots. This grotesque version of Britain of the late 1970s – the last years of the Callaghan administration – conflated with the first strike-filled years of Thatcher's reign, shows Anderson as totally cynical and despairing about the aspirations of the Left, expressing only contempt for a despised British establishment. In fact, his anguish about the chaotic state of the nation here extends to a totally pessimistic view of the human condition itself.

A much quieter film, Richard Eyre's *The Ploughman's Lunch*, deals directly with Thatcherism. Subsidised by Channel 4, this sardonic, literate and stylistically conventional movie perceptively satirises London media life, as well as the political and social climate of Thatcher's Britain. The film centres around an ambitious, opportunistic BBC radio news editor of working-class origins, James Penfield (a subtle, muted performance by Jonathan Pryce), who avidly pursues class, status and an unattainable upper-class woman, Susi (Charlie Dore). Penfield, an unpleasant and even repellent character, represents a fitting anti-heroic figure for an ethos that eschews social concern and commitment in favour of the celebration of individual success. Penfield can pretend his working-class parents do not exist when it suits his purposes. He remains passively remote from his dying mother, the emotional desperation of a colleague and the moral fervour of the Greenham Common women. He also displays a gift for adapting his political convictions to the person he is talking

Stranded in the countryside, journalist James Penfield (Jonathan Pryce) is cornered by the Green-ham Common protesters, to whom he promises press coverage, in *The Ploughman's Lunch* (1983)

to – turning into a proponent of imperial Britain and the invasion of Suez when talking to his conservative publisher, and anti-Suez and sympathetic to socialism when talking to a left-leaning historian.

The Ploughman's Lunch does more than focus on one driven careerist's saga. Eyre totally entwines James' fortunes with a pointed critique of the moral emptiness of British public life. The BBC news staff meetings function as gatherings of wary, cynical professionals who lack any moral or intellectual response to the news. They aim to find the right balance, to provide a great deal of soft news and avoid contro-versial stories, like the Greenham Common women, that could upset the bland social order they wish to convey. In other spheres, book publishing turns into merely the packaging of commercial products, while advertising creates fabricated pasts like the supposedly eighteenth-century 'ploughman's lunch' – invented in the 1960s in some London marketing office.

The 'ploughman's lunch' is a metaphor for all the falsifications – private and public – that Penfield and other men on the make in Thatcher's Britain construct. Penfield diligently writes a book on Suez, revising its humiliating history so that it can be viewed as a predecessor worthy of the imperial Falklands victory. To top all these fabrications off, Eyre seamlessly fuses footage of the 1982 Tory Party conference in Brighton with his fictional story. At that conference, Margaret Thatcher makes political capital by invoking the successful Falklands invasion as a sign of the renewal of the British spirit – one more powerful example of how hype and promotion substi-tute for reality. Like most of the 1980s films critical of Thatcher, *The Ploughman's Lunch* offers no defined leftist or other specifically political alternative to her ethos. The only socialist in the film, Ann Barrington (Rosemary Harris), a middle-aged histo-

Rosemary Harris plays Ann Barrington, an academic socialist whose life is at odds with her politics, in *The Ploughman's Lunch*

rian, lives a life of affluence and total comfort in a grand Norfolk house, while still indulging in empty, reflexively leftist critiques of the Labour Party. The prototype of the academic socialist, her insulated, privileged everyday life is totally at odds with her political convictions. While the Greenham Common protesters' moral passion is treated sympathetically, they are still seen as ineffectual and a touch absurd (see Quart 1985).

A richer, more emotionally complex and optimistic work than *The Ploughman's Lunch*, one that provides a direct and corrosive critique of Thatcherism, is Mike Leigh's *High Hopes* (1988). Leigh, a much more original, idiosyncratic director than Eyre, and a man rooted in experimental theatre, uses little camera movement and builds the film around a minimal and loosely-structured narrative. In *High Hopes* Leigh evokes the social mood and class tensions of Thatcher's London through the actions and interactions of his seven main characters – three couples and the ageing, isolated mother of the film's main character, Cyril. In creating his slice of London, he moves from satire to farce to genuine pathos. The central, most sympathetic and nuanced characters in the film are Cyril (Philip Davis) and Shirley (Ruth Sheen). Shaggy-haired, left-wing, bohemian and marginally linked to the working class, Cyril smokes pot, reads Lenin for Beginners, and works at a dead-end job as a motorcycle messenger. An alien in Thatcher's Britain, he is a man without interest in money and status, one who must angrily adjust to being treated as invisible by an impersonal, profit-obsessed society. The couple even own a cactus named Thatcher.

Cyril, choked with feelings of class resentment, still does obeisance to Marx and his vision of society. Although committed to social change, he ruefully admits that he sits on his backside in despair because he just is not sure what to do politically. Shirley may be bucktoothed and ungainly, but her radiance and warmth make her seem beautiful at times, and she is connected to the world in a more concrete and knowing and less ideological way than Cyril. Leigh displays little use for leftist slogans or sentimentality. A woman-friend of Cyril and Shirley's who anxiously spouts leftist rhetoric about changing the world and going to help the peasants in Nicaragua looks like someone whose politics function more as a psychological lifeline than as a thought-out commitment. The film's animus, however, is not directed at the Left, but at the other two couples, who adapt, in different ways, to the Thatcherite ethos.

Leigh uses the snobbish Tory couple who live next door to Cyril's depressed, disconnected mother, Mrs Bender (Edna Dore), as venomous comic caricatures to send up gentrification and Thatcherite social callousness. The wife, Laetitia (Leslie Manville), conveys the brittle, harsh inhumanity of a pint-sized Thatcher, as she briskly advises Mrs Bender to buy her house so she can resell it for a nice profit. The couple use expressions like 'tip-top' and 'post-haste' – sounding like extras from *Brideshead Revisited* – though much of their manner derives from aspiration and mimicry rather than inheritance. Mrs Bender is obviously an embarrassing neighbour for this upwardly mobile couple to have – a melancholy, downscale, working-class widow, one whose presence only lowers their street's property value.

The third couple centres around Cyril's hysterical, nouveau-riche sister, Valerie (Heather Tobias), a shrill, overdressed vulgarian who puts her make-up on with a trowel. Valerie's husband is a lecherous lout of a used-car dealer, and they predictably live in an overstuffed, garish suburban house. But despite Valerie's success, at least along Thatcherite lines of making money and acquiring material goods, she remains unsure of her class position and painfully tries to imitate Laetitia's yuppie dress and manner. (The traditional class structure and style still carry a great deal of social weight in Britain.) Leigh's portrait of a leopardskin-coat-wearing Valerie

Shirley (Ruth Sheen) and Cyril (Philip Davis), a left-wing, working-class couple in Mike Leigh's *High Hopes* (1988)

sometimes goes over the top, but the pathos of days spent exercising, consuming and hungering for affection from her abusive husband gives the stereotype some redeeming poignance.

In contrast to his satiric treatment of the smug, odious Tory couple and the unhappy, selfish Valerie and her boor of a husband, Leigh depicts Cyril and Shirley in a more naturalistic fashion. They demonstrate more than a single dimension, and their intimate behaviour – talking, fighting, having sex – feels utterly genuine. Leigh holds out a touch of hope for Cyril and Shirley in a society riven with avarice and lack of compassion. By the film's conclusion, Cyril clearly knows that this society will not suddenly be transformed in accordance with the high political hopes he still holds in his head: pursuing Marx's vision of a classless society is now merely, in his words, like 'pissing in the wind'. But he is not defeated; in fact, without the film providing any explanation for the emotional change, he feels more serene, more willing to come to terms with life's injustice and have a child with Shirley – something he previously refused to do. *High Hopes* provides no political alternative to Thatcherism, but it suggests ways to live more humanly, even amid the social inequity and meanness of Thatcher's Britain. Those grander high hopes of radical political change no longer have much viability, but Cyril balances his political disillusionment with the more modest hope of building a humane and caring life with Shirley (see Quart & Quart 1989).

In addition to *High Hopes*, other British films deal directly with Thatcherism, like Chris Bernard's small fable *Letter to Brezhnev* (1985) and David Drury's *Defence of the Realm* (1985). The former centres around two working-class women who feel permanently imprisoned in a depressed Liverpool suburb, until ironically a Russian sailor arrives to offer one of them hope. The latter film, a well-made, paranoid thriller, poses direct political questions about the functioning of Thatcher's police-state-like security services, and the conservative press's willing collaboration with their murderous activities.

More imaginative and intellectually resonant than most of the British films of the 1980s were Stephen Frears and Hanif Kureishi's literate and ironic *My Beautiful Laundrette* (1985) and *Sammy and Rosie Get Laid* (1987). Both films depict Thatcher's Britain as dominated by racism, greed and social injustice, but they eschew an orthodox leftist perspective for a more ambiguous, unpredictable point of view. Frears and Kureishi avoid sentimentalising victims of prejudice or economic deprivation and, though men with leftist sympathies, equally subvert both schematic leftist thinking and respectable authority. Their commitment is to an anarchic, impulsive and sexual life, and consequently they are sympathetic to characters with size and panache – even if they turn out to be capitalist rogues and authoritarian executioners. In fact, the only unqualified villain in the two films is an absurdly posh-accented, arrogant Margaret Thatcher.

Other directors, like Marek Kanievska and Michael Radford, use the past implicitly to criticise present-day Britain. Kanievska's decorative *Another Country* (1984), set in an archetypal public school in the 1930s (though it could be England of the 1980s), views the sadism and power games that dominate student life as morally bankrupt and ominous apprenticeships for future political power. Radford's *Another Time, Another Place* is a luminously composed exploration of the clash of cultures – expressive, emotionally open Italian POWs versus chill, repressed Scots – in rural northern

Scotland in 1944. The film, less concerned with depicting the reality of Scottish life during World War Two, strongly affirms a woman's sexuality and humanness as she struggles to break from the constraints of a dour and rigid community. Both *Another Time, Another Place* and Radford's imaginatively visualised version of Orwell's novel *Nineteen-Eighty-Four* (1984) place their emphasis on human feeling, love and the inner life as antidotes to either a constricted communal life or the horrors of collectivism and state terrorism. Radford's films abhor repressive dogmatism, rejecting all political ideologies and systems for a belief in the freedom to express all the contradictory and flawed elements that being human entails. Stating that Britain in the 1980s is too complex a phenomenon for any ideology to explain, Radford claims that we inhabit a world where 'all the things we were taught to believe have crumbled away' (quoted in Park 1984: 100). For Radford, the only belief system functioning in Britain in the 1980s was Thatcherism, an ideology that utterly repelled him.

Directors and screenwriters like Leigh, Frears and Kureishi may not exactly echo Radford's sentiments, but they too convey that both the Thatcher ethos and the traditional leftist political alternatives to her rule were no longer viable in the Britain of the 1980s. Cultural and social structures that once reverberated morally and politically – like left-wing politics, the unions, the church and even the class system – no longer played the same social role. In her desire to transform Britain into a more assertive, efficient, profit-oriented society, Margaret Thatcher created a world of rapidly changing, often socially and morally alienated values, a world that severed itself from many of the institutions and norms that once dominated British society. For eleven years she controlled and shaped the British political and social landscape, looming as a larger-than-life figure in the consciousness and vision of some of its best film directors. Most of their films expressed a revulsion with Thatcherism; still, their anger rarely turned to vaporous and schematic polemics, evolving instead into the complex formal texture and imagination of art. Thatcher never provided direct help to the film industry, but her powerful, often oppressive, presence moved British filmmakers to burn brightly for at least one decade.

WORKS CITED

Anon. (1990) 'The Thatcher Record: To the Victor These Spoils', *Economist*, 24–30 November, 17–20.

Leadbeater, Charlie (1990) 'A Head without a Heart', *Marxism Today*, July, 16–17.

McFarlane, Brian (1986) 'A Literary Cinema? British Films and British Novels', in Charles Barr (ed.) *All Our Yesterdays: 90 Years of British Cinema*. London: British Film Institute, 120–42.

Park, James (1984) *Learning to Dream: The New British Cinema*. London: Faber and Faber.

Quart, Leonard (1985) 'The Ploughman's Lunch', *Cineaste*, 14, 3, 48–9.

Quart, Leonard and Barbara Quart (1989) 'High Hopes', *Cineaste*, 17, 2, 47, 56–7.

Roddick, Nick (1985) 'If the United States Spoke Spanish, We Would Have a Film Industry', in Martyn Auty and Nick Roddick (eds) *British Cinema Now*. London: British Film Institute, 3–18.

Young, Hugo (1989) *The Iron Lady*. New York: Farrar Strauss Giroux.

2. THE LAST NEW WAVE: MODERNISM IN THE BRITISH FILMS OF THE THATCHER ERA

Peter Wollen

Author's note: When I wrote the original essay for this volume, Derek Jarman was very much with us. Sadly, he passed away on 19 February 1994. He is missed.

– Peter Wollen

Independent filmmakers of the 1980s reacted strongly against the effects of Thatcherism. They responded to the imposition of market criteria in every sector of society, to political authoritarianism, to the 'two nations' project of Thatcherism, and to the leading role of the City, in films as various as Laura Mulvey and Peter Wollen's *Crystal Gazing* (1980), Terry Gilliam's *Brazil* (1985), Derek Jarman's *The Last of England* (1987), Stephen Frears and Hanif Kureishi's *Sammy and Rosie Get Laid* (1987), Mike Leigh's *High Hopes* (1988), Reece Auguiste's *Twilight City* (1989) and Peter Greenaway's *The Cook, the Thief, His Wife and Her Lover* (1989). Paradoxically, these are all London films, precisely because of the success of Thatcher's polarisation of the country between North and South – a polarisation that, as shown in the films, is doubled within the metropolis itself. Their roots can be traced back to the 1960s – to the art world, the satire boom, experimental theatre and the post-1968 avant-garde. It was in these areas that a modernist impulse had finally made itself felt in British culture and had eventually combined with an emphasis on the visual dimension of television, theatre and film. Together, these films provide a definitive picture of the Thatcherisation of London.

Negatively, Thatcherism has aimed to destroy the postwar Keynesian settlement, dismantle the public services provided by the state, and eliminate obtrusive foci of political opposition. Positively, Thatcherism combines three elements: (i) an economic 'unregulated market' neoliberalism; (ii) a politically neoconservative authoritarianism; and (iii) a social 'two nations' project, dividing the country geographically, between North and South, and socially, in terms of the labour market, between a de-unionised 'peripheral' sector and a 'core' company union sector. The 'two nations' project, of course, hits ethnic minorities especially hard and encourages a sharp division between 'inner city' and suburb. Thatcherism is a modernising movement in a very specific sense. It aims to modernise the finance, service, communications and international sectors of the economy, but not domestic manufacturing industry or civil society. New 'core' industries, largely dependent on international capital, are consolidated in the South, while the North of the country is left as a peripheral, decaying hinterland. The South, organised around the City of London, traditionally the hegemonic pole of the economy, is increasingly decoupled from domestic manufacturing industry. Thus Thatcherism, terrified that the City will lose even more of its world role, given the continuing relative decline of the British economy, has an Atlantic rather than a European outlook in its international policy and aims to provide the point of entry into Europe for American and Japanese capital. Money rather than goods are paramount. Socially and visually, the citadels of international capital are abruptly juxtaposed with the decay of London's old industries and docklands.[1]

The Thatcher years provoked a long-delayed efflorescence of British film, still largely unrecognised in Britain itself. It can be seen, I believe, as a 'British New Wave', coming long after the idea of a New Wave had crumbled away in most other European countries. The first New Wave, of course, exploded on the world from France in the 'Miraculous Year' of 1959, which launched Truffaut's *Les Quatre Cents Coups*, Resnais' *Hiroshima Mon Amour* and Chabrol's *Les Cousins*. Godard's *A Bout de Souffle* followed in 1960, also the year of *L'Avventura*, the first film of Antonioni's trilogy. This, in turn, drew attention to the work of Pasolini and, soon, Bertolucci. A few years later, Fassbinder, Syberberg and Wenders were grouped together as the core of a somewhat belated 'German New Wave'. Since then critics gathered at festivals around the world have sought out 'New Waves' wherever they could, broadening their net to include the Third World and hailing the Brazilian, African and Chinese 'New Waves'. No one thought of looking again at Britain, which, having missed the bus in the 1960s, could hardly expect a second chance. Besides, the British were notoriously unvisual, unartistic and uncinematic. What was it Truffaut had said? 'Aren't the words "Britain" and "Cinema" incompatible?'[2]

It has been argued that the 'Angry Young Men' films of 1959–63 were the 'British New Wave', rather than the 'Jeune Cinéma Anglais', as the French, who certainly ought to have known, dubbed it at the time.[3] Yet surely to call these films New Wave is both inappropriate and misleading. First, the idea of a New Wave was intimately linked to the project of directorial 'authorship'. A good case can be made for Lindsay Anderson as a bilious but authentic 'auteur' (something he himself might well deny in a fume of irascibility), but nobody has made a serious claim for the auteurist credentials of Reisz, Richardson, Schlesinger and others. In fact, it would be much more plausible to argue for the producer-director duo of Relph and Dearden as auteurs, filmmakers whose 'social problem' cycle, beginning with *The Blue Lamp* in 1950 and continuing through, via *Sapphire* (1959) and *Victim* (1961), to *A Place to Go* in 1963, preceded and paralleled the work of the Angry Young Men. Moreover, in 'daring' to deal with race and homosexuality, for whatever headline-grabbing reasons, they showed greater courage, prescience and, indeed, political sense than their more celebrated and supposedly more progressive and innovative younger colleagues.

Second, the idea of a New Wave involved putting film first and not subordinating it to literature or theatre, as Truffaut argued in his notorious polemic against adaptation in *Arts* magazine. The Angry Young Men films, however, plainly put film second. Their success was directly derived from the success of the original plays and novels by Osborne, Amis, Braine and Sillitoe. *Look Back in Anger, Room at the Top,*

The Entertainer, A Taste of Honey, Saturday Night and Sunday Morning, and *The Loneliness of the Long Distance Runner* came out in their original forms between May 1956 and September 1959. The film versions, which came out after a three-year interval, between 1959 and 1962, clearly depended on the pre-publicity and acclaim already generated by their literary sources for their initial impact. Moreover, Woodfall Films, beginning with *Look Back in Anger* (1958), set a pattern by having the original writers first collaborate on the film scripts with professional scriptwriters and then write them entirely. Osborne, Sillitoe and Delaney all wrote their own scripts for the film adaptations of their work. The same procedure was followed with *This Sporting Life* (1963), written by the author of the novel, David Storey (and directed by Lindsay Anderson), and with John Schlesinger's *Billy Liar* (1963), written by Keith Waterhouse and Willis Hall, based on their own play of Waterhouse's novel. This film of an adaptation of an adaptation is about as far from Truffaut's ideal of auteurism as you can get.[4]

Third, both critics and the directors themselves explicitly justified the Angry Young Men films in terms of 'realism'. Their attitude reflected an old shibboleth and plaint of the British cinema establishment, both in production and reception, best summed up by Michael Balcon's programmatic preference for 'realism' over 'tinsel'.[5] This system of value, though most strongly entrenched on the Left, ran all the way across the political spectrum. For the Right, as with the Left, the aesthetic preference for realism was bound up with nationalism. 'Tinsel', of course, was identified with Hollywood escapism and, in contrast, realism evoked local pride and sense of community. It meant showing ourselves honestly to ourselves, rather than indulging in other people's alien and deceptive fantasies. British critics praised films they liked in terms of their realism and damned those they did not as escapist trash. The French New Wave, however, aimed to transcend this shallow antinomy. The third term that made this possible was, of course, 'modernism'. The films of Resnais and Godard, even when adaptations, placed themselves clearly in a modernist tradition, as did Truffaut's crucial *Jules et Jim* (1962). Resnais, to take the most obvious example, collaborated with writers like Robbe-Grillet and Duras. The *Cahiers* group followed the path blazed by the Nouveau Roman and recognised Jean Cocteau as their godfather. Yet in Britain filmmakers fetishised the second-rate novels of regionalists, realists and reactionaries.

The history of modernism in Europe followed a definite geographical pattern, which reflected an underlying historical reality.[6] The more a country felt the ambition to catch up economically and culturally, the more an aggressively avant-garde section of its intelligentsia embraced and radicalised a version of modernism. After the collapse of the old absolutist regimes, avant-garde artists often rejected the search for new modes of personal expression in favour of a depersonalised rationalism or functionalism. They attempted to subordinate the arts to industrial and technological needs and imperatives, and to merge the artist with the masses. Thus in backward Russia, the avant-garde moved rapidly from symbolism to futurism and then, after the impact of the October Revolution, to constructivism. In Italy futurism developed its own technocratic ideology and, in Germany, expressionism gave way to the Bauhaus. In France, where the *ancien régime* had been toppled more than a century before, cubism was followed by the much weaker current of purism, around Le Corbusier, but also, more significantly, by surrealism. The surrealists, like the constructivists or the later Bauhaus artists, lined up on the left politically, and yet reacted with hostility to the norms of modern industrial development, unlike their counterparts in revolutionary Russia or Germany. In Britain, after the brief flurry of vorticism, modernism never took root in any lasting way.

Britain, of course, was both the homeland of the Industrial Revolution, the pioneer of manufacturing capitalism, and the European country with the most remote and attenuated experience of absolutism. Modernism, in its pure form, appealed to very few in Britain, especially not in England. England's most committed modernists were very often expatriates – Eliot, Pound, H.D., Wyndham Lewis. In the visual arts, vorticism rapidly dissolved and modern currents were smoothly amalgamated into the English landscape tradition, as in the work of Ben Nicholson or Henry Moore. A mild and heavily romanticised anglicisation of surrealism surfaced briefly and then sputtered to a halt. In the world of literature and in taste-setting journalism, there was a bloodless transfer of power to the Bloomsbury group, within the traditional intelligentsia itself, and an increasingly emollient modernism was assimilated into the ongoing high culture with hardly a break. Indeed, the most effective protagonists of modern literature – Eliot and Leavis – argued for modernism in frankly traditionalist terms. Far from wanting a break with the past, they saw modernism as the culmination of a long national literary history. This history now needed only to be reassessed retrospectively, rather than brusquely overthrown. Moreover, modernism was treated as something that had already happened and been absorbed, rather than as an ongoing project.[7]

Modernism first impinged on British film culture during the silent period with the London Film Society and the journal *Close Up*. But the coming of sound quickly wiped out these tender plants, as it did much stronger film avant-gardes elsewhere. The *Close Up* circle, around the writers Bryher and H.D., produced Kenneth MacPherson's *Borderline* (1930), financed by Bryher (then married to MacPherson), and starring H.D., alongside Paul and Eslanda Robeson. It remains the one outstanding British avant-garde film of the period. However, *Close Up* folded shortly thereafter, and its contributors lost heart and dispersed.[8] Meanwhile, after the collapse of the London Film Society, its moving spirit, the irrepressible Iris Burny, left for New York in 1930.[9] In New York she met Philip Johnson at a cocktail party and soon afterward she was hired by Alfred Barr to run the new Museum of Modern Art's film programme. Thus the modernist impulse was transferred from London to America, where the Museum played a crucial role in the survival of avant-garde film through the 1930s, enabling it to resurface again in the 1940s. In Britain, of course, this did not happen.

The Film Society's most significant outcome was its impact on Alfred Hitchcock, a habitual and doubtless punctual attender at screenings. There Hitchcock not only mingled with the cultural elite but also absorbed modernist aesthetic ideas, which he later attempted to nurture within narrative film. Hitchcock experimented with sound in his first talking picture, *Blackmail* (1929), but soon retreated into conformity. Nonetheless, once he felt his career in the industry was secure, both in Britain and subsequently in the United States, he cunningly contrived a place for experimental ideas within commercial genre films – the Salvador Dali dream sequence in *Spellbound* (1945), the ten-minute takes in *Rope* (1948, produced by another Film Society alumnus, Sidney Bernstein), the 'pure cinema' project of *Rear Window* (1954), the montage murder sequence in *Psycho* (1960), and so on. Hitchcock's collaborator,

Ivor Montagu, whom he met through the Film Society, also worked with Eisenstein, and many echoes of Eisenstein appear in Hitchcock's own work. But, in general terms, Hitchcock seems to have drawn the conclusion that modernist experiments were best contrived as a kind of illicit contraband, which he could smuggle in and secretly enjoy, while lapping up the praise and the dollars for his success within the mainstream of the industry.

During the 1930s, the surviving vestiges of 1920s modernism were channelled into the state-sponsored British documentary movement. John Grierson, a Scot, remained more open to modernism than other British producers and hired co-workers (like Alberto Cavalcanti, a Brazilian, and Len Lye, a New Zealander) who had impeccable experimental film credentials: Cavalcanti's *Rien que les Heures* (1926) was a landmark of the French avant-garde and Lye had made his abstract film *Tusalava* for the London Film Society in 1928. Nonetheless, the main drift of Grierson's project was to subordinate modernism (in its Russian form) to realism and to national propaganda. Grierson was impressed by Eisenstein's vision of an epic, silent cinema based on the masses and achieving its dramatic effects through formal means rather than character identification, and he believed it could be transposed to fit British documentary and propaganda film. Grierson's documentaries aimed to represent the society at large rather than particular individuals. They were meant to inform rather than entertain. In this context, he could draw productively from Eisenstein and Pudovkin. Similarly, other modernists could have a role to play within his team. Thus, in this unlikely setting were to be found artists like Lye, W. H. Auden (who wrote the voiceover for *Night Mail*, 1935), and Humphrey Jennings (a chief organiser of the London surrealist exhibition of 1936).[10]

To critics at the time, Grierson's efforts seemed to combine the realism they desired with a prudent preservation of modernist elements in an acceptable, marginal role. Meanwhile, Alexander Korda became the standard-bearer for narrative film in Britain, launching a series of costume dramas celebrating the popular high spots of British history and a cycle of extravagant imperialist epics, mainly directed by his brother, Zoltan Korda.[11] Korda's initial success with *The Private Life of Henry VIII* (1933) sprang from a canny combination of grandiose costume spectacle with music-hall comedy, but he was never able to repeat it, and his backers, Prudential Insurance, abruptly withdrew their support in 1937. Korda, however, did succeed in inspiring the British cinema world with the idea that they could and should set their sights on Hollywood as a model to be emulated. He pointed the way toward Rank's brave attempt to take on Hollywood after the war and, more recently, the pathetic false dawn of David Puttnam. Meanwhile, British cinema continued to churn out a series of 'quota quickies': George Formby vehicles and vernacular potboilers for the domestic audience. But when the deadly grip of heritage drama and pierhead comedy finally broke down during the 1939–45 war, it was romanticism, and not realism, that carried the day: whether the operatic Technicolor romanticism of the Archers and Gainsborough or the contorted black-and-white 'man-on-the-run' romanticism of the 'spiv' film and Carol Reed.[12]

The war years saw a revival of English romanticism in response to the need for an idealised reaffirmation of British history and shared values (as perceived within the dominant ideology) and, on the other hand, for release into fantasy and dream to relieve the stress, hardship and agony of war.[13] During the war, film production was necessarily limited, but nonetheless the national mood is much better conveyed by the visual ambition and expansive romanticism of Olivier's *Henry V* (1944) than by the restrained grittiness of Coward and Leads' *In Which We Serve* (1942), however much the critics may have welcomed the realism they felt that it conveyed. After the war was won, still sheltered from American competition, British cinema blossomed. This period saw not only Powell and Pressburger's trilogy of *Black Narcissus* (1947), *The Red Shoes* (1948) and *Gone to Earth* (1950), in which a series of intensely desirous women are thwarted and finally plunge over the edge to their death, but also Carol Reed's trilogy of *Odd Man Out* (1947), *The Fallen Idol* (1948) and *The Third Man* (1949), in which appealingly desperate heroes are caught in paranoid labyrinths of pursuit and betrayal.

It is important to stress the strength of this 'new romanticism', as the parallel movement in painting and poetry is called, because it partly explains the success of the Angry Young Men films in the next decade. In 1945 the top box-office film was *The Seventh Veil*, a sublimely over-the-top drama of female desire, classical music and psychoanalysis. The same year, Cavalcanti, having left Grierson's documentary unit, made a small masterpiece of the grotesque in *Dead of Night* and followed this up, in 1947, with *They Made Me a Fugitive*, the definitive expressionist 'man-on-the-run' film. Thus even a hero of 'documentary realism' showed himself the master of 'docklands romanticism' (along with Robert Hamer and *It Always Rains on Sundays*, 1947). British films, none of them remotely 'realist', dominated the domestic box office for four straight years, until American political and economic power became irresistible and the British finally capitulated to Washington arm-twisting and a Hollywood boycott in 1948.[14] Both *The Third Man* and *Gone to Earth* were co-productions with Selznick and, apart from them, the most impressive films from 1949 onward were Hitchcock's transatlantic *Under Capricorn* (1949), Dassin's *Night and the City* (1950) and Huston's series of 'runaway productions' beginning with *The African Queen* (1952). The stage was now set for the critics at last to welcome a truly 'realist' counterblast to Hollywood, one that simultaneously reacted against the romanticism and aestheticism of earlier British film.

However, the Angry Young Men were not the only cultural countercurrent of the 1950s. In 1956, the same year that *Look Back in Anger* was produced at the Royal Court Theatre (8 May), the exhibition 'This Is Tomorrow' opened at the Whitechapel Gallery (8 August).[15] This was the culmination of the work of the Independent Group of artists, architects and critics and the emblematic beginning of British pop art. Both the Angry Young Men and the Independent Group, founded in 1952, reacted strongly against the diluted modernism of the traditional intelligentsia, a decaying amalgam of Bloomsbury and Cold War pieties. However, while the Angry Young Men turned back toward a provincial Little Englandism, the Independent Group openly welcomed American consumer culture in their struggle against the English countryside and the villa in Tuscany, celebrating science fiction, Hollywood movies, tailfins and advertising. The Angry Young Men were resentfully anti-American, although they did energise their English populism with a taste for traditional jazz, uncontaminated either by Tin Pan Alley or by post-bebop modernism. 'Trad' enlivened the soundtracks of Reisz's *Momma Don't Allow* (1955) and Richardson's *Look Back in Anger*. Visitors to 'This Is Tomorrow', on the other hand, were greeted by a giant Robbie the Robot (from the sci-fi movie *Forbidden Planet* (1956), and a wall montage celebrating CinemaScope.

A leading proponent of the Independent Group's work, Lawrence Alloway, went on to become a kind of godfather to the auteurist film magazine, *Movie*, in the early 1960s.

Pop art was a way to outflank the dominant elite culture by turning simultaneously to popular consumer culture and to the avant-garde tradition. Reyner Banham, for instance, carefully placed pop technophilia in the context of the modern movement, and Richard Hamilton, the pioneer pop artist, turned back to Marcel Duchamp as a revered ancestor. Pop broke through to a wider cultural audience with the 1961 appearance of a new phalanx of artists, the Young Contemporaries, encouraged by Alloway, and then Ken Russell's benchmark television show, *Pop Goes the Easel*, the following year. In retrospect, we see that the non-existent British 'New Wave' of the time would have been much more closely linked to pop than to the Angry Young Men. Pop prefigured the 1960s transformation of British culture. When the transformation came, however, it was expatriates who showed the way, at least as far as the cinema was concerned: Richard Lester, especially with *The Knack* (1965); Joseph Losey, who made *Modesty Blaise* (1966); and Antonioni, whose *Blow-Up* (1967) became the archetypal film of the decade. These directors aligned themselves much more closely with their French counterparts. Their scripts derived from absurdism rather than realism – Harold Pinter or *The Goon Show*. Local directors appeared very late in the decade – Cammell and Roeg's *Performance* was shot in 1968, but its distributors cravenly delayed its release until 1970. Alongside Roeg, John Boorman and Ken Russell both developed into 'auteurs', but basically they were neoromantics (low-key and high-key, respectively), clearly anti-Kitchen Sink, but only incidentally modernist.[16]

Jimmy Porter (Richard Burton) and Helena Charles (Claire Bloom) in Tony Richardson's film version of John Osborne's 'angry young man' play about rebellious youth, *Look Back in Anger* (1958)

We can better see the long-term importance of the 1960s for British film in the subsequent work of Derek Jarman and Peter Greenaway. Both went to art school in this period, Jarman after getting a literature degree at London University, in deference to his family, and Greenaway in going to university, in defiance of his family. Jarman and Greenaway both set out to make films within the visual arts tradition. The dominant painters in Jarman's world were gay – David Hockney and Patrick Procktor. He was also close to Ossie Clarke on the fashion scene, which interlocked with the art world during the 1960s. Hockney's significance, of course, sprang not only from his success as a painter, but also from his public declaration of homosexuality and its increasingly crucial presence in his art. Jarman himself, however, was not a pop painter, but a landscapist who moved toward abstraction. His early paintings show monoliths on English 'west country' hills – descendants of Paul Nash or Henry Moore. Jarman is deeply attached to the landscape around Swanage in Dorset (which appears many times in his films), where he spent many childhood holidays and whose unique features Paul Nash also celebrated in his surrealist paintings. Jarman's own landscape *tour de force* at Prospect Cottage on Dungeness, a garden of Elizabethan flowers, stones and driftwood, over which looms a massive nuclear power station, recreates the surrealist world of Chirico, with the respect for the 'genius loci' always felt by Nash. There is a lasting tension in his work between a delirious neoromantic Englishness and a pop modernism, always in touch with 'street culture'. His two influential teachers at university were Eric Mottram, who introduced him to William Burroughs' *Naked Lunch*, and Niklaus Pevsner, who directed him to Gothic cathedrals, Lincoln, Canterbury or Ely. The eerie elegiac tone of his recent films has its roots in this metaphysical historicism and in his deeply ambivalent nostalgia for childhood, fed by an intransigent anger and a will-to-resist rooted in gay culture.[17]

In his films, rather than his paintings, Derek Jarman first articulated the gay world in which he lived, its tastes, routines, extravagances and crises. Filmmaking began for him as a personal art of home movies, strongly contrasted with his professional work as a set designer for Ken Russell. The crucial turning point came when he turned down Russell's invitation to design *Tommy* (1975) and determined instead to make his own first feature, *Sebastiane* (1976). What strikes me now about *Sebastiane* is no longer its place as a pioneering transposition into film of age-old visual motifs aestheticising beautiful, tormented boys in Mediterranean settings, but its 'high camp' silver Latin dialogue track. To me, this makes the film like an opera, whose libretto is in a foreign language, foregrounding the role of performance and visual composition. Dialogue has always seemed an awkward necessity for Jarman, and he has increasingly been happiest with pre-existing literary texts – *The Tempest* (1979) or *The Angelic Conversation* (1985) – or, as with *War Requiem* (1989), musical texts. (Here he carries out Michael Powell's old ambition of the 'composed film', in which the music preceded the filming, as in episodes of *Black Narcissus* or, of course, *The Red Shoes*.)[18] Greenaway, on the other hand, is fascinated by words and overloads his soundtrack with dialogue, sometimes as though the characters were mouthpieces for an abstruse disputation taking place outside the film.[19]

Peter Greenaway was much more directly influenced by 1960s pop artists, such as R. B. Kitaj (after whom a star is named in *Drowning By Numbers* (1988)) and Tom

Phillips, the creator of *A Humument*, with whom he collaborated on his television film *Dante's Inferno* (1989), the pilot project for *Prospero's Books* (1991). In Greenaway's case, the fascination centres on artists who explore the relationship between words and images, between literature and painting. Greenaway discovered Kitaj's paintings at the same Marlborough Gallery show in 1963 that Derek Jarman also visited. Like Greenaway, Kitaj maintains an impenetrably enigmatic relation to his sources. Like Greenaway, too, he is drawn to the arcana of old engravings, incunabula, emblems or maps. Kitaj has sought to people his paintings with imaginary characters, like those in novels, who appear in a series of works. In the same way, Greenaway has his caste of imaginary characters, presided over by Tulse Luper, who crop up in film after film, sometimes in central roles, sometimes as fanciful marginalia. At heart, Greenaway, like Kitaj, is a collagist, juxtaposing images drawn from some fantastic archive, tracing erudite coincidental narratives within his material, bringing together Balthus and Borges in a bizarre collocation of eroticism and *trompe l'oeil* high modernism. Kitaj also, of course, is a cinephile, through whose painting, *Kenneth Anger and Michael Powell* (1973), we can trace a strange connection between the myth-worlds of Greenaway and Jarman.[20]

At first sight, Derek Jarman and Peter Greenaway have little in common. Indeed, Jarman is notorious for his vitriolic attacks on Greenaway. Yet both were products of 1960s art schools, both were trained as painters and still are painters, both developed a strong visual style and dedicated themselves to making personal films marginal to the populist mainstream of the industry, both pay court to narrative while shamelessly revealing that their true interests lie elsewhere. Both can be seen, in a certain sense, as modernists. Both, in another sense, can also be seen as neoromantics, steeped in a personal vision of the English landscape, endlessly revisiting and rejecting the temptations of Victorianism and antiquarianism, returning much more winningly to their memories of childhood, mediated through home movies and family snapshots for Jarman, and through pored-over children's book illustrations for Greenaway. Jarman accuses Greenaway of succumbing to antiquarianism in *The Draughtsman's Contract* (1982), a vice he attributes first to Poussin and thereafter to the Victorians. In contrast, he cites his own *Caravaggio* (1986), with its contemporary references on image and soundtrack, its obvious debt to Pasolini, its inauthentic modernity. But Greenaway does not see *The Draughtsman's Contract* as authentic. On the contrary, he reacts angrily to a comparison with Kubrick's *Barry Lyndon* (1975): 'My film is about excess: excess in the language, excess in the landscape, which is much too green – we used special green filters – there is no historical realism in the costumes, the women's hair-styles are exaggerated in their height, the costumes are extreme. I wanted to make a very artificial film.'[21] In the same interview, he dismisses *Chariots of Fire* (also Jarman's most hated film) as reactionary and lacking any real aesthetic, even that of a *Saturday Night and Sunday Morning* (1960).

The difference between them, of course, lies in their divergent strategies for avoiding antiquarianism. Jarman explicitly modernises, introduces contemporary references and false touches, interprets Caravaggio's life and art through a filter of topical and personal preoccupations and tastes. Greenaway, on the contrary, exaggerates the archaism, pushing all the elements into an unreal and peculiarly inauthentic realm of caricature and pastiche, trying to turn a Restoration comedy into *Last Year at Marienbad* (1961). *Prospero's Books* follows in the same tradition by recreating the high Renaissance world of masque, pageant and emblem in exaggerated splendour, while at the same time placing the play within Prospero's mind and experimenting with video effects and infography. The risks run by the rival strategies are clear. Jarman opens himself to the charge of anachronistic travesty, Greenaway to that of lavish overindulgence. When I saw *The Draughtsman's Contract* at its premiere at the Edinburgh Film Festival, I was nauseated by the excess of Englishness, the hyperbolic heaping of English language on English acting on English landscape on English country-house murder on English preciousness and whimsy, the dilettantish celebration of eccentricity and games-playing. The modernist dimension of Greenaway's work, the side that takes us toward Hollis Frampton's *Zorn's Lemma* (1970) or toward the Oulipo writers in France,[22] toward an intricate conceptualism or a Nabokovian dandyism, can appear over-ingenious and willfully bizarre – another re-run of Lewis Carroll, yet with its shadow side made ever more apparent in erotic tableaux and Jacobean cruelty.

Derek Jarman is much more intimately linked to 'New Romanticism'. His most prominent disciples (John Maybury and Cerith Wyn Evans) were part of the 'Blitz crowd' and his own work is related not only to this 'club scene' new romanticism,[23] but to a much deeper, more long-lasting tradition: to the medieval poets, the Elizabethans (not only Marlowe and Shakespeare, but magicians, alchemists and herbalists), Blake and Shelley, the late Victorians, the Apocalyptics and, of course, Michael Powell and Emeric Pressburger. Modernism in Britain has prospered precisely in alliance with the underground currents of this broad national-romantic strain in the culture. Neoromanticism fitted intimately with the experience of the war, in poems by Edith Sitwell, Dylan Thomas or T. S. Eliot, in drawings or paintings by Moore and Piper, in films by Humphrey Jennings and Powell and Pressburger. This wartime mood still runs through Jarman's films, especially *The Last of England* with its recurrent imagery of a blitzed and burning London, recalling also the Great Fire of 1666, the burning of the Houses of Parliament painted by Turner, and the burning down of his own studio. 'Fire turned nasty.' It was no longer the comforting glow of childhood hearth and picnic bonfire. The palette of *The Last of England*, too, like that of Jarman's more recent paintings, is all tarry black and fiery red, made to look like cathedral stained glass.

Whereas the mainstream of romanticism has always expressed and consolidated national myths, Jarman subverts them. Underlying the imagery of the blitz and the wasteland lies a critique of a destructive society and government – in a word, of Thatcherism. The desolate cityscape is contrasted with the imagery of the garden, as the state terrorism of *Jubilee* (1977) was contrasted with the closing masque of *The Tempest*, the two films linked through the role of two Renaissance magicians, John Dee and Prospero. Jarman's political commitment draws on the sense of an alternative tradition, on the great homosexual texts – Plato's *Symposium*, Shakespeare's sonnets, the paintings of Caravaggio. At the same time, it is inseparable from his day-by-day involvement in the gay world, in the struggle against Clause 28 and the solidarity of gay men in the face of AIDS as they confront an authoritarian and homophobic regime whose leader's insistent moral appeal was to 'Victorian values' and against the 'permissive society'.[24] The key turning point, for Jarman, came with the Royal Jubilee of 1977 and its riotously sinister shadow, punk. Jarman's *Jubilee* is a protest against the whole horrendous notion of the 'second Elizabethan age', the backdrop of national grandeur and creativity against which Britain's economic and cultural decline was played out for 25 years. After that, of course, Thatcherism came as a movement not of renewal, but of vengefulness against everything she disapproved of that had somehow still managed to survive.

Peter Greenaway emerged from a strangely contradictory background. On the one hand, he worked for the government Central Office of Information, making films meant to express the British way of life, and, on the other, he made idiosyncratic 'structural films' in his own free time. His affinities are with 'international' modernism – before making *The Draughtsman's Contract*, he screened films by Fellini, Bertolucci, Rohmer, Straub and Resnais for the crew, so that they could understand his intentions. At the same time, he secretly remade his own earlier *Vertical Features Remake* (1979), in which a group of film scholars try to reconstruct a lost film from a series of surviving views. Greenaway is also close to movements in modern art and music that employ modular and serial structures. Like many conceptual artists, he is fascinated by fists, grids, catalogues, counting games and random procedures, which appear in his work as 'coincidences' or 'accidents'. He is also fascinated by mysteries and their concomitant troop of red herrings, deceptive riddles and false trails, the stock-in-trade of the peculiarly English form of the cerebral detective story. His films are made under the twin signs of the taxonomy and the enigma. Such an aesthetic is perhaps strongest in an intrinsically non-realist art like music, but even in literature and painting it subordinates content to formal preoccupations, so that subject matter often seems no more than a pretext. The structure comes first and the content – say, a series of fictions – is then fitted into it, a lesson Greenaway learned from John Cage. This school of modernism, unlike neoromanticism, was historically decoupled from politics, yet, under the pressure of Thatcherism, Greenaway too turned to political invective in *The Cook, the Thief, His Wife and Her Lover*.

Greenaway's antipathy toward Thatcherism stems from an ethical and aesthetic dislike for the philistinism and vulgarity of her regime, her exaltation of the profit motive, her determination that art and scholarship should only be supported if they served an economic function, her authoritarianism, her social philosophy of frugality and order for the poor combined with greed and license for the rich. Thus an expensive restaurant was a logical setting for his film, a place where Spica's own authoritarianism, greed and licence can be publicly indulged. Moreover, one of Greenaway's recurrent preoccupations is with the food chain, the process of ingestion of the weak by the strong and the dead by the living, in curious configurations of cruelty and death with sex and dinner. At the same time, the restaurant is symbolically a cathedral, a cinema and an art museum, the chef its officiating priest and artist. As in other Greenaway films, the woman is the controlling character, bent on revenge on the world of men, destroying the figure of the artist en route. The brutalisation of an innocent child recalls that of Smut in *Drowning By Numbers* (1988), a gruelling moment when a ludic *commedia dell'arte* is suddenly transformed into a macabre Jacobean drama. Indeed, as Greenaway puts it,

> The Jacobeans were looking over their shoulder at the grand Elizabethan age; Britain still looks over its shoulder at the Great Empire. In Jacobean times, syphilis was the new sexual scourge; we now have AIDS. There's a certain comparison in that sexuality has become complicated, so there's a similar spirit of melancholy. The same sensation

of fatalism exists *vis-à-vis* the sort of cruelty we see every day, especially cruelty in the home, the abuse of children, and so on.[25]

From their very different angles, Greenaway and Jarman unexpectedly converge on a surprisingly similar standpoint.

Both Greenaway and Jarman made key films for the British Film Institute (BFI) Production Board, under Peter Sainsbury: *The Draughtsman's Contract*, suggested by Sainsbury, who asked Greenaway whether he had ever thought of making a dialogue film, and later, Jarman's *Caravaggio*. The board had become completely divorced from its experimental function until Sainsbury, former editor of the avant-garde journal *Afterimage*, was appointed in the mid-1970s. Sainsbury became something like a new, but decisively modernist and antirealist Grierson. Toward the end of the 1960s, under the dual impact of New York 'structural film' and the European experiments in narrative of Godard and others, a film avant-garde crystallised for the first time in Britain since *Close Up*. It was built around the BFI, the Other Cinema, the Workshop Movement and the Independent Film-Makers' Association (IFA).[26] Neither Greenaway nor Jarman participated in the avant-garde debates and activities of the time, which they saw, perhaps, as too politically doctrinaire or too potentially time-consuming. In a way, their non-involvement probably made it easier for them to break out of the earlier pattern of their filmmaking, unencumbered by a baggage of past positions and pronouncements. Also, they did not confront Thatcherism head on, as 'political filmmakers', but from a less explicit artistic position within which their political anti-Thatcherism emerged.

Nonetheless, films like those of Greenaway and Jarman should be seen as part of a wider and disparate shift in British film, due in part to a decisive shift toward the visual arts as a source for cinema, and in part to the theoretical and practical consolidation of a film avant-garde in the IFA and at the BFI. The emergence of a post-Godardian 'political modernism' at the BFI, although it never achieved even the limited popular success of Greenaway or Jarman, helped to create an alternative pole of attraction within British cinema and thus the space between mainstream and countercinema that they later occupied.[27] Greenaway and Jarman are much closer in background and outlook to other directors emerging from the BFI and the workshops than they are to the upscale television drama and advertising directors who constitute the rump of the 'film industry' left behind in Britain after the more ambitious of them have been called to the Coast. The other important condition, of course, was the fabulous collapse of Puttnamism and the flight of its leader to Hollywood, where his pretensions were ignominiously liquidated. 'The British are coming' indeed.[28]

Thatcherism, by breaking the mould of British politics and carrying through radical right-wing cultural policies, directed, in essence, against the legacy of the 1960s, succeeded paradoxically in politicising filmmakers who had been formed during the comparatively liberal years of Wilson, the decade of sexual liberation, the last hurrah of welfare Keynesianism, and the belated entry of modernism into the general culture. This 'delayed modernism', however, proved resilient enough to survive into the 1980s. It decisively influenced a generation then in a position to make oppositional films first for the BFI, later for Channel 4, and eventually for independent producers within the industry or in Europe. As a result, Britain saw an efflorescence of filmmaking paralleled only in the 1940s. Britain finally produced the 'Last New

Wave', a series of uncompromising films made by original, oppositional, visually oriented modernist auteurs. It was worth waiting for.

NOTES

1 This analysis of Thatcherism emerges from debates carried on by a number of authors. See especially the following: Andrew Gamble (1988) *The Free Economy and the Strong State*. Basingstoke: MacMillan; Stuart Hall (1988) *The Hard Road to Renewal: The Crisis of Thatcherism*. London: Verso; Bob Jessop, Kevin Bonnett, Simon Bromley and Tom Ling (1988) *Thatcherism*. London: Polity Press; Scott Newton and Dilwyn Porter (1988) *Modernisation Frustrated*. London: Unwin Hyman; and Henk Overbeek (1990) *Global Capitalism and National Decline: The Thatcher Decade in Perspective*. London: Unwin Hyman. For the general anti-Thatcherite cultural efflorescence under Thatcherism, see Robert Hewison (1989) *Future Tense*. London: Methuen. Films coming from outside London, it should be noted, like Bill Forsyth's Scottish films or the Liverpudlian *Letter to Brezhnev* (1985), seem strangely less bitter than the London films, although a vein of cynicism underlies the mood of astringent comedy and wry fantasy. Northern Ireland has been marginalised in the cinema, as in the political arena, although Alan Clarke's extraordinary television work there represented the most startling and successful convergence of political with formal preoccupations in any of the media.

2 These words are quoted without citation in Roy Armes (1979) *A Critical History of the British Cinema*. London: Secker and Warburg. They are requoted parodically in Peter Greenaway's *The Draughtsman's Contract* (1982), with 'painting' substituted for 'cinema'. For another version, see also Truffaut's remark that there is 'something about England that's anti-cinematic', in François Truffaut (1969) *Hitchcock*. London: Panther.

3 Jacques Belmains (1967) *Jeune Cinema Anglais*. Lyon: Premier Plan, 44.

4 On the Angry Young Men and their impact on the cinema, see Harry Ritchie (1988) *Success Stories: Literature and the Media in England 1950–1959*. London: Faber and Faber; and Robert Hewison (1981) *In Anger*. London: Weidenfeld and Nicolson. John Hill (1986) *Sex, Class and Realism: British Cinema, 1956–63*. London: British Film Institute, provides a comprehensive survey of the movement in film.

5 See Robert Murphy (1989) *Realism and Tinsel*. London: Routledge, which takes its title from Michael Balcon's pamphlet *Realism and Tinsel*, based on a talk given to the Film Workers Association in Brighton in 1943. This is available in Michael Balcon (1947) *25 Years in Films*, ed. Monja Danischewsky. London: World Film Publications. In his talk, Balcon especially stressed the contribution Grierson's unit had made as 'the men who kept realism going on the screen' and the potential for a new type of film bringing a realistic treatment to 'story elements' within the industry.

6 See Peter Wollen (1990) 'Scenes from the Future: Komar and Melamid', in *Between Spring and Summer*. Tacoma, WA: Tacoma Art Museum/Boston: Institute of Contemporary Art.

7 For the postwar history of modernism in Britain, see Alan Sinfield (1989) *Literature, Politics and Culture in Postwar Britain*. Oxford: Basil Blackwell. He is also very illuminating on the sexual and class politics of the Angry Young Men.

8 For *Close Up* and *Borderline*, see Roland Cosandoy (1985) 'Re-assessment of "Lost" Film', *Afterimage*, 12, which contains a full bibliography. See also Anne Friedberg (1983) 'The Film Journal *Close Up*', PhD dissertation, New York University.

9 For the Film Society, see Jen Samson (1986) 'The Film Society, 1925–1939,' in Charles Barr (ed.) *All Our Yesterdays: 90 Years of British Cinema*. London: British Film Institute.

10 For Humphrey Jennings, see Mary-Lou Jennings (1982) *Humphrey Jennings*. London: British Film Institute.

11 Sir Alexander Korda can be seen as one of the roster of émigré knights described in Perry Anderson (1968) 'Components of the National Culture', *New Left Review*, 50, along with Sir Isaiah Berlin, Sir Ernst Gombrich, Sir Lewis Namier and Sir Karl Popper. Yet Korda, it should be noted, worked with the revolutionary Bela Kun regime in Hungary and was a refugee from counterrevolutionary dictator Admiral Horthy. Later, however, he became an intimate and patron of Churchill and his circle.

12 For the music-hall, pierhead and seaside tradition, best exemplified by George Formby, the ukelele-playing hero of the Beatles and Morrissey, see Murphy (1989). Murphy's chapter 'The Spiv Cycle' also provides the best introduction to this riveting British equivalent to film noir. A 'spiv' was a petty racketeer involved in the postwar black economy. He wore flash ties, suits with wide lapels and a sneer or grin.

13 For wartime and postwar romanticism, see especially David Mellor (1987) *A Paradise Lost*. London: Lund Humphries; and Robert Hewison (1977) *Under Siege*. London: Weidenfeld and Nicolson.

14 The best brief treatment of the British struggle against the economic power of Hollywood, led by Harold Wilson, is in Murphy (1989).

15 See *This Is Tomorrow Today* (1987) New York: P.S.1, Institute for Art and Urban Resources; and, for the subsequent shift in British popular culture, Dick Hebdige (1988) *Hiding in the Light*. London: Comedia.

16 For a general treatment of the 1960s, see Robert Hewison (1986) *Too Much: Art and Society in the Sixties, 1960–75*. London: Methuen.

17 The indispensable sources for Derek Jarman are his two books of journals, *Dancing Ledge* (1984), London: Quartet, and *Modern Nature* (1991) London: Century. See also the special issue of *Afterimage* of 1985, 'Derek Jarman … of Angels and Apocalypse', *Afterimage*, 12. I have also drawn from Derek Jarman (1986) *Derek Jarman's Caravaggio*. London: Thames and Hudson; Derek Jarman (1987) *The Last of England*. London: Constable; and Derek Jarman (1989) *War Requiem*. London: Faber and Faber.

18 Michael Powell was inspired by Friedrich Feher's film *The Robber Symphony* (1936), which is described by Graham Greene in his review in the *Spectator*, 24 May 1936, reprinted in Graham Greene (1980) *The Pleasure-Dome*, Oxford: Oxford University Press.

19 For Greenaway, I have drawn mainly from Peter Greenaway (1990) *Papers*, Paris: Dis Voir, which contains a selection of his artwork with his own commentary, and Greenaway (1988) *Fear of Drowning By Numbers*, Paris: Dis Voir. A number of Greenaway's scripts are also published.

20 For Kitaj, see Marco Livingstone (1985) *R. B. Kitaj*, Oxford: Phaidon Press. Kitaj did actually introduce Kenneth Anger and Michael Powell to each other: 'I brought Anger and Powell together because they admired each other. They're both quite mysterious and since I introduced them, I painted them together in their disjunction.'

21 See Peter Greenaway (1984) 'Meurtre dans un jardin anglais', *Lavant-scène cinema* (Paris), 333. The translation of Greenaway's remarks is my own.

22 For the Oulipo group of writers, see *Oulipo* (1986) ed. Warren E Motte Jr, Lincoln: University of Nebraska Press.

23 For new romanticism and Blitz culture, see Caroline Evans and Minna Thornton (1989) *Women and Fashion: A New Look*. London: Quartet.

24 Derek Jarman is one of a number of gay filmmakers who made films in Britain during the Thatcher years, including Terence Davies, Isaac Julien, John Maybury, Ron Peck and Cerith Wyn Evans.

25 See Gary Indiana's interview with Peter Greenaway, in *Interview* (1990), 20, 120–1, on the occa-

sion of the New York release of *The Cook, the Thief, His Wife and Her Lover*.

26 Reliable sources are few for this period in British cinema. For the black workshops, see especially Mbye B. Cham and Claire Andrade-Watkins (eds) (1988) *Blackframes: Critical Perspectives on Black Independent Cinema*. Cambridge, MA: MIT Press; and Coco Fusco (1988) *Young, British and Black: The Work of Sankofa and Black Audio Film Collective*. Buffalo, NY: Hallwalls/Contemporary Arts Centre.

27 See D. N. Rodowick (1988) *The Crisis of Political Modernism*. Urbana: University of Illinois Press.

28 'The British are coming!' was the media slogan propagated after *Chariots of Fire* won an Oscar. It is strange that the next British Oscar sweep, for *The Last Emperor*, had no discernible impact whatever in Britain, presumably because its director was Italian. Conversely, a director like Ridley Scott, even though he has retained his personal and working ties with Britain, has been systematically neglected. Yet Scott's vision of the city in *Blade Runner* (1982) has much in common with its British counterparts.

3. IMAGES FOR SALE: THE 'NEW' BRITISH CINEMA

Thomas Elsaesser

THE THATCHER YEARS: HARD TIMES, INTERESTING TIMES

The British cinema during the 1980s – the Thatcher Years – enjoyed a Renaissance. Indeed, early on in the decade even Hollywood helped to celebrate its rebirth: Oscars for *Chariots of Fire* (Hugh Hudson, 1981); the appointment of its producer, David Puttnam, as director of production at Columbia Pictures; more Oscars for *Gandhi* (Richard Attenborough, 1982). The 1980s also saw notable bits on the art cinema circuit with *Letter to Brezhnev* (Chris Bernard, 1985) and *My Beautiful Laundrette* (Stephen Frears, 1985), recognition for auteurs like Peter Greenaway, John Boorman and Nicolas Roeg; plaudits in Berlin for heretic iconoclasts like Derek Jarman; and commercial successes for international directors like Stephen Frears, Ridley Scott, Adrian Lyne and Alan Parker. In addition, a more hard-bitten, controlled professionalism among directors eclipsed the volcanic and fizzling talents of a Ken Russell and a Lindsay Anderson from the previous decades. This group, by and large, opposed the ideological rigidities of Thatcher, matching the Iron Lady's temperament with an equally steely determination not to whine or indulge in left-wing romanticism.

During the decade, more British films were made than at any time since the 1950s, or at least more British films attracted international awards or coverage. In Britain the cinemas were filling up again, albeit for American blockbusters, but whatever the attraction, a revival of audience interest might just, in the long run, be good for the British movie business, as well. One could begin to talk of a 'British film culture' without having to invoke François Truffaut's famous quip about 'British' and 'cinema' being a contradiction in terms. Movies were also helped by the lively interest television took in the cinema, thanks to a popular preview programme like Barry Norman's 'Film' on BBC1, the retrospectives on BBC2's 'Film Club' and 'Moviedrome', the 'South Bank Shows' devoted to filmmakers, 'The Media Show' on Channel 4, and the co-production/co-financing or in-house filmmaking of television, especially BBC's 'Screen Two' and Channel 4's 'Film on Four' series, with a helpful hand from the British Film Institute (BFI) Production Board. Out in the streets, however, the scene became further depleted: fewer and fewer cinemas, even among the Rank/EMI-Cannon duopoly, and a dying out of independent neighbourhood cinemas as well as art houses.

Director Alan Parker (on the set of *Mississippi Burning*, 1988), one of the British directors to achieve international success during the 1980s

In the country at large, millions of Britons during the Thatcher era were living through hard times. Others found them interesting times, because her government brought about polarisations in the body politic not seen since the late 1920s: the definitive break-up of a social consensus that had maintained a common discourse about what was important to the national interest across the political spectrum. With Thatcher, the very terms by which to voice dissent were challenged, a point of some importance when considering the different political styles that emerged: from Arthur Scargill's miners' strike to David Owen's Social Democrats, from the militant faction on the Liverpool City Council to Nicholas Ridley on Germany. In the cinema's case, the different filmmaking styles (too readily lumped together as 'postmodern') broke with the consensus idiom *par excellence*: 'realism'. In short, the Thatcher years implicitly and explicitly asked what it meant to be British – or English, Scottish, Irish or Welsh, or to be from the North, the Midlands or the South. The decade also questioned what it meant to be a British filmmaker. The polarisations along lines of class, of race, of region, of nationality and of language recalled similar break-ups elsewhere in Europe. They make the 1980s a period of momentous social shifts well beyond Thatcherism and support the view that violent social tensions are often the best soil for the flowering of resilient, contesting and confrontational arts, obliging artists to rediscover themselves as social counter-forces and moral consciences.

An obvious topic would be to investigate whether one can trace the break-up of the consensus in the cinema of the 1980s, as well. Yet equally relevant is whether the kind of self-questioning of national identity just hinted at can be distinguished from another response, no less prominent in the 1980s: self-promotion, also pursued in the name of national identity. Given the increasing dependence of the arts on money (a condition always true of the cinema) and the fact that those granting money increasingly demand that the arts demonstrate their usefulness, what might be the status of such a national identity, especially where it defines itself in economic terms: as competitive edge, conquest of markets and brand-name awareness, while nonetheless relying on images and stories rather than goods and services for its meaning and substance?

NOT ANOTHER BRITISH CINEMA RENAISSANCE...

Screenwriter Colin Welland's cry 'The British are coming' at the Oscar ceremony for *Chariots of Fire* set the tone for the decade, releasing a flood of pent-up emotion and producing acres of print about the British film renaissance. But whenever the word 'renaissance' crops up in the context of the British cinema (as it seems to do at least once every decade), one needs to be wary. Chances are the film industry is in deep trouble. This was the case around 1984–85 when, still flushed with the success of *Chariots of Fire*, a string of media events culminating in the British Film Year of 1985 persuaded the public to see not the small acorn but the mighty oak tree: to ignore the continuing decline of an indigenous film industry, the decreasing share of British-made films in British cinemas, and an exodus to Hollywood of directors, cinematographers and specialists in many filmmaking crafts (especially sound, sets and animation).

Scanning the titles trumpeted as New British Cinema at the 1984 London Film Festival, one wonders if what took place was a large-scale re-labelling of the goods, a quick fix for the deep-seated structural ills of mainstream filmmaking. Suddenly, half the drama output of British television found itself named 'cinema'. While some 'Plays for Today' deserved to be called movies (*Rainy Day Women*, 1984, scripted by David Pirie, for instance), even more television films should never have been showcased in the cinema, although co-production deals (sometimes with foreign companies) made this obligatory. Thus, Chris Peachment could write about *Loose Connections* (Richard Eyre, 1984), 'What we have here is something that would not be diminished by showing on video. Which may be perfectly acceptable to its director ... but is not what one would hope to say about something consciously made for the cinema' (1984: 152). More damning still, Jeremy Isaacs, then head of Channel 4, thought the efforts by the independent filmmaking sector fell between both stools: 'too slight for the cinema, too slack for television' (1984: 118), while for the critic John Brown a major vehicle of the film industry, *The Dresser* (Peter Yates, 1984), despite its 'elaborately promoted status (The Royal Film, the Oscar nominations) as a big screen movie [could not disguise the fact that it] operates as a big screen extension of television traditions' (1984: 190).

A renaissance implies a renewal. What was it that was stirring, moving, breaking through frozen ground? Talent? Commercial success? Big Themes? Big Names? The organic metaphors flowing from those panegyric pens homogenised divergent if not contradictory phenomena. In the case of British cinema in the mid-1980s, these ranged from fiscal changes affecting investment depreciation (the end of tax shelters, in short), to judicious programming (film critic Derek Malcolm's term of office as director of the London Film Festival proved particularly rich in this respect), to taking in an anniversary (fifty years of the BFI in 1983), to the trial-and-error period of a new television network (Channel 4's buying and commissioning policy), and to the low rental rates of home video recorders and prerecorded tapes (making Britain by the early 1980s 'the largest home video market in Western Europe', according to *American Film*, May 1983).

Talk of a renaissance, however, rekindled the question of what a national cinema could be, what it has been, and who needed it. The British film industry always had problems asserting itself economically against overpowering Hollywood competition. Interestingly, in the periods when it held its own, or whenever a discernible strategy emerged (during the war years, or the 1950s), its success sprang as much from an ideological move as from an economic boost. This is what one learns from the classic studies. *A Mirror for England* was the programmatic title of Raymond Durgnat's influential book, and Charles Barr showed in what elaborate ways 'projecting Britain and the British character' was Michael Balcon's motto at Ealing Studios. In other words, whether during the war or immediately after, propaganda, patriotism and 'projection' have functioned as integral parts of a successful national cinema.

Reporting on the 1981 Berlin Film Festival's retrospective of Balcon's work, David Robinson marvelled at 'just how rich the British cinema was in the 1930s and 1940s', and concluded that it had to do with 'craftsmanship and a sure and determined sense of a national identity ... The films have a sort of confidence that they can sell themselves without recourse to vast budgets, or running after "international" (that is American) appeal' (*The Times*, 27 February 1981).

Robinson was not alone in thinking that an 'emphasis on British themes gives ... films the sinew of authenticity'. The writer Alan Bennett put it equally succinctly:

> Behind a lot of the questions that are raised lurks an unspoken one: how do we make it big in America? Risking being hauled before Colin Welland in the Barnes Magistrate's Court, charged with insulting behaviour, I'd like to ask why do we want to? ... [T]he European directors I admire ... don't eat their hearts out because they're not big in Arkansas. Why should we? Mrs Thatcher has the answer, but does she know anything about films? (1984: 122)

To which one might reply that she may not have known about films, but her speech writers knew a thing or two about self-promotion. She projected 'British themes' and the 'sinews of authenticity' pummelled out of flabby jingoist nostalgia, or more humbly put, she constructed national myths out of the bric-a-brac of history, xenophobia and paranoia.

THATCHER'S BRITAIN: AN INVENTION OF THE MEDIA

The dilemma when writing about cinema in the age of Thatcher is quite simply this: the Thatcher years were an invention of the media, or at the very least, the result of a complex and often collusive love-hate relationship between the Thatcher government, the press and television. Most commentators agree that the connection between politics and television – not just in Britain – has become too close for comfort for democracy. But since the connection between film and television has become even more inextricable, it is almost impossible to construct for the cinema during this decade a straight opposition between confrontational artists and complaint public opinion, nor indeed for those working in the audiovisual media, an opposition between the hard times for some and the interesting times for others.

What remains most vividly about the decade is the so-called Saatchi effect. In politics, it pinpointed the close ties between the Conservative Central Office and a well-known advertising agency: the massive deployment, from within No. 10, of the Prime Minister's press secretary Bernard Ingham, and the promotion and preferment of flamboyant industrial entrepreneurs or 'boardroom buccaneers' such as Lord Hanson (of the Hanson Trust), Lord King (Chairman of British Airways) and Lord Weinstock (Chairman of GEC). These men, a newspaper once pointed out, Margaret Thatcher rewarded as Queen Elizabeth I once rewarded Francis Drake. For the cinema, the Saatchi effect blurred the fines between the different kinds of self-awareness: that which probes and that which promotes. When Norman Stone, writing for Rupert Murdoch's *Sunday Times*, made his much-publicised attack on filmmakers like Derek Jarman and Stephen Frears ('Sick Scenes from English Life'), he quite simply hated what they showed. Clearly alien to Stone was the idea that a filmmaker's shocking or disturbing images might be essential to making a certain reality visible, not just to the eye but to one's moral and emotional senses. Stone could assume, without questioning it, that at issue was England's image in the world, since national cinema worked as advertising: the agency should look after the client.

On the other hand, as the high-risk business for self-made men and buccaneers *par excellence*, the film industry should have appealed to the Thatcher philosophy. Yet even Puttnam and Attenborough found it hard to catch the Prime Minister's ear when it came to mitigating, with the help of central funds, the effects of abolishing the Eady Levy, the tax write-offs and other economic measures detrimental to the film industry. In one sense, of course, the film industry in any European country always looks toward state support, as did the New German Cinema; the French government also directed massive aid to its film industry. In Britain, government perceived the film lobby as looking for 'handouts', and thus as anathema to free-marketeers. But equally in the pursuit of new (and this means American) markets, British cinema should have enjoyed the government's benevolence on a par with Plessey, Westlands or Rover Cars. After all, Britain under Thatcher became a nation of national brand names, company logos, icons and slogans: identity under the reign of 'The Image'.

How then can one read the relations between British cinema and Thatcherism? When neither official rhetoric nor central government supported the small but nonetheless real impact of British films internationally, the whole spectrum, from Alan Parker to David Puttnam, from Dennis Potter to Peter Greenaway, from Derek Jarman to Stephen Frears, turned scathingly anti-Thatcher. But did this necessarily mean that Britain in the 1980s had either a critical, self-questioning or a combative, society-questioning cinema?

WHAT 'WE' CAN SELL TO 'THEM'

The answer must be, both and neither. Both, insofar as one can easily name dozens of films highly critical and satirical, sombre and desperate about the state of Britain. Neither, insofar as the terms of the debate about the cinema shifted sufficiently to make 'critical' and 'combative' almost irrelevant notions. Superficially at least, the debate on both sides concerned markets, box office, image and impact. As to 'why we want to make it big in America', for instance, film journalists had no doubt. Perhaps the Thatcher ethos was well understood and accepted. More likely, the home truth had sunk in that no successful European film industry can make films for its own market alone. Investment calculated on a purely national revenue basis makes the home-grown product look too cheap to be attractive to domestic audiences, those who vote with their feet for pictures with production values. On the other hand, journalists like Margaret Hinxman thought that 'precisely the qualities that have made *Chariots of Fire* such a hit across the Atlantic' were the ones apparently advanced by Rank, Lord Grade and EMI for turning down David Puttnam when he approached them for financing: 'It has no name stars in it, its subject was sport, above all, it was too British' (*Daily Mail*, 31 January 1982). Here, then, appears another dilemma: either too British or not British enough. Yet this presents too easy a juxtaposition. At issue is what kind of Britishness 'we' could sell to 'them', in turn balancing an appeal to 'insider knowledge' about England and Britain with what the world knew, or thought it knew, about Britain.

Such a proposition raises a number of further points. First, we must differentiate between the projection of what one could call a 'social imaginary' of Britain and the projection of a 'national imaginary', one for 'us' and one for 'them'. The distinction might even mark off television productions from film productions, with the latter necessarily destined for an international audience. Mamoun Hassan rightly points out that, as far as television goes, 'international sales provide the jam' because the bread and butter is a national audience. The BBC has to justify its licence fee, while the paymasters of commercial television are 'the advertisers, [who] wish to sell their goods ... in Birmingham, West Midlands, and not Birmingham, Alabama' (1984: 116). But he underestimates the quite tangible 'commercial good will' that tourism, the publishing trade, luxury cars, or British quality knitwear and leather goods derive even from the relatively paltry sums changing hands between American PBS stations and ITV for *Upstairs Downstairs* or *Brideshead Revisited*. From television to films, and from style magazines to record sleeves, the Thatcher years taught the British media a crucial lesson: the importance of an image culture, rather than a film culture.

FILM CULTURE: A FOREIGN IMPORT?

I once argued that Britain lacked a film culture from the grass roots up, as existed in France: meaning a large number of filmgoers who could recognise a travelling shot by Vincente Minnelli or a sequence edited by Sam Fuller. Equally important, I thought, was a generation of cine-literate as well as cinephile writers and directors. Hence the early enthusiasm for Chris Petit (a film critic turned director), whose reputation as a director always seemed slightly higher among the cinephiles than their judgement of his films, and the high praise for David Pirie (a film critic turned scriptwriter): '*Rainy Day Women* is a film ... highly conscious of its choice of vocabulary, operating within unfashionable dialects in the face of a dubious art-house accent from draughtsman to ploughman, putting its energy into story-telling and discovering its themes in the process' (Brown 1984: 190).

But I now wonder whether an emphasis on a film culture that, with the advent of television, risks becoming either scholastic or antiquarian, if it insists on filmmakers being cine-literate (knowing the 'language of cinema') or cinephile (quoting from John Ford or Jean-Luc Godard), misconstrued the role of a tradition. During the years between 1968 and 1975, when a new generation of British film critics struggled to have the study of film accepted as a valid intellectual endeavour, the dialogue of the deaf between a certain journalistic establishment and the university film theorists narrowed the options of a film culture: on one side, the demand for a 'materialist' practice and a countercinema, on the other the condemnation of semiology and psychoanalysis as the 'Screenspeak' of 'pod-people'.

One could also think of another kind of divide – perhaps more appropriate for the age of media globalisation: that between the insider's and the outsider's view of Britain, where the outsider could well be from Scotland, Ireland or Liverpool, and the insider from Hollywood. Historically, the 'outsider-as-insider' view of Britain has often proved most memorable, as in Joseph Losey's films, especially in his collaborations with Harold Pinter, which epitomise an image of Britain in the 1960s that still survives, even if it never achieved cult status. To the Losey-Pinter partnership one should add Roman Polanski's *Repulsion* (1965) and *Cul de Sac* (1966), as well as Jerzy Skolimowski's *Deep End* (1970): films where the pastiche element has, over the years, taken on a patina that gives them a truth missing from the films of Lindsay Anderson or John Schlesinger.

The precise relation of Britishness to a (cinema- or television-based) film culture is important, even if one argues that a strong national cinema must feed on its predecessors and thus stand in a vampiric relation to what has gone before. Identity and pleasure in the cinema remain connected to questions of narrative, the art of repetition and recognition. One strategy of both television and the cinema as socially significant forms of self-representation might well be the energy either medium puts 'into storytelling and discovering its themes in the process' (ibid.). But film culture partakes also of the pleasure of the quotation and the in-joke, the reworking of known styles, genres, idioms and themes. Imitations, irony, remake, pastiche, parody are all modes of sustaining a sense of cultural identity or a myth of the nation.

NATIONAL AUDIENCES, OR...

What of the national audience for either British television or British cinema, insofar as the cinema still has such an audience? Does it care about national identity when it comes to entertainment? For viewers in the north of England, the lifestyles in *Dynasty* or *L.A. Law* are about as real as the lifestyles of the Yuppie stockbrokers living in London's Dockland or the Home Counties. Is the 'national cinema' question, then, more than a figment of someone's (the critics') imagination, or a promotion ploy of doubtful use for products not marketed by way of genre or star? The unclassifiability of a production range drawn from television drama, film/TV co-productions, commercial feature films and former film-school debuts is self-evident. But it is equally self-evident that the mid-1980s 'renaissance' was tied up with the showcasing of large numbers of British films at jamborees like the London Film Festival.

Festivals are the Olympics of the show-business economy, even though not all are as market-oriented as the Cannes Film Festival. What competes at festivals are less individual films than film concepts, film ideas, sales angles, or what Stephen Heath called a film's 'narrative image' (Heath 1981: 44). Created by the press back-up, by promotional activity that suggests several sources of appeal or cultural access in a film, these images can be generated by sheer numbers (if diversity is tied together with a label) or, more frivolously, by emphasising a newsworthy item either in a film or surrounding it. What counts at festivals is novelty, discovery, the element of surprise. With the paying public afterward, it is more a matter of what they already know or recognise, the familiar that they discover in the different. A native public, therefore, may be flattered by the attention that others – other critics, other media, other audiences – give to the homegrown product or talent, as was the case with *A Fish Called Wanda* (Charles Crichton, 1988). The most celebrated heroes, therefore, often win their highest accolades abroad.

Critics thought the hype surrounding the British contingent at such festivals was rather over the top: 'The current rash of hyperbole about the new British cinema will fade. Of course much of the TV drama "showcased" at the London Film Festival was merely routine. The pendulum always swings too far at first' (Millar 1984: 121).

Yet bulk remains crucial in launching a national cinema. The New German Cinema emerged internationally at the 1974 Cannes and 1975 New York festivals, mainly from the sheer number of films by three or four directors. These filmmakers' earlier work fed distribution demands, which in the case of Fassbinder amounted to some ten or twelve films. Producers or directors must have sufficient films, for demand once generated must be met quickly. Hence the close interdependence of film and television as delivery systems, neither of the same narrative material nor of a necessarily different experience, but of two distinct cultural discourses continually implying and pointing to each other. In the case of British films in the 1980s, the persistent danger was that if films never circulated outside television, then the associations evoked by the label 'British Cinema' would fade; if the label exists successfully, but the industry cannot provide enough product to fit it, then television will offer its product under the label: both were the case, with diminishing returns for the idea of a national cinema. The objective conditions for the renaissance, therefore, were not so much the existence of Channel 4 and its commissioning policy, but the coexistence of Channel 4, the BFI Production Board, the National Film Finance Corporation, and two or three risk-taking producers (David Puttnam, Simon Perry) and production companies (Virgin, Chrysalis, Palace) living 'inside the whale' of all the available sources of film financing. Their films – by the very heterogeneity of cultural and economic values that entered into the filmmaking process – were open texts, changelings rather than bastards, traveller's cheques rather than forgeries in the currency markets of film culture.

Therefore, as far as a 'brand image' is concerned, Britain faced an interesting dilemma. In its efforts to promote a particular national cinema, it stood somewhere between Germany and France. Despite the nouvelle vague, French filmmakers over and over define themselves (positively or negatively) by reference to their own cinematic traditions, their cosmopolitan international film culture, and a heavily theorised cinephilia. Think of Eric Rohmer and Bertrand Tavernier at one end, and of *Jean de Florette* and *Cyrano de Bergerac* on the other. In West Germany, where an idea of a national cinema imposed itself only in the 1970s, diverse directorial talents accumulated enough films to appear before an international art-house audience as a group whose work reflected on the country from which they came. What could Britain offer in the way of either image or group identity to an art cinema audience? In Germany, it was invariably a director-star combination (Fassbinder and Hanna Schygulla; Herzog and Klaus Kinski; Wenders and Bruno Ganz) or 'trilogies' that provided genre association; in Britain, films are one-offs, with occasionally an 'engine' to pull a few others in its train. Could this add up to a national cinema? On the other hand, British media products, in terms of an industrial infrastructure, are poised not between competing European cinemas, but between commercial Hollywood and commercial television, with the independent sector in both film and television up until the mid-1980s (prior to the quota) much more marginalised than the French or Italian art cinema. The British film industry rests on a strong technical base and unrivalled craftsmanship in certain specialised areas – heavily used by the Americans as long as sterling was weak against the dollar. Its television industry is highly competitive and sufficiently funded to buy what talent and services it needs from the theatre, the film industry or the literary establishment.

The real crisis for a new British cinema, therefore, came in the distribution and exhibition of material produced for television as well as for the cinemas. Without the tradition of an art cinema, British society only slowly incorporated the institutions (Regional Film Theatres, film magazines) necessary to create a coherent image for different kinds of film at their point of reception and consumption. The two major distribution/exhibition chains always preferred to handle American films, partly because they could acquire, in addition to the film, the advertising, promotion and marketing directly with the product. Such films prove much easier to handle than something that needs not only a market but an image, as well. By contrast, the biggest French distributor, Gaumont, undertook a vast expansion and diversification programme that made it both desirable and necessary for a distributor to invest in the production even of art-house films, something that Rank and EMI have been notoriously reluctant to do and for which the stakes in Britain may indeed be too high.

Gaumont expanded and diversified into new areas of filmmaking only to the degree that it could distribute these films adequately – be it by exporting to Italy, Germany and the United States, or by splitting their Parisian and provincial theatres into ever more mini-units. It gave the company a higher turnover of films, but also allowed them to keep a 'sleeper' in repertory without clogging up the schedules for their blockbusters. Gaumont's extraordinary monopolistic position and strong vertical integration meant that this policy benefited both production and exhibition. In Britain, it seems that the smaller, London-based distributors/exhibitors (Artificial Eye, the Screen group, and the Gate cinemas) tried something very similar: to acquire enough venues to enter the market as a biggish buyer, which in turn gave them the number of films that makes programming policy respond to variable and unpredictable demand.

...NATIONAL IMAGINARIES

With this in mind, we might return to our topic: national cinema. If we exclude what I earlier called the 'social imaginary' of television and concentrate on the 'national imaginary', the cinema of the 1980s stands in a highly instructive relation to what precedes it, while it also helps us to identify how the cinema under Thatcher is distinctive. We can read a number of motifs, narratives and images as a kind of identikit rather than an identity of Britain, and can construct from them mythologies, or mythemes. But does such an emphasis on the recycling and recombining of already existing images not risk collapsing filmmaking entirely with that obedient manipulation of images and references one now identifies as the curse and legacy of the Thatcher image culture? Perhaps. Yet what would it mean to oppose this image culture with a stern recall to realism and a search for that favourite catchword of the New German Cinema, 'authentic images'? In Britain's case, this would be a call for images of misery and degradation, of unemployment and urban blight, of pollution and police harassment, of violence and racism. But is this not a retreat to another kind of conservatism, no less nostalgic than Heritage England or Edwardiana, and no less demagogic than the Enterprise Culture?

British cinema celebrates its renaissances with such regularity because it always functions around another polarisation – what one might call an 'official' cinema and an 'unofficial' cinema, a respectable cinema and a disreputable one. The renaissances always signal a turning of the tables, but only to change places, not the paradigms. Official: Basil Dearden, Noel Coward, David Lean; unofficial: Powell and Pressburger, Gainsborough melodrama. Official: Ealing comedies; unofficial: Carry On comedies. Official: *Room at the Top* (1958), *Saturday Night and Sunday Morning* (1960), *This Sporting Life* (1964); unofficial: Hammer horror, *For King and Country* (1964). *Official: Sunday Bloody Sunday* (1971); unofficial: *Secret Ceremony* (1968). One could go on … official: *The Ploughman's Lunch* (1983); unofficial: *Brazil* (1984); official: *Chariots of Fire* (1982); unofficial: *Hope and Glory* (1988). Sometimes it appears as if the same films get made every twenty years or so: *Local Hero* (1983), a remake of *Whisky Galore* (1949) and *The Maggie* (1954); *The Ploughman's Lunch*, a remake of *Room at the Top* (or, as Charles Barr has pointed out, of *Darling*, 1965); and *Chariots of Fire*, a remake of *In Which We Serve* (1942).

This Jekyll-and-Hyde, yin-yang quality of the British cinema, first analysed by Raymond Durgnat, has in its 'realism versus romanticism' version become one of the orthodoxies of academic film studies. Its deeper psychic economy, as it were, rests in the fact that for every mythic or cliché image of Britain, there is a counter-cliché. Rare are the films that let both myth and countermyth assert themselves, which is why *Brief Encounter* (1945) has such a special place in the canon. One of the main changes in the 1980s is that more films meshed the traditions: under Thatcher, reality itself became fantastic, for some a fairy tale (*A Room with a View*, 1985), for most a nightmare (*Jubilee*, 1976; *No Surrender*, 1986; *Sammy and Rosie Get Laid*, 1987; *The Last of England*, 1988). Others saw the future as high-tech and shabby at the same time: *Brazil*, for instance, a very British film by an American director (Terry Gilliam), not dissimilar from *Blade Runner* (1982), a very American film by a British director (Ridley Scott).

For much of the 1980s, the mythemes remained in place. On one side: home counties, country house, public school, sports, white flannel, rules and games; Edwardian England, Decline of the Empire, Privilege and Treason; male bonding, female hysteria. On the side of the countermyth: Scotland, Liverpool, London; dockland, clubland, disco, football, punk, race riots, National Front; working-class males, violent and articulate; working-class women, sexy and self-confident. No one would mistake this as realistic, yet the films that fit the scheme range from *The Draughtsman's Contract* (1982) to *Letter to Brezhnev*, *A Passage to India* (1984) to *The Last of England* (1987), *Another Country* (1984) to *My Beautiful Laundrette*, *The Long Good Friday* (1979)

BBC Radio journalist James Penfield (Jonathan Pryce) dictates his story on the Falklands crisis in *The Ploughman's Lunch* (1983), an example of Britain's 'official' cinema

to *Educating Rita* (1983). Most of these images of Britain sell better in Birmingham, Alabama, than in Birmingham, West Midlands, because they encapsulate what 'we' try to sell to 'them'. But on closer inspection, one sees that the films that did well in both places, whether coming from the 'official' or the 'unofficial' cinema, gave the myths a special edge, mixed the stereotypes in unexpected ways, or enacted the cliché to poignant perfection. Thus, they released a rich cultural sediment of meaning by which members of a national and historical community explain themselves to themselves and express themselves to others. In effect, the density or cross-hatching of references has assumed the place of 'realism'. Consider, for instance, how little relation to the historical facts the prevalence of stories about public school spies and traitors has. It is not only since the advent of satellites that spies have become irrelevant to information gathering or to national security. Yet because the complex of playing fields – Oxbridge, homosexuality – is able to articulate and negotiate such a number of important oppositions and contradictions (traitors to one's class/traitors to one's sex/traitors to one's country), its reality to Britain is of a different order than merely historical or sociological, and therefore we can expect some version of it even to survive the end of the Cold War.

MATERIALISATIONS OF THE IMAGE

During the 1980s, British films and television have successfully marketed and packaged the national literary heritage, the war years, the countryside, the upper classes and elite education. In a sense, they emulated the British record industry, rock musicians and the rag trade, a lesson the Americans learned quickly after World War Two, when commerce started following Hollywood rather than the flag. That the communication and media industries participate in the commodity exchange systems of capitalism should not surprise anyone who knows about ownership and control in these industries, and that images, clichés, narratives are now fully caught up in the same game simply takes the process to its logical conclusion. Like the natives in Third World countries who impersonate themselves for the sake of the tourists, Britain appears the victim of its own sophisticated media-making, the materialisation of its own imaginary. Feeding from the myth and the countermyth in equal measure, the images give a semblance of verisimilitude to its public life by the sheer diversity of recognisable stereotypes.

Such a circulation of representations is useful politically (as the Thatcher government knew full well) insofar as it fixes a complex and shifting reality (for example, nationhood and social cohesion at times of crisis and decline) into images commonly accepted as true and meaningful as soon as they crop up everywhere, forcing even the opponent to do battle on the same terrain. Britishness in the cinema may thus be a synthetic myth, but it remains no less powerful for that because it is held in place by binary oppositions and polarities that attract each other. Due to the violence of the social tensions that the uneven distribution of the wealth generated by North Sea oil brought to almost all regions and communities of the British Isles, Britain during the 1980s was probably the most colourful country in Europe. In this respect, the 1980s were a rerun of the Elizabethan or the Victorian age, if only by virtue of the immense contrasts between rich and poor, energy and waste, violence and ostentation. But when history returns, to paraphrase Marx, it usually does so as tragedy and farce. No wonder, perhaps, that Dickens was the author most often adapted on television during the period, or that when Margaret Thatcher finally resigned, the main evening news programme was followed by a montage of the day's images to a text made up of quotations from Shakespeare's history plays.

One tends to imagine little effective political opposition to Thatcher, but in the years to come we may recognise the wealth of talent in writing and journalism that etched the decade's image in acid. Much of the talent found its way into television, less into the cinema. But film, after all, was not about documentation, information, investigation, or even satire (all the province of television), but rather about myth and the stereotype, both beyond realism and fantasy and closer to allegory and to games played according to the rules. Yet both the myths and countermyths of the British cinema strongly speak of Britain as a class society, maybe even a caste society.

In this respect, at least, less has changed during the Thatcher years than might at first appear. While her social policies broke up one kind of consensus, another was formed, one using the same elements but striking from them a different coinage. Hence the impression that in the New British Cinema the sum of the parts, at least for now, is greater than the whole. The cinema under Thatcher contributed greatly to an unmistakably British image culture, but perhaps not so much to a film culture. Once more, talking about British cinema implies a look at British television, for the national imaginary hides, but also implies the social imaginary. But that is another story.

Author's note: This essay includes portions of my 'Images for England (and Scotland, Ireland, Wales...)', published in *Monthly Film Bulletin*, September 1984, in a three-part investigation of the present state of British cinema (the other essays in the series were by Raymond Durgnat and Charles Barr). I wish to thank the British Film Institute for permission to use the material.

WORKS CITED

Barr, Charles (1977) *Ealing Studios*. London: Cameron and Tayleur.

Bennett, Alan (1984) 'My Scripts, Where Wheelchairs Make Up the Armoured Division, Are Not Ready-made Movie Material', *Sight and Sound*, 53, 2, 121–2.

Brown, John (1984) 'Home Fires Burning', *Sight and Sound*, 53, 3, 188–90.

Durgnat, Raymond (1970) *A Mirror for England*. London: Faber and Faber.

Hassan, Mamoun (1984) 'Journalism and Literature Use Words...', *Sight and Sound*, 53, 2, 116.

Heath, Stephen (1981) 'Narrative Space', in *Questions of Cinema*. London: Macmillan, 19–75.

Hinxman, Margaret (1982) *Daily Mail*, 31 January.

Isaacs, Jeremy (1984) 'If We Can Sustain the Impetus...', *Sight and Sound*, 53, 2, 118.

Millar, Gavin (1984) 'I for One Am Not Going to Wait Around...', *Sight and Sound*, 53, 2, 120–1.

Peachment, Chris (1984) 'London/Munich Loose Connections', *Sight and Sound*, 53, 2, 151–2.

Robinson, David (1981) 'Berlin Festival Report', *The Times*, 27 February.

Stone, Norman (1988) 'Sick Scenes from English Life', *The Sunday Times*, 10 January.

4. HISTORY WITH HOLES: CHANNEL 4 TELEVISION FILMS OF THE 1980s

Paul Giles

This essay examines how Channel 4 contributed to British filmmaking in the 1980s and how involvement with television affected the aesthetic shape of many British films during this era. The writer and director Mike Leigh, interviewed in *American Film* (1989), claimed that during the 1970s and 1980s in Britain 'all serious filmmaking was done for television' (Fitch 1989: 12). Leigh exaggerated here, of course; still, media critics in the United States usually fail to appreciate how extensively British cinema remains institutionally and artistically bound with the London stage and television companies. In America, the typical television movie appears as an inexpensive B-movie programme negotiating some current social problem and containing the most conventional narrative forms of romance and melodrama.[1] British television broadcasts this kind of material, too, but during the 1980s the medium also offered space to many of the country's best writers and directors, whose films for the small screen surpassed most 'British cinema' during this period.

Commentators too often frame the study of television with an apocalyptic, all-encompassing rhetoric, from Raymond Williams' notions of continuous 'flow' in the early 1960s, through Marshall McLuhan's 'global village' later that decade, to Jean Baudrillard's postmodernist reduction of television to a flattened medium 'delivering its images indifferently, indifferent to its own messages' (1988: 50). But as John Caughie argues, these theories of television 'universalise a local, national experience – the US Experience – as the essence of television' and ignore how this experience is constituted differently in other countries (1990: 48). British television, for example, exists within a tradition of state-approved public service. Since its establishment by Royal Charter in 1922, BBC Television, which has been on the air since 1936, has carried no advertising and remains financed by the government's annual licence fee charged to all owners of television sets. The second BBC channel, BBC2, was set up in 1964 to complement the programme schedules of its senior partner. Before the advent of Channel 4 (1982) the only other option available for British viewers was their local station of Independent Television, a network that began broadcasting in 1955, financed principally by advertising. Independent Television consists of fifteen regionally-based companies presided over by the Independent Broadcasting Authority (IBA), subsequently renamed the Independent Television Commission

(ITC). We must recognise, therefore, that market forces have never competed freely within British television. In 1984, the market-oriented Thatcher government passed its Cable and Broadcasting Act, which allowed a more general expansion of cable and satellite television, but progress during the 1980s was slow. By the spring of 1990, only about 93,000 homes subscribed to cable services. Satellite television started up later, in February 1989, though by spring 1990 it reached about one million homes.[2] By August 2003, by contrast, almost half of all homes in the UK had access to non-terrestrial channels, though the licence fee was still in place and this tradition of public service broadcasting retained at least some of its power.

Two obvious difficulties characterise the British model of broadcasting in the Thatcher era: first, a relative lack of choice for the consumer; second, the perennial threat of government interference. The BBC has always jealously guarded its editorial independence, though the 1980s demonstrated how such independence is a precarious business. The Conservative government vituperatively criticised the BBC for its insufficiently 'patriotic' reporting of the Falklands War and the US bombing of Libya; it openly exercised political influence in the appointment of BBC governors and administrators; it pressured all the television companies to censor a number of supposedly 'obscene' broadcasts. Indeed, in 1988 the government established a 'Broadcasting Standards Authority' to develop a stringent code on representing sex and violence. Yet, as Colin MacCabe shrewdly remarked, the scrutiny that any given medium receives from the censors is a sure index of its cultural importance at a particular moment in history. To say British television in the 1980s was subjected to political censorship also testifies to the psychological and aesthetic power of the medium, its ability to help shape the way people think. In this sense, the circumscribed nature of consumer choice offered potential advantages for ambitious writers who understood television as a public arena for fiercely contesting meaning and ideology.

Thus British television offered considerable inducements to filmmakers: substantial financial rewards, a highly visible medium, a captive audience. The viewing figures, as David Hare has said, were 'crazy'; anywhere from three million to twelve million people would watch a single work on a single evening (1982: 49). A conservative figure of eight million roughly equates to filling an average-sized theatre in London every night for six years. Americans accustomed to flicking past fifty television channels may find it difficult to appreciate the power each individual broadcasting station wields when only four of them existed, as in Britain during most of the 1980s. In this sense, the situation appeared more like American television in the network-dominated 1950s than in the US cable market of the 1980s. Accordingly, British television filmmakers felt, as Alan Bennett put it, that they were 'addressing the nation' (Bennett et al. 1984: 121); the 1980s was the last golden era for public service broadcasting in Britain in the sense that makers of television programmes could be confident of how even their minority products would reach a huge audience. Like Bennett, Stephen Frears remarked that he made *My Beautiful Laundrette* (1985) for Channel 4 because he wanted a large number of people to see and talk about the film (see Howkins 1985: 239). The statistics reinforce this emphasis upon television as the focal point of social narratives and popular memory during the 1980s. For instance, 74 per cent of the British population at this time never visited a cinema (Lane 1986: 36), but every British adult in 1988 watched on average over 25 hours of television each week (Harvey 1989: 61). As a consequence of these institutional structures of public broadcasting that were developed after World War Two, British television generated what John Caughie called 'a collectively shared experience' (1986: 168), a discourse predicated upon the compulsive pleasures of familiarity and communal recognition. The most successful British television films internalised these communal aspects of television, allowing audience members to witness these easily identifiable aspects of popular memory; yet, such films also interrogate those comfortable assumptions, inducing the audience to reconceive its perspectives upon past and present in new and unsettling ways.

The whole question of what constitutes 'successful' television, as Charlotte Brunsdon notes, became an unfashionable academic issue during Thatcher's reign (1990: 59), as television studies focused more upon the sociological conditions of transmission than upon the semiotics of the televisual text. Various studies of audience responses to standard light entertainment made up the most influential works in this area, with a few notable exceptions: Caughie sought to define 'the specific ways in which representations are produced on television and the ways in which they circulate' (1985: 98), while Brunsdon herself expressed renewed interest in the development of 'a televisual aesthetic' (1990: 69) and stressed the 'importance of retaining the notion of text as an analytic category' (1990: 63). Promoting a critical discourse about television, however, should not involve simply erecting 'taste' or 'discrimination' or 'quality' as fetishes in themselves. Much of what passes for 'quality television', especially old-style BBC serialisations of 'classic' novels, exhibits mediocre aesthetic qualities. Such a critical discourse depends rather upon aesthetic quality, the recognition that certain texts bear a density and a complexity that actively challenge the viewer to reflect upon them. Television art, like all good art, ranges beyond mere fine 'taste'; it possesses the power to startle, to challenge, to make its audience think. The best television fiction does just this. Yet the medium's artistic achievements remain mostly invisible because we lack an appropriate critical language to describe them.

Gavin Millar articulates one potentially useful strategy in response to this critical lacuna, totally eliding the television origins of such works: he simply claims these television films as 'part of the British cinema' (Bennett et al. 1984: 120). Quite apart from the different modes of production, though, exhibition and distribution restrictions ensured that few of these works circulate widely among an international film audience. How many American reviews of British cinema in the 1980s include the BBC film An Englishman Abroad (1983), written by Alan Bennett and directed by John Schlesinger, or Saigon: Year of the Cat (1983), directed by Stephen Frears from David Hare's script? These remain two of the finest British films of the decade, made by two internationally renowned film directors. Extraordinarily, though not entirely unpredictably given the intense ratings wars between the major networks at this time, these films ran against each other on different channels during the same Tuesday evening, 29 November 1983: An Englishman Abroad was scheduled from 9.25 to 10.30pm on BBC1, Saigon: Year of the Cat from 9.30 to 11.30pm on ITV. The subsequent unavailability of both films for many years, however, testifies to the chronic accessibility problems that beset the study of television fiction. After the critical success of An Englishman Abroad – a poignant reconstruction of the exile suffered by Guy Burgess (Alan Bates) after his exposure as a Soviet spy – screenwriter Alan Bennett ruminated on how some of his earlier works directed by Frears for London Weekend Television (LWT) might have 'fared almost as well' had they enjoyed exposure to 'a better class of critic' at the London Film Festival before their fleeting television incarnation, as was the case with *An Englishman Abroad*. Now, complained Bennett, these old films 'languish in the archives of LWT with no prospect of ever being seen again' (Bennett *et al.* 1984: 122). Because of the attention it garnered, *An Englishman Abroad* was issued on videotape by BBC Worldwide Publishing some years later. But most of Bennett's other work for television has not enjoyed this kind of dissemination, and it remains a paradox that although television films frequently enjoy a very wide audience at the moment of their first appearance they do not usually have the kind of archival afterlife accorded to books, which are of course easily found in libraries, or even to theatre scripts.

One of the innovative aspects of Channel 4, which began broadcasting on 2 November 1982, was the way it institutionalised this close relationship between television and film production, both in the 'Film on Four' series and, later on, through the channel's financial investment in feature films under the 'Film Four International' umbrella. However, Channel 4's modes of production differed importantly from earlier television practices. Whereas the BBC and Independent Television previously produced their own dramatic material and purchased viewing rights to films after their theatrical release, Channel 4's charter required the broadcasting of programmes made by independent suppliers. Hence Channel 4 defined itself more as a 'publishing house', a policy stemming from the Annan Committee's report in the late 1970s, which recommended some decentralisation within broadcasting institutions. John Ellis argues that this policy of broadening the production base and increasing access to the screen for underrepresented minority interests was one of the last political by-products of the pre-Thatcher era. Although Channel 4 opened three-and-a-half years after Thatcher assumed power, says Ellis, its essential organising principles were laid down earlier, so that the station remains 'inflected by Tory ideology but not born of it' (1986: 11). Thus the government established Channel 4 as a non-profit body, a subsidiary of the Independent Broadcasting Authority. Funded indirectly through advertising, the new channel was to arrange its programme schedules to complement existing Independent Television services.

Had Channel 4 started a couple of years later, its tone would probably have been very different. The Conservative government's parliamentary bill 'Broadcasting in the '90s: Competition, Choice and Quality', published in November 1988, proposed that by the early 1990s Channel 4's advertising airtime should be sold on a competitive basis separately from the Independent Television authorities, a move that would inevitably force the station to attune itself more toward demands of the mass market in its quest for a larger overall share of the audience. Significantly, though, this government white paper described Channel 4's programming record as 'a striking success' and recommended that by 1992 the BBC and Independent Television should follow the fourth channel's example by obtaining 25 per cent of their original programmes from independent producers. This report marked a distinct change from the early 1980s, when Conservative politicians accused the home secretary of 'letting the loonies on the air'. Then, Cabinet Minister Norman Tebbitt informed Jeremy Isaacs, first controller of Channel 4, that 'the different interests you are supposed to cater for' were not those of 'homosexuals and such,' but rather 'Golf and sailing and fishing' (Isaacs 1989: 65–7). In its early days, when it enjoyed a reputation for being both highbrow and liberal, Channel 4 frequently became the target of the populist right-wing press and was often involved in the kind of censorship controversies that beset all of British television at this time. The arguments in the mid-1980s over screenings of Derek Jarman's films *Sebastiane* (1976), *Jubilee* (1977) and *Caravaggio* (1986) remain the most obvious examples of this inquisitorial climate that hovered over Channel 4 in its early days.

Nevertheless, between 1981 and 1990 Channel 4 partially funded the production of some 170 films by independent companies, and it quickly became a major player in the impecunious arena of the British film industry. By Hollywood standards, of course, the resources available to Channel 4 were miserly: David Rose, the first commissioning editor for fiction, made twenty films in his first year for a total of £13 million, the average budget of one Hollywood feature (Park 1982/83: 8). Usually production companies released these films first in the theatres, thereby gaining enough critical notice and reputation to make their subsequent appearance on television something of a special event. A few films arrived in theatres after their television appearance, usually with unhappy financial results. Toward the middle of the decade, after several failures on the commercial cinema circuit, Channel 4 supported fewer films entirely from its own finances, instead collaborating on the funding with organisations such as the Goldcrest Company, the National Film Finance Corporation, and others. Still, the general prominence of Channel 4 cannot be denied: ten out of the 28 British features made in 1984 had Channel 4 investment (Ellis 1990: 376), and the company gradually developed a strong presence at film festivals. At Cannes in 1987, for example, David Rose accepted the Rossellini Award for the contributions made by Channel 4 to filmmaking, while in the same year the British journal *Sight and Sound* congratulated Channel 4 for providing 'filmmakers with a continuity of financial support not seen since the heyday of Michael Balcon's Ealing Studios' back in the 1940s (Kent 1987: 260). By the end of the 1980s, other British television companies started to emulate their example, with both Granada and the BBC co-producing more and more feature films.

As with the Ealing cinema, we can identify a particular kind of aesthetic style as characteristic of the Channel 4 movie in the 1980s. John Ellis describes Ealing comedies as negotiating a series of 'aspirations and utopian desires', wherein the petit-bourgeoisie express their resentment against an increasingly bureaucratised postwar world (1975: 115). Channel 4 films work with something similar, insofar as they often juxtapose what is foreign, strange or sinister with the safe haven of the drably domestic. Although 'Film on Four' offerings addressed many potentially disturbing themes, they usually framed and contained them by structures of reassuring normalcy. For instance, in *Another Time, Another Place* (1983), director Michael Radford visually represents the Italian prisoners of war billeted upon an isolated farm in Scotland from the crofters' point of view, so that the Italians come to seem devils dressed in black, satanic figures who carry pitchforks over their heads as if wearing diabolic horns. The sexual knowingness of these Italians tantalises Jane (Phyllis Logan), her marital misery reinforced by a sense of geographical isolation. Jane's laconic husband, Finlay (Tom Watson), responds less sympathetically to the glamour of foreignness: he will, he says, be 'thankful to be rid of them lot' now that the war is ending. Phyllis, left to gaze longingly out of the window, tells

The allure of the foreign: Jane (Phyllis Logan) dances with Luigi (Giovanni Mauriello) in *Another Time, Another Place* (1983)

herself, 'There's other days, and other places.' Yet as the heavy weight of famili-arity associated with the BBC radio programmes that waft over this bleak Scottish landscape implies, for Phyllis, other times and places will exist only in her fantasies. Recognition of these old BBC favourites binds the viewer into complicity with that sense of repressive familiarity that the film disseminates, and hence engenders an air of fatalism. Such styles of fatalism or inertia are characteristic of many different types of television production. As theorists of television situation comedy show how its narratives traditionally rotate upon an axis of transgression and restitution, with 'order' re-established after the mild allure of the forbidden, so Channel 4 films in the 1980s often follow a similarly conservative pattern, albeit in a more sophisticated way.[3]

The form of this threat varies, of course: homosexuality in *Another Country* (1984), *Maurice* (1987), *Prick Up Your Ears* (1987); West Indians and the drug culture in *Playing Away* (1986); Jewishness in *Sacred Hearts* (1984); Americans in *Stormy Monday* (1987) and in *The Dressmaker* (1988); the Soviet Union in *Letter to Brezhnev* (1985). The latter movie features a Liverpudlian girl (Alexandra Pigg) who defies her family and British consular advice by flying to Russia to pursue a Soviet sailor she met during a night on the town. Scripted by Frank Clarke and directed by Chris Bernard, this film features a creative team that also worked on the Channel 4 soap opera 'Brookside', again set in Liverpool. This authorial link with Brookside helps explain the film's sensitivity to Elaine's domestic plight, shut up in her parents' deadly suburban house where the continuous noise of the television only partially drowns out the perpetual family quarrels. To put it another way, *Letter to Brezhnev* deals more convincingly with containment than with escape. As Martin Auty has written, the public mind associates television with 'naturalism' and cinema with 'the realm of fantasy' (1985: 63), and, in the terms of this hypothesis, *Letter to Brezhnev* fits more comfortably with its televisual than with its cinematic characteristics.

It would not, then, be difficult to argue that Channel 4 films of this era implicitly reinforce dominant conservative national ideologies, however much they explicitly seem to challenge such concepts. Jeremy Isaacs' contention that these films should reflect 'our preoccupations here in Britain' rather than be geared for 'a bland international market' (Bennett *et al*. 1984: 118) uneasily overlaps those 'national concerns' articulated by William Whitelaw, patriarchal home secretary at the time of Channel 4's inception. Whitelaw, a loyal member of Thatcher's government for many years, wanted a channel that would provide space for 'minority interests,' a television station 'somewhat different, but not too different' (Docherty & Morrison 1987/88: 11). Clearly Whitelaw's views of 'national concerns' were not synonymous with the 'preoccupations' of Isaacs. The former, concerned frankly with repressive tolerance, remarked that 'if they don't get some outlet for their activities, you are going to run yourself into more trouble' (ibid.). Isaacs, on the other hand, had no obvious vested interest in television as a means of social control. But for many radical filmmakers, these positions stood too close to each other for artistic comfort. Directors such as Chris Petit, Derek Jarman, Alan Parker and Lindsay Anderson, all outspoken in denouncing the general timidity of British cinema, found such pusillanimity reinforced by the unwelcome restrictions imposed by television production codes. Jarman openly associated Channel 4's small-screen cinema with the Thatcherite 'little England' of the 1980s, complaining that the 'TV men' only wanted films to 'complement the ads' (1987: 86) and accusing fellow directors such as Frears and Peter Greenaway of conformity to the demands of the television medium. Petit similarly scorned British cinema as being merely 'television hardback' (Walters 1987: 62), while Alan Parker described Channel 4 as a cage within which the trapped filmmaker beats frantically against the bars (see Houston 1986: 153). More thoughtfully, Anderson addressed what he saw as the restrictions of the Channel 4 medium in a 1989 interview: 'I think the real difference is the kind of subject liable to be financed by Channel 4, which leads to some of the new British films being a bit lacking in the ambition one associates with a cinema film. There is a certain restriction of imagination or idea, rather than the feeling that if you make a film financed by television you have to restrict it in terms of technique or style' (Pratley 1989: 95).

What I want to argue, however, is that the whole issue of television aesthetics should be seen as more complex than Anderson suggests here. Despite those confining parameters and the structural containment observed in many Channel 4 movies, the best of these make skilful and sometimes experimental use of their small-screen medium, creatively exploring the whole idea of limits. Here aesthetic complexity becomes a crucial critical factor: while most television films simply reflect the dominant ideology, the most illuminating reflect back actively upon it. In Mike Leigh's *High Hopes* (1988), to take one example, the thematic as well as formal emphasis rests on physical claustrophobia and psychological immobility. The central characters find themselves locked into a round of urban poverty and obligations to cantankerous relatives, the grotesque scenario peppered with frequent cups of tea and trips to the lavatory. This theatre of embarrassment challenges its onlookers by

The theatre of embarrassment: Shirley (Ruth Sheen), Cyril (Philip Davis) and Cyril's mother (Edna Dore) look over the rooftops of London in *High Hopes* (1988)

bathetically subverting the expectations of cinematic narrative and engendering a sense of queasy familiarity, a recognition of the film's disconcerting proximity to the trials of daily living. This is not, said Leigh, a form of naturalism, but rather 'heightened realism' (Fitch 1989: 12): Leigh draws the viewer into uncomfortable empathy with his landscapes, exploiting the medium of television as a repository of the banal and the everyday to valorise that empathy. Despite its abjuring of the transparent window of naturalism, *High Hopes*, as Gilbert Adair says, produces 'an effet du réel' (Adair 1988/89: 65), an illusion of verisimilitude inextricably interwoven with the structures of television and predicated upon a mimetic relay of ordinary domestic life. Leigh made most of his films in the 1970s and 1980s exclusively for television, and, though *High Hopes* played in cinema theatres, it remains a film crucially informed by a televisual perspective.

From this point of view, we can recognise the automatic preference for cinema over television as little more than nostalgia for a more traditionalist aesthetic ideology. In 1984 Mamoun Hassan, then managing director of the National Film Finance Corporation, inveighed against what he took to be Channel 4's 'hybrid' form of cinema by claiming television as more akin to 'journalism', and cinema to 'literature':

Television films and programmes have to be topical; cinema films have to be more universal than timely ... Television is at its best dealing with concepts, explaining and describing (it is no accident that the drama documentary is the preferred form of television drama); cinema is at its best when it concerns itself with the ineffable, with that which cannot be expressed. (Bennett *et al.* 1984: 116)

One hears this kind of reactive idealism – 'universal', 'the ineffable' – repeatedly in critiques of early Channel 4 films; but, as Fredric Jameson remarks, such fetishising of cinema over television is reminiscent of quests for that original 'aura' of a unique work of art that Walter Benjamin famously claimed had been undone by the twentieth-century age of mechanical reproduction (1990: 217).

A similar blind assumption of 'cinematic' principles led Mike Poole to criticise *High Hopes* on the grounds that 'what is always absent … is any capacity for change – in Leigh's world people are denied any kind of development' (1982: 29). The model Poole implicitly invokes is the 'aura' of cinematic narrative style grounded upon enigma, resolution, fluidity and change. The cinema, paradigmatically a medium of the gaze, forces an audience to identify intensely with the action and to be transported by it. Television, by contrast, establishes itself upon the casual glance, upon interaction with its viewers, upon recognition rather than identification.[4] As Herbert Zettl says, 'We look at the movie screen, but into the event on television' (1978: 5). Such a distinction risks relapsing into overly essentialist divisions between the two media, when, of course, the thrust of this essay suggests points of intersection between them. The point remains, however, that the ideological lens of an earlier art form has too often misrepresented Channel 4's films during this period. Pauline Kael, for example, complained that *High Hopes* 'isn't really conceived as a narrative of film. It's conceived as a group of skits that the director will extend and fuse' (1989: 96–7). Yet such rejection of linear sequence is entirely commensurate with a medium that prioritises montage over hermeneutic resolution. Television, says Sandy Flitterman-Lewis, 'provides a fragmentary and discrete series of microstagings' (1987: 193); by contrast, classical cinema foregrounds processes of sequential development, what Stephen Heath calls 'narrativisation' (1981: 43).

We can see obvious examples of this different emphasis in the most widely watched television serials. The 'plots' of *EastEnders* or *L.A. Law* exist as open-ended and amorphous; the narrative lines flow and converge, sometimes turning repetitively back upon themselves, but rarely reaching the cathartic climax we expect in a cinema production. The pattern in television serials reflects that in *High Hopes*, where any clear-cut resolution to the dramatic situation would seem artificial. Camille Paglia observes that television is 'a genre of reruns, a formulaic return to what we already know' (Paglia & Postman 1991: 51); I would suggest that the best television films harness this expectation of familiarity to comment upon the repetitive or compulsive aspects of national life. In many of these films, we find that the *mise-en-scènes* possess a statuesque quality reinforced by the relative immobility of the camera. Shots of action across the screen remain far less common than in old-style movies, and this restrictive idiom represents the less fluid, more humdrum environment that television so well epitomises. Television's reliance on dialogue rather than exotic or spectacular visual effects also contributes to this mood of confinement. In the case of *The Dressmaker*, a 1988 film set in wartime Liverpool, such confinement connotes a gothicised repression, a deathly refusal by Aunt Nellie (Joan Plowright) to face her niece's emerging sexuality or the changing social world outside. Of course, such formal processes do not, in themselves, ensure the excellence of television films. While the most challenging texts interrogate their audience's expectations of familiarity and force them to reconsider what such familiarity means, other films tend merely toward banality, a soap opera-like reworking of the already too well known.

Claiming that television films by definition surpass cinema films would be as falsely absurd as the opposite assertion. Yet we should understand that the aesthetic principles of television and film are not directly interchangeable, any more than those of painting and photography may be substituted.

The conjunction of two distinct modes of production fosters this illusion of realism in television films. On the one hand, television gives the spectator an impression that what he or she is watching happens 'live': this, says Jane Feuer, binds the viewer into an imaginary presence, 'a sense of immediacy and wholeness' (1983: 16). On the other hand, film engenders an impression of historicity: the idea that these events once took place in the material world. David Hare writes about his great preference for film over videotaped television productions precisely because video lacks that 'visual finesse' and 'stylistic density or texture' (1982: 48) that enable film to imply a complex historical world, the very stuff of Hare's fiction. Margaret Morse theorises this difference in terms of film's assimilation of the Renaissance rationalisation of perspective, designed to represent the truth of an object in space, rather than a television studio's two-dimensional surfaces, which eliminate all such spatial depth (1985: 6). Consequently, television drama shot in a studio on videotape has a more atemporal feel, as though everything takes place in a vacuum. Back in 1977, when he was producing *Licking Hitler* for television, Hare spurned the use of video and declared himself willing to wait a whole year until one of the film slots became available at BBC Birmingham. Hare was supported on this occasion by his producer, David Rose, then head of drama at BBC Birmingham, later to become commissioning editor for fiction at Channel 4; Hare remarked gratefully that Rose's 'allegiance to the film system is absolute' (1982: 47). Crucially, this televisual ontology of the live event, when crossed with the historicity of film, produces an illusion of the past unfolding as if in the present, as if happening 'live'. A great many of the Channel 4 films made in the 1980s portray the past, not so much in a simple 'nostalgia-deco' way (Jameson 1990: 225) but rather in a manner that maintains a complex, bifurcated perspective shifting between past and present. These films foreground the difficulties of a contemporary representation and reclamation of the past, and highlight the elaborate apparatus locking Britain into its historical destiny. But their force also derives from how they translate history into a feigned simultaneity with the here and now, drawing upon television's fictive authorisation of its discourse as a current event.

The frequent announcement after the opening title sequences of 'another time, another place' can be seen as one of the clearest distinguishing characteristics of these Channel 4 movies: 'Spring 1954, London' in *Dance With a Stranger* (1984); 'Michaelmas Term 1909, Cambridge' in *Maurice*; 'The North of Scotland, Fall 1944' in *Another Time, Another Place*. Other films immediately seek to establish a specific historical time and place by easily identifiable signs: a bus headed for the Welsh town of Pwllheli together with Helen Shapiro singing 'Walking Back to Happiness' in *Experience Preferred but Not Essential* (1982); newsreels of the 1948 England-Australia cricket internationals in *P'Tang Yang Kipperbang* (1982); icons from the Festival of Britain and Queen Elizabeth II's coronation in *Prick Up Your Ears*; BBC shipping forecasts and the 'Billy Cotton Band Show' on the radio in *Distant Voices, Still Lives* (1988). Such icons spark off communal memories to establish a bond of identity between the text and its viewers. Yet the best of these films engage in a complex dialectic of familiarity and defamiliarisation, a dialectic probing and problematising the hallucinatory images of the past evoked. Hare's 1985 film *Wetherby*, for instance, juxtaposes two different time periods, the 1950s and the 1980s, and elucidates seemingly inexplicable events of the present in terms of that deterministic historical continuity established by the film's images of the repressive 1950s, when ubiquitous family tea parties mask gaping sexual insecurity. The opening sequence of this film – mostly financed by Channel 4 – features a discussion about Richard Nixon: 'Do you remember?' 'It wasn't so long ago.' 'Only ten years.' 'It's funny how people forget.' This conversation anticipates the general tone of Hare's film, concerning the burdens of time, the vagaries of memory and the perplexities of decoding and reordering the past. John Caughie suggests that the cinema elicits audience identification with its protagonists by the classic point-of-view shot, but that television fiction relies more upon the reaction shot, the audience witnessing knowledge dispersed to a wider group of characters (1990: 54). This style of reaction shot permeates *Wetherby* and Hare's other television fiction, his emphasis falling upon groups of people responding to forces of history and events not of their own making.

Dramas set in the past have represented part of television's staple diet for many years, as countless BBC adaptations of Victorian novels readily testify. More specifically, D. L. LeMahieu (1990) writes about how the Edwardians seem like 'imagined contemporaries' of late twentieth-century Britons: LeMahieu argues that the popularity of films such as *A Room with a View* (1985) which had Channel 4 involvement – and television serials like *Upstairs, Downstairs* and *Testament of Youth* exemplify how British conservatism sought to annex this supposedly golden era as an arcadian valorisation of its own traditionalist time. This wish fulfilment pure and simple, along with a similar kind of synthesised nostalgia, permeates several of the Channel 4 films, particularly in the 'First Love' series that David Puttnam's Enigma company produced for television: Philip Saville's *Those Glory, Glory Days* (1983), about a young girl's fanatical support for a London soccer team in the early 1960s, and Desmond Davis's version of Edna O'Brien's novel *The Country Girls* in the same year. These examples demonstrate excessively domesticated television films, the kind of production Lindsay Anderson and Derek Jarman railed against.

Yet in the Channel 4 film *Wish You Were Here* (1987), written and directed by David Leland, different perspectives begin to emerge. Though this story concerns a rebellious girl growing up in East Anglia (the film is based loosely on Cynthia Payne, who was actually brought up in Bognor Regis, West Sussex) during the 1950s, the iconography of nostalgia remains rigorously framed by narrative structures weaving in and out of time. Leland shifts from the end of the war in 1945 to the picture palace movies of the 1950s to account for the claustrophobic climate of postwar Britain. The film self-consciously reconstitutes past time: the inhabitants of this seaside town loom out from the screen in statuesque fashion, as though caught in a series of still photographs; a plethora of shots heightens the style of projection and displacement that refracts objects through doorways and windows, as if to signify how this film is peering back on the 1950s from the distant vantage point of the 1980s. Moreover, Leland replicates the ways in which Lynda (Emily Lloyd) remains inextricably bound up with her dreary heritage by allowing the film's audience to empathise with the cultural icons represented here. The fish-and-chips stands, the Gracie Fields photo-

Magic realism: Joely Richardson as the young Jean Travers, with Robert Hines as Jim, her 1950s lover, in *Wetherby* (1985)

graphs, the sentimental war movies – all of these serve to lock the viewers, like Lynda herself, within the contours of collectively-shared experience and popular memory. In this sense, Leland's film – whose very title implies nostalgia – crystallises that urge toward identification and recognition that, as Caughie suggests, the discourse of television customarily trades upon, promoting a sense of transference that allows the audience to witness these fictional scenes as if they were real. *Wish You Were Here* amalgamates its aesthetic self-consciousness with these more choric aspects of television, harnessing the medium's ability to involve its mass audience in a series of binding recognitions, yet also keeping the audience slightly off balance so that these recognitions are not transmitted merely in an unproblematic manner.

We can understand this dialectic of familiarity and defamiliarisation in television fiction's reconstitution of the past as a mode not of realism but of magic realism. Refusing the glossy fetishes of simplified nostalgia, magic realism introduces 'history with holes, perforated history' (Jameson 1990: 130): it insists on the structural disjunction between past and present that exists simultaneously with any attempt to reconstitute the lost objects of other eras. Many of the most effective Channel 4 films of the 1980s did not simply fictionalise history; they also implicitly commented on how history itself becomes fictionalised. Thus magic realism's disjunction between event and memory, between the object and its name, expanded into a broader investigation of how national mythologies are created, how history is reinvented and rewritten, sometimes unscrupulously. Richard Eyre's Channel 4 film *The Ploughman's Lunch* (1983) remains the most obvious example of this, with its suggestion that the Suez crisis and the Falklands War were both repackaged for the history books like commodities in the advertising market. The film's theme of manufactured appearances is underscored by its scenes shot at the Conservative party conference in Brighton, an event notoriously staged with great care for the national television cameras. As if to re-emphasise the interdependence of film and television in this production, Eyre's team received permission to shoot footage at this conference only through Channel 4's contacts with Independent Television News (Forbes & Pulleine 1983: 235).

The distorting mirrors of the television medium again function self-reflexively in the Channel 4 serial *A Very British Coup* (1988), which features a beleaguered Labour Party Prime Minister (Ray McAnally) eventually going on television to complain about the media conspiracies undermining his administration. A more international reworking of this theme, the deflection of history into Machiavellian fictions, can be found in Tom Stoppard's treatment of the Polish Solidarity crisis, *Squaring the Circle* (directed by Mike Hodges), screened by the 'Film on Four' series in May 1984. Described by Stoppard as 'an imaginative history', this film was shot entirely in the studio with an assortment of gimmicky, alienating devices to reinforce the narrator's assertion: 'Everything that follows is true, except the words and the pictures' (see Woolley 1984: 33). The film depicts Lech Walesa (Bernard Hill) playing elaborate mind games with the old Russian bureaucrats as he tries to establish freedom in Eastern Europe. As with *The Ploughman's Lunch*, Stoppard's work represents politics as a series of elaborate intrigues, a deadly playing field where the disjunction between the rhetoric of the image and the more intangible processes of history is always teasingly apparent.[5]

Such displacement of history into fiction takes on a kind of ontological status in television films of the 1980s. Television films train their glance back on television itself, exploring the contradictions inherent in this medium's own recycled vision of the world. In this way, the fictional dialectic of familiarity and defamiliarisation exposes those fissures and ambiguities latent within the nation's domesticated understanding of history. *Letter to Brezhnev* undermines the stereotypes of 'evil' Russians regurgitated by the news media back in the pre-glasnost days; *Prick Up Your Ears* provides a more hard-edged, sexualised angle on the cutesy commodification of Brian Epstein and the Beatles in the 1960s; *Saigon: Year of the Cat* painfully undercuts official American rhetoric about the Vietnam War by portraying the evacuation from this lost city as undignified and frightening. A memorable moment occurs in this film when the American ambassador (E. G. Marshall), who sets himself up to launch into a grand speech about his country's contribution to the Vietnam cause, suddenly finds himself brusquely hustled away by his troops because there simply is not time. This bifurcated perspective, where rhetoric and image fail to confirm the validity of each other, also appears in several of the most effective BBC serials of the 1980s: in Troy Kennedy Martin's *Edge of Darkness* (1985), which concerns itself with the ruthless cover-ups perpetrated by British intelligence in order to protect the state's illegal experiments with nuclear energy; in Alan Bleasdale's *The Monocled Mutineer* (1986), which plays off the military and political machine of World War One against a startling sense of the ragged resistance to that organisation among ordinary soldiers.

All of these texts, especially the BBC serials, attracted predictable political controversies; yet in this decade television broadcasts found themselves becoming increasingly politicised, whether they actively sought such a status or not. A widespread anxiety appeared about the Thatcher government aggressively restricting freedom of information, with television – the prime conduit of this information society – becoming a central target for censorship.[6] Richard Collins observes that the government at this time 'made unprecedently explicit use of its powers ... to prohibit transmission of particular messages' (1989: 6), most notably in banning television appearances by speakers on behalf of Sinn Fein and the Ulster Defence Association, two lawful political organisations. The heavy-handed nature of this legislation contributed to a wide-ranging feeling of unease in liberal circles. As Harold Pinter, hardly an extremist, put it: 'When the Conservatives came to power, one of their platforms was that they wanted to save the country from state control ... What has actually taken place is that no state power has ever been stronger in this country' (quoted in Ford 1988: 6).

For 'stronger', we might perhaps substitute the phrase 'more apparent'. Sally Hibbin, producer of *A Very British Coup*, points out that the whole idea and apparatus of the state became more visible when the postwar political consensus in Britain fell apart, leading to far sharper disagreements about what should constitute national security interests. Consequently, the Thatcher government provided a milieu where television films like *A Very British Coup* and *Edge of Darkness* could no longer be dismissed as 'just a paranoid fantasy, left-wing conspiracy theory' (Petley 1988: 96).[7] As Malcolm Bradbury recognised, many British fictions of this time 'are filled with strange conspiracies that frequently became curiously true' (1990: 8). Hence television, necessarily implicated within the apparatus of this information society, lost any vestige of political innocence. The television screen no longer was a mere window on the world, what John Ellis called 'a safe means of scanning the world outside' (1982: 170); by the 1980s, this screen appeared more sinister as a medium that was, in a metaphorical sense, watching the viewer, helping to construct his or her psychological attitudes by its carefully regulated flow of information. This phenomenon was not confined exclusively to Britain, of course, as the ingenious screen performances of Ronald Reagan at the same time demonstrated, but it was exacerbated in Britain because of the nation's status as a small, centralised country with relatively few channels of information. In this sense, the Channel 4 work of Peter Greenaway

The distorting mirrors of the media: the Prime Minister (Ray McAnally) with his simulacrum in
A Very British Coup (1988)

– discussed in detail elsewhere in this volume – could be seen as a meta-text for British television films of the 1980s. Greenaway's emphasis in *The Draughtsman's Contract* (1982) and elsewhere on both obfuscation and decoding, on the construction and unravelling of a pictorial puzzle, might be understood as a metaphor for the Thatcherite televisual medium where all the assumptions of 'naturalism' needed to be problematised and all the sutures of conventional representation probed.[8] In the 1980s, Thatcher's own public image was a larger-than-life figure. She became almost a caricature of herself, like 'a duchess in a farce or a pantomime dame', as Angela Carter described her (1983: 8). Consequently, analysing her political power in similarly simplistic or iconic terms, rather than seeking to address its larger cultural context, remains a danger. This occurred in several Channel 4 films that tried too hard to comment upon Thatcherism: *Stormy Monday*, to take one example, used the conceit of 'America week' in Newcastle-upon-Tyne to sprinkle its *mise-en-scène* with large rosettes of Thatcher and Reagan, along with a caricatured speech on the values of self-reliance by the city's Thatcherite mayor (Alison Steadman). This kind of satiric scenario, however, ignores the possibility that most people who voted for Thatcher did not, in abstract terms, support such a dogmatic stance on 'self-reliance', nor even admire the Prime Minister personally; opinion polls tended to suggest that many supported her for a much more complicated variety of social and economic reasons. It is true that Thatcher liked to portray herself iconically, as the guiding philosophical spirit of Britain in the 1980s, but the actual historical situation was surely more complex than this. Ironically, then, films overtly hostile to Thatcher, such as *Stormy Monday*, colluded in the rhetorical force of this image she invented for herself, even in opposing it politically. This difference between manifest and latent political content is well illustrated in *Wetherby*, which David Hare claims as a deliberate attempt to evoke the tone of Thatcher's Britain (see Hiley 1985: 64). At one dinner party scene during this film, Stanley Pilborough (Ian Holm) proffers a psychoanalytical explanation of the Prime Minister's behaviour, claiming she is taking vengeance upon the country out of a series of private obsessions. More convincing than this, however, are the impersonal elements in Hare's film: its analysis of time, history and memory, together with its projection of how the past flows inexorably into the present. Often the most perceptive critiques of Thatcher's Britain came when directors and writers kept the pantomime villain herself at a safe distance, or when – as in *Wetherby* – Thatcher represented a cumulative product of postwar British history rather than just a grotesque aberration.

Thatcher resigned as Prime Minister in November 1990, and during the subsequent decade the landscape of television broadcasting in Britain changed considerably. The BBC, no longer under such direct and intense political pressure, became more adventurous and eventually moved into the financing of feature films themselves, supporting distinguished works such as *Mansfield Park* (1999) and *Iris* (2001), while gradual increases in the penetration of cable and satellite meant that all the network channels began having to address the general problem of a more fragmented audience. David Aukin succeeded David Rose as Head of Channel 4 Films, also in 1990, and he came under increasing pressure to deliver success at the box office, which to some extent he achieved with such productions as *Four Weddings and a Funeral* (1994), *The Madness of King George* (1994) – the latter scripted by Alan Bennett – and *Trainspotting* (1995). There were also, however, some spectacular flops, notably *Charlotte Gray* (2001), a prestige production featuring Cate Blanchett which cost £14 million to make and grossed only £1,567,000 in the UK and $668,000 in the US. After a rebranding as Film Four Limited in 1998 to coincide with the launch of the television station's digital channels, the company's distribution and international sales departments were closed down in 2002 and the film production unit brought back within the much more modest aegis of Channel 4's overall programming budget.

In retrospect, Film Four's ambitious attempts after the Thatcher years to produce international cinema can be seen as less effective than the Channel 4 films of the 1980s, which, like the Ealing cinema of the late 1940s and early 1950s, flourished through creating an idiosyncratic aesthetic style out of the circumscribed conditions associated with their particular mode of production. Channel 4 films in the Thatcher years marked an implicit acknowledgment of the specific terrain of their aesthetic medium and of the ways in which this medium worked with the discourses of social convention, popular history and communal memory. A hard-edged negotiation with such discourses helped to produce that dialectic between familiarity and defamiliarisation characteristic of the best television films of this decade, perhaps the last decade in British television history when narratives could depend upon attracting huge audiences and in exploiting formally the resources of communal memory. As David Hare observes, the idea of eight million invisible people simultaneously watching a television production is so disorienting, so hard to conceptualise, that authors and critics sometimes contain this bewilderment by imagining that viewers cannot distinguish between superior works of fiction and 'dog food commercials' (1982: 49). But, suggests Hare, the truth of the matter is very different: the television film of this era functioned as a uniquely democratic art form, unique in bridging general accessibility with the power to reshape people's perceptions and so, potentially, to change their lives.

NOTES

1   For a recent analysis of American television movies, see Laurie Jane Schulze (1986) 'Getting Physical: Text/Context/Reading and the Made-for-Television Movie', *Cinema Journal*, 25, 2, 35–50.
2   Figures on cable and satellite television are taken from Feist & Hutchison (1990: 63) and the ITN Factbook (1990: 935).
3   On situation comedy, see, for instance, Mick Eaton (1978/79) 'Television Situation Comedy', *Screen*, 19, 4, 61–89.
4   In making this distinction, I follow Ellis (1982: 137–8).
5   *Squaring the Circle* is a classic example of a major work by a major writer that is, at the present time, almost invisible because of the lack of accessible television libraries.
6   Media censorship in Britain was particularly prevalent during the Falklands War. For an account of this, see Harris 1983.
7   The quotation comes from Lynda Myles, producer of *Defence of the Realm* (1985), another film about government suppression of information. Myles said that this film, directed by David Drury, 'turned out to be extremely prophetic' in relation to Thatcher's Britain (see Petley 1988: 96).
8   Many films that addressed issues of representation were shown in Channel 4's 'Eleventh Hour' series, a showcase for more obviously avant-garde works that were screened for smaller audiences late at night. In this essay, however, I have chosen to concentrate upon the more well-known and widely-seen Channel 4 productions.

WORKS CITED

Adair, Gilbert (1988/89) 'Classtrophobia: *High Hopes*', *Sight and Sound*, 58, 1, 64–5.
Auty, Martyn (1985) 'But Is It Cinema?', in Martyn Auty and Nick Roddick (eds) *British Cinema Now*. London: British Film Institute, 57–70.

Baudrillard, Jean (1988) *America*, trans. Coos Turner. London: Verso.

Bennett, Alan, Mamoun Hassan, Jeremy Isaacs and Gavin Millar (1984) 'British Cinema: Life before Death on Television', *Sight and Sound*, 53, 2, 115–22.

Bradbury, Malcolm (1990) 'Write Angles', *Listener*, 15 February, 8–9.

Brunsdon, Charlotte (1990) 'Television: Aesthetics and Audiences', in Patricia Mellencamp (ed.) *Logics of Television: Essays in Cultural Criticism*. Bloomington: Indiana University Press, 59–72.

Carter, Angela (1983) 'Masochism for the Masses', *New Statesman*, 3 (June), 8–10.

Caughie, John (1985) 'On the Offensive: Television and Values', in David Lusted and Phillip Drummond (eds) *TV and Schooling*. London: British Film Institute, 53–66.

____ (1986) 'Popular Culture: Notes and Revisions', in Colin MacCabe (ed.) *High Theory/Low Culture: Analysing Popular Television and Film*. Manchester: Manchester University Press, 156–71.

____ (1990) 'Playing at Being American: Games and Tactics', in Patricia Mellencamp (ed.) *Logics of Television: Essays in Cultural Criticism*. Bloomington: Indiana University Press, 44–58.

Collins, Richard (1989) 'White and Green and Not Much Read: The White Paper on Broadcasting Policy', *Screen*, 30, 1/2, 6–23.

Docherty, David and David Morrison (1987/88) '…Somewhat Different, but Not Too Different', *Sight and Sound*, 57, 1, 10–13.

Ellis, Jack C. (1990) *A History of Film*, third edition. Englewood Cliffs, NJ: Prentice-Hall.

Ellis, John (1975) 'Made in Ealing', *Screen*, 16, 1, 78–127.

____ (1982) *Visible Fictions: Cinema, Television, Video*. London: Routledge and Kegan Paul.

____ (1986) 'Broadcasting and the State: Britain and the Experience of Channel 4', *Screen*, 27, 3–4, 6–22.

Feist, Andrew and Robert Hutchison (1990) *Cultural Trends*, 6 (August).

Feuer, Jane (1983) 'The Concept of Live Television: Ontology as Ideology', in E. Ann Kaplan (ed.) *Regarding Television: Critical Approaches – An Anthology*. Frederick, MD: University Publications of America/American Film Institute, 12–22

Fitch, Janet (1989) 'Review of *High Hopes*', *American Film*, March, 12.

Flitterman-Lewis, Sandy (1987) 'Psychoanalysis, Film, and Television', in Robert C. Allen (ed.) *Channels of Discourse: Television and Contemporary Criticism*. Chapel Hill: University of North Carolina Press, 172–210.

Forbes, Jill and Tim Pulleine (1983) 'Crossover: McEwan and Eyre', *Sight and Sound*, 52, 4, 232–7.

Ford, Anna (1988) 'Harold Pinter: Radical Departures', *Listener*, October 27, 4–6.

Hare, David (1982) 'Ah! Mischief: The Role of Public Broadcasting', in Frank Pike (ed.) *Ah! Mischief: The Writer and Television*. London: Faber, 41–50.

Harris, Robert (1983) *Gotcha! The Media, the Government and the Falklands Crisis*. London: Faber.

Harvey, Sylvia (1989) 'Deregulation, Innovation and Channel 4', *Screen*, 30, 1/2, 60–79.

Heath, Stephen (1981) *Questions of Cinema*. New York: Macmillan.

Hiley, Jim (1985) 'The Wetherby Report', *Observer* Magazine, 10 March, 64–5.

Houston, Penelope (1986) 'Parker, Attenborough, Anderson', *Sight and Sound*, 55, 3, 152–4.

Howkins, John (1985) 'Edinburgh Television', *Sight and Sound*, 54, 4, 238–9.

Isaacs, Jeremy (1989) *Storm over 4: A Personal Account*. London: Weidenfeld and Nicolson.

ITN Factbook (1990) London: Michael O'Mara.

Jameson, Fredric (1990) *Signatures of the Visible*. New York: Routledge.

Jarman, Derek (1987) *The Last of England*, ed. David L. Hirst. London: Constable.

Kael, Pauline (1989) 'The Current Cinema', *New Yorker*, 20 February, 95–8.

Kent, Nicolas (1987) 'Commissioning Editor: David Rose Interviewed', *Sight and Sound*, 56, 4, 260–3.

Lane, Stewart (1986) 'Out Dated', *Listener*, 24 April, 36.

LeMahieu, D. L. (1990) 'Imagined Contemporaries: Cinematic and Televised Dramas about the Edwardians in Great Britain and the United States, 1967–1985', *Historical Journal of Film, Radio and Television* 10, 243–56.

MacCabe, Colin (1988) 'The South Bank Show Lecture: Is Television About to Enter the Dark Ages?', *Listener*, 11 February, 10–12.

Morse, Margaret (1985) 'Talk, Talk, Talk – The Space of Discourse in Television', *Screen* 26, 2, 2–15.

Paglia, Camille and Neil Postman (1991) 'She Wants Her TV! He Wants His Book!', *Harpers*, March, 44–55.

Park, James (1982/83) 'Four Films for 4', *Sight and Sound*, 52, 1, 8–12.

Petley, Julian (1988) 'Review of *A Very British Coup*', *Sight and Sound*, 57, 2, 95–7.

Poole, Mike (1982) 'Improvising the Real', *Listener*, 2 September, 29.

Pratley, Gerald (1989) '35 Days in Toronto', *Sight and Sound*, 58, 2, 94–6.

Walters, Margaret (1987) 'Safe British Cinema', *Listener*, 17–24 December, 62.

Woolley, Benjamin (1984) 'Being Poles Apart', *Listener*, 24 May, 33.

Zettl, Herbert (1978) 'The Rare Case of Television Aesthetics', *Journal of the University Film Association*, 30, 2, 3–8.

5. THE REPRESSION OF COMMUNITIES: VISUAL REPRESENTATIONS OF NORTHERN IRELAND DURING THE THATCHER YEARS

Brian McIlroy

> I remember once, in the early days of the troubles, the local RUC received a call one wintry night from a Protestant farmer reporting intruders on his property. As the patrol car turned into his drive, they saw a colour television plonked smack in the middle of the road. One constable got out to remove it – and was blown to kingdom-come. In Ulster, the medium really is the message.
>
> – John Naughton

John Naughton's striking anecdote above inspired me to explore the ways in which film directors and screenwriters approached the subject of Northern Ireland's violence during the years 1979–90. The Thatcher years produced many works that still require contextualisation. 'The troubles' in Northern Ireland (which 'started' in 1968–69) have certain inbuilt impediments as a film topic, primarily the sheer complexity of Ireland's history with, and governance by, Great Britain. Margaret Thatcher came to power with mainstream opinions on Northern Ireland's position in the United Kingdom; as long as the majority of the population of the northern six counties wished to stay under British rule, she would defend that desire. In effect, this policy (which the Labour Party also endorsed) put the British government and the Irish Republican Army (IRA), who seek to reunite the country against the wishes of the majority Protestant population of Northern Ireland, on a collision course for over twenty years. Thousands have suffered injury and death from this guerrilla war.

The claims for separation from the United Kingdom were helped by the rampant constitutional anomalies. For example, in Northern Ireland, unlike England, Scotland and Wales, the major political parties – Conservative, Labour, Liberal Democrats – never were allowed or encouraged to form local branches. Instead, political parties in Northern Ireland reflect specifically the Irish/British dimension: the Ulster Unionist Party (UUP) and the Democratic Unionist Party (DUP), supported mainly by the Protestant population, argue for the continued connection to Great Britain; the Social Democratic and Labour Party (SDLP) and Sinn Fein, supported mainly by the Catholic population, argue for a gradual move to a United Ireland. Sinn Fein is the political representative of the Provisional IRA.

In the midst of Thatcher's election campaign in 1979, her close friend and shadow secretary of state, Airey Neave, was murdered by the Irish National Liberation Army

(INLA), a more left-leaning organisation than the Provisional IRA. Thatcher, in her early period of office, instructed her ministers to seek a peaceful internal arrangement within Northern Ireland. Meanwhile, she inherited from the Labour government a slew of problems concerning special category status for terrorist prisoners. This special status officially ended in April 1980, and was quickly followed by the 'blanket' protest (in which prisoners refused to wear prison clothing), which turned into a series of hunger strikes. The most famous hunger striker, Bobby Sands, was elected a Westminster MP in a by-election, while he was starving himself to death.

Thatcher refused to grant special status to terrorist prisoners, and after ten men died, the IRA leaders called the strike off.[1] Though this emotional battle was a propaganda victory for the IRA, it also showed the resolve of Thatcher, a woman not afraid of confrontation, as she proved again during the British miners' strike and the Falklands War. On the political front, plans for 'rolling devolution' for Northern Ireland never garnered much interest, but in 1982 a local assembly convened after province-wide elections. The Catholic nationalist parties declined, however, to take their seats, leaving the Unionists to talk to themselves.

Instead of attending the assembly, the constitutional nationalists (led by John Hume of the SDLP) discussed matters with elected representatives from the south of Ireland. These talks resulted in the New Ireland Forum Report released in 1984, which called for three main options to be considered by the British and Irish governments. Thatcher's negative response, later coined the 'Out, Out, Out' speech, was characteristically to the point: 'I have made it quite clear – and so did Mr Prior when he was Secretary of State for Northern Ireland – that a unified Ireland was one solution that is out. A second solution was confederation of two states. That is out. A third solution was joint authority. That is out. That is a derogation from sovereignty. We made that quite clear when the Report was published' (Kenny 1986: 82).

Her strong criticism came only a month after a bomb attempt on her life at the Conservative Party Conference (October 1984) killed five people, so Thatcher was in no mood for fudging the issues. Nevertheless, a great deal of hard bargaining behind the scenes over the next year led to an ingeniously worded (it avoided defining the present status of Northern Ireland) Anglo-Irish Agreement, one signed in November 1985. This agreement gave a formal voice, for the first time since the formation of the Northern Ireland province in 1921, to Southern Irish elected representatives in the running of the province. Although restricted to matters of security and the treatment of the Catholic nationalist community, it offended the Unionist parties who refused to recognise the legitimacy of the agreement and began to encourage acts of civil disobedience. The accord represented an attempt to isolate the IRA and its violence. For the remainder of her term, Thatcher's ministers sought to strengthen the accord in spite of Protestant resistance. This policy included banning all terrorist spokespeople from appearing directly on television.[2] Through all these complex political negotiations, 'the troubles' ebbed and flowed. In retrospect, from the vantage point of 2006, Thatcher's legacy is a mixed one, for her confrontational style clearly worsened the situation, yet her willingness to sign the Anglo-Irish Agreement provided a base for the later, and more comprehensive, Good Friday Agreement of 1998.

As befitting the confrontation of the period, it is unsurprising that most films made between 1979 and 1990 dealing with Northern Ireland invariably grapple with IRA violence, as well as the violence that happens in response. They usually fall within the thriller genre, since it contains all the ingredients necessary for conspiracy, intrigue, murder and star-crossed lovers. Belfast's rugged streets move characters from innocence to experience. In many ways, this tendency to use generic conventions and formulas betrays a conservative choice: it emphasises the universal quality of a film's narrative and, in so doing, avoids a concerted attempt to demythologise the Northern Ireland 'problem'. But given cinema is a powerful cultural force in society, it remains important, first, to point out how films underwhelm or repress history and politics, and second, to understand how they also undermine specific communities. So the haphazard group of films dealing with Northern Ireland follows a fatalistic aesthetic, much in the same way as Polanski's *Chinatown* (1974) convinces us that societal corruption so pervades our world that it swallows up the individual seeking to do good.

The history of films dealing with Ireland as a whole has been well charted in a series of books published since the late 1980s (Rockett *et al.* 1987, Slide 1988, Curran 1989, McIlroy 1989 and 2001, McLoone 2000, Pettitt 2000, Barton 2004, Barton & O'Brien 2004). We see from these works that Ireland's struggle with Britain for independence has attracted many filmmakers: from Brian Desmond Hurst's *Ourselves Alone* (1936) through Michael Anderson's *Shake Hands with the Devil* (1959) to David Lean's *Ryan's Daughter* (1970). These films look at violence within Ireland, among Irish people, and conclude that compromise is possible for those who are not fanatics. Of the three directors above, only Hurst was an Irishman. English and American filmmakers tend to bring Ireland to the Irish. Like many other small countries sharing a common language with a larger country, Ireland's national images have been foisted upon it by outsiders. John Ford's *The Quiet Man* (1952), for instance, remains a favourite among Irish viewers of all ages: it presents a flattering, romanticised version of the country, an escapist revision of reality through rose-technicolor spectacles.

The film that influenced many screenwriters and directors considering Northern Ireland as a subject is Carol Reed's *Odd Man Out* (1947). The pursuit of an IRA gunman through the streets of Belfast provided Reed with a convenient metaphor to explore the metaphysical themes of the outsider – and of salvation. Reed's combining of the thriller genre with film noir allows him to suggest the universal aspect of the gunman's actions, and some viewers have been disappointed at the apparent lack of a political statement from the film (Hill 1987; McLoone 2000). This unwillingness to be historically or locally precise springs, they argue, not only from a fear of being accused of partisanship but also from a fear of confusing the non-Irish audience, those not expected to understand the by-ways of Irish politics as containing vital information for narrative resolution. Yet a close reading of the film and of certain scenes in particular actually argues the reverse, that Reed is much more detail-oriented than he is given credit for, and his clear preference is for constitutional nationalism (McIlroy 2001).

Although one can say very little about the Northern Ireland situation without someone attacking the critic as misguided and/or prejudiced, it seems important to take a stand on delineating the problems of representation. The easiest and most conventional method of approaching the conflict opens filmmakers and critics to charges of sectarianism because it too neatly divides the warring groups into three camps: (i) the Catholic community and its paramilitary off-shoots (particularly the IRA and the INLA); (ii) the 'security forces' (the British Army; the locally recruited Ulster Defence Regiment (now disbanded); the Royal Ulster Constabulary (RUC) (now renamed the Police Service of Northern Ireland)); and (iii) the Protestant community and its paramilitary offshoots (particularly the Ulster Defence Association and the Ulster Volunteer Force). Such a framework allows a filmmaker, particularly in the field of documentary, to give the impression that the security forces either keep the warring factions apart or, indeed, the reverse, keep them fighting and thereby prevent a solution. Immediately, readers may object to the use of the words 'Catholic' and 'Protestant', preferring the less religious terms 'Nationalist' and 'Unionist'. But it remains a fact that Catholics populate the vast majority of Nationalist organisations, and Protestants the Unionist groups. Most filmic representations accept this generalisation of Northern Ireland's simmering political scene. To term someone a Protestant or a Catholic in this context conjures up a whole history of social, economic and political attitudes not confined to religious affiliation.

Grave misconceptions and misunderstandings between the two communities in Northern Ireland have spread to the film representations of the people in Ulster, and to that extent, film and television drama production has often added to the mystification. By dividing my subsequent discussion into the three sections mentioned above, I will take the sectarian positions 'by the throat', as it were. The first, and most 'appealing' to filmmakers, is the depiction of the Catholic community and the paramilitary organisations emanating from it.

THE CATHOLIC COMMUNITY AND THE IRA

The majority of film and television productions dealing with the province focus on the minority population of Roman Catholics in Northern Ireland, a subject area prone to censorship. A television drama reviewer in 1982 commented that 'in television alone, upwards of forty programmes have been suppressed in part or in whole during the past decade' (Poole 1982: 33). One of the most famous cases of censorship was the BBC film *Real Lives* (1985), which profiled two Irish extremists, one Protestant and one Catholic. The furor over the initially-banned film resulted from Martin McGuinness's (of Provisional Sinn Fein) voiced opinions in favour of an organisation (the IRA) that in 1984 almost murdered the Prime Minister and most of her cabinet colleagues. A letter from the home secretary sent to the BBC Board of Governors indicated his concern over the film's possible transmission. The board voted against the screening. In reaction, journalists led a one-day strike at the BBC, protesting the blatant intervention of the Thatcher government. Matters worsened when Thatcher appeared on a news programme and thanked the board for their 'judicious' decision not to screen the documentary. On the surface, it appeared that the Board of Governors had bowed to government pressure, and the IRA received yet another propaganda victory. In the heat of the moment, commentators overlooked that until the last few years of Thatcher's term, the British government had allowed the reporting of Sinn Fein. By contrast, the Irish Republic banned Provisional Sinn Fein access to broadcasting in 1975 because of its unequivocal support of the 'armed struggle'.

Most films blindly accept the assumption that the Catholic community is an oppressed minority. Since the IRA casts itself as the protector of this beleaguered community, filmmakers deal with the IRA. At the start of Thatcher's term of office, three films with references to the IRA caused considerable comment. Two of these, with American directors but diverse financial backing, were the most direct and explicit. Arthur MacCaig's *The Patriot Game – A Decade Long Battle for the North of Ireland* (1979) utilised television footage from a number of international television stations to build its visual argument that the British troops present in Northern Ireland continue to play the role of imperial oppressors. The film vehemently supports the IRA armed struggle, ostensibly showing how history makes it inevitable. According to the *Variety* review in 1980, the Irish Northern Aid Committee, subsequently investigated by the American authorities over allegations that it transferred money directly to the IRA, used the film as a fundraiser. So controversial was the film that two special screenings were held in the Royal Court Theatre in London in June 1979, since most British distributors declined to handle the picture.

Dealing with the IRA also functions as the main subject of the two other films released in 1979: John Mackenzie's *The Long Good Friday* and Tony Luraschi's *The Outsider*. In a sense, they reveal the 'tentativeness' of a British production versus the 'boldness' of a foreign-financed production, a general thesis advanced by John Hill (see Rockett *et al.* 1987).

John Mackenzie's film looks primarily at gangsterism in 1970s London. Bob Hoskins plays working-class mobster Harold Shand, who makes good by sheer graft and appropriate violence, a precursor to Spica in Peter Greenaway's *The Cook, The Thief, His Wife and Her Lover* (1989). Shand, the nouveau riche, eventually runs into an older, more efficient 'family', that of the IRA. As the screenwriter conceived it, 'The hero would be a Thatcher man gone mad – the ultimate self-made capitalist and utterly patriotic' (Keefe 1984: vi). The problem with the film from an Irish nationalist perspective is that IRA violence simply functions as a form of gangsterism (which to many British governments it has always been characterised). In this way, the film reflects a British *realpolitik*. The history of the film's postproduction reveals that financial backers were uneasy with the depiction of the IRA as this unstoppable, incorruptible force. Mackenzie never helps the audience move beyond gangsterism because he never investigates the IRA. It is, in effect, the evil *deus ex machina*. What is fascinating is that the IRA infiltrates the underworld in Britain and is treated as an inexplicable, though amazingly efficient, force. This attitude of respect tinged with repulsion remains the essential British view today.

Tony Luraschi's *The Outsider* focuses on young Irish-American Michael (Craig Wasson), who, filled with songs and stories from his Irish-born grandfather, comes to Northern Ireland to join the IRA. Michael accompanies the IRA on special missions, including the murder of a magistrate. The naive American soon learns that the IRA and the British army stay caught in a struggle without regard for the kind of romanticised idealism Michael exhibits. Luraschi presents the IRA as a duplicitous group of men who use the young man for their own purposes. Ironically, Michael's grandfather turns out to have been the sinner of all Irish sinners: an IRA informer. Brutal, violent and direct, *The Outsider* nonetheless bravely questions the presence of the British army, the shadowy role of the Ulster Defence Regiment, the interrogation techniques of the RUC, as well as the kangaroo courts of the IRA. This film, too, ran into distribution problems because of its topicality, especially scenes where police torture a blind IRA sympathiser.

Danny (Stephen Rea), in pursuit of revenge, clutches the weapon that has replaced his saxophone-playing career, in Neil Jordan's *Angel* (1982)

The first truly remarkable Irish-directed 'Northern Ireland feature' was released in 1982. Neil Jordan's *Angel* has received a great deal of attention from commentators who validate its aesthetics by remarking that both sides in the Northern Ireland 'troubles' are condemned. Danny (Stephen Rea), the sax player, becomes a gunman for reasons of revenge after a Protestant gang murders a deaf-mute he has befriended. Some critics argue that the specifics of religion/allegiance are unclear; but, a knowledgeable viewer knows that because the policeman is the ring-leader of the gang, this is almost certainly a Protestant paramilitary group.

Interestingly, the clue of a clubfoot sets off Danny's search for revenge. A non-specific Irish saying to determine religion is to ask whether someone kicks with the 'other' or 'left' foot. In this instance, the culprit kicks with a malformed foot! The film's underlying premise is that police corruption and murder (represented by the Protestant community) destroy Danny's humanity and lead him to violent acts. Danny is, then, the IRA, 'the people' radicalised into action. Literally, he is a son without parents, one who finds his voice – first by sax-playing and then by gunplay. He eliminates the 'cancer' of Protestantism and contentedly leaves a Jewish head of police – significantly called Bloom (a cute Joycean echo) – to sort out the mess at the end.

Pat O'Connor's *Cal* (1984), taken from Bernard MacLaverty's novella of the same name, follows the literary source very closely and traces a young Catholic boy's story. He and his father are the only Catholics left on a Protestant street and suffer accordingly. The film also looks at how a young Catholic man becomes involved in the operations of the IRA. Not unlike many reluctant activists, Cal (John Lynch) is seduced into working for the IRA – half through threats and half through promises that if he complies with 'small jobs' he will be left alone to live his own life later. The IRA leader, Skeffington (John Kavanagh), presents his involvement through his crippled father, a parallel to the crippled father of the murdered RUC man for whose death Cal is partly responsible; Skeffington's father once was heavily committed to the cause of national liberation. Through his choice of characterisation and shooting style, O'Connor indicates how the IRA leaders see themselves as fighting some kind of holy war. Skeffington, for example, is strangely puritanical and disapproves of bad language. At one point, Cal meets the IRA leader in a pigeon- and bat-infested stone-wall enclosure and, because much of their discussion is shot from above at an angle, it implies that the world of the IRA is unnatural. The brutal representation of the gunman Crilly, who actually murders the RUC man while Cal assists, conveys the sense that the IRA leadership easily manipulates young and violent men who are little more than gangsters.

Both *Angel* and *Cal* were critical and commercial successes, but three films in the 1980s dealing with the Catholic community and the IRA particularly impress because they originate from Irish women: Pat(ricia) Murphy's *Maeve* (1981), Stuart Burge and Anne Devlin's *Naming the Names* (1986) and Anne Crilly's *Mother Ireland* (1988). These three films explore the role of (Catholic) women in the Republican movement. Murphy's film charts the return of Maeve (Brid Brennan) from 'open-minded' England to her Republican 'ghetto', where she finds herself constantly warring with chauvinist ideas from within and without her specific environment. The male soldiers who taunt her on the streets display misogynist attitudes little different from the male Republican leaders and advocates in her own community. By deliberately eschewing a conventional narrative – one feels distanced from much of the supposed linear visual presentation by occasional direct address to the camera and a complicated *mise-en-scène* – Murphy calls into question the patriarchal structures that support the presence of the British army in Northern Ireland, as well as those that support the Republican movement in Catholic Nationalist areas.

In *Naming the Names* (a television film for the BBC), a young Catholic woman, Finn (Sylvestra Le Touzel), is arrested for luring a Protestant judge's son to a park where the IRA apprehends and murders him. The critical event in Finn's life, the Protestant firebombing of her home in 1969, almost kills her guardian grandmother, while Finn is making love with an English journalist. When her grandmother does die a few years later, an orphaned Finn depends on her English boyfriend to keep her from the IRA, though he remains unaware of her predicament. Their break-up seals her fate with the IRA. Circumscribed by the streets of her West Belfast ghetto, Finn repeats only the names of these streets when quizzed by the police for her IRA contacts. The Catholic community, shown to be frightened and impotent in the 1969–70 period, becomes totally radicalised by the mid-1980s, as evidenced by the argument in Belfast City Library between Catholic Finn and Protestant Henry:

Henry: Take Parnell, for example – Charles Stewart Parnell, a Protestant, a leader of the Home Rule, was destroyed by the Roman Catholic clergy over his divorce case.

Finn: He was destroyed by Gladstone, and the English nonconformists … And when has any Protestant movement had a Catholic leader?

Henry: Come on, they're not exactly queuing up at the door, are they?

Finn: How could they be? What of the wars of the constitution?

Henry: That's not relevant.

Finn: A Protestant parliament for a Protestant people. And it's not relevant?! You think
           that's all right? It's economic, rational?

Henry: You get angry very quickly. Who's done that to you, Finn?
           [She gets up and leaves. They both run out into the street and face the large sign
           on the City Hall: 'Belfast Says No' – a reference to the Unionist resistance to the
           Anglo-Irish Agreement].

Henry: Confirmed what they've [the Unionists] always believed. The British government
           are the real Republicans!

Finn: Welcome to Belfast.

The third film, *Mother Ireland,* a documentary video that features many Irish women's attitudes concerning their social and political position in Ireland, achieved a certain notoriety for its interview with Mairead Farrell, one of the three IRA suspects shot dead in Gibraltar by a British SAS unit. She complains that the Republican movement often fails to be fully aware of women's issues. To what extent audiences should feel pleased that Farrell can be just as involved in terrorist activities as any man remains problematic. Nonetheless, her direct engagement with social and political realities reflects the radicalisation of many women in Northern Ireland.

Other Catholic women who dominate the video include Rita O'Hare of the magazine *Republican News;* journalist Nell McCafferty; filmmaker Pat Murphy; feminist Republican activist Bernadette Devlin; and women who supported the Nationalist movement during the War of Independence and the Civil War. Director Crilly forcefully brings out the discrepancy between the Mother Ireland image of compassion and suffering and the reality of modern Irish women who, at least in the Republican movement, demand and receive recognition that violence and feminism can (and do) go hand in hand.

THE SECURITY FORCES

To put it mildly, the screen versions of the security forces in Northern Ireland have not been particularly sympathetic. Yet even here discrepancies exist. So, for example, one group, the Ulster Defence Regiment, has hardly been tackled at all, even though it carried out much of the army-style operations – roadblocks, patrols and the like – in Ulster. Like the RUC, this force is predominantly Protestant in make-up. Their colleagues in the RUC, however, have been more severely treated. For instance, in Ken Loach's *Hidden Agenda* (1990), the police callously murder Irish Catholic and American civilians, violently carry out house searches, and bitterly resent 'foreign' interference. This fact is exemplified by the chief constable of the RUC in the film, Brodie (Jim Norton), who resists the investigation of Kerrigan (Brian Cox) and Ingrid (Frances McDormand). Loach offers no explanation as to why Brodie believes in his cause. Yet to understand the nuances of this particular situation, some background is necessary to discuss it further.

On 12 December 1982, an undercover unit of the RUC murdered Seamus Grew and Roddy Carroll. Grew and Carroll were members of the INLA, an extremist offshoot from the Official IRA. Both men were travelling home to Armagh City when

Police inspector Kerrigan (Brian Cox) and human rights activist Ingrid (Frances McDormand) arrive in a nationalist ghetto to interview an SAS deserter with information incriminating highly placed Conservative politicians, in Ken Loach's *Hidden Agenda* (1990)

a speeding car overtook them and forced them off the road. At close range, Grew and Carroll were shot to death, though neither man was armed nor wanted for any specific crime. Murders like these by the undercover RUC unit led to a police inquiry into what became known as the 'shoot-to-kill' policy in Northern Ireland. Deputy Chief Constable John Stalker of the Greater Manchester constabulary headed an internal investigation authorised to present a report, one recommending what charges, if any, should be laid against police officers in Northern Ireland. Before Stalker could present his findings, he was 'disgraced' back in Manchester by allegations that he kept company with criminals. Though proved false, these allegations removed Stalker from the Northern Ireland investigation.[3]

Commentators and authors put forth many theories to explain this bizarre twist of events, one of the most popular claiming that Stalker found connections between clandestine operations and their authorisation from within the higher levels of the British government. Also in the conspiracy vein, it later emerged that the former Labour Prime Minister Harold Wilson had been the target of a CIA-inspired plan to discredit him. Hearing this, some quickly assumed that right-wing forces actively made conditions conducive for the rise of Margaret Thatcher and her conservative agenda. Loach attempts to combine these two theories in his film *Hidden Agenda*.

In the movie, an American Civil Liberties Union lawyer, Paul Sullivan (Brad Dourif), is killed while uncovering the story behind an ex-SAS soldier, Harris (Maurice Roeves), involved in a conspiracy against Wilson's Labour government in the 1970s. Loach ties the Conservative Party supporters' shenanigans against the Labour Party government of the 1970s (shades of the television series *A Very British Coup* (1988)) with the alleged 'shoot-to-kill' policy in Northern Ireland many years later. He fails, however, to make this connection stick. Two separate issues are (half) addressed here, one well (Conservative Party conspiracy) and one confusingly (the British policy within Northern Ireland). The director stacks the decks from the very beginning. We see policemen make a house arrest, former detainees allege ill-treatment inside police stations, a police/SAS/MI6 unit kill Frank Malloy and the American lawyer with 'efficiency', and British undercover agents kidnap (and kill off-screen) Harris on Dublin's streets – thereby suggesting that Britain continues to 'invade' the Irish Republic.

Loach opens with two quotations: one from Margaret Thatcher states that Northern Ireland is as much part of the United Kingdom as her own constituency, and one from James Lalor, a nineteenth-century Irish Republican, indicates the imperative of Irish independence. To imply that Thatcherism and Conservative Party 'dirty-tricks' supporters in the 1970s remain part and parcel of an alleged 'shoot-to-kill' policy in Northern Ireland without investigating IRA violence and murder makes one question the ethics of Loach's intertwining of fictional filmmaking and politics. His film seems more an exercise in political correctness, a response to recently published material (Doherty 1986) than a true engagement with the real issues (many of which can be usefully scanned in Ryder 1989). Loach's negative depiction of the RUC stands with good filmic company. The corrupt police in *Angel* are involved in murder, and, in *Cal*, the police rather earnestly beat up the Catholic protagonist for his part in the murder of one of their own. The graphic murder of the RUC man in *Cal*, replayed often in flashback to underscore the protagonist's guilt and desire for redemption, never contextualises nor explains the province's problems.

In *Naming the Names*, a policeman interrogates Finn while others watch through closed-circuit-television surveillance, as a policewoman stands silently beside her and looks on disapprovingly. Policewomen are noticeably missing in most contemporary films dealing with the RUC. Perhaps filmmakers and writers feel their presence weakens the frame they hang around the picture of Northern Ireland: male, Protestant security forces exploiting and repressing female, Catholic civilians, including feminist Republican activists, as seen in such films as Murphy's *Maeve* and *Anne Devlin* (1984) and Crilly's *Mother Ireland*. To be sure, the presence or numbers of policewomen do nothing to subvert patriarchal structures, but they do complicate the rather simplistic accusations of misogyny at the root of Protestant policing. *Maeve*, through its distancing devices, does point out that the Republican movement finds it extremely difficult to integrate women.

The British army in action appears as background 'filler' in nearly every film dealing with Northern Ireland. Some television documentary programmes isolate their experience, but only a few narrative fictional films have similar goals. Alan Clarke's *Contact* (1985, BBC Screen 2), based on his own recorded experiences in Belfast and South Armagh while he was in the British Parachute Regiment, captures precisely the tension and boredom of patrol and rest periods. The soldiers are young, violent, frightened and curious all at the same time. One striking scene serves to sum up this weird atmosphere: after a comrade dies in action, the soldiers move toward the dead man, as if finding it psychically necessary to see the injuries inflicted. Every sound on patrol represents possible danger, and Clarke makes the audience feel almost continuously on edge.

Karl Francis' *Boy Soldier* (1986), one of the less conventional male treatments of the British army, looks critically at the ridiculous go-between status of the army.

Unique here is the Welsh emphasis. Without Channel 4, funding for this project would not have been secured, and it comes across as one of the more sophisticated treatments of the British army in recent years. Wil (Richard Lynch), a young Welsh soldier serving in Northern Ireland, sees his best friend killed on the streets. In a state of panic, he shoots a young man brandishing a knife. The public unrest at this 'civilian murder' demands Wil's sacrifice. Clinging to his principles of honesty, Wil refuses to lie for expediency and subsequently suffers maltreatment from his English army superiors who see little difference between the Irish and the Welsh. The process of brutalisation, carefully traced by Francis, suggests that ultimately the army is an inappropriately blunt instrument to use in the delicate Northern Ireland situation. But Francis also suggests that the real value the army offers for working-class British males resides in its sense of a close community.

THE PROTESTANT COMMUNITY AND ITS PARAMILITARY OFFSHOOTS

One must look hard for a likeable or sympathetic Protestant character in films dealing with Northern Ireland; in fact, one rarely discovers a well-rounded protagonist or antagonist. Quite simply, filmmakers display little interest in developing approaches to the Protestant community, preferring to rely on comfortable stereotypes. For example, the Protestant voice is painfully missing in Loach's *Hidden Agenda:* the one million Protestants of the North of Ireland remain invisible in his constellation. Images of Protestantism are conveyed merely by a long shot from a high window during the 12 July celebrations (when the Protestants commemorate the victory over Catholic James II by Protestant William of Orange in 1690), and by the chief police officer Brodie who 'resists' Kerrigan's investigation. What other Protestants we see are involved in violence or implied bigotry.

In O'Connor's *Cal*, the Protestant family members with whom the Catholic boy interacts are severe, distrusting and terribly cosy with the trigger-happy security forces. Protestant youths assault Cal in another example of Protestant intimidation. In Peter Smith and Alan Bleasdale's otherwise comic *No Surrender* (1985), a Protestant terrorist threatens a former comrade with exposure of his daughter's mixed marriage with a Catholic. Finally, we see the more 'liberal' Protestant murder his more 'extreme' former colleague, a hardly sympathetic portrayal despite the screenwriter's intent to achieve it. Violence, and malicious violence at that, seems integral to most filmmakers' conceptions of the Protestant male community.

This contention opens up a new area: how have filmmakers considered Protestant women and violence? As Richard Kearney (1988) observes, Edward Bennett's *Ascendancy* (1981) and Kieran Hickey's *Attracta* (1983) show male violence paralysing and repressing women to an extent that they assume mythic proportions – essentially the all-suffering Mother figure. Of course, given the blatant pro-Republican bias of Anne Crilly's *Mother Ireland,* Protestant women simply are excluded from the video documentary. But this view of Irish Protestant women fails to account for the violence that radicalised certain women to join the security forces.

Only *Naming the Names* offers an interesting portrayal of an Irish Protestant, even though reviewers misread the character as English (Pascal 1987). Henry Kirk (Michael Maloney), the son of a local judge, is studying Irish history at Oxford University. While at home, he travels to the Catholic Falls Road Bookshop to look at their Irish collection in search of materials for his PhD thesis. The bookshop assistant, Finn, is steeped in Irish history but, given the *de facto* separate education systems in Northern Ireland for Catholics and Protestants, from a purely Republican perspective. Finn and Henry form a romantic attachment, both claiming that they have English partners. In this way, writer Anne Devlin emphasises the love-hate relationship both Irish Catholics and Protestants have with the English mainland.

Finn delivers the two volumes of R.M. Sibbert's *Orangeism in Ireland and Throughout the Empire* (1914–15) to Henry, and this history of Orangeism written by an Orangeman sparks a lively debate. In the midst of their discussion, Henry utters the Protestant position rarely articulated verbally or visually on television and film:

Finn: You think that's all not irrelevant now? Gladstone and Home Rule?
Henry: No, no, Gladstone tended to dismiss the Protestants as a bigoted minority.
         Successive British governments are making the same mistake.
Finn: What is your thesis, briefly, in a line?
Henry: The Protestant opposition to home rule was rational. Because at the time Ulster
         Protestant industries, linen, shipbuilding, were dependent on the British market.
         Home rule would have ruined Ulster financially.
Finn: But it wasn't just about money, was it?
Henry: No, no. The Protestants were also worried about being discriminated against in a
         largely Catholic state.
Finn: They were worried?
Henry: Yes, I think those fears were justified.[4]

The fact that I must quote a dialogue interchange to establish a Protestant Unionist ideological position is significant. No filmmaker in Britain and Ireland in this period thoroughly investigated a visual representation of the Protestant community, one that reaches beyond the easiest of stereotypes.[5] If anything, filmmakers fetishise what they conceive as minority opinions. This reductiveness creates terribly unbalanced fictional renditions, despite the painstaking efforts of local television stations to provide fair treatment of each community in current affairs and news programmes (Cathcart 1984). Consequently, violence and the issues surrounding it in Northern Ireland received an extremely skewed representation between the years 1979 and 1990, a time during which a minority oppositional cinema has dominated our perceptions.

Over the Thatcher years, mainstream filmmakers became more assertive and aggressive in their representations of the Northern Ireland 'problem'. Films and videos toward the end of Thatcher's 'reign', such as Ken Loach's *Hidden Agenda* and Anne Crilly's *Mother Ireland*, confidently and directly criticise the British government's role in Northern Ireland. These films, in particular, struggle with a complicated politics; yet they often fail to provide a stimulating visual treatment. At the other end of the spectrum, films concerned primarily with character continued to do well at the box office, including Neil Jordan's *Angel* and Pat O'Connor's *Cal*. These films repress history and politics for fear of distancing the non-Irish audience. In general, filmmakers and videographers have served well the ideological position of the Catholic nationalist community in Northern Ireland. The position of the security forces has been sketchily treated. The Protestant unionist community has largely been ignored.

Although narrative films can arguably play a crucial role in the cultural reconcilement of Northern Ireland's communities, we find neither comfort nor proof in the productions made during the Thatcher years. We do, however, see bolder attempts than hitherto in articulating anti-British politics.

NOTES

1   A useful blow-by-blow account of the hunger strikes may be found in Liam Clarke (1987) *Broadening the Battlefield: The H-Blocks and the Rise of Sinn Fein*. Dublin: Gill and Macmillan.
2   In the post-Thatcher era, 'talks about talks' appeared to promise a new agreement involving all mainstream political parties, but in mid-1991 these meetings broke down, leaving Thatcher's legacy in place.
3   In addition to Doherty (1986), useful books on various aspects of the Stalker case include the following: Peter Taylor (1987) *Stalker: The Search for Truth*. London: Faber and Faber; The Committee on the Administration of Justice (1988) *The Stalker Affair: More Questions Than Answers*, second edition. Belfast: CAJ; John Stalker (1988) *Stalker*. London: Harrap; Kevin Taylor with Keith Mumby (1990) *The Poisoned Tree*. London: Sidgwick and Jackson; and David Murphy (1991) *The Stalker Affair and the Press*. London: Unwin Hyman.
4   Until the 1990s, The Republic of Ireland remained one of the most conservative countries in Europe. In 1983 and 1986, respectively, access to abortion and divorce were rejected in referendums. The latter issue, in particular, confirmed Protestant fears of a united Ireland.
5   The appearance in 1990 of Thaddeus O'Sullivan's *December Bride*, which focuses on the rural Protestant community of the Strangford Lough area, is a remarkable exception. One might also make a reasonable case for the 'Protestant sections' of Mike Leigh's *Four Days in July* (1984).

WORKS CITED

Barton, Ruth (2004) *Irish National Cinema*. London: Routledge.
Barton, Ruth and Harvey O'Brien (2004) *Keeping it Real: Irish Film and Television*. London: Wallflower Press.
Cathcart, Rex (1984) *The Most Contrary Region: The BBC in Northern Ireland, 1924–1984*. Belfast: Blackstaff Press.
Curran, Joseph (1989) *Hibernian Green on the Silver Screen: The Irish and American Movies*. New York: Greenwood Press.
Doherty, Frank (1986) *The Stalker Affair*. Dublin: Mercer Press.
Hill, John (1987) 'Images of Violence', in Kevin Rockett, Luke Gibbons and John Hill (eds) *Cinema and Ireland*. London: Croom Helm, 147–93.
Hitch, John (1980) 'The Patriot Game – A Decade Long Battle for the North of Ireland', *Variety*, 18 June, 18, 24.
Kearney, Richard (1988) 'Nationalism and Irish Cinema', in *Transitions: Narratives in Modern Irish Culture*. Manchester: Manchester University Press, 173–92.
Keefe, Barrie (1984) *The Long Good Friday*. London: Methuen.
Kenny, Anthony (1986) *The Road to Hillsborough: The Shaping of the Anglo-Irish Agreement*. Oxford: Pergamon Press.
McIlroy, Brian (1989) *World Cinema 4: Ireland*. Trowbridge: Flicks Books.
_____ (2001) *Shooting to Kill: Filmmaking and the 'Troubles' in Northern Ireland*. Richmond, BC: Steveston Press.

McLoone, Martin (2000) *Irish Film: The Emergence of a Contemporary Cinema.* London: British Film Institute.

Naughton, John (1985) 'The good spies come back', *Listener,* 10 January, 33–4.

Pascal, Julia (1987) 'Personal Troubles', *Listener,* 5 February, 31.

Pettitt, Lance (2000) *Screening Ireland: Film and Television Representation.* Manchester: Manchester University Press.

Poole, Michael (1982) 'The Long March', *Listener,* 4 November, 33.

Rockett, Kevin, Luke Gibbons and John Hill (1987) *Cinema and Ireland.* London: Croom Helm.

Ryder, Chris (1989) *The RUC: A Force Under Fire.* London: Methuen.

Slide, Anthony (1988) *The Cinema and Ireland.* Jefferson, NC: McFarland.

6. RE-PRESENTING THE NATIONAL PAST: NOSTALGIA AND PASTICHE IN THE HERITAGE FILM

Andrew Higson

The cultural status of British films in the mid-1980s was relatively high, with commentators celebrating what they saw as a revival of British production. This celebration was in part an acknowledgement that British films were once more forces to be reckoned with in the international market place. While the obligation to succeed internationally requires to some degree an effacing of the specifically national, certain films of the 1980s used the national itself – or at least, a version of the national past – as their prime selling-point. Images of Britain and Britishness (usually, in fact, Englishness) became commodities for consumption in the international image market. The films I have in mind are the cycle of quality costume dramas, or what I will refer to here as 'heritage films'. My interest in these films is in the way in which they represent the national past, and in how these representations might have functioned for their spectators. I will argue that the past is displayed as visually spectacular pastiche, inviting a nostalgic gaze that resists the ironies and social critiques so often suggested narratively by these films.

The numbers of feature films produced in Britain each year had been falling steadily since 1972, to an all-time low of just 24 films in 1981. They picked up again in the mid-1980s, when the average number of films produced each year was more than double the output of 1981. In total, 487 British films were produced between 1980 and 1990 inclusive. Of those films, some 43 were costume dramas with some sort of British connection (either the film was set in the British Isles, or it dealt with the English abroad), and with a pre-World War Two setting (although some of them also had the occasional present-day interlude, from which vantage-point the past was recalled). In other words, around one in every 11 films produced in Britain in the 1980s was a 'British' costume drama with a pre-World War Two setting. Most of those films – 26, to be precise – were set between the 1880s and 1930s, with another eight taking place in the early or mid-nineteenth century. Only a small number were set in an earlier period.

It would therefore not be unreasonable to conclude that one of the most significant production trends in British films of the 1980s was the costume drama, and especially films set in the late nineteenth and early twentieth centuries. The trend was initiated by a number of relatively high-profile films released in the early 1980s, including *Tess* (1979), *The Elephant Man* (1980), *Chariots of Fire* (1981), which won the Best Picture Oscar, *The French Lieutenant's Woman* (1981) and *Ghandi* (1982), as well as two films set much earlier, the Arthurian epic *Excalibur* (1981) and Peter Greenaway's breakthrough art-house hit, *The Draughtsman's Contract* (1982), set in 1694. The period drama trend was given renewed energy in the mid-1980s with the release of David Lean's epic *A Passage to India* (1984), the Cannes prize-winner *Another Country* (1984) and Merchant-Ivory's hugely successful *A Room With a View* (1986), closely followed by *A Handful of Dust* (1987), *Maurice* (1987) and *Little Dorrit* (1987). The costume dramas that appeared at the end of the decade, such as *The Fool* (1990) (Christine Edzard's follow-up to *Little Dorrit*), *December Bride* (1990) and *Robin Hood* (1990) were perhaps less successful either with critics or at the box office, although Kenneth Branagh's *Henry V* (1989) achieved a higher level of visibility. This mix of low-budget art-house films and more mainstream although still relatively modestly budgeted fare is typical of the trend – and of course the higher the budget, the more likely it is that Hollywood was involved.

Equally typical is the fact that many of these films are adaptations. Indeed, the vast majority of the films that make up this production trend are adaptations, 27 of them adaptations of novels. Some of those adaptations work with canonical works of the past, such as Shakespeare's *Henry V*, Charles Dickens' *Little Dorrit* and Evelyn Waugh's *A Handful of Dust*, with the most frequently adapted author being E. M. Forster (*A Passage to India*, *A Room with a View* and *Maurice* – with two more appearing in the early 1990s, *Where Angels Fear to Tread* (1991) and *Howards End* (1992)). Other films were adapted from more recent but still critically acclaimed work, such as Julian Mitchell's play *Another Country*, John Fowles' *The French Lieutenant's Woman*, J. L. Carr's *A Month in the Country* and Bruce Chatwin's *On the Black Hill* (both made into films in 1987), and Maggie Hemingway's *The Bridge* (adapted as a film in 1990).

The only director to make more than two of the films that fall into the British costume drama production trend was the American James Ivory, with *Quartet* (1981), *Heat and Dust* (1982), *A Room with a View* and *Maurice*. With the international cross-over success of the visually lush but actually very modestly budgeted *A Room with a View*, his company, Merchant Ivory Productions, came to dominate critical debate about the costume drama trend from the late 1980s. This essay, first published in 1993, was one of the first academic interventions in that debate (although see also Wollen 1991, which was published shortly before I finished writing the original version of this essay). As such, it is very much a product of its moment. I have continued to work on Anglo-Hollywood costume dramas of the 1980s and 1990s over the last decade, although the way I now write about those films has changed in some ways since this essay was first published – not least because others have challenged the way I present the films here. Even so, although I have written a new introduction and conclusion, I have the left the rest of the essay pretty much as it was, since it has become a standard reference point in the debate about these films. For a more recent presentation of my thinking about these films, and indeed of the thinking of others, I refer readers to my book *English Heritage, English Cinema: Costume Drama since 1980* (2003; see also Higson 1996 and 2001). Among other things, this book provides a filmography of British costume dramas of the 1980s and 1990s, a survey of the critical debate about these films, and an in-depth analysis of the commercial context of the production trend. (Another useful survey of the 1980s heritage film can be found in Hill 1999.)

In what follows, I focus on a small group of quality costume dramas that deal with the English upper and middle classes in the early decades of the twentieth century (*Chariots of Fire, Another Country, A Passage to India, A Room With a View, A Handful of Dust* and *Maurice*) – and, by way of contrast, one film set in the mid-nineteenth century that deals as much with the poor as with the middle classes (*Little Dorrit*). As noted above, my interest in these films, when I first wrote this essay, was in the ambivalent ways in which they seemed to represent the national past, for both domestic and foreign audiences.

The heritage cycle and its particular representation of the national past is in many ways symptomatic of cultural developments in Thatcherite Britain. The Thatcher years, of course, coincided with an international capitalist recession that accelerated Britain's decline as a world economic power, but that also saw the growth of multi-national enterprises, including the European Community. Inevitably, these processes disturbed traditional notions of national identity, which were further upset by the recognition that British society was increasingly multiracial and multicultural. At the same time, the government adopted political and economic measures, often sharply contested, that tended to encourage high unemployment, marked inequalities of income and standards of living, and a more general social malaise among the dispossessed that drifted periodically into social unrest.

The heritage cycle is of course only one strand in the British cinema of these years, and it can usefully be contrasted to other British films like *My Beautiful Laundrette* (1985), *Letter to Brezhnev* (1985), *Passion of Remembrance* (1986), *Sammy and Rosie Get Laid* (1987) and *Riff-Raff* (1990). These films are set firmly in the present, away from the centres of power, in an unstable and socially divided post-imperialist and/or working-class Britain, where identities are shifting, fluid and heterogeneous. The heritage films, on the other hand, provide a very different response to developments in Thatcherite Britain. By turning their backs on the industrialised, chaotic present, they nostalgically re-construct an imperialist and upper-class Britain (or its other side, the picturesque poverty of *Little Dorrit*). The films thus offer apparently more settled and visually splendid manifestations of an essentially pastoral national identity and authentic culture: 'Englishness' as an ancient and natural inheritance, *Great* Britain, the *United* Kingdom. It would be wrong, however, to suggest that these films resonate unequivocally with Thatcherite politics. They are too ambivalent to sit easily in such an equation and in various ways propose more liberal-humanist visions of social relations, at least at the level of dialogue and narrative theme. It is this tension between visual splendour and narrative meaning in the films which makes them so fascinating.

Heritage films operate at very much the culturally respectable, quality end of the market, and are key players in the new British art cinema, which straddles the traditional art-house circuit and the mainstream commercial cinemas in Britain. These are the sort of films that are invited to festivals and that win prizes. They are discussed in terms of an authorship that, at least in the case of the literary adaptations, is doubly coded – in terms of both film director and author of the source novel. Their audience is primarily middle-class and significantly older than the mainstream film audience, and they appeal to a film culture closely allied to English literary culture and to the

Reproducing Englishness: cricket practice, in *Another Country* (1984)

canons of good taste (see Higson 2003: 101–6). The hand-to-mouth production base of these films, along with the terms of their reception and circulation, indicate that they function within a *cultural* mode of production, as distinct from Hollywood's *industrial* mode of production (Elsaesser 1989: 3; see Higson 2003, chaps 3 and 4, for an account of the commercial context of these films): their significance is accounted for culturally rather than financially, even though several of them (including *Chariots of Fire*, *A Passage to India* and *A Room with a View*) were in the end considerable box-office successes relative to their budgets.

We must also recognise that this cycle of films, as with so many recent British films, depends on television in a variety of ways. Several were partially funded by television companies: *A Room with a View* and *Maurice* by Channel 4, and *A Handful of Dust* by London Weekend Television, for instance. Hugh Hudson and Charles Sturridge, the directors, respectively, of *Chariots of Fire* and *A Handful of Dust*, came from the television industry. All of the films arguably owe as much to the tradition of the BBC classic serial and the quality literary adaptation on television as they do to the filmed costume drama or to art-house cinema (on the classic serial, see Kerr 1982). Thus, in addition to the films already mentioned, the cycle of heritage adaptations should also perhaps include prestige television serials of the 1980s, such as *Brideshead Revisited* (1981) and *The Jewel in the Crown* (1983), the former directed by Sturridge. Indeed, Channel 4's policy – and its influence on the policies of other television companies – of co-funding filmed dramas for a theatrical as well as a tele-visual release, rather than funding serialised drama on video, temporarily replaced the television classic serial in the mid-1980s, while employing many of its aesthetic conventions for the films that emerged.

John Corner and Sylvia Harvey argue that the radical economic and social reconstructions of Britain in the 1980s required the Thatcher government to find novel ways of managing the conflict between old and new, tradition and modernity. They identify the key concepts in this process as 'heritage', with its connotations of continuity with the past and the preservation of values and traditions, and 'enterprise', with its connotations of change and innovation. The terms are vitally interconnected: 'What has come to be called "the heritage industry" is itself a major component of economic redevelopment, an "enterprise", both in terms of large-scale civic programmes and the proliferation of private commercial activity around "the past" in one commodified form or another' (1991b: 46). One of the more obvious manifestations of official concern with the values and properties of the past can be found in the National Heritage Acts of 1980 and 1983. As Patrick Wright shows, these acts reworked concepts of public access and use in terms of commodification, exhibition and display, encouraging the forthright marketing of the past within a thoroughly market-orientated heritage industry (1985: 42ff; see also Hewison 1987, and Higson 2003: 48–53). The heritage industry has thus developed as a vital part of contemporary tourism and related service industries such as the leisure industry, which of course embraces cinema.

The heritage film and its reconstruction of the past thus represents just one aspect of the heritage industry as a whole. Of course, the heritage impulse, 'one of the most powerful imaginative constructs of our time' (Samuel 1989a: xii), is not confined to Thatcherite Britain, but is a characteristic feature of postmodern culture. The heritage industry may transform the past into a series of commodities for the leisure and entertainment market, but in most cases the commodity on offer is an image, a spectacle, something to be gazed at. History, the past, becomes, in Fredric Jameson's phrase, 'a vast collection of images' designed to delight the modern-day tourist-historian (1984: 66; see also Urry 1990, chaps 5 and 6). In this version of history, a critical perspective is displaced by decoration and display, a fascination with surfaces, 'an obsessive accumulation of comfortably archival detail' (Wright 1985: 252), in which a fascination with style displaces the material dimensions of historical context. The past is reproduced as flat, depthless pastiche, where the reference point is not the past itself, but other images, other texts. The past as referent is effaced, and all that remains is a self-referential intertextuality (Jameson 1984: 60ff). Yet, at the same time, the sense of pastness and historicity are important, for as Andreas Huyssen (1981) suggests, the search for tradition is a vital feature of the contemporary response to the felt failure of modernism.

The heritage films, too, work as pastiches, each period of the national past reduced through a process of reiteration to an effortlessly reproducible, and attractively consumable, connotative style. The films turn away from modernity toward a traditional conservative pastoral Englishness; they turn away, too, from the hi-tech, special-effects dominated aesthetics of mainstream popular cinema. Where Hollywood in the late 1970s and 1980s specialised in the production of futuristic epics, the heritage film prefers the intimacy of the period piece, although their visual splendour lends them an extravagant, epic scale. The postmodernism of these films is actually an anti-modernism that clothes itself in all the trappings of classical art – but the more culturally respectable classicisms of literature, painting, music, and so on, not the classicism of Hollywood (indeed, the image of American-ness against which Britishness/Englishness is contrasted in *Chariots of Fire* is explicitly techno-logical and machine-like).

The image of the past in the heritage films has become so naturalised that, para-doxically, it stands removed from history: the evocation of pastness is accomplished by a look, a style, the loving recreation of period details – not by any critical historical perspective. The self-conscious visual perfectionism of these films and their fetish-isation of period details create a fascinating but self-enclosed world. They render history as spectacle, as *separate* from the viewer in the present, as something over and done with, complete, achieved. Hence the sense of timelessness rather than historicity in relation to a national past which is 'purged of political tension' and so available for appreciation as visual display (Wright 1985: 69). As Cairns Craig suggests, this is 'film as conspicuous consumption' (1991: 10) – or rather, because it is only images being consumed, it is a *fantasy* of conspicuous consumption, a fantasy of Englishness, a fantasy of the national past.

Yet at the same time, the version of the national past offered is above all a modern past, an imaginary object invented from the point of view of a present that is too distasteful to be confronted head-on. Thus Raphael Samuel shows how Christine Edzard's *Little Dorrit* produces a Dickens for the 1980s, despite, or perhaps precisely because of, the care taken to reproduce period details. Samuel contrasts the 1980s Dickens, which seeks to conserve the heritage of Victorian values, with the grotesque realism, the 'dark Dickens' of the 1940s, when the Victorian period was being re-viewed as problematic and repressive. Thus Edzard's film cleans up the city's slums and workshops, its inhabitants and their authentically period costumes: 'The arte-facts so lovingly assembled turn the London of [Edzard's] film from a prison-house – Dickens' guiding metaphor – into a showcase of period delights' (1994: 423). The film effaces the gothic aspects of the novel in favour of a conservationist urban pastoral in which 'London is ... a playground, and poverty – provided it is safely period – picturesque' (1989b: 284).

In a move typical of the heritage industry (see Wright 1985), these key films in the *national* cinema of the 1980s are fascinated by the private property, the culture and values of a *particular* class. By reproducing these trappings outside of a materialist historical context, they transform the heritage of the upper classes into the national heritage: private interest becomes naturalised as public interest. Except, of course, these are still films for a relatively privileged audience, and the heritage is still refined and exclusive, rather than properly public in the sense of massively popular. The national past and national identity emerge in these films not only as aristocratic, but also as male-centred, while the nation itself is reduced to the soft pastoral landscape of southern England untainted by the modernity of urbanisation or industrialisation (or, in the case of *Little Dorrit* or *The Fool*, a tasteful urban pastoral). In each instance, the *quality* of the films lends the representation of the past a certain cultural validity and respectability.

These films share a particularly strong group style, not least because of the degree to which they work as pastiches. The central intertextual focus of the cycle, and of the broader historical genre which informs these films (see Higson 1995, chap. 4), is, as noted above, undoubtedly the adaptation of literary and theatrical properties. In the case of adaptations of canonical texts, the 'original' is as much on display as the past it seeks to reproduce. The literary source material, of course, functions as an

A Dickens for the 1980s: the picturesque poverty of *Little Dorrit* (1987)

important selling point, playing on the familiarity and prestige of the particular novel or play, but also invoking the pleasures of other such quality literary adaptations and the status of a national intellectual tradition. The genre can also invent new texts for the canon by treating otherwise marginal texts or properties to the same modes of representation and marketing.

The genre involves much more than simply the adaptation of literary or dramatic texts and plunders the national heritage in other ways, too. Almost all of these films contain a recurrent image of an imposing country house seen in extreme long shot and set in a picturesque, verdant landscape. This image encapsulates much that is typical of the films as a whole, and indicates that the notion of heritage property needs to be extended to cover in addition the types of ancient architectural and landscape properties conserved by the National Trust and English Heritage, and the costumes, furnishings, *objets d'art* and aristocratic character-types that traditionally fill those properties. These properties (the term, with its theatrical connotations, seems more than appropriate) constitute the iconography of the genre. In what is both a bid for historical realism (and visual pleasure) and a function of the nostalgic mode (seeking an imaginary historical plenitude), the past is delivered as a museum of sounds and images, an iconographic display. This iconography brings with it a particular moral formation and set of values, which the films effortlessly dramatise at 'significant' historical moments.

The intertextuality of the heritage cycle is also particularly noticeable in the casting of the films. The same actors play similar roles and class-types in several different films, bringing a powerful sense of all the other heritage films, costume dramas and literary adaptations to each new film. In fact, these films draw on two groups of actors: on the one hand, established actors who specialise in character parts (Denholm Elliot

(*A Room With a View*, *Maurice*), Judi Dench (*A Room With a View*, *A Handful of Dust*), Maggie Smith (*A Room With a View*), Simon Callow (*A Room With a View*, *Maurice*)) and who bring with them all the qualities and connotations of the British theatre tradition; on the other, various younger actors virtually groomed for their parts in the heritage films (Helena Bonham Carter (*A Room With a View*, *Maurice*, *Where Angels Fear to Tread*), Nigel Havers (*Chariots of Fire*, *A Passage to India*), Rupert Graves (*A Room With a View*, *Maurice*, *A Handful of Dust*, *Where Angels Fear to Tread*), James Wilby (*Maurice*, *A Handful of Dust*), Hugh Grant (*Maurice*)).

Set against the intertextual, generic qualities of these films are the discourses of authorship and authenticity, which stress originality and uniqueness rather than similarity and repetition. These discourses work in various ways: the literary adaptations strive to reproduce the tone that distinguishes the book, to respect the 'original' text and the 'original' authorship. The period films, which, of course, include the literary adaptations, seek to reproduce the surface qualities that define the pastness of the particular period. Yet, at the same time, there is a foregrounding of filmic authorship, too, the attempt to make a unique and original film. Each strategy is a means of stressing authorship, originality, authenticity – but the authenticities are not all of the same category, each potentially pulling in a different direction, while the generic qualities *deny* the sense of originality altogether. Paradoxically, the preoccupation with authorship, the display of good taste and a self-consciously aesthetic sensibility, are themselves generic qualities that bind the films together. Literary authorship, the process of writing itself, is foregrounded in the recurrent narrative episode of a character writing or reading a letter or a book, either aloud or in voiceover, thus celebrating the purity of the word. Literary adaptations also, of course, foreground the authenticity of the 'original' by their effort to reproduce dialogue from the novel

The iconography of heritage Englishness: white flannels, summer hats, Edwardian fashion (watching cricket in *Maurice* (1987))

for characters in the film, or to transpose the narrative voice of the novel to the speech of those characters. There is also a studied reference to and reproduction of other art objects and art forms – classical paintings, statues, architecture and music all add weight to the tasteful production values of these films.

Narratively, the films move slowly and episodically rather than in a tightly causal manner; they demonstrate a greater concern for character, place, atmosphere and milieu than for dramatic, goal-directed action. There is also a preference for long takes and deep focus, and for long and medium shots, rather than for close-ups and rapid cutting. The camera is characteristically fluid, but camera movement is dictated less by a desire to follow the movement of characters than by a desire to offer the spectator a more aesthetic angle on the period setting and the objects that fill it. Self-conscious crane shots and high-angle shots divorced from character point of view, for instance, are used to display ostentatiously the seductive *mise-en-scène* of the films. This is particularly clear in the Merchant-Ivory films. In *A Room with a View*, there is a typical interior shot of Lucy playing the piano at the Pensione Bertolini: Lucy, the ostensible focus of *narrative* interest, sits in the background, while artefacts and furnishings fill and frame the foreground; the camera gracefully, but without narrative motivation, tracks slowly around one splendid item of furniture to reveal it in all its glory. In the same film, the shots of Florence are always offered direct to the spectator unmediated by any shots of characters within the diegesis looking at the view. Such shots, in fact, *follow* the views, rather than preceding and thus motivating them. Insert shots of Cambridge function similarly in *Maurice*, having only a minimal function as establishing shots. In this way, the heritage culture becomes the object of a public gaze, while the private gaze of the *dramatis personae* is reserved for romance: they almost never admire the quality of their surroundings. Heritage culture appears petrified, frozen in moments that virtually fall out of the narrative, existing only as adornments for the staging of a love story. Thus, historical narrative is transformed into spectacle; heritage becomes excess, not functional, not something to be used, but something to be admired.

All in all, the camera style is pictorialist, with all the connotations the term brings of art photography, aesthetic refinement and set-piece images (Higson 1995: 48ff). Though narrative meaning and narrational clarity are rarely sacrificed, these shots, angles and camera movements frequently exceed narrative motivation. The effect is the creation of heritage space, rather than narrative space: that is, a space for the display of heritage properties rather than for the enactment of dramas. In many respects, therefore, this is not a narrative cinema, a cinema of storytelling, but something more akin to that mode of early filmmaking that Tom Gunning (1990) calls 'the cinema of attractions'. In this case, the heritage films display their self-conscious artistry, their landscapes, their properties, their actors and their performance qualities, their clothes, and their often archaic dialogue. The gaze, therefore, is organised around props and settings – the look of the observer at the tableau image – as much as it is around character point of view.

The use of flamboyantly-designed intertitles in *A Room With a View*, while emphasising the episodic nature of the narrative, suggests another affinity with very early cinema. It redundantly indicates narrative action before it takes place, and in so doing interrupts the actual telling of the tale and highlights the artifice of the diegesis. Indeed, such films often seem more concerned to *show* the 'original', whether a novel or a period, a building or a landscape, than to tell an internally coherent tale. As Samuel notes of *Little Dorrit*, 'the film resembles nothing so much as a series of cameos in which the chapters of the book are replayed as scenes' (1989b: 281).

The emphasis on spectacle rather than narrative draws attention to the surface of things, producing a typically postmodern loss of emotional affect: emotional engagement in a drama is sacrificed for loving recreations of the past, or rather, beautifully conserved and respectfully observed spectacles of pastness. This is particularly odd in dramas which are in almost every case organised around a romance, an imagined romance, or a romantic triangle, and that include a fair share of narrative coincidence, fateful intervention, and obstacles thrown in the path of love. But, if this is the stuff of melodrama, in this case emotions are underplayed, while sensationalism and contrivance are tastefully obscured. The excitements of the love story lie submerged by the trappings of the period piece.

A more generous reading of these films might suggest that, in the displaced form of the costume drama, the heritage film creates an important space for playing out contemporary anxieties and fantasies of national identity, sexuality, class and power. Temporal displacement and cultural respectability license the exploration of taboo subjects such as the homoerotic passions of *Another Country* and *Maurice*. Such films may then produce a pointed critique of the limits of the present social and moral formation. After all, the nostalgic perspective always involves a dialogue between the imagined past and a vision of the present; it never simply talks about the past. Like Forster's novels, several of the films dramatise a vision of liberal-humanist values in a materialistic world, and Alison Light argues that 'the return to Edwardian England in the 1980s [is] as much a rejection of Thatcherism and its ethics as a crude reflection of it'. She suggests that 'what the films have picked up on is the romantic longing within liberalism for making unions despite differences of nationality, sexuality, social class' (1991: 63). Thus, if the films seem at first to attempt to escape from the cultural heterogeneity of contemporary Britain by celebrating a class apparently secure in its self-knowledge and self-sufficiency, it is clear that they also dramatise the effort of different social identities to connect with one another across cultural and social boundaries, so re-invoking the liberal consensus. Thus, we have the gay love affairs of *Maurice* and *Another Country*, the trans-class relationships of *Maurice* and *A Room with a View*, and the inter-ethnic friendships of *Chariots of Fire* and *A Passage to India*.

Peter Widdowson (1977) argues that Forster sought to affirm his liberal vision through art, and one might suggest that the tasteful artistry of the heritage films enables them to affirm such a vision. But there are problems with applying this argument to the films. In their concern for authenticity and fidelity in the reproduction of pastness and the 'original' text, they fetishise artistry, as well as the past itself – or at least its filmic image. The strength of the pastiche in effect imprisons the qualities of the past, holding them in place as something to be gazed at from a reverential distance, and refusing the possibility of a dialogue or confrontation with the present. Even those films that develop an ironic *narrative* of the past end up celebrating and legitimating the *spectacle* of one class and one cultural tradition and identity at the expense of others through the discourse of authenticity, and the obsession with the visual splendours of period detail. *Mise-en-scène* and drama thus work against each other in their construction of the national past: images of permanence, tradition, grandeur and continuity counteract the narratives of impermanence and cultural fluidity, and the ironies of the Forsterian voice. Undoubtedly, Forster's novels are also overly concerned with Englishness, but rarely is that identity framed as permanent and unchanging. On the contrary, Forster argues for a liberal-humanist refashioning of Englishness, rather than a simple assumption of an already formed national identity. Indeed, he savagely derides as sham the suburban middle-class Englishness of the Halls in *Maurice*, yet their household in the film is rendered desirable in its accumulation of the antique collector's signs of Edwardian period style: 'the society which Forster is criticising becomes almost involuntarily an object of veneration' (Hollinghurst 1987: 1225).

Many of the novels and other stories which provide the sources for the heritage films of the 1980s have some edge to them of satire or ironic social critique, and the films in various ways try to reproduce this sensibility. But it seems clear that it is the pictorial qualities of the exotic period settings that have attracted the filmmakers as much as the moral critique. As a consequence, that which is in the source narratives abhorrent or problematic becomes prettified, elegant and seductive. For instance, while the owners of Hetton Hall in *A Handful of Dust* constantly worry about the unfashionable qualities of their vast gothic pile, and the money it takes to maintain it, in the film the hall is positively alluring and resplendent. As one reviewer comments, 'The Duke of Norfolk's country seat, Carlton Towers [which stood in for Hetton Hall] … is the star of stars' (Walker 1988: 32). The pleasures of pictorialism thus block the radical intentions of the narrative.

The conservationist desire for period authenticity rarely equates with the desire for faithful adaptations of the source text in the literary adaptations. Indeed, in the adaptations of the Forster and Waugh novels, contemporary social satires and comedies of manners are transformed into period pieces. Similarly, Samuel argues that, in the case of *Little Dorrit*, 'the film's preoccupation with period effects is singularly at variance with Dickens himself, who was notoriously cavalier in his treatment of history and contemptuous of notions of heritage' (1989b: 283). Samuel goes on to claim that Dickens was not a period novelist, but drew ideas, images and characterisations from different historical periods, self-consciously fabricating the fiction and creating 'a fantasy of Victorian England' (ibid.). While Forster is indeed a writer 'who manifests and is attentive to the social and historical context out of which he derives' (Bradbury 1966: 3), he is not a novelist of place, but rather of ideas and manners. Place, setting and *mise-en-scène* in Forster are dealt with in very general terms, rather than observed with the obsessively detailed eye of the art directors of the films adapted from his novels. The novels explore what lies beneath the surface of things, satirising the pretentious and the superficial, and especially those who are overly concerned with keeping up appearances rather than acting according to the passions of the heart. The films, however, construct such a delightfully glossy visual surface that the ironic perspective and the narrative of social criticism diminish in their appeal for the spectator.

A Room with a View, for instance, can be read as a satire on the repressions of the middle classes and a reaffirmation of generative, life-giving forces. As a critique of Victorian values, it may well be nostalgic for the emotional simplicity and libidinal spontaneity of the fairy tale romance. But in the film, Maggie Smith plays the repressive life-denying figure of Catherine Bartlett so powerfully, so charismatically, that

The attractions of performance, the delights of high camp: Daniel Day Lewis as Cecil Vyse in
A *Room With a View* (1986)

it becomes once more attractive. The film delights in her performance of Victorian
primness, as it delights in the equally excessive performances of Simon Callow and
Daniel Day Lewis. Similarly in *Maurice*, Clive Durham (Hugh Grant) becomes a far
more attractive and fascinating character than Maurice (James Wilby) himself, partly
because of Grant's boyish good looks and sublimely camp performance full of exaggerated gestures and mannerisms. Yet it is Maurice's sensibility that the narrative
requires us to share; indeed, the film purports to criticise all that Clive eventually
represents. Clive is, in the final analysis, horrified by Maurice's sexuality; he cannot
confront it, preferring instead, like Catherine Bartlett, to save face, to keep up a
respectable appearance, to look the part.

Forster's satirical impulse is also undercut in *A Room With a View*. On one level
it is there, for instance in George's (Julian Sands) description of Cecil (Day Lewis) to
Lucy (Helena Bonham Carter): '[Cecil] wants you for a possession, something to look
at, like a painting or an ivory box, something to own and display. He doesn't want
you to be real and to think and live.' But in the end, the film adopts Cecil's pretensions, displaying its possessions and making every effort to fashion each image 'like
a painting'. The film attempts to criticise people who have a fear of being seen doing
the wrong thing, encapsulated in Cecil's anxious, furtive looks about him before he
kisses Lucy, his fiancée, for the first time; the other side of this fear is a love of being
seen and admired by the right kind of people, as when Cecil looks around the gathered society at his mother's house for the nods of appreciation at *his* good taste as

Lucy plays the piano. Yet the film itself circulates in society in the same way, desperately wanting to be viewed by the right kinds of audiences, ceaselessly displaying its good taste in just as knowing a way as Cecil.

But if satire or moral critique require an ironic distance from the characters and their settings, surely this is achieved in the refusal of psychological depth and emotional engagement? Surely such shallow characterisations as the emotionally empty and materialistic protagonists of A Handful of Dust, and their desire to keep up appearances, can be read as representations of ironically superficial characters? Indeed they can, except that all that these figures, and the space they inhabit, are so lovingly, beautifully and seductively laid out that a desire for the other, for the lost perfection of the spectacle, narrows any ironic distance that may have been intended. Period authenticity and heritage conservationism represent precisely the desire for perfection, for the past as unimpaired paradigm, for a packaging of the past that is designed to please, not disturb. Satire, however, requires the contrary, the tainting of the paradigm and the disturbance of perfection.

Forster's novels were themselves, of course, nostalgic narratives, but the desire for period authenticity tends to refashion the nature of the nostalgia. Forster yearned for a mid-Victorian golden age rather than what was for him the Edwardian present. His novels respond to a felt crisis in liberal-humanist values and play out a pastoral concern for a passing rural England, one encroached on by industrialisation, suburbia and London society. They demonstrate 'a profound, almost mystical, response to the English countryside and its living embodiment of the past [but] perceive it to be in the process of radical and destructive change' (Widdowson 1977: 58). At the end of Maurice, as he and Alec go off into the greenwood, Maurice realises that 'they must live outside class ... But England belonged to them. That, besides companionship, was their reward. Her air and sky were theirs, not the timorous millions' who own stuffy little boxes, but never their own souls' (Forster 1972: 208–9). England, in other words, is a pastoral scene without the trappings of class celebrated in the films, but the scene is already impaired by the spread of suburbia. The Forster films, on the other hand, look back nostalgically to an Edwardian golden age. The greenwood of Merchant-Ivory's Maurice and the ruralism of A Room with a View, the pastoral community of Summer Street, and the sincerity, companionship and moral support of the bourgeois family are offered as part and parcel of the period they depict; they have not yet become the lost objects of nostalgic desire. The pastoral of the films therefore invents a new golden age, one that the novels depict as already tainted and unstable.

The narratives of Chariots of Fire and Another Country try to avoid this problem through their flashback structures, suggesting that the nostalgia of the representation is actually that of the ostensible narrator: Aubrey Montagu (Nicholas Farrell) in Chariots of Fire and Guy Bennett (Rupert Everett) in Another Country. The latter, closeted in a dingy Moscow flat surrounded by the trappings of Englishness (the Harrods mug, the cricket ball, the old school photographs), looks back on his last years at a highly privileged English public school during the 1930s. Here, as in Maurice, the nostalgic image of a perfect national past is deliberately set up, only to be destroyed – 'flawlessly staged then condemned' (Finch & Kwietniowski 1988: 77) – by uncovering its shortcomings, especially its systematic exploitation and abuse of gay men. But at the same time, there is a lingering desire to celebrate that past in the loving recreation of the period piece. The film tries to contain this residual nostalgia by projecting the tale as Bennett's memory. But the vision of the past rapidly becomes the film's central diegesis, the range and scope of camera shots used suggesting that it is our vision rather than the partial vision of a character. Even before the possibility of a flashback is established, the title sequence creates a nostalgic perspective by cutting between a delightful English pastoral scene and the grey concrete of Bennett's Moscow apartment block. The tastefully melancholic music and the image of passing through a dark tunnel before being able to appreciate the full glory of the pastoral scene further underlines the sense of recalling a cherished but lost memory.

Other heritage films also create the nostalgic experience. Thus the imperialist fantasies of national identity found in the cycle of films and television programmes about the Raj, such as *A Passage to India* and *The Jewel in the Crown*, and other films looking at the last days of the British Empire in Africa, such as *White Mischief* (1987), can be seen as conservative responses to a collective, post-imperialist anxiety. Retreating from the social, political and economic crises of the present, they strive to recapture an image of national identity as pure, untainted, complete and in place. Yet like so many nostalgic narratives, they return to a moment of stability and tranquillity in the social order as they themselves chart the process of decay, the fall from this utopian national ideal: in most cases, they chronicle the corrupt and decadent last days of imperialist power, a period when that power was already coming under attack, the pure identity becoming tainted, and the culture in decline. As a whole, the heritage films deal with the last of England: not just the end of Empire, but the betrayal of the nation in *Another Country*; the corrupt decadence and moral decay of the upper classes in *Another Country* and *A Handful of Dust*; the death of liberal England; the efforts of the aristocracy to make way for new blood in *Chariots of Fire* (see Johnston 1985). The idea of heritage implies a sense of inheritance, but it is precisely that which is on the wane in these films: there can be no issue from the sexless and/or homosexual relationships of *Maurice* and *Another Country*; the son is killed in *A Handful of Dust*; Brideshead is destroyed; and in almost every case, there is a marked absence of strong father figures. Nostalgia is then both a narrative of loss, charting an imaginary historical trajectory from stability to instability, and at the same time a narrative of recovery, projecting the subject back into a comfortably closed past.

The nostalgic narrative of *Another Country* illustrates just this complexity. At the end of the film, the journalist interviewing Bennett asks if he misses anything. Bennett hesitates; choral music fades in, and he replies, 'I miss the cricket!' End of film. The choral music here conjures up memories of the first scene of the flashback to the 1930s, a memorial service in the school quadrangle and the site of Bennett's first over-determined gaze at his loved one, Harcourt (Cary Elwes), another boy at the school. Cricket also conjures up a specific memory, again of a particularly passionate exchange of looks between Bennett and Harcourt on the cricket field. If only those perfect scenes could have lasted forever, the system in place, homosexual desire able to live a secure, passionate, if closeted life! If only the past in all its perfection could have remained in place, unimpaired. But the film goes on to show that this image of perfection is indeed already impaired, the product of a militarily authoritarian system that is openly corrupt and exploitative.

In these films, however, the sense of impending narrative-historical loss is always offset by the experience of spectacular visual pleasure. Their reconstructions of the national past feast on the spectacle of authentic objects, clothing and other signs of an apparently secure heritage, contrasted with the often fearful exoticism of other cultures. Thus even a film like *A Passage to India*, which purports to criticise British imperialism, shows the cinematic spectacle of the British in power. The theatricality of the Raj, and the epic sweep of the camera over an equally epic landscape and social class is utterly seductive, destroying all sense of critical distance and restoring the pomp of Englishness felt to be lacking in the present. Similarly, *Another Country*'s critique of the details of class power, and the whole system of privilege, inheritance and tradition, is lost in the welter of period detail. As Craig puts it, 'The death of inheritance ... is counteracted by the seeming permanence of the architecture, landscape and possessions that fill the screen' (1991: 11). In *Maurice*, Forster describes Clive Durham's country house as on the verge of decay, rather than magnificent: 'it struck [Maurice] once more how derelict it was, how unfit to set standards or control the future' (1972: 209). In the film, the outhouses are decrepit, ladders are everywhere because the house is being repaired, and the sitting-room ceiling is leaking ('Why is my house falling down?', asks Clive), but the crumbling inheritance is never foregrounded as much as the remaining magnificence of the house: the splendour of the society in place always undercuts images of the last of England. Visual effect, the complete spectacle of the past, becomes an autonomous attraction in itself, once more displacing any narrational qualities the *mise-en-scène* may have.

'The national past,' Patrick Wright argues, 'is capable of finding splendour in old styles of political domination and of making an alluring romance out of atrocious

The *mise-en-scène* of power, the perfection of posture: schoolboy style in *Another Country*

colonial exploitation' (1985: 254). The comment seems particularly appropriate for the heritage genre, one that obsessively constructs (often upper-class) romances around authentic period details. Class, gender and race relations, and the values of the ruling elites, are in effect re-presented as just so much *mise-en-scène*, elegantly displayed in splendid costumes, language, gestures and all the props (the properties) of the everyday life of one or another class. The history of exploitation is effaced by spectacular presentation. The past becomes once more unproblematic, a haven from the difficulties of the present.

The *mise-en-scène* of power, the theatricality of the Raj, the spectacle of privilege: these films construct a fantasy of extravagance, decadence, promiscuity and passion (frequently, of course, a homoerotic passion: there is a continual insistence on the pleasures of the male body). If such a fantasy is in some ways a critique of the more mundane and repressive present, that critique is always contained by being accessible only through a facade of class privilege firmly set in the past. But that facade, constructed in the self-conscious artistry of these films, is itself extravagant. The discourse of authenticity is treated so seriously, and taken to such lengths, that it becomes almost self-parodic: the meticulous period piece as knowing artifice and extravagant frivolity. From this point of view, the films scale the heights of camp, which Susan Sontag defines as 'the theatricalisation of experience' (1983: 114). In a passage which seems designed to comment on the heritage cycle, she suggests that 'camp art is often decorative art, emphasising texture, sensuous surface and style at the expense of content' (1983: 107). Such art requires a peculiarly intense but superficial gaze from its admirers. In *Another Country*, for instance, Bennett's gaze at his loved one is so intense and self-conscious that it becomes almost a parody of desire. The look is always knowing; there is never any doubt that both the subject and the object are aware of the look, as too are the spectators of the film. What is

The knowing theatrical gaze: Guy Bennett (Rupert Everett) eyes his loved one in *Another Country*

remarkable is the theatricalisation of the gaze, its exaggerated, camp quality. It is this same knowing theatrical gaze for which the heritage films of the 1980s display their wares.

One of the key features of the Thatcher years was the denationalisation of the economy, a process that was justified in terms of the concepts of enterprise and competition. Inevitably, there was a certain cultural denationalisation, as well. The privatising ethics of popular capitalism shifted the emphasis from community values and notions of consensus and collective identity to the values of individual enterprise and the marketplace. The production of new market-led identities thus challenged long-standing class-bound and deferential notions of national identity. As Corner and Harvey suggest, the self-made individuals of the enterprise culture 'refuse the certainties of the old patrician aristocratic order, they overturn the stately world in which everyone knows their place and they challenge, in the process, the rules of noblesse oblige' (1991a: 8).

These challenges to the traditional settlement of national identity are to some extent compensated for in the fantasy worlds of the heritage films. They thus provide a platform from which either a liberal or a more traditionally conservative critique of the Thatcherite project could be mounted. This raises the important question of how well these films accord with the official management of heritage in the 1980s. Margaret Thatcher herself both called for a return to 'Victorian values', and, during the Falklands War, invoked the spirit of Churchill and World War Two. It is notable, however, that very few British films of the 1980s dealt with World War Two in heroic mode. Likewise, few of the most prominent heritage films of the 1980s were actually located in the Victorian period, and of the ten or so costume dramas that were, none tell stories of nineteenth-century entrepreneurs on the make, accumulating vast private fortunes at the expense of public welfare – even though it is surely Victorian capitalism and the dramatic industrial transformations of that period which provide the ideal role model for Thatcherism. Similarly, while heritage films tentatively narrate the stories of enterprising and innovative individuals who reject convention – after all, these are virtually requisites of a classical narrative structure – narrative development is in the end downplayed. Nor is enterprise generally couched in overtly competitive and materialistic terms, except perhaps in the case of *Chariots of Fire*, with its aggressive plea for meritocratic justice; but even here, the expected climax of individual competition is set to one side in favour of a jingoistic national struggle at the Olympic Games. Other films, especially the Forster adaptations, are in various ways critical of the sort of materialistic society that Thatcherism promoted – yet, at the same time, these films visually celebrate the possessions of the upper classes.

Corner and Harvey suggest that Thatcherism 'has at once challenged, popularised and commodified the values of a more ancient, patrician and rural conservatism' (1991a: 14); this is a more than apt description of the function of the heritage films of the 1980s. Many of them do criticise the values of this upper-class Englishness in various ways, as we have seen; but they popularise this social formation as one whose possessions are worth acquiring, or at least admiring. They also popularise this social formation as one in which the contemporary spectator might find refuge from the radical and often problematic transformations of the 1980s. Yet the liberal-humanist visions of social union in so many of these films implicitly criticise rather than celebrate the values of the marketplace, suggesting a flight from Thatcherism rather than concord with its Victorian antecedents or its contemporary effects. The ambivalence of these films to both the past and to the Thatcherite present is, as we have seen, the ambivalence of nostalgia. On the one hand, there is the reassurance of apparent continuity with the past; on the other, the societies depicted are often already in decline, even if visually the suggestion is otherwise.

In closing, it is worth noting another group of contemporary British costume dramas dealing with the more recent past, including such films as *Dance With a Stranger* (1984), *Wish You Were Here* (1987), *Hope and Glory* (1988), *Distant Voices, Still Lives* (1988) and *Scandal* (1989). These films concentrate on the everyday lives and memories of 'ordinary people', and in many cases pushed female characters to the fore, to some extent therefore democratising the genre and offering a rather different range of narrative pleasures and identifications. The converse of this, however, is that their representation of the past remains in a conservationist mode such that even the *mise-en-scène* of ordinariness delights the eye, and invites the collector's curiosity.

Looking back on this essay from the vantage-point of 2006, I still find the reading of the films I put forward persuasive – but I am now very much aware that it is just one reading, and that other audiences have read the same films in different ways, and indeed taken issue with the readings I advance here. In my more recent work on heritage cinema, I have adopted a perspective much closer to reception studies and have tried to attend to the range of readings and audience responses these films have generated. For some audiences, for instance, these films are clearly extremely moving rather than emotionally disengaged, which thereby puts into question the Jamesonian reading of these films. Clearly too, while several of the costume dramas on which I have focused offer male-centred narratives, the production trend as a whole offers a range of pleasures and sensibilities that appeal particularly to female audiences. These are some of the issues I explore in my book *English Heritage, English Cinema: Costume Drama since 1960*.

Author's note: The original version of this essay could not have been written without the many discussions I had about these films with students and colleagues at the University of East Anglia. I would also like to acknowledge my particular indebtedness to Patrick Wright's book listed below.

WORKS CITED

Bradbury, Malcolm (1966) 'Introduction', in *E. M. Forster: A Collection of Essays*. Englewood Cliffs, NJ: Prentice-Hall, 1–14.

Corner, John and Sylvia Harvey (eds) (1991a) 'Introduction: Great Britain Limited', in John Corner and Sylvia Harvey (eds) *Enterprise and Heritage: Crosscurrents of National Culture*. London: Routledge, 1–20.

_____ (1991b) 'Mediating Tradition and Modernity: The Heritage/Enterprise Couplet', in John Corner and Sylvia Harvey (eds) *Enterprise and Heritage: Crosscurrents of National Culture*. London: Routledge, 45–75.

Craig, Cairns (1991) 'Rooms Without a View', *Sight and Sound*, 1, 2, 10–13.

Elsaesser, Thomas (1989) *New German Cinema: A History*. London: British Film Institute/Macmillan.

Finch, Mark and Richard Kwietniowski (1988) 'Melodrama and *Maurice*: Homo is Where the Het Is', *Screen*, 29, 3, 72–80.

Forster, E. M. (1972 [1908]) *Maurice*. London: Penguin.

Gunning, Tom (1990) 'The Cinema of Attractions: Early Film, its Spectator and the Avant-Garde', in Thomas Elsaesser with Adam Barker (eds) *Early Cinema: Space-Frame-Narrative*. London: British Film Institute, 56–62.

Hewison, Robert (1987) *The Heritage Industry: Britain in a Climate of Decline*. London: Methuen.

Higson, Andrew (1995) *Waving the Flag: Constructing a National Cinema in Britain*. Oxford: Oxford University Press.

____ (1996) 'The Heritage Film and British Cinema', in Andrew Higson (ed.) *Dissolving Views: Key Writings on British Cinema*. Andrew Higson. London: Cassell, 232–48.

____ (2001) 'Heritage Cinema and Television', in Dave Morley and Kevin Robins (eds) *British Cultural Studies: Geography, Nationality and Identity*. Oxford: Oxford University Press, 249–60.

____ (2003) *English Heritage, English Cinema: Costume Drama since 1980*. Oxford: Oxford University Press.

Hill, John (1999) *British Cinema in the 1980s*. Oxford: Oxford University Press.

Hollinghurst, Alan (1987) 'Suppressive Nostalgia', *Times Literary Supplement*, 6 November, 1225.

Huyssen, Andreas (1981) 'The Search for Tradition: Avant-Garde and Post-modernism in the 1970s', *New German Critique*, 22, 23–40.

Jameson, Fredric (1984) 'Post-modernism, or the Cultural Logic of Late Capitalism', *New Left Review*, 146: 53–92.

Johnston, Sheila (1985) 'Charioteers and Ploughmen', in Martin Auty and Nick Roddick (eds) *British Cinema Now*. London: British Film Institute, 99–110.

Kerr, Paul (1982) 'Classic Serials – To Be Continued', *Screen*, 23, 1, 6–19.

Light, Alison (1991) 'Englishness', *Sight and Sound*, 1, 3, 63.

Samuel, Raphael (1989a) 'Preface', in R. Samuel (ed.) *Patriotism: The Making and Unmaking of British National Identity*, vol. 1, *History and Politics*. London: Routledge, x–xvii.

____ (1989b) 'Docklands Dickens', in R. Samuel (ed.), *Patriotism: The Making and Unmaking of British National Identity*, vol. 1, *History and Politics*. London: Routledge, 275–85.

____ (1994) 'Who Calls So Loud?' Dickens on Stage and Screen', in *Theatres of Memory*. London and New York: Verso, 413–25.

Sontag, Susan (1983) 'On Camp', in *A Susan Sontage Reader*. London: Penguin, 105–19.

Urry, John (1990) *The Tourist Gaze*. London: Sage.

Walker, Alexander (1988) 'Review of *A Handful of Dust*', *Evening Standard*, 9 June, 32.

Widdowson, Peter (1977) *E. M. Forster's 'Howards End': Fiction as History*. London: Sussex University Press/Chatto and Windus.

Wollen, Tana (1991) 'Over Our Shoulders: Nostalgic Screen Fictions for the Eighties', in John Corner and Sylvia Harvey (eds) *Enterprise and Heritage: Crosscurrents of National Culture*. London: Routledge, 178–93.

Wright, Patrick (1985) *On Living in an Old Country*. London: Verso.

7. FREE FROM THE APRON STRINGS: REPRESENTATIONS OF MOTHERS IN THE MATERNAL BRITISH STATE

Mary Desjardins

Hope and Glory (1987) and *The Krays* (1990) are two internationally successful British films made in the latter part of Margaret Thatcher's political rule which offer images of mothers compatible with a number of the possible representations of the 'maternal' constructed in psychoanalytic discourse and its appropriation by feminist discourses. *Hope and Glory*, for instance, features the Oedipal mother, as its young male protagonist struggles to find adult role models in an increasingly feminised British home front during World War Two. The mother in *The Krays* suggests one version of the phallic woman psychoanalysis has described as the pre-Oedipal mother holding life and death powers over the defenseless infant. Along with her own mother and sisters, Violet Kray usurps the place of the patriarch, infantilises her sons, and willfully ignores their brutalisation of other men. Because she despises how men have oppressed women, she seeks to banish all rivals to her son's power and to the power she holds over her sons.

This essay explores these representations of the maternal, but one should not apply psychoanalytic concepts to these films in an ahistorical context. In fact, what interests me about these two films is how their positioning of mothers as central forces in the narratives seems significant in the historical context of 1980s Great Britain, a period in which both Prime Minister and monarch are women and mothers. Although I will ultimately offer some suggestions in regards to that significance, the questions here have more to do with how the discursive field of Thatcherite Britain has negotiated an understanding of the maternal in relation to the state. Two questions seem central to this understanding: (i) What does it mean to represent the maternal in films in a nation whose political agenda is to free the people from what Thatcher identified as 'the apron strings of the governess state' (quoted in O'Shea 1984: 22), in other words, to free them from a state rhetorically figured as an infantilising maternal? (ii) How does a government in the process of constructing a contemporary popular memory that will reassert an older, glorious national identity mobilise representations of the maternal to that end?

Both questions concern political and representational strategies and/or values with which the Thatcherite government became notoriously associated. The right-wing Conservative government under Thatcher's rule as Prime Minister from 1979 to 1990 was characterised by a dismantling of many of the institutions and symbolic supports of the previous coalition and Labour governments. This entailed a rejection of 'big government' – pejoratively termed by many as the welfare state and by Thatcher as the governess or nanny state – through an increased privatisation of state-owned companies and housing, a weakening of trade unions, a lifting of controls on foreign exchanges and a levying of a poll tax that lessened taxes for the wealthy and increased the tax burden for the working and middle classes. In a provocative essay on Thatcher politics and the film *The Ploughman's Lunch* (1983) Tony Williams argues that the implications of such a rejection was a movement of 'national consciousness toward social Darwinist "Victorian values"' (1991: 11).

In privileging government policies that on the social level resembled Darwin's 'scientific' precept of evolution as 'survival of the fittest', Thatcher's regime eliminated another set of Victorian values: 'the cult of True Womanhood', which heroicised traditional maternal capacities because they were supposedly morally superior to those which enabled men to compete in an exploitative marketplace. In other words, in the Thatcher years, competition among free enterprisers replaced a maternal state seen as infantilising and therefore incapacitating its citizens. The government's contribution in constructing a contemporary popular memory that reinstates an earlier, powerful national identity based on 'pluck' (self-initiative) and imperial values is crucial to the successful 'maturation' of British citizens. Restoration of an earlier national identity similar to that held by Britain during and right after World War Two, for example, means a national identity forged before the women's movement, when women were most manipulated as producers and reproducers by a series of nationalistic pronatalism propaganda.

This essay focuses on *Hope and Glory* and *The Krays*, not only because the films pay most attention to the historical specificity of the maternal, but also because they suggest World War Two as a crucial moment or reference point for real, social women as well as a contemporary popular memory for Britain. Of course, for many feminist historians and scholars of film noir and the woman's film, World War Two also represents a privileged historical moment. At that time, twentieth-century women entered a public consciousness constructed in part by powerful mass media institutions in the form of radio and the cinema. As the films under discussion suggest, women were also able to figure in the private unconscious during this period. In both *Hope and Glory* and *The Krays*, mothers on the home front substitute for absent or weak patriarchs, increasing the psychic hold between mother and child. The films' perspectives on the value of such a substitution differ, as do the ways they participate in the construction of a contemporary popular memory of World War Two. *Hope and Glory*'s production of memory of the war presents a unified ground for past and present, whereas memory of that period represented in *The Krays* consists of a contradiction between the dominant contemporary meanings of the war and the particular disruptive memories that cannot find their place in the public field.

My conceptualisation of 'popular memory' is derived from a series of written exchanges in the 1970s on the British Telefilm *Days of Hope* (1975) (see McArthur 1981; MacCabe 1981a; 1981b; Tribe 1981) from work done by the Popular Memory Group associated with the Centre for Contemporary Studies in Great Britain, and from the British Film Institute's 1983 Summer School on 'National Fictions: Struggles over the Meaning of World War Two'. Work of the latter two groups was given impetus by the Falklands War of 1982, when, as Colin McArthur argues, 'the left and liberal opinion generally experienced what could only be described as a deep sense of shock at the massive resurgence of a regressive definition of British national identity' (1984: 54). McArthur and other participants in the BFI Summer School further argue that 'the central historical experience in this refurbished national identity was World War Two and the overarching rhetoric of its enunciation by the Thatcherite government was Churchillian' (ibid.). In other words, the Thatcherite government at once constructed and drew upon a popular memory of Great Britain and World War Two to support its contemporary claims about war and the nation. Popular memory functions here as 'a version of the past which connects it up to the present so as to produce popular conceptions' of who a particular people or nation are, where they have come from, and why their society is as it is (Dawson & West 1984: 9).

The popular memory of World War Two constructed within the Thatcherite years positions the war period as part of an unfolding destiny of the British people. Memory is a work of discovery, confirming a unified subject. One concern of the various scholars analysing this construction is to replace the aforementioned notion of memory and history with one that sees history as 'something perpetually constructed in a specific juncture' (Tribe 1981: 321). This understanding of popular memory can help to place the mythology of World War Two in the terms and conjunctures constructed in the war years themselves, as well as in the Thatcherite period in which the films under discussion were produced and received. This understanding remains attentive to 'disruptive' memories of the war as well as to those belonging to the dominant public field, to the displacements affected by and the pressures resulting from the need to rearticulate the past in the present, with both the past and present national history the process and result of popular struggle.

Both *The Krays* and *Hope and Glory* begin with self-conscious evocations of the process of memory and history. *Hope and Glory*, the autobiographical film of director John Boorman's childhood experiences in wartime London, when his mother took over as head of the family in his father's absence, begins with a newsreel of Chamberlain's admittance that appeasement has failed. *The Krays*, the biographical film of the notorious Kray brothers, gangsters who loved their mother 'too much' and terrorised London in the 1960s, begins with the voiceover narration of the Krays' mother, as she recounts a dream in which she is a bird keeping her egg warm and safe. The beginning of *Hope and Glory*'s narrative, with newsreel footage of events securely ensconced in public memory, holds the promise of exposing how the filmic institution mediates history and memory, while the beginning of *The Krays* clearly positions its conception in the personal, and since this specific memory is of a dream, as a manifestation of the unconscious. That *Hope and Glory*'s construction of popular memory of World War Two begins with a self-reflexive gesture and with an event recognisable to the collective does not ensure that public struggle will be represented or serve as some kind of model of representation in its status as a set of contradictions. *Hope and Glory*'s beginning with the failure of appeasement is, however, quite significant. Chamberlain's shameful policy provides the 'lack' motoring the war in popular mythology during World War Two, and in Thatcherism's construction of memory of World War Two in the postwar period. In the words of Graham Dawson and Bob West:

Thatcherism has reworked the meanings of that moment when appeasement collapsed, so as to re-establish continuity with that previous glorious history: a continuity now broken, not by the disasters of 1940, but by the period of the postwar consensus, 1945–79. Britain has fallen from 'her' previous supremacy, but can be great again. The Thatcher government is the self-appointed heir of the glorious past. (1984: 9)

Hope and Glory marks its difference from the Thatcherite rhetoric of greatness by constructing a memory of the war from the point of view of the child, a subject

Mothers on the home front substitute for absent or weak patriarchs, increasing the psychic hold between mother and child, in John Boorman's *Hope and Glory* (1987)

whose experiences are usually excluded in representations of war and popular memory. Boorman stated in interviews that he made the film as a tribute to the wartime contributions of his mother and aunts. As typically ignored or underrated experiences, the activities and feelings of women and children work to fragment 'consciousness into a contradiction between one's preferred general meanings and the displaced, but persistent, particular memories, which if brought to life, can be most disruptive' (quoted in Dawson & West 1984: 11). So in the film, the young Boorman and his sisters actually wish for war and bombings as a kind of liberation from the strictures of their ordered bourgeois life, his older sister becomes sexually active, and his mother expresses desire to be with men outside of monogamous marriage. These 'persistent, particular memories' could disrupt a popular memory in the process of smoothing over contradiction or inadequately representing the experiences 'which impede identification and the fusion of the personal and the general' (ibid.). They could expose the partiality or contradictions within the consensus politics of the war.

But ultimately the film fuses the personal lack with the social or national lack, with both resolved in fullness and unity. The shame of appeasement is resolved by a war in which class differences supposedly eroded, in which the people supposedly kept 'a stiff upper lip', and in which, in Churchill's rhetoric, 'the native soil' was protected from invasion. The 'lack' of the young Boorman in *Hope and Glory* is an inadequate Oedipalisation due to the absence of fathers on the home front. So one of the film's memories potentially disruptive to a national popular memory – the experiences of mothers, sisters and aunts – also functions as the source of the boy's insecurity and embarrassments. Boorman makes it clear throughout the film that mothers and other women have become a problem. The young boy squirms and chafes at signs of the feminised home front: watching the love story film he must sit through, witnessing his older sister having sex in a public place, overhearing his mother confess her love for his father's best friend. These traumas, and thus the boy's lack, are resolved when the mother's desire for infidelity is met with the literal destruction of the home – just after she confesses her love to her husband's friend on a train, the family's home is bombed. The bombing forces her and the family to the home of her father, a misogynist who fills the gap left by the absent father, and constantly gives the boy lessons in how to undermine what he sees as an increasingly feminised culture.

The grandfather's house on the River Thames serves as both the pastoral paradise of Churchill fantasy and the place where the young Boorman has his first experience with the British film industry. The pastoral paradise of England, securely in the hands of the patriarch, serves as the site where Boorman will find his vocation in film – destiny of Britain and destiny of the Oedipally-resolved male individual converging at the film's conclusion. Past and present, individual and collective popular memory of the war come together as Boorman finds the man in the boy. Mother will be under the eye of her father, and the older sister, now pregnant, will marry her soldier boyfriend on the country estate. Women, who during the war were producers, wives, mothers, lovers, nurses and soldiers, now will be confined to the institution of motherhood, contained within marriage or the care of secure patriarchs.

The Krays, directed by Peter Medak, puts a different value on the substitution of mothers for absent patriarchs on the home front, and because it cannot fully contain the disruptive memories of these mothers on the home front, exposes the gender

Young Boorman and the grandfather, a misogynist who fills the gap left by the absent father in *Hope and Glory*

and class problematics of the coalition politics of the war and even exposes the core of resentment that the Thatcherite government tapped in the later postwar period. While the opening memory of *The Krays* positions the maternal in a mythical space – in a dream of and by the all-nurturing mother – and thus works to further mystify it, the film also contains evidence of the inextricable connection between gender and class, and of their specificity in history. If the opening memory, which will be repeated at the end of the film in voiceover during mother Violet's funeral, succeeds in making the maternal an eternal, then at other points it counters that construction with memories of specific historical moments when women have been most oppressed and repressed by patriarchy. For example, in one scene, the young Kray boys huddle with their mother and aunts in a World War Two air-raid shelter, while their maternal grandfather entertains the crowd with stories of Jack the Ripper. This kind of construction of memory, though conveyed by a male, contains a memory of male violence against women (and women of a certain class) that fuels feelings of resentment against men. Not only is it just as potent a myth as the one of the simultaneously frightening and loving phallic mother, but it is also a historical reality. The film constantly reminds us of the difference between psychic fantasies and historical realities and when the two might converge. Violet Kray often self-mockingly compares herself to the wicked mothers of fairy tales, but the violence of the Kray boys and their male cronies and rivals results in actual murder and intrigue. Reggie even becomes the embodiment of an evil maternal when he 'mothers' his young wife to the point that she commits suicide. Violet even sees this coming. As much as she loves her son, she says, Frances (Reggie's wife) must learn to kick back at men, like she has.

Frances (Kate Hardie) and Reggie (Martin Kemp) before Reggie 'mothers' Frances to the point of suicide, in *The Krays* (1990)

The film also abounds with memories of World War Two that disrupt the unified image of that war in popular memory. Violet and her mother constantly remind men that they are children only thinking that they are in control, for it was actually women who fought the war and continue to do so in the home every day. In one scene, Violet's husband responds to these assertions by claiming that she knows nothing of war, since she was confined to the home during those years. When she claims that the home is full of death and heartache that he would know nothing about, he moves to strike her. Violet threatens to slit his throat if he touches her, and the twins jump to her defence. These memories, shown in the process of construction around the quotidian, provide a charge to what might be considered utterly banal motherly and housewifely activities. In this way, the film mimics and then perversely transvalues the British government's discursive strategies during the war and postwar periods that made the homefront a site of battle winnable by mothers.

One memory of the war years, evoked by Violet's sister Rose, who is the Kray twins' most beloved aunt, serves as an excessive disruption not only in terms of its content (disrupting the popular memory of the war), but also as a narrative disruption, coming after the happy moment of Reggie's wedding and precipitating Rose's death. Back at Violet's house after Reggie's wedding, Rose tells of recently hearing a man on the bus boasting of his war experiences. As the camera slowly tracks in on her face, Rose has a tortured recollection:

It was the women who had the war, the real war. The women were left at home, sitting in the shit, not in some sparkling plane or gleaming tank. They should have been with me when old Pauline Wooley went into labour ... seven hours of screaming ... and then

I had to cut the baby's head off to save the mother's life. She died anyway ... So much blood. And the abortions! Poor girls. One day they'll drain Victoria Park Lake. And you know what they'll find? What glorious remnants of the Second World War? Babies ... Bullets and dead babies. Men! Mum's right; they stay kids all their fucking lives and they end up heroes or monsters. Either way, they win. Women have to grow up. If they stay children, they become victims.

Ironically, it is this Aunt Rose and Violet who help keep their men in a state of prolonged adolescence. But if the film suggests that strong mothers are responsible for male violence – another way of containing the maternal by claiming its subversion of the social order – it also intimates that if mothers and aunts train their male children to kill other men, it is due as much to class resentment as to gender vengeance.

This suggestion also disrupts the popular memory of World War Two – from its inception during the war through the present – as won because of a coalition government on the national level and a putting down of class boundaries on the local level. But, in reality, society constantly struggled against dissolution, and the lower classes felt resentment because they were making greater sacrifices than the upper-class 'partners.' These failures are never adequately addressed in either the popular memory of World War Two constructed during the war or in the Thatcher years.

In the latter period, the Conservative government located failure in the postwar consensus period, with its concessions to unions and creation of a welfare state. Thatcher's government wanted to liberate Great Britain from 'the apron strings' of the maternal state through privatisation and promotion of free enterprise. In *The Krays*, Violet, her sisters and their mother locate failure in the coalition government of World War Two as they identify over and over again the oppression of women during the war. They also attack the postwar consensus years, as they reward the Kray twins for gaining social status not through identification with working-class unionisation, but through a vicious pursuit of individual success and power in the marketplace, even if the marketplace must be taken by force. The film perversely suggests that Violet Kray had the idea for 'mothering' free enterprise rather than having the welfare state 'mothering' the lower classes before Margaret Thatcher did, all while doing the everyday duties of mothering and keeping the family together. 'For what is the real driving force in our society?' asked Mrs Thatcher in 1979. 'It is the desire for the individual to do the best for himself and his family' (quoted in Ogden 1990: 337).

Violet Kray hates her slacker husband because he is a man and because he deserted during the war, but most of all because his cheating has gotten him nowhere in terms of social mobility. If men of a certain class cannot succeed lawfully, Violet cannot understand why they do not do so outside the law. She knows that men have the power no matter what side of the law they are on, and that women have no power except as mothers. She agrees with Rose that if women stay like children they become victims of the patriarchy, as does Reggie's wife Frances.

What does a film like *The Krays* suggest in a national and historical context in which a female Prime Minister tried to free the 'people' from a supposedly infantilising maternal state? Violet Kray uses the maternal to promote free enterprise. In many ways, Violet allies herself with the Thatcher philosophy that respects and gives Spartan nurturing to those who succeed through individual initiative. But neither the film nor Violet is so naive as to suggest that success through individual initiative is

Violet's (Billie Whitelaw) closeness to her sons Reggie and Ronnie (Martin Kemp and Gary Kemp) is terrifying at both the private and social levels in *The Krays*

ever achieved without power that oppresses certain groups – whether that power be an infantilising maternal that Violet can exercise over her sons, or patriarchal power that could jeopardise Violet and her matriarchal clan. She chooses to bind her sons to her so that patriarchal power will be exercised over other men.

At its conclusion, the film brings these gender and class issues together in a cross-cut sequence that confuses which one has primacy. As the twins commit their most brutal crimes, those that will consolidate their power and send them to prison, where they remained working-class heroes (Reggie died in October 2000) – Violet sits at home watching a documentary of World War Two on television. The murders are intercut with images of Violet watching and sobbing as a popular memory of World War Two is constructed through the media and she finds her experience, once again, left out. As the television documentary ends, the boys come home, Violet turns to them and recounts the dream of her bird-like protection of her boys, which was the film's opening. Personal memory – for Violet, a mythology of a powerful maternal – resists the public, media-made memory that marginalises disruptive recollections. It is through such strategies – the constant contextualisation and recontextualisation of the personal memory and historical moment – that *The Krays*, more successfully than *Hope and Glory*, suggests the process of popular memory in all its contradictions.

I am not suggesting, however, that the depiction of the maternal in *The Krays* is radical or even necessarily progressive. The film's image of the mother can be appropriated by the spectator for a misogynistic or homophobic response. The film shows Violet Kray's closeness to her sons as having terrifying implications for both the private and the social.[1] Because the film suggests that Ronnie Kray, the homosexual twin, is the more violent of the two, classic homophobic and misogynist depictions of homosexuality and the maternal are potentially revived. It could be argued, however, that the depiction of homosexuality in this film is less concerned with the influence of the maternal (despite the mother's centrality) on sexual 'deviance' and more concerned with exposing a 'homosocial economy' of the male gangster society as a 'doppelgänger' of the ordered society of Thatcher's Britain, which rejects the maternal. Moreover, the film's focus on the victimisation of women and mothers by men, which is seen as a historically specific victimisation, makes the film a valuable text for an understanding of how the mother can be the subject and

The 'homosexual economy' of the gangster group as doppelgänger of Thatcherite Britain, in *The Krays*

object of a historical representation, rather than dismissed or vilified as the 'eternal unclean' of the abject.

The strategies in *Hope and Glory* and *The Krays* that centralise, but also evaluate, maternal and female concerns evidence many of the ambivalences Western societies feel about women in power since World War Two, growing especially intense in ambivalence since the women's movement. Janice Winship has traced the debates about women's power in postwar Britain, arguing that the dominant discourse tried to reconcile a notion of 'we the nation' with 'we women' through constructing peace as a battle only women (especially mothers) could help to win (1984: 197). This included figuring a popular image of Queen Elizabeth (crowned in 1953) as both ruler and devoted wife and mother (1984: 208–10). While this imaging has continued to the present (with the Queen's ruler image predominating during various IRA crises, her mother image predominating in a tabloid press concerned with the social foibles of her various sons- or daughters-in-law), the introduction of a woman Prime Minister in the configuration of British ruler-mothers with Thatcher's election in 1979 brought many of the culture's resistances to feminism to the foreground. This was not because Thatcher represented feminism, but because, despite (perhaps because of) her own rise to power, by serving as one of its greatest detractors, she expressed the feelings of many. Her remark in 1978 that 'the feminists have become far too strident and have done damage to the cause of women by making us out to be something we're not' (quoted in Ogden 1990: 341) is representative of the position on women's rights and sexual difference that Thatcher took in her eleven years in office.

It is also representative of a culture that increasingly believes that we live in a post-feminist age, when feminism and the movements of other marginalised groups are no longer needed as positions of political resistance to the dominant culture. That feminism is no longer, or perhaps was never, needed is supposedly proved by the fact of Thatcher's election. Likewise, that feminism (and socialism) has gone 'too far' and now given benefits to the undeserving is proved by an underclass that demands rights rather than working for them. When Thatcher remarked before her election, 'You get on because you have the right talents' (ibid.), she encapsulated the philosophy of free enterprise that would be invoked in her own country and in the United States whenever programmes helping marginalised groups were weakened or dismantled. Whenever this attitude about winning through individual initiative was clothed in nationalistic terms reminiscent of the Churchillian rhetoric of World War Two, Thatcher and her constituents participated in the state's construction of public memories.

The self-conscious positioning of mothers within narratives constructed around the bitter-sweetness (as in *Hope and Glory*) or the disruptiveness (as in *The Krays*) of memory must be seen in this context of a culture coming to terms with the place of feminism in a resurrected free enterprise world where even women can be leaders. *Hope and Glory* suggests its place for feminism when it recalls the mystery of women from the safety of nostalgia and a fully Oedipalised male adulthood. *The Krays*, looking back at the war, postwar and 'swinging London' period of British history, exposes the connection between free enterprise and criminality that is surely as relevant to Thatcher's Britain as Coppola's *Godfather* saga (1972, 1974, 1990) was to Watergate and post-Watergate America. Although it pictures the terrifying power of the maternal familiar to misogynistic representations of mothers, the film also provides an outlet for the anger and for the memories of mothers who fought a war every day in the home. *The Krays* suggests, with a kind of irony and cynicism that seems particularly relevant to a historical context in which a woman can claim with no irony that 'you get on because you have the right talents', that women can only save themselves from victimisation if they control men to act in the name of capitalism on women's behalf.

NOTE

1   In an essay on Thatcher and Ruth Ellis (the last woman to be executed in Great Britain), Jacqueline Rose (1988) argues that the collective fantasy of state violence that characterises Thatcherite Britain is connected to a collective misogynist fantasy that puts women on the very edges of the social. Ellis, who admitted calculating the murder of her lover, threatened to expose the constructedness of women as hysterics (as not responsible for their actions) and the connection between rationality and violence. Thatcher's defence of capital punishment is representative of a collective attempt to mask aggressivity from within by making violence appear from the outside, in the form of the Law. But Thatcher's supremely rationalised discursive strategies for defending capital punishment also threaten to deconstruct the oppositions between reasoned law and violence.

WORKS CITED

Dawson, Graham and Bob West (1984) 'Our Finest Hour? The Popular Memory of World War Two and the Struggle over National Identity', in Geoff Hurd (ed.) *National Fictions: World War Two in British Films and Television*. London: British Film Institute, 8–13

McArthur, Colin (1981 [1975/76]) '*Days of Hope*', in Tony Bennett, Susan Boyd-Bowman, Colin Mercer and Janet Woollacott (eds) *Popular Television and Film: A Reader*. London: British Film Institute, 30–59.

____ (1984) 'National Identities', in Geoff Hurd (ed.) *National Fictions: World War Two in British Films and Television*. London: British Film Institute, 54–6.

MacCabe, Colin (1981a [1976]) '*Days of Hope* – A Response to Colin McArthur', in Tony Bennett, Susan Boyd-Bowman, Colin Mercer and Janet Woollacott (eds) *Popular Television and Film: A Reader*. London: British Film Institute, 310–13.

____ (1981b [1977]) 'Memory, Phantasy, Identity: *Days of Hope* and the Politics of the Past', in Tony Bennett, Susan Boyd-Bowman, Colin Mercer and Janet Woollacott (eds) *Popular Television and Film: A Reader*. London: British Film Institute

Ogden, Chris (1990) *Maggie: An Intimate Portrait of a Woman in Power*. New York: Simon and Schuster.

O'Shea, Alan (1984) 'Trusting the People: How Does Thatcherism Work?', in Martin Langan and Bill Schwarz (eds) *Formations of Nation and People*. Oxford: Blackwell Synergy, 19–41.

Rose, Jacqueline (1988) 'Margaret Thatcher and Ruth Ellis', *New Formations* 6 (Winter), 329.

Tribe, Keith (1981 [1977/78]) 'History and the Production of Memories', in Tony Bennett, Susan Boyd-Bowman, Colin Mercer and Janet Woollacott (eds) *Popular Television and Film: A Reader*. London: British Film Institute, 319–26.

Williams, Tony (1991) '*The Ploughman's Lunch*: Remembering or Forgetting History', *Jump Cut*, 36, 11–18.

Winship, Janice (1984) 'Nation before Family: Woman, the National Home Weekly, 1945–1953', in Martin Langan and Bill Schwarz (eds) *Formations of Nation and People*. Oxford: Blackwell Synergy, 188–211.

PART TWO
FILMMAKERS DURING THE THATCHER ERA

8. POWER AND TERRITORY: THE EMERGENCE OF BLACK BRITISH FILM COLLECTIVES

Manthia Diawara

Margaret Thatcher conducted the whole affair with absolute control. She pretends to be charming, and seductive, and on observation, I could see that she uses her gender in terms of being feminine, listening to men, in the ways she'd ask questions, and then she'll be like a mother and tell the men off.
— Isaac Julien, 'Downing Street Seminar', in *Diary of a Young Soul Rebel* (1991)

I think it means that people are really rather afraid that this country might be swamped by people of a different culture. The British character has done so much for democracy, for law, and done so much throughout the world that if there is any fear that it might be swamped, then people are going to be rather hostile to those coming in. We are a British nation with British characteristics. Every country can take some minorities, and in many ways they add to the richness and variety of this country. But the moment the minority threatens to become a big one, people get frightened.
— Margaret Thatcher, quoted in *Handsworth Songs* (1986)

The period 1985 to 1991 constitutes a black film movement in Britain that is as significant politically and aesthetically as the Brazilian Cinema Novo, the French New Wave and the Argentinian Third Cinema. This essay will delineate some of the constitutive elements of the new black British renaissance cinema in order to categorise it as a movement. For the sake of diasporic specifity, I will concentrate on the films of three film collectives: Ceddo, Sankofa and Black Audio. The black British renaissance cinema, like surrealism in the 1920s and Cinema Novo in the 1960s, presents itself with themes of discontinuity, boundaries, political agendas and aesthetic manifestos that set it apart from British experimental cinema, the earlier black British films and the films of the black diaspora.

Many commentators already characterise the black British renaissance cinema of the 1980s as a movement; one of these is Jim Pines, the first journalist and cultural practitioner to seriously explore collectives such as Ceddo, Sankofa and Black Audio. The notion of 'movement' is also explicit in Kobena Mercer's articles on black British cinema. In 'Recoding Narrative of Race and Nation', for example, Mercer states that 'the prolific activity of the black independent film movement stands out as an area of development in contemporary film culture that is unique to Britain in the 1980s' (1988: 4). In his introduction to *Questions of Third Cinema*, Paul Willemen describes black British cinema as constituting 'the most intellectually and cinematically innovative edge of British cultural politics' (Pines & Willemen 1989: 28). Alison Butler, for her part, sees in films such as *Handsworth Songs* 'the hope that we are witnessing the arrival of new artistic forms and cultural movements' (1988: 19). Finally, one must acknowledge the centrality of the theoretical writings by Stuart Hall, Homi Bhabha and Paul Gilroy, around which pivot notions of identity, ambivalence, Englishness and diasporic aesthetics crucial to an understanding of black British cinema.

THE HISTORICAL AND POLITICAL CONTEXT OF THE MOVEMENT

The history of the black British renaissance film of the 1980s has to be traced back to the emergence of the so-called minority arts in Britain since the mid-1970s. The riots associated with the 1976 and 1981 Notting Hill carnivals were followed by strategies of containment. Such policies resulted both in a militarisation of the police against black youth in British cities and in the setting aside of funds for minority artists by the National Art Council, the Greater London Council, the British Film Institute, Channel 4 and arts councils of local governments. Naseem Khan's 1976 report, entitled 'The Arts Britain Ignores', recommended the establishment of the Minority Arts Advisory Service (MAAS), which could encourage multiculturalism in Britain by recognising 'immigrant arts' and by providing creative spaces in schools and art centres for 'minority artists'. To put it in Kwesi Owusu's words, 'MAAS would construct and maintain an up-to-date register of groups and publicise immigrant arts, and act as a pressure group to see through the implementation of the report's recommendations' (1986: 49). Naseem Khan, instrumental in setting up the agency, also acted as its *de facto* head, aided by a committee of black and immigrant artists.

While many artists benefitted from funds generated by the Naseem Khan report, the idea of 'minority art' angered black artists afraid of being ghettoised as a problem to be nurtured and protected in British society. Thus some artists challenged the new multiculturalisms, claiming that 'they collapse different cultural and artistic forms into a melting pot without necessarily acknowledging their individual modes of expression, and without challenging institutional and attitudinal racism, which deprecates their quality by racial stereotyping' (Owusu 1986: 43).

In 1982, barely a year after the 1981 Notting Hill riot, the Greater London Council (GLC) sponsored a conference to re-evaluate black artists' access to media production. Black artists remained critical of how the GLC and the newly created Channel 4 television underfunded their creative projects, or put white artists and producers in charge of representing black issues to the public. Imruh Caesar, a black independent filmmaker at the GLC conference, brought out the need for 'black people to become the subjects, rather than merely objects, of the camera' (Owusu 1986: 86). The conference participants also criticised the timidity of Channel 4 for not yet committing itself to the training of black youth in directing, camera work and production. Channel 4's documentaries and television series, such as *Eastern Eye*, *Ebony* and *Black on Black*, also received criticism for not going far enough to address black spectatorship in British television. As Jim Pines pointed out, some black spectators of Channel 4 magazines on the black experience argued that 'programmes like *Black on Black* and *Eastern Eye* should be more propagandist in their orientation. In other words, given the dynamics of race politics in Britain at the moment, you should be concerned with putting across black political and cultural views which are explicitly in opposition to the white mainstream' (1983: 7). By propagandist, Pines meant creating counter-images to ITV shows like *Love Thy Neighbour*, *Mind Your Language* and *Mixed Blessings*, which portray racist stereotypes of black people in Britain. Channel 4's policy of non-racist situation comedies such as *No Problem* aimed to undermine images of black people as muggers, as lazy and shiftless, instead positing images of black people that emphasised their good citizenship, their hard work and their ordinariness. In other words, black spectators defined their relation to Channel 4 by demanding positive images; such images were supposed to be necessary to combat mainstream television's construction of black people. They wanted Channel 4's cameras to shift the blame away from black youth by revealing and denouncing the Metropolitan Police's construction of the youths' image as muggers and drug pushers in order to survey and punish it.

Both the GLC and Channel 4 responded to black artists' criticism by setting aside funds for training black youth in their desired mediums and helping them set up collective film and video workshops. Such workshops, after all, helped to keep the youth off the streets and reduced the chances of further uprising by a people affected by racism and unemployment. As Isaac Julien puts it, 'It also has to be noted why we are here, the struggles of black communities which have taken to the street to express their frustration, are continued and mirrored in other spaces, i.e. cinema' (quoted in Auguiste *et al.* 1988: 36). In the early 1980s, black film and video workshops also had to overcome the obstacle of virtually closed unions. For black people and women, as Jim Pines puts it, the Association of Cinematograph, Television and Allied Technicians (ACTT) 'traditionally has been a highly protective union – indeed, it is a closed shop and reputedly one of the most difficult unions to get into. For those on the outside, the problem is that without a union card it is practically impossible to get employment in the industry' (1983: 20).

THE MANIFESTOS OF THE MOVEMENT

The early phases of the black workshops were marked by a search for a film language capable of expressing the many experiences of black people in Britain. At first the young filmmakers used conference sites to distinguish their positions on representation and aesthetics from, on the one hand, those of previous black filmmakers in Britain and the diaspora, and the white independent cinema of Britain and Western Europe, on the other. They also used the newly created workshops to screen films by Sembene Ousmane, Haile Gerima, Charles Burnett and Julie Dash, which they discussed with audiences and compared to the practices of Third Cinema as amplified and applied to African, Asian and black American films by Teshome Gabriel's book, *Third Cinema in the Third World: The Aesthetics of Liberation* (1982). Sankofa and Black Audio Film/Video Collective were particularly interested in film theory and the applicability of Laura Mulvey's various writings on narrative cinema and visual pleasure, Homi Bhabha's notions of ambivalence and hybridity, and other uses of Lacan and Althusser in *Screen* and *Framework* in the late 1970s and early

1980s. The diaspora influence was linked to the works of African Americans such as June Jordan, whose *Civil Wars* (1982) helped the young black British to theorise policing in their own context, Manning Marable, Cedric Robinson, James Baldwin and black women writers; the Caribbeans included C. L. R. James, George Lamming, Wilson Harris, Frantz Fanon, Aimé Cesaire, Edward K. Braithwaite and Derek Walcott; the African influences included Ngugi Wa Thiongo and Sembene Ousmane. Crucially, however, the works of Stuart Hall and Paul Gilroy and the publications in the journal *Race and Class* were the most immediate influences on the new black British cinema. By 1986, when the collectives were internationally famous for films such as *Territories* (1985, Sankofa), *Passion of Remembrance* (1986, Sankofa) and *Handsworth Songs* (Black Audio), a new film language had been forged that marked a significant departure from race relation films that constructed black presence in Britain as a problem, from white independent cinema that rendered race invisible, and from diaspora and Third Cinema films that lacked cinematic pleasure and took ambivalent subject positions.

Position papers and artistic and political manifestos by John Akomfrah, Martina Attille, Karen Alexander and Reece Auguiste outline the programmes of the new black British cinema; they insist on its specificity within the larger context of independent filmmaking in Britain. In 1983, John Akomfrah's article in *Artrage* announced the birth of Black Audio Film/Video Collective. For Akomfrah, the collective was created to address three main areas in film activities. First, they questioned the mainstream media's representation of black people: 'to look critically at how racist ideas and images of black people are structured and presented as self-evident truths in cinema. What we are interested in here is how these "self-evident truths" become the conventional pattern through which the black presence in cinema is secured' (Akomfrah 1983: 29).

In the second place, Akomfrah posits Black Audio's need to inventory the 'available techniques within the independent tradition and to assess their pertinence for black cinema. In this respect our interest did not only lie in devising how best to make "political" films, but also in taking the politics of representation seriously' (ibid.). By adding the dimension of the 'politics of representation' to their agenda, Black Audio problematised the whole notion of black people's 'relation to images'. They demonstrated that the issue of representation was not resolved by simply shifting from negative images to positive images. Positive images, they believed, were as embedded in stereotypes as negative images, and only a politics of representation could account for the filmmaker's relation to the images that he or she arranged on the screen. As Stuart Hall put it:

> How things are represented and the 'machineries' and regimes of representation in a culture do play a constitutive, and not merely a reflexive, after-the-event, role. This gives questions of culture and ideology, and the scenarios of representation – subjectivity, identity, politics – a formative, not merely an expressive, place in the constitution of social and political life. (1988: 28)

Finally, Akomfrah described the need for a collective practice in Black Audio's approach to film, as opposed to privileging the director as the sole creative force in a film. The collective approach emphasised the division of labour among the producer, the director, the persons in charge of distribution and publicity, the audience for the film, and so on. To put it in Akomfrah's own words:

> The strategy was to encourage and emphasise collective practice as a means of extending the boundaries of black film culture. This would mean attempting to de-mystify in our film practice the process of film production; it would also involve collapsing the distinction between 'audience' and 'producer'. In this ethereal world filmmaker equals active agent and audience usually equals passive consumers of a predetermined product. We have decided to reject such a view in our practice. (1983: 29)

The three points Akomfrah put on the table for Black Audio Film/Video Collective helped them address the issue of stereotypical representation of black people by the police and the media in Thatcherite Britain, as well as to posit the possibility for the emergence of a film style specific to black Britons. For Akomfrah, a theory of difference was necessary both for deconstructing structured presence/absence of black people in the media and for the grounding of a politics of representation that was not fixed: 'The search is not for "the authentic image" but for an understanding of the diverse codes and strategies of representation' (1983: 30).

Martina Attille of Sankofa Film Collective explained that her group was first concerned with the experience of black people and policing in Britain. To better understand this phenomenon, they investigated the strategies of containment, the varieties of black communities, and systems of power and control. According to Attille, 'despite the diversity of black life in Britain, images of black people are defined in very narrow terms and contained as problematic' (1988: 53). Sankofa's goal was, therefore, to bring the multiple identities and values of black subjects out of the shadows in order to expose the stereotypical images mobilised by the police to maintain black youth as the problem in Britain. Sankofa Film Collective used the notion of pleasure and multiple subject positions as elements of their film language, giving voices back to black people and revealing the diversity of their lives in Britain. For Attille, a pleasurable cinema is necessary to draw people into the film:

> We wanted the film to appeal to young people, the politically aware and those who could become politically aware, a film for Europe about being young and black in Britain at a time of uncertainty. We also wanted the film to retain its original integrity, e.g. the realities of policing in its broadest sense – and to assert the politics of being a black woman, always active. (Ibid.)

Sankofa Film Collective also emphasised gender and sexual politics as constitutive elements to shape their film language. For Attille, putting gender and sexuality in the foreground was one of the ways Sankofa distinguished itself from the first generation of black filmmakers: 'Sankofa's particular character in terms of race, gender and sexuality meant that the unfinished business of the 1960s/70s (black, gay and feminist movements) was something that we felt needed prioritising in the present, particularly in relation to those three areas of experience' (1988: 54).

Finally, the new black film collectives' search for a specific identitary experience in Britishness expressed itself in a specific film language that made them question the prevailing styles in diaspora and Third Cinema films, as well as in the British independent and West European cinema. No doubt the theories of Third Cinema, particularly Teshome Gabriel's application of the concept to the films of Sembene Ousmane and Haile Gerima, opened up the possibilities for an alternative film practice in Britain. As Reece Auguiste put it at the Commonwealth Institute conference on Cultural Identities in 1986, the historical antecedents of the black film renaissance were 'the early period of British black independent film production from Lionel Ngakane's allegorical *Jemima and Johnny* (1974), to the 1980s, with the films of Henry Martin, Horace Ove, Imruh Bakari Caesar and Menelik Shabazz, and the political and aesthetic intervention of Third Cinema, as a countermovement in film, which is critical of its own position, as it is of European cinema' (1988: 33).

However, for Auguiste, neither Third Cinema, with its emphasis on oppositional film style, nor the old British black independent films, which focused on race as a problem in Britain, adequately encompassed the hybrid and creolised space that was the subject of the new black cinema. As Auguiste put it:

> Debates around Third Cinema have not in my view sufficiently addressed developments in the cinema by diasporic subjects living and working in the metropolitan centres of London, Paris, New York, etc. Thus it becomes immensely problematic when films from Britain are incorporated into this all-embracing conceptual framework called Third Cinema practice. Such a process does not allow adequate space for a critical evaluation of the distinctiveness of films emerging from Britain and other Western metropolitan centres. That level of analysis and critical reflection is most needed. (1988: 215)

Similarly, Cassie McFarlene explained the difference between an earlier black British film like *Burning an Illusion* (1981) and the films of the black British renaissance like *Passion of Remembrance* and *Handsworth Songs* by arguing that the former is embedded in the discourse of ethnic absolutism, while the latter emphasise multiple subject positions. As McFarlene put it, '*Burning an Illusion* was made at a period during which there emerged a new ideology of ethnic absolutism which focused on the black cultural formation in Britain as homogeneous. The question of the racial/cultural identity of black people in the Diaspora was at this period given priority over other factors arising out of the history of settlement' (1987: 29). For McFarlene, a shift occurred with films by Sankofa and Black Audio, which were more in conversation with the independent white leftist experimental filmmaking, the recent developments in theory, as well as the latest issues raised by black women writers in the United States. McFarlene saw the emergence of a unique consciousness among the new wave of black filmmakers with regard to blackness and Britishness, gender and sexuality, desire and pleasure – issues that before were marginal in black films.

The black film renaissance distanced itself from independent British and Western European films, too, by emphasising black subjecthood and notions of pleasure that were banned in the films of such directors as Peter Gidal (*Close Up*, 1983), Lezli-Ann Barrett, Laura Mulvey, Peter Wollen, and others. While the white experimental cinema did away with the subject and notions of identity, the black British deployed diasporic memories in their films. As Isaac Julien put it:

> On the left of avant-gardism is pleasure, which the avant-garde self denies, clinging to the purism of its constructed ethics, measuring itself against a refusal to indulge in nar-

rative or emotions and indeed, in some cases, refusing representation itself, because all these systems of signs are fixed, entrenched in the 'sin or evil' of representation. The high moral tone of this discourse is based on a kind of masochistic self-censorship which relies on the indulgence of a colonial history and a post-colonial history of cinema of white representations based on our black absence. The problematic that surfaces when black filmmakers experiment with the idea of black film text and the subjective camera, is that subjectivity implies contradiction. But this is not, in itself, fixed. (Quoted in Auguiste *et al.* 1988: 36)

THE BRITISH CINEMA IS DEAD, LONG LIVE BLACK BRITISH CINEMA

To turn now to the themes that unify black British renaissance cinema as a movement I shall emphasise policing and diasporic aesthetics in the films. These themes are differently represented to question Englishness and blackness in the films, as well as to address the problematics of sexuality, class relations and belonging in Britain. The representation of policing in the films draws from the treatment of the same subject by Stuart Hall and others (*Policing the Crisis: Mugging, the State, and Law and Order*) and Paul Gilroy (*There Ain't No Black in the Union Jack*), as well as from the uprisings against the police in Handsworth, Brixton and Tottenham. The filmmakers intend to depict not only the manner in which the police and the mainstream press construct stereotypical images of black people in Britain and force the population to accept these images, but also the ways in which bodies are sexually constructed and maintained in certain positions. *Territories*, for example, depicts an image of two gay men dancing on the British flag under the watchful eyes of a policeman. Britishness as English puritanism is contested in this scene through the defiance of police surveillance and an appropriation of the Union Jack by black people and gay men.

The figuration of policing in the films takes on two levels defined by Paul Gilroy as the archaeology of representations of law-breaking. The first level shows the efforts by the police and the mainstream press to construct and maintain a monolithic and fixed image of black people in Britain, while the second level deconstructs the first one and posits the possibility of multiple black subject positions. The first one links blackness to crime and argues that black law-breaking is un-English and therefore constitutes the main evidence that black people are unworthy of belonging to the nation. The second level reveals the police's bias against black people by focusing on 'the supportive relationship between the police and the local white residents harassed by the noise' (1987: 97). It constructs an image of the law that suppresses black culture in its attempt to preserve a monolithic Britishness. The extent to which black people are seen as a threat to Britishness is shown in a television address by Margaret Thatcher that is quoted in *Handsworth Songs* and that serves as the second epigraph of this text.

Following Gilroy's work, films like *Handsworth Songs*, *Territories*, *Passion of Remembrance* and *The People's Account* (1986, Ceddo) show both the Thatcherites and the Labour Party colluding to maintain that black law-breaking distances them from authentic Englishness. *Handsworth Songs*, for example, represents the riots of Handsworth by placing its cameras with the mob, instead of placing them behind the police. Thus we see the police and the mainstream press as they approach their 'victim'. In one scene, the cameras track down a group of helmeted policemen as they chase and trap a black man with long dreadlocks. Parts of the scene are shown in slow motion as the police finally catch the Rasta man who vainly tries to escape them. The filming of the scene puts emphasis on the police outnumbering the man in dreadlocks, and on the brutality of the police against the helplessness of the man.

Also, in *Territories*, the police's representation of the streets as dangerous for elderly white women is turned against itself. In one scene, an old white woman clinging to her purse and looking frightened crosses a street full of young black males. The camera stays on her until she reaches the other end of the street, then the scene is reversed, sending her back to the beginning. Interpreted from the perspective of black youth's contestation of their construction by the police, this scene embodies several meanings. To begin with, it appropriates the discourse of the police and addresses the fears of the white woman, for whom the image of young black male connotes rape and mugging. In this sense, the presence of black youth turns the streets into hell, and crossing from one end to the other becomes a painful and long journey for the law-abiding white woman. But, by running the same image in reverse, the film literally deconstructs the stereotypic police construction of black youth. The image in reverse, because it is comical – or a bad joke at the expense of the old woman – unseats the authenticity of the image of the black youth the police have created in the woman's mind. As Gilroy argues, 'the struggle over signs and images [between the police and the black artists], particularly those which involve blacks, has become more important for the maintenance of order than the actual law-breaking that they denote' (1987: 109). *Territories* uses the theme of policing to 'recompose' the signs of blackness and Britishness in Britain and to lift blackness from the pathological space created by police files.

Such films denote the theme of policing and black youth's resistance to it through recourse to images of burning buildings in Brixton, Handsworth and Tottenham. Just as these buildings in smoke have come to symbolise black resistance in films like *Who Killed Colin Roach* (1983), *Handsworth Songs*, *Passion of Remembrance*, *Territories* and *The People's Account*, the names of black people, such as Colin Roach, Keith Blakelock, Cherry Groce and Mrs Jarret, whose deaths are associated with the riots, have also come to symbolise black martyrdom in Britain.

Without doubt, the strongest indictment of policing comes from *The People's Account*, a film about the community's view of the 1985 riot in Broadwater Farm, Tottenham. Using interviews with people from Broadwater Farm, the documentary looks into the historical and contemporary relationship between black people and the police, their social and economic conditions, and the role the media, in collusion with the police, have played to 'distort and undermine the fundamental reasons for the uprisings' (Ceddo press release, 1986). *The People's Account*, now famous for being censored by the Independent Broadcasting Authority (which must give its stamp of approval before films can be shown on British television), focuses mainly on policing, which distinguishes it from other films of the movement dealing with several themes at the same time. It compares the police's treatment of black people in Britain to the treatment of black people in the apartheid system of South Africa. It accuses the police of 'terrorist raids against Black communities', describes black people as victims of police racism, and calls the events of Broadwater Farm a 'classical example of self-defence by the [black] community'. *The People's Account* is also known for its use of *uprisings* in the place of *riots* to underscore black people's revolt against discrimination, exploitation and policing. Ceddo Film/Video Workshop considers film to be a guerrilla weapon in the general perspective of uprisings, just as Bob Marley's music was considered to be a weapon of liberation. It is in this sense that Ceddo film crews have been present among the crowd to film the police at the uprisings in Handsworth, Brixton and Tottenham. Original footage from Ceddo archives can be seen in films like *Handsworth Songs* and Sankofa films.

The theme of the black diaspora figures importantly in many of the films. The filmmakers represent the diaspora as a way of resisting the pathological construction of blackness by mainstream media and of positioning blackness as a third and hybrid space that can be opposed to the ethnic absolutism of Englishness and other ethnicities in Britain. As Gilroy put it, 'Black Britain defines itself crucially as part of a diaspora. Its unique cultures draw inspiration from those developed by black populations elsewhere. In particular, the culture and politics of black America and the Caribbean have become raw materials for creative processes which redefine what it means to be black, adapting it to distinctly British experiences and meanings' (1987: 154). For Stuart Hall, diasporic narratives often construct cultural identity either as 'hidden histories, true essences of Caribbeanness or Africanness inside the many other more superficial or artificially imposed "selves", which people with a shared history and ancestry hold in common' (1989: 69); or as difference and rupture, 'points of deep and significant difference which constitute "what we really are": or rather – since history has intervened – "what we have become"' (1989: 70). While the first narrative empowers itself through archivism, excavation and continuity, the other valorises fragmentation, hybridity and rupture. In either case, the filmmaker articulates his or her identity with different types of presences: African, American, Asian and European.

Films like *The Passion of Remembrance*, *Handsworth Songs*, *Territories*, *My Beautiful Laundrette* (1985), *Twilight City* (1989) and *I'm British But...* (1989) and construct diasporic space as a third space. By third space I mean the familiar notion of hybrid spaces that combine the colours and flavours of different localities, and yet declare their specifity from each of those localities. In *My Beautiful Laundrette*, the Asian presence and the English presence are combined to produce a third space, which is occupied not only by the youth of Asian descent, but also by the white youth of the punk generation.

The construction of a third space is the subject of narrative deployment in *The Passion of Remembrance*. On one level, the youth construct their black Britishness through recourse to the black American funk style of the 1970s and the sexual politics legitimised by British feminism and post-structuralism, and by making a movement away from the 1970s reggae and the 1960s-derived black British nationalism and white British ethnic absolutism. On another level, *The Passion of Remembrance* constitutes a third space as the space for women and homosexuals whose struggles were not sufficiently highlighted during the civil rights movement. It is in this sense that heterosexuals seem lost in the open spaces of the film, while women lead the way.

Diasporic narratives are also used in the films for didactic and celebratory purposes. In films such as *Omega Rising: Woman of Rastafari* (1988) and *Time and Judgement* (1989), the African and Caribbean presences are emphasised in order to bring hidden histories out of the shadows. In *Time and Judgement*, director Menelik Shabazz combines images of Marcus Garvey, Haile Selassie, Nelson Mandela and the Queen of Sheba with Afrocentric poems and images to denote how, after 400 years of oppression, the African people 'rose up with the rod of Moses and passed judgement' against 'Babylon'. In *Omega Rising*, Ceddo travelled through Britain and Jamaica to reveal the role of women in the Rastafari movement that many consider patriarchal and sexist.

In films such as *Handsworth Songs*, *Testament* (1989) and *Looking for Langston* (1989), the African and American presences are questioned in order to envision their usefulness to the material conditions of black British identity formation. The narrative of *Looking for Langston*, for example, empowers itself by conjuring up Hughes and other figures of the Harlem renaissance. The film is looking back at that discourse of the turn of the century in order to empower its own discourse of the present, namely, black Britishness. In *Handsworth Songs*, Black Audio inserts enigmatic foot-age of Malcolm X in Birmingham to point to the similarities of white racism and black struggle in the United States and Britain. In *Testament*, too, the protagonist ques-tions the 'presence Africaine' in the make-up of black British identity by travelling to Ghana and articulating her British identity with the pan-Africanism of Nkrumah.

Other important thematisations of the diaspora in the films involve religion (*Omega Rising*, *Time and Judgement* and *Dreaming Rivers* (1988)), languages, music and cos-tumes of African, American and European presences. All these diasporic narratives are used to situate black people inside and outside Britishness, to delineate points of identification with blackness, and to mark the fluidity of identitarian positions.

In closing I would like to return to the beginning of this essay, which places the black British film movement between 1985 and 1991. Is it possible that identity politics no longer maintain their efficacy and that broader political coalitions are be-coming more urgent? Perhaps the critique of essentialism, too, has influenced new narratives that privilege what Gianni Vattimo calls 'weak thought'. It is also possible that the subsequent decision by Channel 4 not to support the workshops has precipi-tated the demise of the movement. One might also point to the return to authorship, implicit in the fame associated with names such as Julien, Akomfrah and Shabazz, as an indicator of the end of an era. At any rate, the end of *Young Soul Rebels* (1991) marks a new era in black British filmmaking. As the four main characters get out of their couches and begin to dance, it becomes clear that they are tired of identity, sep-arate communities and Thatcherite Britain, and that they are leaving all that behind.

WORKS CITED

Akomfrah, John (1983) 'Black Independent Film-making: A Statement by the Black Audio Film/Video Collective', *Artrage: Inter Cultural Arts Magazine*, 3/4 (Summer), 29–30.

Attille, Martina (1988) 'The Passion of Remembrance: Background', in *Black Film, British Cinema*, ICA Documents 7. London: Institute of Contemporary Art, 53–4.

Auguiste, Reece (1989) 'Black Independents and Third Cinema: The British Context', in Jim Pines and Paul Willemen (eds) *Questions of Third Cinema*. London: British Film Institute, 212–17

Auguiste, Reece, Isaac Julien and Martina Attille (1988) 'Aesthetics and Politics: Working on, Two Fronts', *Undercut: The Magazine for the London Filmmakers' Co-op*, 17, 32–9.

Butler, Alison (1988) '*Handsworth Songs*', *International Documentary*, Winter/Spring, Ceddo Press

Release, 19–22.

Gabriel, Teshome (1982) *Third Cinema in the Third World: The Aesthetics of Liberation*. Ann Arbor: University of Michigan Press.

Gilroy, Paul (1987) *There Ain't No Black in the Union Jack*. London: Hutchinson.

Hall, Stuart (1988) 'New Ethnicities', in *Black Film, British Cinema*, ICA Documents, 7. London: Institute of Contemporary Art, 53–4.

____ (1989) 'Cultural Identity and Cinematic Representation', *Framework*, 36, 68–81.

Hall, Stuart, Charles Critcher, Tony Jefferson, John Clarke and Brian Roberts (1987) *Policing the Crisis: Mugging, the State, and Law and Order*. London: Macmillan.

Julien, Isaac and Colin MacCabe (1991) *Diary of a Young Soul Rebel*. London: British Film Institute.

Khan, Naseem (1986) 'The Arts Britain Ignores', in *The Struggle for Black Arts in Britain*, edited by Kwesi Owusu. London: Comedia.

McFarlene, Cassie (1987) 'Toward a Critical Evaluation of Black British Film Culture', unpublished paper, BA Film, Photography and Television, London College of Printing.

Mercer, Kobena (1988) 'Recoding Narratives of Race and Nation', in *Black Film, British Cinema*, ICA Documents, 7. London: Institute of Contemporary Art, 4–14.

Owusu, Kwesi (1986) *The Struggle for Black Arts in Britain*. London: Comedia.

Pines, Jim (1983) 'Channel 4: A Pandora's Box for Blacks?', *Artrage*, 3/4, 2–5.

Pines, Jim and Paul Willemen (1989) *Questions of Third Cinema*. London: British Film Institute.

9. ENCOUNTERS WITH THATCHERISM: FOUR WOMEN FILMMAKERS

Deborah Tudor

During Margaret Thatcher's tenure as Prime Minister, women filmmakers explored various public and private roles of women through documentary, narrative and avant-garde screen practices. The work of Sally Potter, Ngozi Onwurah, Pratibha Parmar and Beeban Kidron exemplify responses to particular aspects of women's lives during the Thatcher years, offering four different ways of re-presenting political and cultural issues affecting women. To understand how these films respond and produce resistance, it is necessary to sketch out two discourses that contextualise the films' production: how Thatcherite discourse constructed dominant ideas about class, race and gender to form the political culture in which these films function, and how the work of feminist film critics provide the theories that both informed and developed from film practice. This essay considers the work of these filmmakers within both those historical contexts, drawing upon analyses of Thatcher's rhetoric and policies and upon feminist film theory. Examining the Thatcher government's actions in the Falklands War – including a brief history of British immigration law – demonstrates how these procedures are linked to racism and sexism, and provides an understanding of how the effects of Thatcher's social and economic policies upon women establishes the political context of these filmmakers' works.

THATCHERISM: IMPERIALISM AND IMMIGRATION

The Falklands War created a resurgence of imperial feeling. Post-imperial Britain in the 1980s was not a major world power; however, Britons still felt that the country's voice had major, if indirect, international influence. When faced with an overt challenge like the Falklands crisis, the government felt it necessary to assert British military power in a very direct way; the alternative, an admission of the inability to act militarily, would mean 'nothing less than a public acknowledgement of a dreaded Third World national status' (Femenia 1996: 126). Thus, the Falklands crisis was viewed in Britain as a means to restore and renew the idea of the British nation, a function of ideological nostalgia that ignored the contemporary diminishment of Britain's international standing by looking to the 'glory of the imperial past' (Femenia 1996: 122) that was founded upon and linked to racism throughout the twentieth century.

An explicit link between the British imperial hangover and racism emerges through two types of legislation that attempt to exert government control over complex negotiations of race, particularly at the intersection of blackness and citizenship.

The first type of legislation consisted of a series of Acts aimed at bringing immigration under control. Britain shifted its legal definition of citizenship for Africans and Asians born in Commonwealth nations several times during the post-World War Two era. Laws tightening immigration control for Africans and Asians were passed in 1962 and 1968. These and similar acts continually redefined an 'allowable immigrant' by reducing or eliminating immigration categories for those without particular work skills or for those without previously-established family ties to Great Britain. Although government officials denied that racist ideas fuelled these acts, Cabinet papers recently released to the public reveal a sustained concern about the influx of more Asians and Africans into Britain. The Notting Hill riots of 1958 were interpreted as 'evidence' that 'traditional British tolerance to immigrants from Asian and African countries, even those who were part of the Commonwealth, and therefore traditionally assumed to have at least limited rights to emigrate to Britain, was stretched beyond reasonable limits' (Pilkington 2003: 211). The 1981 British Nationality Act restricted rights of dependents, fiancés and spouses of British citizens to settle in Britain (Pilkington 2003: 219). Such legislative shifts throughout the last century exemplify the ambivalent relationships between white and black Britons and underline the indistinct nature of black British citizenship.

The second type of legislation negotiating blackness and citizenship was a series of Race Relations Acts, such as those of 1965 and 1968, which attempted to combat racial discrimination in public accommodations, housing, employment and commercial services. The 1976 Race Relations Act extended the 'definition of racial discrimination to include indirect forms and thus encompass organisational practices, which had a disproportionately adverse effect on a particular group (Pilkington 2003: 231). The contradiction of the two types of legislation was apparent. Labour Party member Roy Hattersley noted that immigration policy has created 'the impression that we cannot afford to let them in. And if we cannot afford to let them in, those of them who are here already must be doing harm' (quoted in Pilkington 2003: 243). This language indicates that immigrants were conceptualised as a threat within the borders, and this type of discourse became specifically tied to the military action in the South Atlantic.

The Falklands crisis is a crucial part of race politics in the 1980s. This military action highlighted and built upon an existing rhetoric of invasion and war traditionally invoked to describe immigration. For example, the presence of black immigrants in Britain had been described by a hostile language, in metaphors like 'the enemy within, the unarmed invasion, alien encampments, alien territory and new commonwealth occupation' (Gilroy 1987: 45). It is important to remember that this discourse was activated in the name of defining Britishness and, even more importantly, to discuss who had rights to British citizenship. These issues also emerged through the Falklands military action, one that reinvigorated notions of Empire. Such actions re-emphasise race and power, which were foundation blocks of Empire. The nature of this conflict drew attention to the exact type of connection that existed between the British and the Falklanders.

One of Margaret Thatcher's statements about the rationale for military action further elucidated the governmental mindset about this connection. On 3 April 1982 Thatcher said: 'Nor have we any doubt about the unequivocal wishes of the Falkland Islanders, who are British in stock and tradition, and they wish to remain British in allegiance' (quoted in Femenia 1996: 139). The identification of the white Falkland Islanders as 'British in stock' defines their claim to being British not through residency in British-governed territory, but through race. After the crisis was over, the Falkland Islanders were granted British citizenship. Further, Thatcher drew parallels between the conflict in the South Atlantic and domestic 'subversive' activities, like labour actions and other activities that did not 'match the spirit' of the reborn Britain (Gilroy 1987: 51).

Clearly, Thatcher's government was concerned with internal and external racial politics. The tightening of immigration and the call to arms for the Falkland Islanders both reveals the ways in which the government sought to control race in Great Britain. Sometimes, Thatcher's remarks even seemed to blame immigration for the rise of far right-wing white movements, like the National Front. In 1978, for example, she remarked that 'some white people felt swamped by people with a different culture' and spoke of these fears 'driving some people to the National Front, a party considered to be at least talking about the problems' (quoted in Pilkington 2003: 219).

THATCHERISM: GENDER RHETORIC AND SOCIAL POLICIES

Margaret Thatcher was the first woman to head a political party in Britain and to become Prime Minister. Her accomplishments would seem to represent a very public victory for feminism. However, Prime Minister Thatcher consistently disassociated herself from feminist discourse, preferring to represent herself as an individualist. She saw her accomplishments as something outside the ordinary lives of British women, not representative of any particular movement. Thatcher's particular embodiment of 'femininity' in her role as Prime Minister was as the 'exceptional woman', a model that suppressed the notion that women could be a political class with specific issues (Wilson 1987: 224). Her preferred self-designation promotes an 'individualistic ethos of high achievement and financial success (that) glossed over structural inequalities' (quoted in Nunn 2002: 41–2).

The irony of her position is reflected in her personal history. Several times, Thatcher experienced incidents of class and gender discrimination that impeded her political advancement. At Oxford, she became President of the Conservative Association, but as a woman was denied the chance to join the Oxford Union. Membership in the Union would have helped develop her debating skills and allowed her to make useful contacts, as it had done for many other politicians like Harold Macmillan and Edward Heath. She also lacked independent wealth; her family had trouble with her fees for Oxford, and she had to defer running for office until the salary for Members of Parliament was raised from £600 to £1,000 per year. Clearly, in a political system of training and practice designed for upper-class men, a middle-class woman like Margaret Thatcher faced many 'structural inequalities'. This contradictory image of Thatcher combines with economic policies that strengthened traditional gender definitions (male as property owner) and an overall rhetoric that defined women as full-time housewives, a role no longer occupied by the majority of women in Britain.

Thatcher articulated a 'two roles of women' position that derived from the stances of British governments since the 1960s. She indicated that women (by nature and by culture) had two jobs to do in life: (i) as wife and mother, and (ii) as public employee (Wilson 1987: 204–5). This concept helped Thatcher consign feminism to the past. Her insistence that women's struggles were no longer necessary established her rhetorical position that the Tory Party was the 'modern' party. And, as such, best able to include change into its programme. This positioning aligns with an attack on 'old-fashioned' dogmas of trade unions, marxists and feminists. In a 1981 interview for Thames Television News, she stated that there was no longer any necessity for legal changes to prevent sexism: 'After all, I don't think there's been a great deal of discrimination against women for years' (quoted in Nunn 2002: 38). Through Thatcher's pronouncements and the resulting social agenda put forth by her party, the Conservative government 'proclaimed that class, race, sexual and gender oppressions were largely irrelevant' (McNeil 1991: 229).

Although a strong public discourse aimed at promoting a retrogressive attitude toward women characterised the Thatcher years, the exact nature of Thatcherism as a political philosophy and set of practices remains disputed. Some analysts see a coherent ideology with emphasis on liberal economics and regressive social policies whose coherence serves as an explanation of the 1979 election of a Tory government. This approach assumes that 'disillusionment with Socialism and progress had willed the whole populace to the right', a view which developed after Thatcher's election and prompted by disbelief on the British left that people could actually vote for Thatcher (Wilson 1987: 199). This view also promotes a notion of Thatcherism as inherently hostile to women, with economic policies and 'values' rhetoric specifically aimed at pushing women back into the home.

A second view of Thatcherism maps a loose alliance of various groups that produced a political programme riddled by contradictions between its social and economic policies. Elizabeth Wilson argues that the 'Thatcherite ideology' position ignores the role of previous Labour governments in constructing some of the 'tenets' of Thatcherism, such as the abandonment of commitment to full employment (1987: 200). With reference to the specific economic position of women, Wilson finds the Thatcherite thesis most troubling and inexact. She finds Thatcherism's overall impact on women seems to be less than on men economically, for example. She also convincingly demonstrates the fact that Labour in the 1970s echoed the Tory position on 'family values' and 'stability of the home' (1987: 204). However, while arguing that the Thatcherite programme is neither a unique nor new 'back to the home' approach to women's role in public life, she admits that the public rhetoric of prominent party members placed great emphasis on 'family values' and the centrality of family life (1987: 203). Because both parties emphasised this 'familialist' ideology, Wilson argues that the impact of the Conservative policies affecting women were not a great change from the previous government.

Stuart Hall sees a thrust toward social discipline in Thatcherism. This is a punitive philosophy that expresses itself through the dismantling of the welfare state 'crosslaced with the usual moral negatives – teenage pregnancies … drunkenness, sexual offences, and crimes of sadism – all of which can be laid at the door of the welfare philosophy' (1988: 27). The dismantling of the welfare state seems particularly instrumental in returning women to the home, since many employed women in Britain relied on 'state provision for dependent family members (the old, the sick, children)' that allowed them to work outside the home (Barrett 1988: 246). Such emphasis would increase the effectiveness of sustaining a politically regressive public arena, which would include an enhanced rhetoric on maintaining the woman's place in the home.

All critics agree that Thatcher's economic policies affected women in working-class jobs more negatively than women in professional jobs. In effect, Thatcherite economic policies are often credited with creating a 'Two Britains' situation in which the gap between wealthy and poor widened significantly (Hill 1999: 7). The overall loss of jobs in the manufacturing sector was cited as a reason for job loss among poorer women. Also, the wages of full-time working-class women workers were much lower in relation to the average wage for all full-time women workers, 76 per cent of the average wage as opposed to 98 per cent of the average working woman's wages in 1968 (Wilson 1987: 206). This exacerbated class divisions among women (1987: 211). Wilson charges that feminists ignored class and race differences in their situation and that this blindness weakened their analysis and responses to the Thatcher government.

WOMEN'S VOICES: DIFFERENT WAYS OF SPEAKING

Women's film engages with the gender, race and class politics of the Thatcher era in diverse ways. Three of the filmmakers discussed here may be grouped within a tendency of women's cinema that became known as counter-cinema, although they are split between art-house narrative and avant-garde modes of filmmaking. Beeban Kidron's work represents a different tendency, that of the realist documentary. All these cinemas resisted stereotyping of women and sought to redress the cinematic absence of women's images that related to real life.

The various tendencies grouped within the feminist filmmaking movement form part of the lineage of Engaged Cinema of 1960s and 1970s, and follow the efforts of radical filmmaking groups like Newsreel, Dziga Vertov and SLON that shifted into micro-politics and social action movements. Each of the directors discussed in this essay engaged with issues along two axes: those that directly impact women off-screen, and those that concern women's images on-screen. The works of women filmmakers active during the Thatcher years engaged in counter-cinema techniques popularly associated with specific women's films of the 1970s, techniques which redefined gender through textual operations that deconstructed dominant cinematic practice.

In 1973, Claire Johnston authored a germinal article on counter-cinema, 'Women's Cinema as Counter-Cinema', which proposed a cinema that actively opposed main-stream Hollywood through the reworking of narrative and visual strategies. Where Hollywood films proposed an active male gaze and a passive female gaze, feminist counter-cinema narrative strategies placed women at the centre of narrative cause and effect, rather than having active male and passive female characters. Counter-cinema advocates argued for the necessity of reshaping the language of cinema to undermine the apparent naturalness of mainstream mythologies about women. Johnston contended that 'any revolutionary strategy must challenge the depiction of reality: it is not enough to discuss the oppression of women within the text of the film; the language of the cinema/the depiction of reality must also be interrogated, so that a break between ideology and text is effected' (1973: 29). Strategies must counteract mainstream female stereotyping and mythmaking, which are ideological operations of Hollywood-style films (1973: 24–5).

The publication of Laura Mulvey's article, 'Visual Pleasure and Narrative Cinema' in *Screen* (1975), helped open debate about the controlling masculine gaze associated with Hollywood film and its effects upon spectators. While notions of spectator positioning have undergone much redefinition in the years since 'Visual Pleasure and Narrative Cinema' was published, Mulvey's conception of the 'woman as image and male as controller of the look' (1989: 19) provides ways of understanding narrative and visual strategies that inform counter-cinema. Mulvey's own critique of her article states that it was written 'polemically and without regard for context or nuances of argument' (1989: vii). Indeed, the idea of the gaze has been nuanced over the years through an understanding of it as a racialised construction. The 'gaze' is embedded in power relations within white patriarchy, and analysts must account for who is looking at whom, within and across cultures. Attention must be given to who is looking, both characters within the text and those looking at the text in terms of race, class and gender. This would include not just male/female relations, but race, class and colonialist relations. This more nuanced view of the gaze structures our understanding of ways that these same visual and narrative strategies define cinematic representations of race as well as those of gender.

Sally Potter's films are a concrete example of counter-cinema as technique; she uses textual strategies that encourage a contrary type of spectator identification from the audience address commonly used by mainstream cinema directors. This allows her films to counteract the mythological representations of women circulated through dominant cinema. Pratibha Parmar and Ngozi Onwurah work in the avant-garde mode, carrying the ideas of counter-cinema further away from models of dominant cinema, and their films deal very explicitly with race and immigration issues.

The introduction of racial difference into feminist theory in the 1970s–1980s dislocated its dominant white, middle-class bias. Previously, the psychoanalytic and semiotic basis of much feminist film theory was critiqued for its obliteration of race and class as analytic terms. Black feminists argued that women of colour and white women occupy different positions relative to patriarchy, as black men do not attain the same positions of power within patriarchy as white men. As such, feminist analyses of women of colour must emphasise this difference. Holistic analyses of women's roles can discover crucial ways in which race, gender and class interact to form different relationships to a patriarchal society. Black British feminists, such as Hazel Carby, pointed out that 'the existence of racism must be acknowledged as a structuring feature of our relationships with white women. Both white feminist theory and practice have to recognise that white women stand in a power relation as oppressors of black women' (1997: 46). Onwurah and Parmar's experimental work counters white-centric feminist analyses as well as white patriarchal mythologies about women of colour.

Deconstructive textual strategies do not suffice to create feminist counter-cinema. After all, avant-garde films have historically operated in opposition to dominant film practice. Deconstructive films must also operate from a politically oppositional point of view: 'Deconstructive cinema ... speaks from politically oppositional positions or concerns itself with subject matters commonly ignored or repressed in dominant cinema ... deconstructive cinema then may be defined by its articulation of oppositional forms with oppositional contents' (Kuhn 1982: 161). All the films in this essay fit this definition; they deal with marginalisation and oppression in the realms of race, politics, high and popular art, immigration, class and gender.

Not all feminist films of this era, even ones with oppositional content, could be considered counter-cinema. A strong group of realist films, both narrative and documentary, also emerged during the 1970s and 1980s. Such films sought to bring women's experience out of the private realm and to address the lack of diversity in women's cinematic images. Realist strategies made the films accessible to a wide range of audiences, and this aspect of the films was highly valued. This tradition of feminist documentary work aligns with the advent of women's consciousness-raising groups in the late 1960s and early 1970s. The structure of these films emphasised 'biography, simplicity, trust between woman filmmaker and woman subject, linear narrative structure, little self-consciousness about the flexibility of the cinematic medium' (Lesage 1999: 222–3). Beeban Kidron's documentary, *Carry Greenham Home* (1982), provides an example of this mode of filmmaking response to political culture. The films discussed in this essay therefore cover a range of modes. Although their aesthetic and theoretical orientations differ, they resonate with each other in the ways they engage the performance of raced, classed and gendered identities within the framework of Thatcherite Britain.

NGOZI ONWURAH: THE RHETORIC OF MARGINALISATION

Ngozi Onwurah's films consistently focus on the physical body as a site of agency and resistance to patriarchy (and the body politic). Her work has been contextualised within the work of African Diasporic filmmakers (Foster 1997: 24–42), and in terms of its relationship to European and North American avant-gardes (Williamson 1988: 110–12). Here, I want to discuss the ways that her films speak to the terms of performing citizenship in England for women and Afro-Britons during the Thatcher years. Her short films illuminate the lives of black Britons dealing with Conservative immigration and family policies, and notions of 'tradition', all of which contributed to marginalisation. These marginal positions become possible modes of citizenship that exist in contradictory or ambiguous relationships to 'official' citizenship in Britain.

In the 1980s, the British family became a cinematic locus of the state. Questions of identities were explored through films like *Distant Voices, Still Lives* (1988), a film that problematised the white, patriarchal family as a stable site for production of citizens. Mike Leigh's television and film work foregrounded issues of class and family. Television films like *Meantime* (1984) examined life on the dole, and *High Hopes* (1988) looked at class divisions within a family. Representations of a black British family or a mixed-race British family change the grounds of the question, indeed, alter the questions completely.

Two of Onwurah's short films, *Coffee Coloured Children* (1988) and *The Body Beautiful* (1990), present issues surrounding black British families' citizenship. They circumvent the notion of absolutist white/black duality in raced British identity and thereby create representations of the self that resist the easy categorisation of racial stereotypes. This breakdown of exclusive, dichotomous racial categories moves

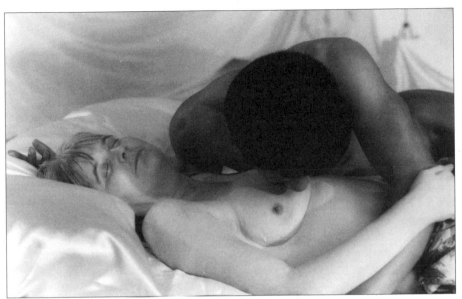

Madge Onwurah's (playing herself) reverie of a young black lover (Brian Bovell) transgresses conservative age and race mores in Ngozi Onwurah's *The Body Beautiful* (1990)

away from an '"essentialising ethnic absolutism" to a more "polyphonic" concept of identity; it marks a step toward the necessary suggestion that black art might begin from the documentation of constructed differences within the fundamental category of blackness' (Paul Gilroy, quoted in Longfellow 1992: 44).

Films that break apart the mythologised, essentialised notion of blackness dominating mainstream film help audiences see beyond the nominal categories of historical media stereotypes. This can help break up the ideological naturalisation that aligns 'whiteness' with 'full citizenship' and 'traditional British identity', a conceptualisation continuously reinforced by dominant cinema. Onwurah's autobiographical films deal with her mixed parentage and manage to resist another cultural and cinematic stereotype, the 'tragic mulatto' by using an amalgam of experimental, autobiographical and ethnographic elements (Foster 1997: 27).

The black family has been a primary site of resistance to oppression (Carby 1997: 46), a traditional source of black strength during the era of slavery, as well as in modern authoritarian states. The black family has also been pathologised by white culture and has served as a source of oppression for black women. *Coffee Coloured Children* depicts a single-parent, mixed-race family. The father is absent; the white mother lives alone with her two children in London. This fictionalised Onwurah family acts as a site for the negotiations of race and British citizenship, a series of compromises and bargains the director depicts as violent and frightening for the family. This film identifies the family as outsiders, as invaders of white Britain. This perception, one that the children must face every day of their lives, spurs them to shame and fosters a conviction that they are exiled from British culture, promoting the internalisation of self-hate which the film expresses in several painful sequences.

The film's syrupy, opening musical sequence presents the idea of multicultural Britain as a 'melting pot' in a utopian way that the rest of the film deconstructs. The manufactured joy of this musical opening contrasts sharply with the rest of the film, which draws upon incidents from Onwurah's childhood to demonstrate the difficulties she and her brother faced growing up in England. Their desire to be British fuses with their desire for whiteness. The film constructs this desire through a motif of shocking scenes that show the children scrubbing themselves with cleansers in an attempt to peel off their black skin. Another recurring image of the fictionalised Ngozi wearing a bridal veil simultaneously puts a white skin over her black face. This links the notion of a young woman's emerging concerns with adult beauty, marriage and family, to the idea of skin colour. These cinematic motifs create powerful images of complicated identities created by the children's oscillation between different groups. The type of mobile identity displayed by the children in this film visibly reminds viewers of the physical and mental dislocation that occurs in immigrant families. The actions of white Britons reaffirm the nomadic quality of immigrant identities and the ambiguous ways in which citizenship plays out in such communities. The children in *Coffee Coloured Children* are '*here*', that is in Britain. However, the acts of the white racists say 'You are *there*, you are not *here*, because here is a white territory and you cannot live here in the same way I can.' This type of dislocation promotes a sense of living in-between two communities, two countries and two worlds. It also denies the existence of the mother, seeing only the father in the children, a mis-recognition that reminds us of racism as a practice of white patriarchy.

Yet Onwurah does not leave the two children trapped in the stereotype of the tragic mulatto, who forever seeks an identity because he or she feels neither black nor white. By revealing the extreme pain of the children onscreen, Onwurah 'turns pain into agency. *Coffee Coloured Children* becomes a weapon against pain and further self-mutilation' (Foster 1997: 28). This agency occurs through the film's representation of the body as the site where the children can resist colonialist, racist ideologies. Onwurah's characters act out against these ideologies in the films as well. Near the end of the film, a young woman burns the wedding veil that she had earlier used as a white skin. This act constitutes a rejection of the trap of the mulatto and of self-hatred. It also symbolises a rejection of the ideologies of marriage and production of children. Gwendolyn Audrey Foster notes that Onwurah's female narrator rejects the circumstances that produce racially-mixed children by announcing that 'the father of my child will be black'. She identifies this as a radical gesture, one that rejects the 'melting pot' ideology and admits that this film cannot change the politics of race (1997: 28–9).

The film demonstrates how the children are repulsed and mocked by whites. White Britons define the 'status' of the Onwurah children as non-British, subhuman, and even 'mongrelised'. This dehumanisation and mongrelisation is made literal through a sequence in which a young white boy smears dog faeces on their apartment door and pushes some of it through the letterbox. The film crosscuts between the white boy's exterior point of view and that of the family inside the flat, watching the faeces being pushed through the letterbox. As the mother cleans the door, the female voiceover informs us that she would never let her children help her clean up after such incidents. The physical and psychological violence of this act establishes the terms within which the family lives. Ms Onwurah's refusal to allow her children to help with the cleaning becomes a maternal act of protection, perhaps one of the few ways she can isolate them from such racist attacks.

Abena Busia locates part of such racist aggression in a British desire to erase their reduced international status as a nation. Since Britain no longer can call itself an imperial power, racism against black British residents provides an outlet to ease such frustrations:

Looked at from anywhere other than a perilously racialised USA, Britain of the 1980s was not a place a black child would voluntarily go. The virulence of the aggression turned against all outsiders, in particular those associated with a faded, once imperial past reminds one more of the USA in the 1970s than the England of my childhood. (1998: 271)

Busia's statement reminds us of the neo-imperialism of the Thatcher era, including the Falklands crisis, as well as the economic policies of Thatcher's administration that encouraged the growth of a divided society with a decaying industrial base. John Hill cites Paul Gilroy's writings on the politics of whiteness during the Thatcher years, which promoted a 'growth of narrow English nationalism [that was] also apparent in the government's "populist" response to race and immigration in which Englishness was characteristically associated with whiteness' (Hill 1999: 15).

This situation provided 'fertile ground towards all those who are vulnerable' (Wilson 1987: 225). This vulnerability attaches to the Onwurah family in several ways. The Thatcher government promoted a political culture dominated by the notion that the family was the only social unit. In October 1987 Thatcher made her now-famous statement that 'There is no such thing as society: there are individual men and women, and there are families'. This rhetoric symbolically eliminates any other recognised institution that could protect families like the Onwurahs. The family becomes the only admitted social unit that could provide protection for the vulnerable women and children of the working classes. In these conditions, a black or mixed-race family was left exceedingly exposed as the target of violence. This economic background that prompted violence matched the public neo-imperialist rhetoric of Thatcher's government, a rhetoric that encouraged a return to notions of a time when a whites-only Britain ruled a large colonial empire. The assumptions of racial superiority that permeate this discourse only strengthen an attitude of racial division. The ideological stigmatisation of mixed-race and immigrant families enhanced their vulnerability to racial attack.

The family is vulnerable in another way as well. The father is absent; the female voiceover states that after her mother and she returned from Nigeria, they never lived as a family again. The film presents an image of a single-parent household. This resonates strongly with Thatcherite social policies concerning immigration and the family. During her tenure, two Immigration Acts (1981 and 1988) restricted immigration. The latter act restricted the rights of UK immigrants to bring family members into the country. By 1991 fewer than 30 per cent of households in the UK were made up of two-parent families. Yet Thatcher's rhetoric focused on 'traditional' family structures. Onwurah combats this cultural and political marginalisation by placing her family at the centre of the narrative.

Questions of identity and the body link *Coffee Coloured Children* and *The Body Beautiful*. Certain tropes recur, notably the present mother, the absent father and the use of the veil. Here, Onwurah transforms the veil from a symbolic wedding garment into an element of the setting, demonstrating another set of ways to look at veiling. The film concerns young Ngozi's relationship with her mother, Madge, who was diagnosed with breast cancer while pregnant with her second child. She refuses chemotherapy to avoid harming the foetus, and undergoes a mastectomy shortly after delivering her son. A few years later, Madge Onwurah develops rheumatoid arthritis. Onwurah uses her own feelings toward her mother and her mother's body to articulate questions about parent/child love and the idea of the mother as sexual being. However, this highly personal and intimate perspective on the family also constructs a politicised image of the mixed-race family through the mother/child dyad, and the film's depiction of racialised desire.

In *The Body Beautiful*, Madge Onwurah plays herself while the character of her daughter Ngozi is split through a visual portrayal by one actress and a voiceover done by another. The 'real' Ngozi remains distant to this personal narrative, hidden behind these two veilings. This dual device separates the highly intimate film from the author as a way of linking it to the larger political world, suggesting that the ideas raised through this narrative can be traced through society at large. The highly personal questions Onwurah poses in the film lead to the revelation that Britons see her only in terms of her father. The definition of a child by the father's status aligns race, gender and citizenship. Race trumps gender as a term of identity formation, and is revealed as the boundary beyond which the category 'British' does not venture. This statement also builds upon the idea of her 'beauty' and signifies the degree to which her body defines her in a patriarchal British society. She may be beautiful, but she is not British. Such definitions bring into play the exoticised roles often assigned to women of colour.

The understanding of her perception as 'black' like her father prompts the character to search for her mother within her. Mother and daughter represent the poles of gendered identity and desirability. The scarring of the mother's body complicates this representation; it is not only a consideration of race and age, but also a more complex unravelling of normative and non-normative physical desire. This leads to a deeper exploration of the ways that bodies can fix women's identities in Western culture. The film presents an episodic portrait of the two women's lives: Ngozi becomes a model, her mother grows older and experiences loneliness. The film explores the issue of loneliness and desire in older women through Madge's voiceover and an extended fantasy sequence of Madge making love to a younger black man.

While looking at a young black man in a café, Madge Onwurah launches into an elaborate sexual fantasy of herself with him. Onwurah shoots much of this sequence through a diaphanous drape, an extended veil that separates the spectator from the image. Through her fantasy, Madge re-enacts her younger self in love with her Nigerian husband, a legitimated married desire that nonetheless transgresses social customs because it crosses racial lines. It becomes, in terms of British citizenship and identity, a type of 'forbidden' desire. Madge Onwurah's ability to enact marriage as a citizen within Britain is difficult if not impossible to fit within the ideology of Thatcherite Britain. This symbolic re-enactment of her married desire should be one that the state promotes as lawful and necessary for begetting citizens.

Onwurah's use of the veil creates several readings for this part of the film. The Onwurahs' married desire produced the mixed-race children who are so 'difficult' for traditional 'white' Britons to recognise as British, so the desire needs to be veiled from sight. Veils also distort vision, representing ways we filter this desire through the racial categories rigidly aligned with British identity. We cannot 'see' this black/white desire without the visual/ideological 'noise'. This firmly places sexual desire within the political realm.

Foster discusses Onwurah's use of the veil as both a 'dialogised signifier of the shroud that silences black women's sexuality' and a 'liberating force, a reclamation of black female space, the female gaze, the scars of the body, and a new skin of self-ownership' (1997: 32). Veils also provide a type of visual 'hide and seek', a cinematic operation examined by Mary Ann Doane, who ruminates about the ways that relationships among several cultural discourses including psychoanalysis, cinema and philosophy structure our understanding of this trope. Her analysis of the veil is linked to the cinematic close-up, a framing that Onwurah largely ignores during this sequence. Doane's argument describes the close-up as the privileged shot in cinema giving access to the image's 'inner self'. A veiled close-up displaces this surface/depth relationship, and what was surface now becomes depth. Face equals soul for the veiled woman (1991: 48–50). Since Onwurah eschews the use of many close-ups, the play of surface and interior remains a distant, troubling image. The veil itself diminishes the spectacular voyeurism of such a sequence, and we are brought to a place where the desire acted out between the older white woman and the younger man becomes culturally difficult to 'see'. Also, the presence of the actual Madge Onwurah in the film creates an uncomfortable intimacy with the character and person's subjectivity – one that audiences may not desire. The veil reduces this intimacy, since it disguises and softens the impact of the images.

Veils also reclaim space. Trinh T. Minh-ha analyses the act of unveiling as one that defies male oppression, while the act of reclaiming the veil can 're-appropriate their space or claim a new difference, in defiance of genderless hegemonic standardisation' (1991: 151). This gives yet another meaning to the veil in this scene. The space enclosed by the veil is a site of resistance in which Onwurah stakes a claim for sexual desire expressed by the character of Madge Onwurah. This use of the veil refutes the idea of transgression, defined by dominant ideologies of race, gender and age, and creates an autonomous space for the character to act in self-defined ways.

The cinematic use of the veil by Onwurah *inverts* the surface/depth relationship when applied in the political context of black/white sexual desire. In the case of Madge Onwurah, her wounded body (surface) has been erroneously assumed to be her substance, her essence. It has become her identity, just as daughter Ngozi's beauty and skin colour are assumed to define her. While such judgements are not the province of only black or only white women, in the case of the Onwurah women, they stamp their position as outside of English society. This positioning fixes the types of citizen-relations that the woman can construct and enact. It is not only Madge Onwurah's scars and age that make her unable to fill the role of a desired lover, but it is her skin colour itself within this particular fantasy relationship and within her marriage. Onwurah 'inverts the traditional European gaze that seeks to encase the body of women, and black women in particular, in an exotic mask, a clinical shroud of medical discourse, and a fetishised object in fashion discourse' (Foster 1997: 33).

In the film, the daughter comes to recognise her mother as a woman and a sexual being. This pierces the veil of familial roles. It is an interesting response to the Thatcher years, as the government's public pronouncements on sexual behaviour and mores contained an attempt to remove the family from the 'unsettling realm of sexuality … This is in line with Thatcher's acknowledgement of the family as the only social unit, which carries the entire weight of socialisation, that is, conservative adaptation to the status quo' (McNeil 1991: 233). Onwurah reinstates the sexual dimension of the family through the progress of mother/daughter interactions. Autonomous female desire cannot exist within this definition of the family, because the woman's function is to contain any potentially disruptive sexuality by socialising and 'taming' male desire. The images of Madge Onwurah enjoying a sexual encounter with a younger man deny this particular conservative construction of the family in gendered as well as raced terms.

The recognition of her mother as a woman begins in a sequence where the 17-year-old Ngozi and her mother visit a sauna. Except for Madge, all the women in the sauna expose their breasts. Madge's point-of-view shots display her look at the other women's 'whole' bodies. Madge firmly holds her towel to her chest; however, the heat relaxes her into sleep and the towel slips to her waist. A series of reaction shots reveals the women's politely modulated shock at the sight of Madge's scar and her missing breast. One woman leaves. Madge quickly replaces her towel, watched closely by young Ngozi. The daughter's voiceover says that this is the first time she thought of her mother as a woman. Her mother's body, ravaged by arthritis, scarred by cancer, is opposed visually to re-enactments of Ngozi's modelling career. The contrast between the fashion world's acclamations of Ngozi's beauty versus the 'revulsion' with which people view her mother's scar emphasises the body's inextricable link to social definitions of women.

The absence of a breast also signifies the lack of nurturing, an abrupt division from the ability to 'mother', to provide literal sustenance. This highly personal trope simultaneously represents a significant part of the way women in Thatcherite Britain are related to the familial sphere of activity. This in turn, has to be placed within Thatcherite constructions of family and its relation to the state (see Mary Dejardins' essay in this volume for further resonances). The motifs of nurturance and mother/daughter identification are brought to a type of closure at the film's end. Mother and daughter lie entwined on a bed. The voiceover speaks of the recognition of the mother/daughter bond as internal, spiritual and psychological: 'My mother is mirrored in my soul … I am my mother's daughter for the rest of my life.'

Onwurah's work courageously explores the issues that face a mixed-race child in Britain through fictionalised versions of her own family's experience. Her films demonstrate the powerful and detrimental effects that rhetoric and social policy visits on real people.

PRATIBHA PARMAR: VISIBILITY AND SELF-REPRESENTATION

Parmar's films range widely over feminist issues: gay and lesbian identity, immigration and racism. Like Ngozi Onwurah, Parmar, who was born in Nigeria and emigrated to Britain in 1967, provides keen insights on the issues facing immigrant women living in Britain. Her 1990 film *Flesh and Paper* links to earlier works like *Emergence* (1986) through the use of the formal device of an artist reading her own words. The spoken word attains a prominent place in these films, and the use of the verbal realm marks the films' alignment of the idea of physical movement (migration) with storytelling as a mobile form of ideas that articulates nomadic identities.

Parmar's *Flesh and Paper* is a short-form biopic using the idea of journeying to investigate the relationship between the material life and the life of the mind. This film, along with other Parmar works like *Reframing AIDS* (1987), *Memory Pictures* (1989) and *Khush* (1991), was made as part of the lesbian/gay television series *Out on Tuesday* (Foster 1997: 81). It tells the story of Indian author Suniti Namjoshi, who studied in North America and moved to Britain in her forties to begin a relationship with writer Gillian Hanscombe. Initially, Hanscombe and Namjoshi met at a women's conference, and then continued a relationship through letters and the exchange of poems before beginning a life together in Britain.

In one scene, the two women read a type of 'call and response' poem that deals with the way they negotiate differences between their countries of origin. Namjoshi says, 'We can compose ourselves but it's our bodies, not our passports, fit so uncommonly well.' This line articulates the physicality of the relationship between the women, while also reminding the viewer that their national identities are not so harmonious in the political sphere. The poem does not articulate any friction between the two women in terms of their mutual political lives. It recalls the barriers between England and India, the heritage of the colonial past, and the way that these two lovers define themselves through their own interchanges, not through their 'national' identities. It implies a successful negotiation of the power relations between white women and black women; it bespeaks a deconstruction of the old colonialist relations between white English women and Indian women. The poem may also hide an implicit warning that the personal realm should be walled off from the public realm, in which they, as a 'mixed-race', lesbian couple would be perceived as transgressive. The poem's context, the movement of their relationship from paper – the letters they exchanged – to flesh, and the editing of the women sitting harmoniously side by side, points toward a more optimistic reading of the line.

One of Namjoshi's readings reminds us of the everyday reality of immigrants, of the insults and unpleasant incidents while living in a country that identifies them as aliens. Namjoshi reads the story of a cow named Suniti, who resents the attempts of the 'British' cows to Anglicise her name to 'Sue'. Suniti refuses this, an act that stakes her claim to define herself. This act contains a myriad of issues for immigrants. Assimilation, identity and marginalisation by the culture of one's 'new' country all play out in this interchange. Namjoshi intensifies our understanding of this in an interview where she reveals the casual, unthinking racism and patronising attitudes she encountered while in the United States. She recounts a visit to a fellow student's home, where the father complimented her on her white teeth. She did not realise the implications of that comment at the time, thinking it was only social talk. Later, she realised its racist implications.

Interviews with Asian-British women articulate the appreciation that they feel for Namjoshi's works. Crucially, it allows them to find something of themselves; equally important it is written by someone who looks like them, one helping to shape public discourse by giving a voice to a type of multivalent nomadic identity. One mentions how nice it was to find works of literature that were not by white heterosexual men. This comment is followed by one who expresses her happiness at seeing Namjoshi as 'an Indian woman writer presenting herself and the characters in her stories as lesbians'. Such interviews demonstrate that the young women eagerly identify with Namjoshi's life and words. The act of putting this on film allows such identifications wider scope, and it promotes a public realisation of the lack of such images in mainstream culture. Films like *Flesh and Paper* clarify the degree to which entire political classes and their specific issues are often omitted from everyday media representation.

These comments precede one of the scenes featuring a traditionally-garbed Indian dancer, a motif affirming Namjoshi's subjectivity as an Asian lesbian living in Britain. Though this type of image often draws criticism for reinforcing the exoticism of a white colonialist gaze, the scenes of the dancer must be considered within the context of this particular film; a single scene does not exist in isolation, but must be interpreted in the context of surrounding audio-visual materials. The film's discursive construction of a strong pride in one's identity suppresses such a reading. It recasts the dancer's image as a validation of the author, not a reduction of her to a colonialist stereotype.

A brief close-up of Namjoshi provides a transition to the dancer's scene, and situates the dancer within her gaze, not the gaze of the colonial Westerner. Namjoshi provides voiceover: 'In that particular temple, a god slept and a goddess danced. In another temple, a goddess slept and a god danced.' Parmar's editing precludes the gaze of white heterosexual men (mentioned in the literary context above), instead substituting the subjective gaze of Namjoshi as the structure for the following images. This sequence opens up a wonderfully complex idea of identity not only expressed in words (on paper), but also through the material bodies of women – the young Asian women and Namjoshi herself (flesh).

Parmar's films invoke the return of the gaze, an element noted by Foster, who discusses the way that Parmar's films create a 'look back' from the subaltern that disturbs colonialised race relations (1997: 75). The return of a look from the colonised disturbs the balance of power, disrupts the 'dream' or 'fable' of race and colonialism that sustains social relations between colonisers and colonised. For the coloniser, this would indeed result in the chaos referred to in the voiceover, as the mis-recognition practiced upon the colonised would be denied. Such a denial would render chaotic the fabular world of the coloniser, who believes that s/he has the unchallenged and inherent right to assign places to the colonised.

This task of disrupting the gaze, of inverting and destroying stereotypes, still largely falls to independent and experimental filmmakers working alongside, or at the margins of, major media industries. Although international media coverage of formerly colonised nations may seem to be ubiquitous, little attention is paid to cultural specificity of Third World countries; basically, the form of coverage simply echoes and recycles the familiar formats of Western media, without providing a true information flow from other countries. Neither has increased media attention meant the discarding of stereotypes. As Robert Stam and Ella Shohat argue, 'if postmodernism has spread the telematic feel of First World media around the world, in sum, it has hardly deconstructed the relations of power that marginalise, devalue and time and time again massacre otherised people and cultures' (1994: 131). Parmar's films speak back to these relations of power by making visible what was not seen.

SALLY POTTER: CULTURAL DISCLOSURE AND REPOSITIONING

Sally Potter has worked in both experimental film and art-house narrative, of which *Orlando* (1992) is perhaps the best known, and also produced a body of work for television during the 1980s. Her films rewrite the political contexts that mainstream narrative films construct for women characters. This creates new stories about women who refuse traditional roles, and questions the assumption of mainstream cinema's insistence on males as central figures controlling both the narrative and the visuals. Potter's works achieve a great deal of power through their placement within the context of Thatcher's contradictory status in relation to feminism. Potter's work has been reasonably well explored by a large number of film theorists over the years, and her role in the construction of feminist avant-garde narrative cinema is well established. Despite this familiarity with her work, its questioning of specific positions of British women under Thatcherite policies justifies its inclusion in this discussion.

Thriller (1979), a well-known experimental short film, uses feminist counter-cinema techniques to rewrite the narrative of the 1830 Puccini opera *La Boheme*. E. Ann Kaplan identifies Potter as one of the foremost women filmmakers who used new feminist theories focusing on the definition of woman as Other, on the exclusion of women from language, and on construction of sexual difference through the Oedipal process as read by Lacan for feminist film theory in the late 1970s and 1980s. Kaplan emphasises that *Thriller*'s importance lies not just in the way it looks at individuals psychoanalytically, but then progresses to looking at these individuals' social placement (1981/82: 115). The opera's romanticisation of the poor seamstress

Mimi (Colette Laffont) investigates the narrative justifications for her fate in Sally Potter's *Thriller* (1979)

Mimi, who dies of tuberculosis, receives a thorough, vigorous questioning in this film. *Thriller* refuses to assign a traditional place to the female character. Mimi wonders why she had to die and investigates her own 'murder'.

This act of female investigation questions culturally-assigned roles given to women in Western culture's film practice, and the way that mainstream film's construction produces a strong sense of closure for the narrative and the cultural placements of female characters. Potter disrupts *Thriller*'s narrative drive toward closure by the use of stills and prevents a strong cultural closure about 'Mimi' by dividing the character into two portrayals using two actresses: Collette Lafonte, who is black and Rose English, who is white. This displaces the unified white, consumptive heroine whose emaciated form epitomised Romantic ideals of death, morbid beauty and unattainable love. The presence of Lafonte queries the notion of the centrality of white women as objects of desire, and possible subjects of agency. Although Lafonte's Mimi does not overtly speak about race in the ways she speaks about work, romantic love and other female mythologies, her visual presence problematises the idea of the white heroine in Western cinema.

This doubled, fractured Mimi becomes the active central character in her own story, refusing to accept the passive role of dying love object. She questions why she must die, even reading French structuralists to see if they can help her understand her own fate. The Lafonte version of Mimi points out that although she is viewed as a romanticised opera heroine, she is a worker whose labour produces the gowns of both the singers onstage and the wealthy women who adorn the audience. The romantic image obscures her class status. The men see her only as a frail and romantic dying heroine, not as a labourer. Her hidden working-class status is linked to the way the narrative encourages the male characters – and the audience – to see the seamstress. Mimi herself is a product of the romantic narrative, one the men 'consume' as a romantic ideal. Her death closes the romantic adventure with a working-class woman and frees the male characters to find another woman, in another narrative.

Trinh T. Minh-ha defines the cultural need for films with a high degree of closure in terms of consumption: 'The commercial and ideological habits of our society favour narrative with as definite a closure as possible; once the narration is consumed one can throw it away and move on to buy another one' (1991: 147). *Thriller* short-circuits the narrative closure and, by so doing, creates a space in which Mimi refuses to die of consumption, or by being consumed by the audience. It is significant, however, that neither the men nor the audience overtly consider the racial specificity of Lafonte's Mimi. She does make visible something that mainstream cinema has suppressed – the black woman as narrative centre; however, the film does not follow this line of argumentation any further.

Finally, Mimi articulates an alternative ending, one that depends upon surviving the illness. She would grow old, get married, be worn out by childbirth, and be forced to work even harder as a seamstress to support her children. This ending is also indeterminate; it simply continues the narrative line throughout a hypothetical 'life'. None of this, Mimi says, would be 'romantic'. The voiceover emphasises the narrow scope and romantic nature of Western film narrative, its images of women characters, and its embrace of a fantasy world of romance in place of the everyday work of life and human relationships.

Potter's strategies transfer to an analysis of political culture. The theoretical basis for this transference lies in the historical exclusion of women from central places in relation to forces of production, an exclusion that undermined women's social power. This has an 'epiphenomenal counterpart in the female image associated with perennial culture-myths, which are ideological projection of existing social economies' (Gilburt 1973: 5). Under Conservative governments, the continued, heavy emphasis on family values creates a narrative for British women that no longer describes the place of women in society. It is, in fact, one that disguises or devalues the labour of women. As mentioned, Thatcher's policies brought into direct public question the value of labour traditionally identified as 'women's work', such as social workers and teachers who often were stigmatised as part of the problem of creating a 'soft' generation of underclass who demanded benefits instead of becoming heroic individual entrepreneurs. *Thriller* points out the insidious potential of narratives to cover over the social significance of women's lives and confine them to passive stereotypes.

BEEBAN KIDRON: FEMINIST THEORY IN PRACTICE

During the 1980s, Beeban Kidron worked in both British film and television industries. Her documentary, *Carry Greenham Home* covers one instance of Thatcher-era women's political action. The film provides a concrete example of how feminist political action can challenge a society dominated by patriarchal institutions. The Women's Peace Camp at Greenham Common was founded by a group of women who formed around a 'Women For Life on Earth' march from Cardiff to the United States Air Force base at Greenham in 1981. The camp was an ongoing settlement that lasted several years and inspired several Greenham peace groups in British cities over the next two years (Kirk 1989: 267). Greenham actions continued through the 1980s. By 1990, the cruise missiles had been removed from the base and two years later, the government declared the military base redundant. The area is now part of a Greenham Common Trust.

Kidron and fellow filmmaker Amanda Richardson lived at the camp for several months. The documentary they produced has been primarily identified as the observational mode, as defined by Bill Nichols (1991: 38–44). This mode of documentary film takes shape around a repetitive series of representations of the everyday actions of its protagonists. The repeated scenes of the women at the demonstration build up a kind of 'reality effect' over the documentary's running time and guarantee that we are seeing significant, yet representative, moments of the event.

Kidron shot a variety of actions: camp scenes, demonstrators entering the Greenham Common Missile Base, demonstrators outside a court where some of their number are being tried, camp meetings and foreign journalists talking with the protestors. Her choice of documentary mode establishes these events as typical of the women's lengthy political action. The film claims to illuminate the women's daily routine, as well as its significance, to the peace cause and to feminist politics. Barbara Harford and Sarah Hopkins, two of the peace activists who edited the volume *Greenham Common: Women at the Wire* (1984). describe the action in these terms: 'Within male-dominated society, male-dominated institutions and stereotyped male values have determined how all our resources will be used ... a military/industrial complex that cultivates racial fear to boost profits for a fast-expanding armaments trade.' This identifies how a women's peace movement challenges not only the ideologies of war, but also those of patriarchal capitalism and politics.

Gwyn Kirk amplifies how the Greenham Common Women's Group actions were an example of feminist theory in practice. She lists a number of principles of non-violent organisation that operate in the women's camp: personal responsibility, the value of diversity, non-hierarchical organisation and decision-making, communication, coordination and continuity across a wide network, and the value of flexibility (1989: 263). Kidron and Richardson's documentary testifies to the practice of these values through the selection of representative scenes of daily camp life and political actions.

The documentary also gives evidence of the overwhelmingly white involvement in this women's peace action. Harford and Hopkins' study of the Greenham Peace Actions admits that it began as a 'predominantly white, middle-class, heterosexual women's movement', but became one that involved more working-class and lesbian women. They note that by 1983, they were 'beginning to have dialogue with women of colour', and that the labels that divide women are being challenged together with the institutions that promote these divisions. Kidron's film does not focus on women of colour. The class status of women depicted in the film remains obscure, especially to viewers outside Britain who may not be able to read embedded social and verbal codes that function as class indicators.

Women of colour critiqued the political action itself. Pratibha Parmar and Valerie Amos analysed the whiteness of the peace movement in Britain as an indicator that their actions and demands have excluded any understanding or sensitivity to black and Third World women's situations. Their analysis rests upon the fact that black and Third World women around the world fight daily for survival at very basic levels, for food and other necessities of life. The authors point out that in confronting 'for the first time the brutality of the British police [the women] are slowly realising why many black women are not willing to deliberately expose themselves to it when it is an everyday occurrence for them, anyway' (1997: 57).

An opening title informs us that the film begins fifteen months after the start of the protest. Kidron uses titles sparingly throughout the film, to identify certain political actions taken by the women, or to note that some of the women were sent to jail for disturbing the peace. This type of documentary gives little historical or political context about the Women's Peace Camp, or how this action at Greenham Common relates to the larger Women's Peace Movement. For viewers lacking memory of the 1980s, this lack of context diminishes some of the film's impact.

Kidron's choice of approach still offers rewards for the viewer, however. Incidents depicted include a variety of daily camp activities, such as financial and strategy meetings, cooking, caring for a pregnant camper, and communal singing of protest songs. These intimate scenes reveal a strong mutual commitment among the women and the way their mutual solidarity for their cause of nuclear disarmament sustains them through both serious and mundane trials of daily living. The scenes of the women's passive protests, where they do not resist the police who arrest them, emphasises their willingness to take personal responsibility for their political actions.

The accessibility of this documentary approach opens itself to the criticism that it reproduces reality as if it was transparent and, therefore, naturalises the dominant system of representations used to reaffirm patriarchal culture. This issue was central to the debate around representation that occurred in feminist film theory, and realist cinema differs from the counter-cinema approach to filmmaking, which holds the position that it is not enough to show women's actions against oppression on film. Instead, counter-cinema proposed strategies to undermine the politics of the dominant system of visual representation. Kidron and Richardson's film illustrates a second position on feminist filmmaking, one that focused on the ability of audiences to comprehend feminist films.

B. Ruby Rich proposed an alternative classification for films such as *Carry Greenham Home* in 1978. Rich proposed a set of categories for films produced by women that would keep the term 'feminist' from being overused to the point of meaninglessness. Her taxonomy also keeps women's film work from being placed in pre-existing categories, an act of naming that separates the film from other feminist work. One of her names, the 'validative' film, applies to this documentary. A validative film works as a 'legitimation of women's culture and individual lives … it aligns the work with products of oppressed peoples', with the filmmaker as insider (1990: 280). Rich argues that the various *cinema verité* labels, one of which is Nichols' term 'observational documentary', aligns the filmmaker with the exterior observer, 'the oppressing culture' (ibid.). Rich's term suits this work much better than Nichols, as it gives a sense of the position of the women filmmakers that is absent from Nichols' terminology. This term also clarifies the place of this documentary within the context of feminist work.

The film's aesthetics make it accessible, a quality that was a high priority for many feminist documentarians. Julia Lesage points out that feminist filmmakers saw their work as an 'urgent public act' (1999: 223). This documentary, then, is not an exploration of women's psyches, but a record of a group of women who redefine experience to 'challenge the previously accepted indices of "male superiority" and of women's supposedly "natural" roles' (1999: 224). In this sense, the form chosen by Kidron and Richardson acts not only as a record, but as testimony, or in filmmaker Joris Ivens' earlier term, temoignage, to the political point of view of the protestors and filmmakers.

Some discussions incorporated in the film reveal how the practice of feminist daily politics occurs in daily life. At a group meeting, a woman objects to the agenda, stating that some urgent interpersonal issues need to be discussed. When the group decides to remain on the agenda, a couple of women leave as a response to perceived 'insensitivity'. The somewhat detached style of the documentary gives the encounter a low-key quality. No close-ups create dramatic emphasis or heighten tension for the viewer. The lack of emotional intensification helps spectators to look at this as a problem of group interaction, rather than an individualised one-on-one interpersonal situation. This illustrates Lesage's point that these films do not explore individual female psyches.

A title explains that the women of the camp decided to meet in smaller groups in order to address the concerns of some members that their voices were not being heard. The women find a way to balance sensitivity and efficiency in running the camp. This footage addresses a specific concern of the women's movement: how to handle conflict without resorting to patriarchal models. The action of conflict-solving mirrors the larger one of the Peace Action itself, illustrating the way that the women's movement sought to connect the personal and the political.

A series of scenes depicts a large number of individual non-violent actions that demonstrate the scope of the group's political action. Scenes show various groups of women threading the word 'Peace' into the chain-link gate surrounding the Greenham Common Base, sneaking onto the base for a picnic, painting banners, doing sit-ins in front of the gates, singing as they are carted off by police, and keeping a vigil outside the courtroom where members of the group are on trial for breaking the peace. All these actions inform us of the strategies used by the women to draw attention to their cause and peacefully to disrupt the 'business' of the base.

Kidron's film convincingly displays the women's commitment and the range of responses to their lengthy encampment: stoicism, exhaustion, apathy, despair, hope and communal joy. The film validates the women's political experiences, as viewers can examine the daily activities that make up the life of a dedicated peace activist. Through this film, audiences begin to understand the group's commitment and purpose. *Carry Greenham Home* performs a valuable function of bringing the messages of the Greenham women to us twenty years later.

CONCLUSION: PERSONAL EXPLORATIONS AND IDEOLOGICAL CRITIQUES

These films are samples of the responses of filmmakers to government policies and the ideologies underpinning them during the Thatcher era. The multiple forms employed by women filmmakers during this turbulent time construct a set of ideological critiques of the Conservative government's policies that affected the position of women as citizens of Britain. Although no one film addresses all the issues of a feminist critique, as a group these productions do articulate race and class as well as gender. Understanding the context of British political life and the specificities of cultural circumstances illuminates our understandings of even the more abstract experimental films that focus on women's issues. It is also true that the lack of race and class analysis that was felt to prevent truly adequate feminist analysis of the Thatcher governments' impact on women also exists in some of the feminist cinemas operating at the time and, consequently, widens the gaps of misunderstandings among groups of women. The issues that divide women as well as those that unite them needed to be dealt with – and often were ignored.

These films range from intensely personal explorations of how political policies impact upon women's lives (*Coffee Coloured Children*) to validation of women's place in the public political sphere and in resistance to patriarchally-defined institutions (*Carry Greenham Home*). These films yield an alternative set of visions for women's 'place' in public life, one not defined by policymakers and government institutions, but on the ground by women every day.

The documentary and avant-garde films constitute new semiotic maps of territories within Thatcher's Britain: ones of resistance and reclamation. Thatcherite rhetoric assigned women to retrogressive positions within the nation. These films refuse to accept the 'exception-unexceptional' categorising used by the Prime Minister. These films refute Thatcher's assertion that women who have 'not made the grade as men' (Nunn 2002: 40) need to succeed on those terms. These films also perform other important work by linking political policy to daily lives of women outside the upper classes. They express a range of intellectual and emotional responses both to those specific policies, such as the cruise missiles at Greenham, or immigration policy, as well as to the ideologies that underpin women's existence in Britain. This rebuts Thatcher rhetoric that suppressed women as a political class.

The films of Onwurah, Parmar, Potter and Kidron also examine ways that mainstream media usually validate political and cultural mythologies through a range of cinematic strategies. They resist these representations, establishing other cinematic images of women and forms of narrative that raise alternatives to these myths. Value accrues from the success of these films to speak about women in ways that do not fit the contemporary ideologies of Thatcherism. Women's films also create a powerful set of non-traditional narratives that cannot be consigned to the past. All the films discussed in this essay represent specific ways that feminist struggles are ongoing. They resist the idea that feminism is done! Family, race, labour and peace issues – all these appear definitively within the domain of feminist thought expressed in these works.

Parmar's and Onwurah's films also speak to the place of 'the body' within feminist film criticism and practice. Situating women's bodies within discourses of age, class, race and immigration, their films re-affirm the idea of women's bodies as 'sites of political struggle' (Mulvey 1989: xii), an issue that informed early feminist practice. Without such context, the 'body' runs the risk of becoming a phantasm constructed only in feminist theory. Clearly, by creating and strengthening diversity within feminist film practice, these films resist the notion that women can be essentialised, homogenised and contained within political and cultural positions deemed appropriate by Conservative governments.

WORKS CITED

Barrett, Michele (1988) *Women's Oppression Today*, second edition. London: Verso.

Busia, Abena P. A. (1998) 'Relocations – Rethinking Britain from Accra, New York, and the Map Room of the British Museum', in David Bennett (ed.) *Multicultural States: Rethinking Difference and Identity*. London: Routledge, 267–81.

Carby, Hazel V. (1997) 'White woman listen!', in Heidi Safia Mirza (ed.) *Black British Feminism: A Reader*. London: Routledge, 45–53.

Doane, Mary Ann (1991) *Femmes Fatales: Feminism, Film Theory, Psychoanalysis*. London: Routledge.

Femenia, Nora (1996) *National Identity in Times of Crises: The Scripts of the Falklands-Malvinas War*. Cormack, NY: Nova Science Publishers.

Foster, Gwendolyn Audrey (1997) *Women Filmmakers of the African and Asian Diaspora*. Carbondale: Southern Illinois University Press.

Gilburt, Naome (1973) 'To Be Our Own Muse: The Dialectics of a Culture-Heroine', in Claire Johnston (ed.) *Screen* Pamphlet 2. London: Society for Education in Film and Television, 5–13.

Gilroy, Paul (1987) *There Ain't No Black in the Union Jack*. Chicago: University of Chicago Press.

Hall, Stuart (1988) *The Hard Road to Renewal: The Crisis of Thatcherism*. London: Verso.

Harford, Barbara and Sarah Hopkins (eds) (1984) *Greenham Common: Women at the Wire*. London: The Women's Press.

Hill, John (1999) *British Cinema in the 1980s*. Oxford: Clarendon Press.

Johnston, Claire (1973) 'Women's Cinema as Counter-Cinema', in Claire Johnston (ed.) *Screen* Pamphlet 2. London: Society for Education in Film and Television, 24–31.

Kaplan, E. Ann (1981/82) 'Night at the Opera: Investigating the Heroine in Sally Potter's *Thriller*', *Millennium*, 10/11, 115–22.

Kirk, Gwyn (1989) 'Our Greenham Common: A Movement', in Adrienne Harris and Ynestra King (eds) *Rocking the Ship of State: Toward a Feminist Peace Politics*. Boulder, CO: Westview Press, 263–80.

Kuhn, Annette (1982) *Women's Pictures: Feminism and Cinema*. London: Routledge & Kegan Paul.

Lesage, Julia (1999) 'The Political Aesthetics of the Feminist Documentary Film', in Patricia Erens (ed.) *Issues in Feminist Film Criticism*. Bloomington: Indiana University Press, 222–37.

Longfellow, Brenda (1992) 'The Body Beautiful', *Cineaction*, 30, Winter, 43–7.

McNeil, Maureen (1991) 'Making and Not Making the Difference: The Gender Politics of Thatcherism', in Sarah Franklin, Celia Lury and Jackie Stacey (eds) *Off-Centre: Feminism and Cultural Studies*. London: Birmingham Cultural Studies, HarperCollins, 221–40.

Minh-ha, Trinh T. (1991) *When the Moon Waxes Red*. London: Routledge.

Mulvey, Laura (1989 [1975]) 'Visual Pleasure and Narrative Cinema', in *Visual and Other Pleasures*. Bloomington: Indiana University Press, 14–26.

Nichols, Bill (1991) *Representing Reality*. Bloomington: Indiana University Press.

Nunn, Heather (2002) *Thatcher, Politics and Fantasy: The Political Culture of Gender and Nation*. London: Lawrence & Wishart.

Pilkington, Andrew (2003) *Racial Disadvantage and Ethnic Diversity in Britain*. New York: Palgrave MacMillan.

Parmar, Pratibha and Valerie Amos (1997) 'Challenging Imperial Feminism', in Heidi Safia Mirza (ed.) *Black British Feminism: A Reader*. London: Routledge, 54–8.

Rich, B. Ruby (1990) 'In the Name of Feminist Film Criticism', in Patricia Erens (ed.) *Issues in Feminist Film Criticism*. Bloomington: Indiana University Press, 222–37.

Stam, Robert and Ella Shohat (1994) *Unthinking Eurocentrism Multiculturalism and the Media*. London: Routledge.

Williamson, Judith (1988) 'Two Kinds of Otherness: Black Film and the Avant-Garde', *Screen*, 29, 4, 106–12.

Wilson, Elizabeth (1987) 'Thatcherism and Women: After Seven Years', *The Socialist Register*, London: Merlin Press, 199–235.

10. WOMEN'S INDEPENDENT CINEMA: THE CASE OF LEEDS ANIMATION WORKSHOP

Antonia Lant

From the vantage point of the United States the contours of independent British film production in the 1980s appeared narrower than was the case. Economic, technological and cultural factors all contributed to restricted distribution and exhibition patterns in the US, and while American festivals often screened British films, rental agreements rarely followed. Americans, for example, can book Sally Potter's *Thriller* (1979), *The Gold Diggers* (1983), *The London Story* (1987), and films by some of the London-based black workshops (Sankofa and Black Audio Film/Video Collective); but no North American distributors exist for Pat Murphy's *Maeve* (1981) and *Anne Devlin* (1984), feature-length films partially funded by the British Film Institute (BFI) and made in the Republic of Ireland, or for the work of animator Vera Neubauer, or for regional workshops such as Amber Films in Newcastle, or Leeds Animation Workshop (LAW).[1]

Narrow US distribution obscured the breadth of this cinema, but its invisibility also bore the imprint of underlying strata of constraint originating within Britain. Independent cinema distribution is in trouble there, too; at the time of writing the status of Circles and Cinema of Women, the two main British feminist distributors, was changing, and they now may have merged to form Cinenova. Difficulties of national distribution are amplified internationally on other grounds; the lengths, genres, styles, quality and regional character of much filmmaking separates it from an American public. While features remain the standard product for cinema circuits, female feature directors number but few – Lezli-Ann Barrett, Laura Mulvey, Jan Worth, Beeban Kidron, Sally Potter. No British equivalents of Susan Seidelman, Kathryn Bigelow or Penny Marshall exist. No women directed within the admittedly modest commercial sector in the 1980s.[2] When the price of shorts (which women have more frequently made) is also substantial, the reasons for the scarcity of women's films, made or seen, at home and abroad begin to emerge with a vengeance (Merz 1987: 67).

Besides the 'inconvenient' (that is, varied) lengths of women's films, their content may be illegible or uninteresting overseas. The inspirational dictum of the 1970s – 'the personal is political' – has had a powerful corollary: the personal is also local, tied to specific audiences with specific knowledges. Murphy's *Anne Devlin* draws on the folk memory of an Irish heroine and the racism and other strains of Anglo-Irish relations (Gibbons 1986); Creel Films' *It's A' Oor Ain* (1985) concerns Musselburgh miners and women's support groups during the 1984–85 miners' strike, while their *It's Handed Doon* (1986) is a drama/documentary about Fisherow fishwives whose creels (handwoven baskets) carry fish from market to customers; LAW's *Council Matters* presents the arcane structures of a local authority via cutout and cel-animated conversations between an enquiring girl and a latter-day cleaner-cum-witch.

Such films speak to audiences' encounters with the politics of strikes, unemployment and local law and lore, in familiar dialects and landscapes. The regionalism of these works is one of their strengths – the cinema requires an informed audience, in which both film and viewer reverberate with local questions and experience, building audience loyalty and a regional culture of sorts.[3] But this cinema can never translate into a wider purview – the film arena of the United States – and still remain the same.[4] There it risks not being read at all.

The British television market has also shaped distribution patterns for independent cinema; televisual transmission and video rental became its dominant outlet in 1980s Britain.[5] In 1982, with the arrival of Channel 4, a quota of independent film broadcasting was mandated, and became programmed into the regular schedule, most notably in the 'Eleventh Hour' slot, that eponymous, off-peak night-time niche. The early 1980s also saw a meteoric rise in the number of home videocassette recorders in the United Kingdom, swelling from 2.5 per cent of households in December 1980 to 51 per cent in December 1986, and accompanied by further declines in the number of cinemagoers (Lewis 1990: 57). While television, and particularly Channel 4, has been crucial to the survival of British cinema in the 1980s, it has inadvertently often had a countereffect on the international distribution of independent film, because of TV station attitudes that once a film has been aired, its chief, visible life is over. Preparing work for television also affects aesthetic decisions, making a work potentially unsuccessful on 16mm, let alone on 35mm.[6] Lastly, the video modes in the United Kingdom and the United States – PAL and NTSC – are incompatible, prohibiting the export (and, incidentally, the pirating) of tapes without some effort and cost.

The somewhat impoverished picture of independent filmmaking visible across the Atlantic – resulting from the reasons outlined above – belies a unique and distinctive period of production in Britain, especially in the workshop sector. Women have participated in this 'brave cultural experiment', which has now ended (Lovell 1990: 102). Its demise signals one consequence of Thatcherite economic policies, with their emphasis on privatisation, individual consumerism and 'enterprise culture' in which the arts and museums have to run on a profit basis or be subsidised by private monies rather than by citizens' taxes, and in which local authority funds for the arts have been massively cut.[7] Paradoxically the Workshop Movement, emergent in the early 1970s, thrived in the 1980s, on the Association of Cinematograph, Television and Allied Technicians (ACTT) Workshop Declaration (a pact directly funding independent cinema), on monies from metropolitan county councils (including the Greater London Council, which was 'pioneering a new relationship between power and the people' (Hall 1988: 126)), and on the enthusiasm and needs of community activism, rallying around political causes such as the Greenham Peace Camp and the miners' strike. These social actions politicised new groups of women and mobilised cinema and video: *The Miners' Campaign Tapes*, for example, were made through workshop cooperation to spread information and raise funds.

This social network atrophied with the decade. Fewer unofficial community groups came to meet, a result of the privatisation of people as much as property under Thatcher (Leadbeater 1990: 143). LAW's film *Home and Dry?* (1987) states the undermining impact of government policy in bald terms: 'The Government wants us to buy our own houses – once we have a mortgage, we aren't as free to strike.' The landslide Conservative victory of 1983, the defeat of the miners' strike in 1985, the abolition of the metropolitan councils in 1986, and the effective dismantling of the Workshop Declaration in 1991, besides transforming audiences into separate persons, gradually sapped the independent filmmaking sector, even if, in Sean Cubitt's words, 'the taste of a genuinely popular media culture is still in our mouths, and the need to produce it – open, accessible, accountable – has never been stronger' (1986: 13).

This essay will examine the context and conditions of 1980s independent film-making by focusing on Leeds Animation Workshop, a women's film collective based in Yorkshire, active since 1978 and still operating; it predates and survives Thatcher. Its work represents an aspect of British 1980s film culture that usually escapes both academic discussion and international distribution, despite the fact that it is a highly successful cinema in its own right; of all the British film workshops, LAW recuperated the highest proportion of its production costs through distribution in the 1980s, most of it in self-distribution.[8] The outfit could be seen as a brand of enterprise culture, but one functioning by collective endeavour rather than an 'atomised' Tory individualism (Leadbeater 1990: 148). LAW's ten films to date confront major issues of the decade: privatisation (*Council Matters*, 1984, 10min.); nuclear proliferation (*Pretend You'll Survive*, 1981, 9min.); environmental damage (*Alice in Wasteland*, 1991, 12min.); domestic violence and sexism (*Give Us a Smile*, 1983, 12min. and *Out to Lunch*, 1989, 12min.); Third World debt and famine (*A Matter of Interest*, 1990, 13min. and *Crops and Robbers*, 1986, 15min.); childcare provision (*Who Needs Nurseries? We Do!*, 1978, 8min.); the housing crisis (*Home and Dry?*, 1987, 8min.); and worker safety (*Risky Business*, 1980, 15min.).[9] The collective views these issues through the various lenses of feminist, gay, antiracist and socialist politics, encapsulating complex arguments within broad historico-geographical frames in the space of a few minutes – and a few thousand drawings.[10] Dubbed 'Woman's Eye Propaganda', their animated shorts provide contexts for debate, education and organisation, raising questions as much as answering them in their 'get-it-all-in-ism' style.[11]

Because of the range of topics addressed, and because of LAW's consistent output across the decade, a study of their work provides one way of charting the course of recent feminist filmmaking as it engages with the changing political pressures of the 1980s. Of course, examination of a women's animation collective (incidentally the only one in Britain, if not the world) raises questions that differ from those raised by looking at the work of individual filmmakers; matters of funding, audiences, theoretical positions, aesthetic choices, and even quantities of footage apply differently. Other feminist film collectives have operated in Britain in the 1980s, 20th Century Vixen, Red Flannel and Sheffield Film Co-op among them. This brief study could not cover them all.[12] However, it can draw attention to the uneasy coexistence of regional, group filmmaking, sponsored by an unusual union-supported declaration, alongside a rigorous government programme promoting private consumption and the 'centralisation of cultural power' (Cubitt 1991: 124).

My study will analyse LAW's works in chronological order, and will link them to surrounding socio-political movements and sister texts – films by women tackling similar issues in divergent ways. Potter and Mulvey have used cinema to elaborate theoretical issues, particularly questions of realism, filmic pleasure and the impossibility of 'truly' representing women through film despite its analogical force. LAW skirts the stylistic techniques of the avant-garde and the challenge of 'doing theory' through film, largely because of the risk of alienating users. However, their choice of animation can also be seen as a response to those aesthetic and theoretical dilemmas facing filmmakers such as Mulvey and Potter, and expounded most fiercely in *Screen* magazine during the 1970s. Animation's anti-literal quality provided an answer, albeit a different one, to debates about realism, and afforded LAW the opportunity to make a populist feminist counter-propaganda from the Left (Whitaker 1985: 86).

British independent cinema has had a fairly long if shaky lineage, surviving from the Workers' Film Association of the 1930s, through the Free Cinema movement of the 1950s, and into the 1970s. Boosted by the events of May 1968 and the impact of the American avant-garde, the London Filmmakers' Co-op and Cinema Action were making and screening their own (and others') films by 1970, as was The Other Cinema, an alternative distribution outlet and exhibition site.[13] Several in this first wave of workshops were active in the women's liberation movement: the Berwick Street Film Collective (formed in London in 1972), the London Women's Film Group (begun in 1971; makers of *The Amazing Equal Pay Show*, 1974) and Four Corners Films (started in London in 1973) (Whitaker 1985: 85). Their films sought to challenge the politics of gender through documenting sexual inequality and through questioning repertoires of visual culture and their impact in shaping socio-sexual norms. The Berwick Street Film Collective's *Nightcleaners* (1972) aimed to support Women's efforts to unionise as poorly paid contract cleaners, but functioned more as a Brechtian interrogation of documentary filmmaking codes (Johnston & Willemen 1975/76).

A member of the collective, Mary Kelly, subsequently embarked on a massive art project that criticised the institution of motherhood in its social, psychoanalytic, cultural, aesthetic and even historical dimensions. This work, her *Post-Partum Document* (1973–79), incorporated scribble drawings by her child, prints, Lacanian diagrams, typing and quotidian objects (some infamous nappies, and pinned beetles presented to Kelly by her son), while it eschewed representational images of the particular mother and child around whom the whole work turned. The project brought the subject of motherhood into the art gallery, explicitly probing the conjunction mother/artist, as well as the cultural prohibition on carrying out both kinds of production (Pollock 1989, chap. 7).

Laura Mulvey, a member of the London Women's Liberation Workshop (Family Study Group), under which the London Women's Film Group formed, and co-organiser of the 1972 Edinburgh Film Festival's women's event, made *Penthesilea* (1974) and *Riddles of the Sphinx* (1976), with Peter Wollen, during the same period, in addition to publishing her influential article, 'Visual Pleasure and Narrative Cinema' (1975). The latter 90-minute film also scrutinised motherhood, women's work, the need for nursery provision, and representational conventions of all these. (Mary Kelly appears in the film, working on her PPD and interacting with her child.) In *Riddles of the Sphinx*, Mulvey and Wollen disrupt the transparency of the cinematographic medium through off-centred framing (cropping the image of the mother, Louise, to show only her midriff region, thereby denying imagery of her face), 360-degree pans, fragmentation of the mother's 'story' into thirteen parts, and the framing of her story with processed imagery of Egyptian travel footage, footage of solarised female acrobats and a retelling of the Oedipus myth.

The imperatives for the formation of Leeds Animation Workshop and its first film, *Who Needs Nurseries? We Do!*, derive from this same historico-political context: for LAW, too, 'motherhood, and how to live it, lay at the roots of the dilemma', to quote Mulvey in *Riddles of the Sphinx*. *Riddles of the Sphinx*, *Post-Partum Document* and *Who Needs Nurseries? We Do!* are different responses to the same dilemmas of representation, politics and women's daily life. However, while the Mulvey/Wollen film has become a canonical text within the international feminist avant-garde – one of 'The New Talkies' – and while Kelly's work was championed and eventually 'released' as a book, no critical ink illuminated LAW's film, which steadily showed to local and regional action groups, at trade union meetings, at women's meetings and at other community organisations.[14] Indeed, no critical ink has been spilled over LAW's films at all.

They have never entered the critical canon for a number of instructive reasons. First, the various working-class, female, young, old and other audiences to which the films are addressed immediately understand them, even if they balk at them. This clarity of meaning derives from using certain elements of narrative, including cartoon characters, sequences of related events and strong closing images, even if these might not 'resolve' the questions raised by the film. It also stems from the use of accessible, melodic, rhythmic music scored for brass band (in *Council Matters*), electric piano (in *Risky Business* and *Pretend You'll Survive*) and bamboo instruments (in *Alice in Wasteland*), and imagistic sequences that also invite audience engagement through their rootedness in the everyday – the launderette, street, café, factory, supermarket. Closeness to their audience also results from the consultation process integral to the workshop's methods of research and scripting: before making a film they talk to activists, teachers and other potential users to assess their needs, often bringing a draft script and storyboard to meetings. This may be a local process, but also regional, national and even international. For *Council Matters*, town halls in London as well as garbage depots in Yorkshire were visited; for *Crops and Robbers*, the collective met with liberation fighters from Namibia, South America and the South Pacific, as well as supermarket workers in Leeds.

While the films do not consistently deconstruct or dislocate content and representation – and do not engage in the distancing strategies of the filmmaking avant-garde of the 1970s and 1980s and their critics – they do share a feminist content with works such as Kelly's and Mulvey's, and similarly exist outside the mainstream in terms of production, distribution and exhibition. LAW's films are borrowable at libraries and are screened at political meetings, in schools, colleges and education and training sessions – generally at a grass-roots level rather than in cinemas or on television – and for this reason the workshop refers to 'users' of their films, conceiving them as tools to facilitate debate and action.[15] However, the films have been shown in festivals all over the world – in Japan, India, Australia, Africa and Canada, as well as the United States and Europe – and have been requested by resource centres in Colombia, Malaysia, Peru, India and Korea, among other countries. They have been

Freda's Hoovercopter in the Yorkshire landscape, in *Council Matters* (1984)

acquired for television in Germany, France, Holland and Cuba, and during the 1991 Clarence Thomas hearings in the United States, sections of *Out To Lunch* and *Give Us a Smile* were screened by CBS News, as well as by the BBC and ITV, to provide background coverage on the issue of sexual harassment.

What gets lost in documenting the large, individual works of particular artists (the traditional habit of film and art history) is an awareness of the diversity among art practices, and here specifically feminist art practice. Works do not necessarily appear in 'official cultural sites' such as commercial cinemas or academic magazines. In the words of Griselda Pollock and Rozsika Parker, 'there is a necessary relation and inter-change between practical strategies and strategic practices' (1987: 75). In LAW's films, both sides of the equation are at work. Through animation LAW filmmakers refuse the option of seamless, continuity editing and photographic realism; and when using live action or photographic collage elements they throw them into relief as representational, coded systems, rather than as naturally occurring phenomena, by juxtaposing them with animation. These are strategic practices. On the other hand, the humour and transformative power of animation and its cultural associa-tions of accessibility and buoyancy enable the workshop to reach and speak to its users, precluding the necessity for explanatory intellectual amplification (hence the absence of their work in cinema studies scholarship). This is a practical strategy.

Leeds Animation Workshop formed in 1977 when four women with backgrounds in experimental theatre, sociology and education joined forces in Leeds as the Nursery Film Group to campaign for the provision of more state nurseries for chil-dren.[16] Their first film, *Who Needs Nurseries? We Do!* is worth examining in some detail, since its devices have become staples in the group's later filmic transforma-tions of commercial habits of animation into political effectiveness.

LAW films typically present subject matter through an unconventional or traditionally unrepresented point of view.[17] In *Pretend You'll Survive* a housewife confronts
her nuclear nightmares; in *Risky Business* worker Carol sustains a minor industrial
accident and investigates its causes, visiting Mr Potter, the safety officer who waters
his plants as a diversion from employee needs; in *Council Matters* Freda, a char who
uses her vacuum cleaner as a flying broomstick, explains how a local authority functions; in *Alice in Wasteland* Carroll's 'Wonderland' is transformed as the expanding
and shrinking Alice pursues the disposal of rubbish and inspects images made from
torn colour magazines and newspapers, symbols both of damage and re-use; and in
Who Needs Nurseries? We Do! we hear and examine children's gripes.

That film's opening image initiates another LAW strategy – of evoking regional
specificity in setting, characters and audience. In the first drawing we see a cel-
animated journalist spewing the rhetoric of 'balanced' reporting plumily into his
microphone; he professes to be interested in whether more nurseries are needed.
Behind his head, however, looms a large, hand-scrawled poster for scrag end (a
cheap cut of meat). The geographical and class clash of interests, the North/South
divide, are laid out in the juxtaposition of his posh accent with a hinterland meat
market economy.[18] In the film's central section, children convene a large meeting
presided over by three 'chairbabies' who hear divergent opinions from children of
all classes and races on whether they would like to attend a nursery. One pulls
down a screen of statistics and the shrinkage of nurseries since World War Two is
made plain. A reproduced wartime poster ironically suggests how easily daycare was
forthcoming in the past when national security was threatened.[19] In the film's last
image, cel-animated children march rhythmically across the screen, carrying banners
and mowing down the roving southern reporter with whom the film had begun. The

Alice surveys holes in the ozone layer, in *Alice in Wasteland* (1991)

children's drowning out of the southerner, who is concluding, against the evidence, that it is not known whether more nurseries are needed, speaks for the desire of a working class, and of mothers and children, to be heard.

While specific places are never overtly mentioned in LAW's films, local accents, vocabulary and architecture feature prominently, enhancing an address to those close to home; the back-to-backs under Freda's Hoovercopter, the streets outside the factory in *Risky Business*, and the crier for the *Evening Post* in *Give Us a Smile* all sustain the identity of a Yorkshire setting.[20] Further, LAW employs only locally-based people where possible, and completes the entire process of its filmmaking in Leeds.[21] It emphasises local screenings: *Pretend You'll Survive* had its first public showing in the Leeds Trades Club; *Alice in Wasteland* was shown on a video bus touring around Leeds during National Environment Week. By inhabiting non-cinema venues, LAW has tried to expand and find a different audience, hoping 'to get to people who don't go to cinemas, as well as those who do'.[22] These attitudes toward audiences and exhibition are part and parcel of the politics of the women's movement: the determination to pull attention, monies and identities out from under centralised capital authority (Parker & Pollock 1987: 23). The back-to-backs in Leeds are geographically remote from Soho, London, the main location for animated cinema in Britain, but the ideological force of the distance and of its imperial/colonial overtones was made clear again in the 'Looks North' section of a *Daily Telegraph* article on LAW during the making of *Home and Dry?* There Ivor Smullen '*discovers* a defiant six woman group working from a slightly down-at-heels Leeds suburb' (31 July 1987; my emphasis).

Risky Business and *Pretend You'll Survive* followed *Who Needs Nurseries? We Do!*, continuing the use of searing wit and female viewpoints to urge audiences to consciousness, debate and action. In the last frames of *Pretend You'll Survive*, a pun on the derided government pamphlet *Protect and Survive*, a woman rips up images of militarism, transforming them into a banner proclaiming 'Don't Pretend – Protest!' *Risky Business* presents factory accidents resulting from a company's drive for profits at the expense of worker safety. Reggie the Robot, assistant to Carol, spouts excerpts from the 'Health and Safety at Work Act' as Carol challenges management. In a Chaplinesque scene a machine swallows a worker, while in another Carol tussles with a massive dust monster, mindful of the apparently benign uses of cartoons in advertising of the Ajax 'White Tornado' type. Elsewhere Carol finds the workers in contact with VBF, cryptic for 'Very-Ide Bad-For-You-Ene', she discovers.

Both *Pretend You'll Survive* and *Council Matters*, made three years later, highlight the opposing aims of local and central government in Britain under Thatcher. *Council Matters* proposes that city hall, while not perfect, is a resource (unlike private enterprise) that people can use to improve their situation. It is a plea for local democracy, for citizens to get involved. In its image of central government using tax money to foster arms growth, *Pretend You'll Survive* is consistent with this message. This film was made expressly for disarmament campaign groups whose political momentum was growing in protest over the siting of US cruise missiles at Greenham Common during the period of the making of the film; said the collective, 'We set off originally to make a five-minute film about nuclear power but events overtook us in 1979–80'.[23] Only four months after forty women marched from Cardiff to Greenham and spontaneously decided, on 4 December 1981, to set up camp and stay, the film began showing in Leeds.[24]

The experience of making *Pretend You'll Survive*, combined with the newly radi-calised Leeds atmosphere of feminist art practice and politics, propelled LAW into becoming a women-only group, which they have been ever since.[25] The national spotlight had been turned on Leeds (and Bradford) through Peter Sutcliffe's rapes and murders of women committed over several years; dubbed 'the Yorkshire Ripper', he was finally arrested and tried in early 1981. After Yorkshire police had warned women not to go out alone at night for fear of attack, local women's groups, lead by Women Against Violence Against Women, retaliated with demands for a curfew on men as more logical and just. In an obliquely related series of incidents, also in early 1981, Leeds was described hyperbolically as 'the centre of feminist ferment' in the local press after women, signing themselves 'Angry Women', torched three Leeds stores – 'Sex-shop', 'Fantasy,' and 'Cupid' – to protest that 'porn is violence against women'.[26] Thousands of women signed petitions to dissuade Leeds Council from licensing more shops.

The audience and motivation for LAW's fourth and most controversial film, *Give Us a Smile*, grew out of these conditions.[27] It was released in 1983, the same year as Sally Potter's feature-length production, *The Gold Diggers*, and was scored by the same composer, Lindsay Cooper.[28] Just as it is instructive to recognise the shared political motivations of *Riddles of the Sphinx*, *Post-Partum Document* and *Who Needs Nurseries? We Do!*, it is again useful to compare these two apparently different works – one known in the US, the other not – for they both explicitly ques-tion traditions of female representation in photographic pornography, fine art, house-hold magazines and film, by asking what kind of structures link market economy, female imagery and women's struggles.

In Potter's film, shot in Iceland and London, two women, Ruby and Celeste (played by Julie Christie and Colette Lafont), trace their 'origins' in 'the connections between gold, money and women' (Potter quoted in Rosenbaum 1984: 128). The connections prove to be in exploitation and capital; as Ruby puts it, gradually claiming her identity, 'I've been framed.' The film draws on audience knowledge of Christie's career as a star, and on iconography of the white female film heroine, especially that of Griffith's melodramas and film noir. Francophone, black Celeste is a city bank employee who looks behind the figures she pounds into the computer to uncover male stereotypes of bureaucrats, servants, 'anonymous pursuers and street terrorisers' (1984: 129). In one of the more startling moments of the film, Celeste rides on a white charger into a ballroom (the outpatients' hall of the disused Royal Free Hospital) and whisks Ruby away from the tedium of formal dancing with uniformly suited men.

Give Us a Smile, LAW's first film to combine live action with animation, opens with imagery of an anonymous pursuer. His feet follow a woman's down a dark street; shot with live action, the scene is reminiscent of the opening moves of Michael Powell's *Peeping Tom* (1960), with its stealthy piano chords, high-heeled shoes and menacing shadows. The tension continues as now a cel-animated woman also walks a street and passes shops plastered with images of women she cannot understand but uncannily recognises, like Christie's Ruby of *The Gold Diggers*. The collective's angry lyrics accompanying Cooper's score convey the problem: 'Why do the things they say have to dominate my day? ... Every window that I see tries to tell me how to be ... On every shelf I see my face and there isn't any space to be alone.' These words are interlaid with questions to rape victims taken from police reports: 'You are in the habit of going into public houses, are you not?' 'Are you on the pill?' 'What did you expect if you shared a taxi with him?' 'Did you say no when you meant yes?' These are also combined with phrases of street harassment: 'Cor, look at the knockers on that!' 'When did you last have it, luv?' 'Cheer up, it might never happen', and, of course, 'Hey, give us a smile.'

LAW and Potter have both written of their hope of conveying a sense of discovery and pleasure for women through film, of presenting the opportunity for recognition, identification and rethinking. In LAW's words, 'We didn't want women to go away from the film feeling completely depressed … We wanted it to be a positive piece.'[29] Likewise Potter writes that 'ultimately my own desire was and is to give pleasure; to heal the "pleasure time blues" of the opening song whose lines demand: Please give me back my good night out/Please give me back my leisure time' (quoted in Rosenbaum 1984: 129). Potter's image of Celeste bursting in to rescue Ruby is reminiscent in both spirit and iconography of that in *Give Us a Smile* when the tables turn and animated women begin to make their own images. A drawn woman recomposes a television show (for which all the credits are given to 'a man' except wardrobe and make-up) with spray paint, brush and matches. A black-and-white still cartoon of a woman, signed 'a man' again, leaps off the page, out of her bondage, escaping from victim status to the sound of tinkling glass, while literalising the distinction between animated and still cartoons. Another woman transforms typical tabloid headlines of attacks on women into ones of 'Women Fight Back' and 'Fire Guts Porn Shop', borrowed from recent Leeds women's actions. Elsewhere graffiti is added to stocking and cigarette advertisements, making them reveal their sexist suppositions.[30] And a porn shop disappears into crackling animated flames in the film's last shot.

Breaking out of bondage, in *Give Us a Smile* (1983)

Alternative headlines, in *Give Us a Smile*

Whether directing political energy against pornography is tactically sound has been the subject of intensive debate among feminists.[31] What the Leeds film provides through the imagery of animated arson, however, is a 'fantasy of reversal', a release of the feeling of the possibility of change (Williamson 1984: 322). It is a desire parallel to that expressed by Potter for her own film, in her lyrics for its 'theme tune' and in her work's final image of Rosie the Riveter wielding her welding gun in a shower of sparks. While the two films diverge dramatically in length, and while Potter's might be more historically engaged and designated 'an experimental or avant-garde film', and LAW's 'a political film, in the agitational or militant sense' (Wollen 1982: 31), they both insist on the importance of drawing in an audience through the pleasure of music and image, and both use the motif of escape be it from television, a page or a ballroom to express the potential of a different future.

Give Us a Smile was the first of LAW's films to be made under the Workshop Declaration of 1982. This was an agreement between the BFI, Channel 4, the Regional Arts Associations, the Independent Film and Video Association and the Association of Cinematograph, Television and Associated Technicians (ACIF) facilitating funding, security and continuity of employment in the 'cultural and grant-aided sector' of film. LAW was among the first workshops to become franchised and was one of four to be sponsored by the BFI rather than by Channel 4.[32] The declaration boosted LAW's ability to operate an 'integrated practice' of distribution, exhibition, education and training, as well as production. They carried this out perhaps more than any other workshop; as well as producing and distributing their own films they have participated in local, regional, national and international cultural initiatives. They have organised, attended and addressed screenings of their films and those of others; talked to audiences within and outside Britain; held regular training weekends and other courses; and acted as a film resource centre, receiving visitors from several countries, as well as from local districts.

The declaration made all this possible because it offered long-term support and better working conditions (including union maternity leaves and allowances) and allowed collective members to participate in all aspects of production, rotating tasks rather than being forced to respect the usual union-marked divisions of labour.[33] It also allowed filmmakers to pay regular wages, and stated the collective's right to pay equal wages to all its workers. In terms of its provision of a more hospitable climate for film production, the declaration was the single most important event of the 1980s for the workshops. But its positive benefits were eroded by changes that minimised other sources of funding. *Home and Dry?*, the workshop's seventh film, was made just as the defeats of the second half of the 1980s were beginning: the abolition of the Eady Levy in 1985, of capital allowances for British films in 1986 and of the Metropolitan County Councils in the same year.[34] Funding for the film came in under the wire from the Campaign for the Homeless and Rootless (CHAR), themselves sponsored by the Board and Lodging Information Programme of the Greater London Council.

Under Thatcher's housing policy, while some council tenants had become home-owners, homelessness had reached the highest level on record, and council house building had slumped dramatically. The physical and emotional loss of homes was papered over in Prime Ministerial rhetoric: 'The family is the building block of society … It is the preparation for the rest of our life. And women run it' (quoted in Brunt 1988: 19). LAW's film confronts these contradictions – between ample metaphorical and minimal physical homes – via four female animated characters who tend their washing at the local launderette. A lesbian woman, an older single woman and women from the Caribbean and Pakistan whose home is Britain all present their dilemmas – staying in bad relationships for lack of alternative housing, living with the impermanency of bed-and-breakfast policy, not being consulted about their needs, and so on. Their collective anxiety is expressed through a Victorian sampler whose platitude 'No Place Like Home' dissolves into 'Nowhere to Go'. As in *Who Needs Nurseries? We Do!* and *Pretend You'll Survive*, the film ends with images of banners, this time in Bengali and English, urging viewers to discuss, act and protest.

In using female characters and voiceovers to express ideas and means of action, LAW insists that crises in housing, Third World debt and environmental destruction, while on the surface unrelated to gender, have a particular and important impact on women. LAW's films highlight what Elizabeth Meehan has called the 'feminisation' of poverty under Thatcher, with its freezing of children's allowances, complication of access to maternity pay and re-employment and privatisation of health services, which 'encourages the idea women should be at home to care for the sick and elderly' (1990: 197–8).[35] In 1987 *Spare Rib* reported the following impact of 1980s Conservative policy on women: 'Women's unemployment since 1979 has tripled from 327,000 to 934,000. Women are 44 per cent of the workforce, 80 per cent of the low-paid workforce, and two out of three of those in poverty' (Whitlock 1987: 15).

In the face of this evidence Thatcher persistently styled herself a 'Housewife Prime Minister', particularly when addressing a female constituency. In an alliterative 1982 speech she compared running the national economy to running the domestic one: 'Some say I preach merely the homilies of housekeeping or the parables of the

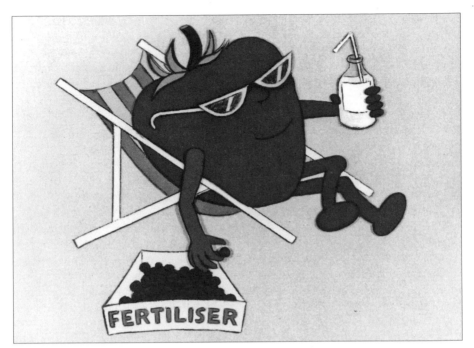

The cultivated strawberry, in *Crops and Robbers* (1986)

parlour. But I do not repent. Those parables would have saved many a financier from failure and many a country from crisis' (quoted in McFadyean & Renn 1984: 111). To the Conservative Women's Conference six years later she argued, 'I cannot help reflecting that it has taken a government headed by a housewife, with the experience of running a family, to balance the books for the first time in twenty years – with a little left over for a rainy day' (quoted in Brunt 1988: 19). Beatrix Campbell points out that in Thatcher's constant reference to the housewife in herself – and its value in sorting out the national economy – she has 'made the domestic visible' (1987: 236). However, in bringing women 'into the political conversation ... as housewives' she renders invisible 'the housewife who is also in waged work and ... blurs the contradictions experienced by the wageless housewife' (1987: 236–7). LAW's films are peopled by the latter categories.

There is a necessary if paradoxical shared ground between LAW's focus on the domestic, everyday experience of their viewers and this housewifely aspect of Thatcher's rhetoric; one uncovers the tracks of the other.[36] And the two politics meet above all in the supermarket, in the motif of shopping, which recurs in Thatcherism's promotions of the promise of individual choice just as it does in LAW's images of connection between women's tasks and international politics. In the collective's words, the shopping mall is 'no longer a morally neutral place'.

As a woman scrutinises products for sale in her Leeds supermarket in *Crops and Robbers* – tea, bananas, sugar – we and she are made aware, through drawing and intercutting, of the origins of these goods outside England, and the human, political and economic price of their journeys to the shelf. In the film Mexico is represented as an outpost of the United States where a cel-animated strawberry (reminiscent of the California raisins), replete with underarm pesticide, is being fattened for export by plane up north while local farmers go hungry. Crayoned cutouts of vegetables march in ranks from Africa and South America to Europe, having decimated the local flora. Through these and other compressed references to plantations, slavery, food aid and colonies we learn 'Imperialism for Beginners', a lesson that animation is superbly equipped to deliver (Petley 1986: 355).

Initially the film's voiceover belongs to First World politicians of the last 500 years, expressing imperialist international sentiments: 'Food is a weapon – it is now one of the principle weapons in our negotiating kit', and, 'Let us remember that the main purpose of American aid is not to help others but to help ourselves.' Pieces are moved around a pseudo-Monopoly board to convey the checks and balances of international trade and capital. This long history and complex network of debts and surpluses weighs more and more heavily on the old woman shopping in Leeds, whose poverty inhibits her consumption, and on the young woman price-tagging food alongside her. Eventually the empire's voice is taken over by subaltern tongues, who call for First World people to recognise the connection between their own deprivations and decisions (in the supermarket) and the exploitation of the Third World. An end to multinational capitalism is demanded, and the entire board is upturned to symbolise this revolution. The final shots show ranks of women, of all ages and colours, marching down the shopping aisles.

In this film a double movement is at work: against the centralisation that makes London/Parliament the holder of the purse strings and the focus of national culture (as in earlier films), but also toward making visible the concerns of working people globally – in Julian Petley's words, 'Poverty is not simply a third world matter' (ibid.). *Pretend You'll Survive*, *Crops and Robbers*, *A Matter of Interest* and *Alice in Wasteland* link the domestic to the international, locating both subject matter and audience within a world picture – all four films abound with images of maps and globes. This geographical and social web is explained as a consequence of both past and present events, of the economic and social history of colonialism as it abuts contemporary struggles, particularly in the later films. In this way LAW is engaging the 'politics of location', alongside Sheffield Film Co-op's *Bringing it All Back Home* (1987), Ngozi Omwurah's *Coffee Coloured Children* (1988), Black Audio Film/Video Collective's *Handsworth Songs* (1985), Sankofa's *Passion of Remembrance* (1986), and so much other independent film of late 1980s Britain, which sees domestic poverty and labour as tied to that of post-colonial countries, and conceives personal histories as part and parcel of international, imperialist ones.[37]

An expanded visual vocabulary expresses the increased complexity of LAW's later analyses: in *Alice in Wasteland*, recycled envelopes, newspaper and rubbish coalesce to form images of sprouting beans and continental drift; other drawings are made directly onto the celluloid, as usual, but thinner paint is used, mixed with glues, to produce watery stains evocative of pollution. *Crops and Robbers* employs pixilation in the movement of elements on the board game (a sort of 3-D animation), live action, cel and cutout animation, and slow-motion footage of a die falling through the air and landing on the board. The inter-mixing of techniques conveys the labyrinthine paths of imported goods as well as the interlacing of the ideas expressed. This general strategy is brought vividly home in a moment of apparent match-on-action; a crayon-drawn, engraved calabash overflowing with mixed tropical fruits cuts to a live-action supermarket scene in which the price-tagger apparently receives the goods, from off-screen, but now they are a uniformly packaged melon monoculture, photographically reproduced. The artisanal quality of coloured drawing borders the processed character of live-action photography in a mimesis of the international politics of food.

Out to Lunch, the last film I want to discuss, is the one that most directly examines the extended life of gender representation. Here pencil-coloured, hinged, cut-out figures and collages of muscle-building and dietary magazine imagery deftly visualise conceptual and physical pressures on women to occupy 'little space', either actually or verbally. Virginia Woolf's premise that 'women have served all these centuries as looking glasses, possessing the magic and delicious power of reflecting the figure of a man at twice his natural size' is printed in white on a black screen in the opening moments of the film. The collective then literalises Woolf's metaphorical image in a café setting. Sitting at a table, a woman listens to a man blathering unintelligible words; his reflection expands in her spectacles as she interjects, 'That's fascinating', 'How amazing', 'Wonderful', 'You're so clever'. The café's animated chalkboard menu resonates with new linguistic significance, punctuating familiar encounters: on offer are 'mussels' or 'slimmer's special', 'ego soufflé', 'honey bun', 'humble pie', 'just desserts', and finally 'piece of cake', as the waitress puts up her feet, having scooped her trying customers into the draining rack and having brushed letters spelling 'manpower' into the bin. At two points the sexual politics of space are expressed through a changed vantage point for the audience, who now see an aerial view of the table. The new vision this unexpected angle creates evokes the spectator's raised consciousness of the gendered significance of daily habits, literally

Aerial view of space invasion, in *Out To Lunch* (1989)

presented by the male 'space invaders' who compress women to the end of the table.

According to LAW, this film campaigns for women to become 'linguistically visible' and aims to 'deepen and accelerate' this process, by sensitising viewers to the woman-reflecting-man syndrome and by dismantling apron-wearing, waitress-style clichés. Margaret Thatcher has been no friend to feminism – her scorn for its efforts and her stated belief that man or woman, 'you get on because you have the right talents' are well documented (quoted in McFadyean & Renn 1984: 111). Yet she does offer a model of a new womanhood: 'She has brought qualities of ruggedness and ruthlessness to femininity which perhaps only men hadn't noticed before in women' (Campbell 1987: 246). She has not reflected men at twice their size but challenged them to housewifely knowledge in order to distinguish her work and express her power. However, while Thatcher's image counters the magnifying woman of LAW's café, hers has not been a pro-woman politics. A single female Conservative Prime Minister is not equatable with collective female empowerment, production and action.

Animation has been an aesthetic choice for other feminist filmmakers besides LAW – Ayoka Chenzira in the US, Vera Neubauer in Britain and Nina Sabnani in India, for example. The reasons for their choice are multi-faceted, linked to practical, economic criteria as well as to questions of representation, gender and politics. Animation is user-friendly: in 1976, when future members of LAW were first considering filmmaking, only a handful of rentable 16mm cameras existed in Yorkshire – live-action filmmaking was not practicable outside London. Animation is woman-friendly: its technology is advantageous to women in whom is so commonly inculcated a fear or revulsion of machinery, a training to run away from it.[39] Animation can be done in low-tech, quiet corners (on the kitchen table, according to British animator Sheila Graber), away from glaring studio lights; it can be a way into cinema. Animation has also been collective-friendly: group decisions are more feasible when few or no actors absorb finances.[40] In Anne Creyke's words, 'Leeds film star Alice is paper thin, remains silent about her professional life and lives in a cardboard box.' Without actors and studio rentals, less pressure exists for on-the-spot decisions. Although animation is very labour intensive, its simpler technology can reduce costs, another allure for independent filmmakers: LAW reckons to spend about £5,000 per minute, while commercial animation costs may that per second for hi-tech, computerised work.[41]

Beyond these practical attractions, animation holds a particular ideological niche in the wider culture that LAW both draws on, and redraws. Animation evokes American studios, fantasy, expensively-produced worlds of immortality and immunity; in LAW's films characters and animals exposed to toxic fumes, intensive farming and radiation simply perish, rather than rebounding like Tom or Jerry. Commercial animation has a repertoire of motifs for signalling femininity – ribbons, curls, frocks, eyelashes exaggerated to the hilt in *Who Framed Roger Rabbit*'s (1988) Jessica Rabbit; one of the challenges for LAW is to find new means of representing women, still recognisable by audiences, without reproducing this constricting menu. The problem is encapsulated in an image from *Out to Lunch* in which an Asian woman is turned down for a waitressing job because the 'uniform' will not fit her. The uniform is a cut-out, aproned drawing of a white, blond woman, with tabs for attachment. It is the uniform Thatcher temporarily dons in her housewifely mode.

Defrocking racism, in *Out to Lunch*

Animation has also been a tool for propaganda – for telescoping messages or transforming familiar images. It has been used to sell goods in advertising and to sell ideologies in wartime. LAW inherits this performance of politics through images and admires Norman McLaren's *Hell Unlimited* (1938), for example. Animation provides LAW with an alternative to talking heads for conveying information succinctly and humorously, in a combination of visual and linguistic forms. Animation is to live action as poetry is to prose, says the workshop representation of a distilled, precise kind. Only through animation may Alice encounter landfill, waste dumps, deforestation, genetic engineering (Cloney Island), ozone depletion and acid rain, all in the space of twelve minutes. It is work in synch with an electorate that thinks 'politically not in terms of policies but images'. Work such as LAW's functions by 'capturing people's political imaginations' in constructing issues 'into an image' (Hall 1988: 260).

One consequence of this compression (certainly the result of attendant economic factors, as well) is the creation of films short enough to be used in the classroom, allowing time for other events to follow screenings, such as discussion or a tandem film. They can take the traditional position of the Disney cartoon before the feature, wittily conveying in a few seconds the chief lessons of Dale Spender or Woolf, disseminating them, and inflecting understanding of adjacent texts.[42] *Crops and Robbers* was shown in a double-bill with *A Question of Silence* in Leeds – two feminist perspectives on shopping-mall politics. LAW films may not be avant-garde in the modernist sense of performing a distancing aesthetic critique of representation, but they can function alongside that avant-garde, emerging from the same politics but into a different ambit. They too find a route away from conventions of realism, but through the hybrid medium of art and photography that is animation.

POSTSCRIPT

Over the winter of 1990 first Channel 4 and then the BFI withdrew their support from the Workshop Declaration, making it essentially inoperable. Thereafter, both Channel 4 and the BFI commissioned individual films and programmes from workshops (as well as any other independent group or individual) rather than having a stake in the long-term running of an outfit (Vale 1989). The special rates and flexible union agreements worked out through the Declaration only made sense alongside a commitment (whether it be from Channel 4, the BFI or other bodies) to continuity of funding for daily running costs and salaries; the Declaration was 'formulated to acknowledge the specific and exceptional conditions prevailing in the cultural and grant-aided sector and [was] designed to encourage the development and growth of stability and permanent employment in this sector' (Anon. 1984: 10). That permanence evaporated: Sheffield Film Co-op went on the dole in June 1991. LAW's last Channel 4-funded film was *Out to Lunch*; their last BBC-funded film was *Through the Glass Ceiling* (1994). Other films envisaged in 1991 – *Hildegard of Bingen* (about the abbess composer), *On the Line* (a lesbian subject), and *Off Your Trolley* (about supermarket decisions) – elicited no funding and remained unmade.

However, LAW manoeuvered through the changed financial straights. They reduced their number of members from six to five in 1991 (with the same five still working there in 2004), and have completed 16 new animated shorts since. Significant support has come through the European Commission and particularly its Daphne Unit, a campaign for protecting women and children from violence: *Home Truths* (1999) examines young people's experience of domestic violence; *Tell It Like It Is* (2000) treats problems faced by young people at school as a result of gender stereotyping and bullying; *Believe Me* (2002, available also in Spanish and German), deals with young people's experience of sexual abuse; *Beyond Belief* (2003) looks at the impact of child sexual abuse on families. Since the mid-1990s the sponsorship of British Government units have supported various LAW projects, most recently films dealing with various aspects of parenting, including step-families (*Joined-up Families* (2003), and parenting from prison (*Dads Inside and Out* (2004)).

LAW still completes all production work, as before, in Leeds. While continuing to shoot on film with a rostrum camera, the workshop is converting to digital editing and to designing for DVD. It now has United States distribution (through The Filmmakers' Library, 124 E. 40th Street, New York, NY 10016) for a suit of four, fairy tale-inspired films about the workplace, narrated by Alan Bennett. (*Through the Glass Ceiling* about equal opportunities at work; *No Offence* (1996) treats sexual and other kinds of harassment at work; *Did I Say Hairdressing? I Meant Astrophysics* (1998) covers women in science, engineering and technology; while *Working with Care* (1999) concerns work, life and caring responsibilities.)

Since the early 1990s, means of access to LAW's work has shifted considerably. The rental market has virtually disappeared, and now free distribution of tapes and DVDs, to libraries as well as professional groups (such as teachers and social workers), is built into initial funding agreements, a pattern which meets funders' needs more effectively.

Author's note: I thank Leeds Animation Workshop for our correspondence and discussions, and for the access they gave me to their films and archive in June 1991. I also thank Women Make Movies and First Run/Icarus for making films available for viewing, and Anne-Marie Smith for comments and especially her bibliographic suggestions. All illustrations are reproduced courtesy of Leeds Animation Workshop, 45 Bayswater Road, Leeds, West Yorkshire LS8 5LF.

NOTES

1 As of 2006, the only LAW films available in the US are through the New York Filmmakers' Library, which has *Through the Glass Ceiling* (1994), *No Offence* (1996), *Did I Say Hairdressing? I Meant Astrophysics* (1998) and *Working with Care* (1999).

2 To suggest the limited scope of that sector, 27 British features were released in 1982, and 34 in 1983. Beeban Kidron's film *Antonia and Jane*, made for television, was theatrically released in the United States in 1991.

3 Sean Cubitt (1991) discusses the challenge that video represents to centralised culture in its potential to build a democratic media network. There are also parallels between the Workshop Movement, in which the ability to record has been in the hands of local, often untrained, people, and the activities and motivations of Mass Observation in the 1930s.

4 See also Ed Buscombe's discussion of the pressures on British television to become more international after 1992 with the removal of trade barriers within Europe. He argues that a federal structure – currently in the form of the decentralised BBC – paradoxically allows for the production of regional fictional television, such as Alan Bleasdale's *Boys from the Blackstuff* and *GBH* (about Liverpool politics), as well as the popular soap opera *EastEnders*. Such regional television will not find a large enough European market after 1992, he argues, and will perish; Ed Buscombe (1991) 'Nationhood, Media, Culture: Britain', paper for the Society of Cinema Studies annual conference, Los Angeles, 24 May.

5 As of 2006, the LAW has just completed transferring all their work to DVD. They now design their work for DVD – with different chapter headings for the DVD menu.

6 This important though sensitive topic is discussed by Whitaker (1985), Williamson (1987) and Lovell (1990), among others.

7 The term 'enterprise culture' is thoroughly analysed, in all its oxymoronic glory, in Caughie & Frith (1990).

8 By the provisions of the Workshop Declaration, under which LAW's films have been made since 1982, any financial surpluses generated through production must be re-invested in the 'activities and infrastructure of the Workshop' (Anon. 1984: 3).

9 Besides these ten films, LAW has made a variety of short animated pieces during the 1980s, including a brief sequence for a Labour Party political broadcast (1980–81); an extended title and end sequence for *Print It Yourself*, a four-part Channel 4 series on community printing initiatives (1984); and an animated logo produced for Scan, a collective of Asian women making videos in London (1986).

10 LAW filmmakers work only in 16mm. Their films usually require between 12 and 24 drawings per second, but over 50 may be used in more complicated, composite frames.

11 Coined by the Halifax *Evening Courier*.

12 Still less the scores of other, mostly unfranchised workshops producing films in Britain in the 1980s. See Cubitt's (1986) discussion of the quantity and types of workshops, distinguishing between those emphasising process and those emphasising product in their filmmaking. About twenty workshops were eventually granted franchises under the declaration in all.

13 Sheila Whitaker excellently surveys this lineage and its recent evolutions. My account is indebted to her essay. See also MacPherson (1980).

14 The expression 'The New Talkies' was coined by the editors of *October*, 17 (Summer 1981) to characterise those films informed by discourses of film theory, psychoanalysis and semiotics, and proceeding from 'the radical critique of representation'.

15 LAW has written substantial accompanying notes for all the films, intended to aid discussion. *Who Needs Nurseries? We Do!*, *Risky Business*, *Pretend You'll Survive* and *Out to Lunch* have aired on Channel 4.

16 Only one of the group, Gillian Lacey, had professional experience in commercial animation – she had worked on *The Yellow Submarine* in a junior capacity, but had abandoned the field and had been teaching in London for seven years before moving to Leeds and becoming active in nursery campaigning. Another important founding member, Jenni Carter, had been a theatre designer working at the Royal Court, London, among other venues, before moving up to Leeds, having a child, and entering the campaign. In 1991, the group had five members: Terry Wragg, Stephanie Munro, Janis Goodman, Jane Bradshaw and Milena Dragic. Terry Wragg was the only member of the original Nursery Film Group still to be part of the collective.

17 Of course, to even talk of point of view implies the presence of characters or coherent personalities within the films, a convention of commercial cinema that a film such as *Riddles of the Sphinx* sought to challenge.

18 The North/South divide is a symbolic one, conveying the division between privilege and non-privilege. As Stuart Hall points out, in another context, the North is not uniform, 'there are plenty of "Southerners" living in the "North"' (1988: 264).

19 Thatcher's Education Act of 1980 was to reduce the number of nurseries further through local authority spending cuts.

20 Islington Borough Council, London, funded a cockney soundtrack for *Council Matters*, amending the script and replacing the original Yorkshire brogue. The need for a new track, recorded by LAW in Leeds using speakers 'imported' from London's East End, suggests how important accent has been in efforts to reach specific sectors of the British audience. As part of LAW's agreement in receiving grants from the local authority, films and videos purchased by residents of the City of Leeds are available at a reduced rate.

21 Until 1983 the collective had to transport all their drawings and props down to London to animate them, since there was no access to a rostrum camera in Leeds.

22 *Leeds Other Paper*, 27 November 1981.

23 Ibid.

24 The women's peace movement, focused through Greenham, became the largest mass feminist campaign of the early 1980s, as Beeban Kidron and Amanda Richardson's film *Carry Greenham Home* (1983) documents. The camp grew to thousands: on 12 December 1982, 30,000 women holding hands circled the 9-mile perimeter fence of the future nuclear weapons base; a year later the missiles arrived as 50,000 women encircled the base.

25 The Leeds Women's Art Programme – for coordinating local women's art-making and study – began in 1981. It was modelled on the Feminist Art Program in California of 1970–71, and was the first such organisation in Britain. The Leeds Women's Photography Project opened in the Pavilion for processing and exhibiting photography in May 1983. Although LAW was not directly involved with these groups, they strengthened the culture of women's artistic practice in the region, as did the exhibition of several sections of Mary Kelley's *Post-Partum Document* in Leeds in 1979, one of their earliest exhibition venues in Britain; see also Parker & Pollock (1987: 33–5).

26 Halifax *Evening Courier* and *Leeds Women's Liberation Newsletter*, April 1981, reprinted in Kanter

et al. (1984: 49), where the group is referred to by the name Sex-Shop Arsonists. Leeds still has a reputation for feminist activism, especially of the pro-censorship variety.

27 A furor blew up when the *Yorkshire Evening Post* printed a misleading front-page headline – 'Leeds "fun" cartoon prompted by the Ripper' – to announce the BFI's grant to the workshop for making the film, all the time capitalising on the word 'Ripper' to sell newspapers and obscuring the specific politics informing the project. The paper even interviewed the mother of one of Sutcliffe's victims for the story (*Yorkshire Evening Post*, 29 May 1981).

28 In an interview LAW recalled the energy given to women's filmmaking generally in Britain when Potter's all-women crew was making *The Gold Diggers* in 1982–83.

29 *Leeds Other Paper*, 21 October 1983.

30 Here the film is indebted to Jill Posener and the graffitists whose work she documents. It also draws on Judith Williamson's *Decoding Advertisements* (1978) and Griselda Pollock's analyses of fine art's traditions of representing women. Pollock was consulted in the making of the film.

31 See especially the divergence of opinion among Stern (1982), MacKinnon (1987), Koch (1989) and Williams (1989).

32 Channel 4 purchased LAW's three earlier films, although *Give Us a Smile* was never broadcast because the particularities of buy-back agreements for animation took until 1991 to resolve. Again the film's length was a problem, since the channel usually paid so much per minute per programme and this film was shorter than most, though more labour intensive. *Out to Lunch* was a commission from the channel's animation department, which later bought the TV rights to *Alice in Wasteland*. As all this suggests, it is their practice of animation that makes LAW anomalous within the workshop sector; they have been alone in that sector in receiving almost no benefits from the Independent Film Department of Channel 4 save a small equipment grant toward the purchase of a second-hand Steenbeck. The other ten workshops to be franchised in 1983 were Amber Films (Newcastle), Birmingham Film and Video Workshop, Cinema Action (London), Four Corners (London), Front Room Productions (London), Newsreel Collective (London), North East Film Workshop (Rosedale, North Yorkshire), Open Eye Film and Video (Liverpool), Sheffield Film Co-op, and Trade Films (Tyne and Wear). By 1985 eighteen were funded, and the black workshops Ceddo, Sankofa and Black Audio Film/Video Collective formed part of this second wave – Ceddo formed in 1981–82, for instance, and became a franchised workshop in 1985.

33 Malcolm Le Grice points out that in eroding the traditional union concept of a division of labour, ACTT was bowing to the inevitable; changes in technology had made 'that division less and less tenable' (Panel Discussion 1984: 7). One can also recognise here the seeds of a weakening of the media unions under the Workshop Declaration, even though it was devised by union members, among others.

34 Parliament and County Hall had become increasingly polarised. Thatcher closed down the GLC and other metropolitan bodies broadly because they were clearly anti-nuclear, left-wing, benign authorities offering power to citizens as best they could (see Hall 1988).

35 Women, employed or not, have not voted in large numbers for Thatcher in any of her three elections (Segal 1983: 214; Hall 1988: 266).

36 For discussions of Thatcherism and feminism see also Gardiner (1983), Segal (1983), Brunt (1988, 1990) and Franklin, Lury and Stacey (1991).

37 'The Politics of Location' was the title of a symposium held in Birmingham in October 1988 at the Midland Arts Centre. The proceedings are largely reproduced in *Framework*, 36 (1989).

38 *Out to Lunch* has been adapted as a book of cartoons for Penguin by Jane Bradshaw, due for publication in 1992. The film was originally titled *Just Desserts*, and briefly *Out of Bounds*.

39 See Cockburn (1985) for a discussion of women's exclusion and discouragement from technical

education and employment, from high school onward.

40 LAW uses actors, at Equity rates, for voiceovers and occasionally on camera.

41 Through the Workshop Declaration the ACTT also agreed to union members working at especially negotiated lower rates because of the special circumstances applying to animation, and in recognition of the general tightness of funding for independent film.

42 Ideas in Dale Spender's *Man Made Language* (1980)were taken up in *Out to Lunch*.

WORKS CITED

Anon. (1984) *ACTT Workshop Declaration.* London: ACTT.

Brunt, Rosalind (1988) 'Conference Darling', *Spare Rib,* 192 (June), 19.

____ (1990) 'The Politics of Identity', in Stuart Hall and Martin Jacques (eds) *New Times: The Changing Face of Politics in the 1990s.* New York: Verso.

Campbell, Beatrix (1987) *The Iron Ladies: Why Do Women Vote Tory?* London: Virago.

Caughie, John and Simon Frith (1990) 'The British Film Institute: Retooling the Culture Industry', *Screen,* 31, 2, 214–22.

Cockburn, Cynthia (1985) *Machinery of Dominance: Women, Men, and Technical Know-How.* London: Pluto Press.

Creyke, Anne (1991) '*Alice in Wasteland*', *Yorkshire Evening Post,* 11 February.

Cubitt, Sean (1986) 'From Workhouse to Workshop', *Arts Express,* August/September, 13–14.

____ (1991) *Timeshift: On Video Culture.* New York: Routledge.

Franklin, Sarah, Celia Lury and Jackie Stacey (eds) (1991) *Off-Centre: Feminism and Cultural Studies.* London: Birmingham Cultural Studies, HarperCollins.

Gardiner, Jean (1983) 'Women, Recession and the Tories', in The *Politics of Thatcherism,* edited by Stuart Hall and Martin Jacques. London: Lawrence and Wishart.

Gibbons, Luke (1986) 'The Politics of Silence: Anne Devlin, Women and Irish Cinema', *Framework,* 30/31, 214.

Hall, Stuart (1988) *The Hard Road to Renewal: The Crisis of Thatcherism.* London: Verso.

Hall, Stuart and Martin Jacques (eds) (1983) The Politics of Thatcherism. London: Lawrence and Wishart.

— (1990) *New Times: The Changing Face of Politics in the 1990s.* New York: Verso.

Johnston, Claire and Paul Willemen (1975/76) 'Brecht in Britain: The Independent Political Film (on *The Nightcleaners*)', *Screen* 16, 4, 101–18.

Kanter, Hannah, Sarah Lefanu, Shalia Shah and Carole Spedding (eds) (1984) *Sweeping Statements: Writings from the Women's Liberation Movement, 1981–83.* London: The Women's Press.

Kelly, Mary (1983) *Post-Partum Document.* London: Routledge and Kegan Paul.

Koch, Gertrude (1989) 'The Body's Shadow Realm', *October,* 50, 329.

Leadbeater, Charlie (1990) 'Power to the Person', in Stuart Hall and Martin Jacques (eds) *New Times: The Changing Face of Politics in the 1990s.* New York: Verso, 137–49.

Lewis, Justin (1990) *Art, Culture, and Enterprise: The Politics of Art and the Cultural Industries.* London and New York: Routledge.

Lovell, Alan (1990) 'That Was the Workshop That Was', *Screen,* 31, 1, 102–8.

McFadyean, Melanie and Margaret Renn (1984) *Thatcher's Reign: A Bad Case of the Blues.* London: Chatto and Windus.

MacKinnon, Catharine (1987) *Feminism Unmodified: Discourses on Life and Law.* Cambridge: Harvard University Press.

MacPherson, Don (ed.) (1980) *Traditions of Independence: British Cinema in the Thirties.* London:

British Film Institute.

Meehan, Elizabeth (1990) 'British Feminism from the Sixties to the Eighties', in Harold L. Smith (ed.) *British Feminism in the Twentieth Century*. Amherst: University of Massachusetts Press, 189–204.

Merz, Caroline (1987) 'Distribution Matters: Circles', *Screen*, 28, 4, 66–9.

Mulvey, Laura (1975) 'Visual Pleasure and Narrative Cinema', *Screen*, 16, 3, 6–18.

Panel Discussion (1984) '"Training" the Independents', *Screen*, 25, 6, 516.

Parker, Roszika and Griselda Pollock (eds) (1987) *Framing Feminism: Art and the Women's Movement 1970–1985*. London and New York: Pandora Press.

Petley, Julian (1986) '*Crops and Robbers*', *Monthly Film Bulletin*, 53, 634, 354–5.

Pollock, Griselda (1989) *Vision and Difference: Femininity, Feminism, and the Histories of Art*. New York: Routledge.

Posener, Jill (1982) *Spray it Loud*. London: Routledge and Kegan Paul.

Rosenbaum, Jonathan (1984) '*The Gold Diggers*: A Preview', *Camera Obscura*, 12, 126–9.

Segal, Lynne (1983) 'The Heat in the Kitchen', in Stuart Hall and Martin Jacques (eds) *The Politics of Thatcherism*. London: Lawrence and Wishart.

Spender, Dale (1980) *Man Made Language*. Boston: Routledge and Kegan Paul.

Stern, Leslie (1982) 'The Body as Evidence', *Screen*, 23, 5, 39–60.

Vale, Jo (1989) 'Screens First: On the Threat to Radical TV', *Guardian*, 22 May.

Whitaker, Sheila (1985) 'Declarations of Independence', in Martyn Auty and Nick Roddick (eds) *British Cinema Now*. London: British Film Institute, 83–98.

Whitlock, M. J. (1987) 'Five More Years of Desolation?', *Spare Rib*, 180 (July), 15.

Williams, Linda (1989) *Hard Core: Power, Pleasure and Machines of the Visible*. Berkeley: University of California Press.

Willamson, Judith (1978) *Decoding Advertisements: Ideology and Meaning in Advertising*. London: Marion Boyars.

____ (1984) 'Give Us a Smile', *Monthly Film Bulletin*, 51, 609, 322.

____ (1987) 'Causes without a Rebel', *New Statesman*, 21 August, 19–20.

Wollen, Peter (1982) *Readings and Writings*. London: Verso.

Wollen, Peter and Laura Mulvey (1976) 'Written Discussion', *Afterimage*, 6 (Summer), 30–9.

11. THE BODY POLITIC: KEN RUSSELL IN THE 1980s

Barry Keith Grant

Ken Russell is commonly known – and most often summarily dismissed – as a director who indulges in visual excess. Unlike many other art-house *auteurs*, most notably Federico Fellini and Luchino Visconti, with whom he is often compared (or more accurately, contrasted), commentators commonly see Russell as vulgar, tasteless, excessive, puerile, misogynist and even misanthropic. Critics established this view of Russell early in his career, at least since his last film for BBC television, *Dance of the Seven Veils* (1970), a biography of Richard Strauss that created a storm of controversy including a parliamentary motion criticising the film's 'viciousness, savagery and brutality' (Baxter 1973: 30). This reputation has remained entrenched ever since. Whatever prestige Russell gained with his third feature film, *Women in Love* (1969), a generally sensitive adaptation of the D. H. Lawrence novel, was largely negated by the two pictures that followed. *The Music Lovers* (1970) and *The Devils* (1971), much more flamboyant than *Women in Love*, displayed all of Russell's more notorious qualities: bold, startling images of eroticism, physical revulsion and violence, a rapid 'kino-fist' editing style frequently incorporating unsubtle shock effects, all combining in what Michael Dempsey vividly described as 'hyperthyroid camp circuses' (1977/78: 24).

Unlike the films of his contemporary Richard Lester, which share a certain visual energy, Russell's work concentrates less on exuberant *jouissance* than the darker aspects of the sexual self. Thus while critics touted the American-born Lester as the cinematic embodiment of 'swinging London' in the 1960s, they perceived Russell as the outrageous *enfant terrible* of British film in the 1970s, a director whose lack of 'restraint' and 'bad taste' violated the decorum of serious British cinema, an aesthetically as well as morally conservative cinema (Manvell 1969: 50; Armes 1978: 33; Ellis 1978: 27) seen as representative of British art and culture generally.

Russell, while aware that the critical rejection of his work is to some extent the result of the British context (Jaehne 1988: 54), has played the part of 'our own abominable showman' (Buckley 1972: 13) with glee. His calculated description of *The Music Lovers* as 'the story of a love affair between a homosexual and a nymphomaniac', for example, exploited the film's commercial potential, but also aroused the ire of cultured Britons. Not insensitive to good promotional hype, Russell embraced the role of *enfant terrible*, even going so far as to 'assault' one of his most vociferous critics, Alexander Walker, on television, and dismissing most others as narrow-minded and irrelevant. In his 1991 made-for-television autobiography, *A British Picture*, subtitled 'Portrait of an Enfant Terrible', the Russell figure sports a rainbow-coloured shock of hair and, although he momentarily considers it, he stead-fastly refuses to change his image.

While his persona has earned him a degree of notoriety, Russell has also been consistently marginalised in historical discussions of British national cinema, despite the fact that his films provide a kind of dialectical response to the sublimated sexu-ality of the Angry Young Men films, the Hammer horror, and the Carry On movies that preceded him.[1] Book-length studies of British film mention him only briefly, or not at all. Conservative critics find him vulgar and disrespectful, while those of the left view his obsession with romantic individualists politically counter-productive. Only a few – most notably Michael Dempsey (1972), John Baxter (1973) and Joseph Gomez (1976) – bother to treat Russell's work with sustained attention. His later films, moreover, received virtually no critical commentary, perhaps because they appear more diffuse and thus less indicative of Russell's auteurist reputation. Of the six that he made in the 1980s, only *Gothic* (1987) and *Salomé's Last Dance* (1988) obviously fit into his distinctive approach to biographies about artists; he made both *Altered States* (1980) and *Crimes of Passion* (1984) in the United States, far from the beloved Lake District, the distinctive English landscape that appears in so many of Russell's films.

But, in fact, Russell's work is neither the distant voice nor still life that critics have deemed it. Given the greater adventurousness in British cinema in the 1980s than when he first came to prominence, particularly in the films of Nicolas Roeg, Derek Jarman (who began his film career as set designer of *The Devils*), and Peter Greenaway, Russell's work of the period lost some of its ability to shock audiences, but it nevertheless remains distinctly British. Indeed, the features that Russell directed in the 1980s not only grow from his earlier work, but also are riven with tensions that suggest significant relations to the historical forces at work in British culture collectively known as Thatcherism.

In what follows, I propose an alternative reading of Ken Russell's work, one that situates his films squarely *within* the British cultural climate of the 1980s rather than marginalising them as an anomalous aberration. The films' thematic tensions, partic-ularly their conflicts between masculine and feminine desire, and the director's own shifting sympathies, express an ambivalence between the need to maintain tradi-tional power structures and the necessity for change that constitute a uniquely rich, unresolved series of cinematic responses to the ideological project of Thatcherism. Russell's excessive style and his frequently campy or mock heroic tone not only exist at odds with the lofty seriousness of his subjects, but also suggest a view of contemporary British life that both embraces the neoconservatism of Thatcherism and resists it.

Typically conceived in terms of a dialectic between realism and fantasy, British cinema's strictest categories collapse in Russell's work. Accordingly, critics discuss him both as a realist (Armes 1978: 300–7) and as a fantasist (Durgnat 1977). The documentary, which has historically been so important in the evolution of British cinema, was largely absorbed into and compromised by the institution of feature filmmaking (Barr 1986: 13; Walker 1986: 155). But virtually alone (with the important exception of Peter Watkins), Russell reversed this influence, redefining British documentary 'restraint' by combining realism with fictional devices to create the biographical 'docudrama'.

Given Russell's distinctive style, which led Stephen Farber (1975) to evoke Dr Johnson's description of the metaphysical poets ('the most heterogeneous ideas are yoked by violence together'), it is not surprising that his films have related uneasily to popular genres. Initially, after two unsuccessful apprentice movies with clear generic affinities, the Tati-like *French Dressing* (1963) and the spy thriller *Billion Dollar Brain* (1965), Russell's earlier films exist in opposition to generic conventions, frequently subverting them. Most obviously, his films about artists deflate the naive reverence of the typical Hollywood biography, which he views as dully conventional (Gow 1970: 9). These movies, employing what Joseph Gomez identifies as a 'tripartite perspective which incorporates the protagonist's own romantic self-image, a more objective view revealed by the perspective of time, and finally Russell's personal vision' (1976: 35), obviously works against the conventional linear narrative of the Hollywood biopic. Many of Russell's films, like the work of Dennis Potter, can also be considered musicals in which he foregrounds the relations between music, dance and sexuality rather than, as in the classic musical, sublimating it. *The Boy Friend* (1972), Russell's homage to the Busby Berkeley musicals of the 1930s, employs camp as a double-edged sword that simultaneously mocks and celebrates the classic Hollywood musical, although ultimately the film attacks the genre that inspired it by contextualising the mounting of the show as a battle among individual egos rather than as a harmonious group effort.

By contrast, the later films position themselves more comfortably *within* the genre system. Most obviously, *Gothic* mobilises a particular form of the horror genre, as signalled by its generic title. In a sense, of course, most of Russell's movies are 'horrifying,' although *Gothic* and *The Lair of the White Worm* (1988) remain his only sustained forays into the horror genre. Less glibly, one might argue that *The Devils* is an anti-horror film, for by demythifying the supernatural it shows the source of horror to be psychological, the result of sexual repression. Although in *Gothic* Russell undercuts the genteel depiction of the discussions between Mary Wollstonecraft Shelley (Natasha Richardson), Percy Shelley (Julian Sands) and Byron (Gabriel Byrne) at the Swiss Villa Diodati that led to the writing of *Frankenstein* (1818), as depicted in *Bride of Frankenstein* (James Whale, 1935), his film nevertheless remains faithful to the genre itself. Thus *Gothic*, appropriately, is filled with the iconography and appurtenances of the gothic story: the heroine running through hallways in flowing white robes, mirrors that reveal ghostly images, spectres in suits of armour, hidden rooms, raging storms, and so on. In the end, typically, the supernatural is explained away as a night of rampant imagination – indeed, one of Mary's visions is modelled on Henry Fuseli's famous painting *The Nightmare* (1781) – and in the film's coda, the following morning is sunny and civil, the group calmly posed for a *déjeuner sur l'herbe*.

Similarly, *The Lair of the White Worm*, its tone more campy than ironic, features many of the stock characters of the horror genre, as well as its conventional thematic oppositions. And if it suggests a victory in the end for the horrific Other, it only provides the 'anti-genre' reversal that already had become conventional in the genre. *Crimes of Passion* also mobilises the horror film, most obviously in the casting of Anthony Perkins, an icon of the genre primarily because of his role as Norman Bates

China Blue (Kathleen Turner) walks the streets in *Crimes of Passion* (1984), a film displaying the visual style of classic film noir

in *Psycho* (1960), as a similarly insanely repressed character.[2] *Crimes of Passion* also demonstrates affinities with film noir, both visually, in its depiction of downtown urban nightlife, and in its narrative, the story of a sexual woman who lures a man away from his wife and responsible domestic existence – perhaps the basic noir plot (Damico 1978: 54). *Altered States* constructs its psychic researcher protagonist, Eddie Jessup (William Hurt), as the conventional mad scientist figure of science fiction who transgresses 'natural' boundaries. In the great cliché of the genre, he experiments in areas men were not meant to know (Bell-Metereau 1982: 171–2).

Genre movies function, on one level, to relieve cultural anxieties (see Neale 1980; Schatz 1981; Grant 1986). One of the primary mythological strategies (Barthes 1972) for doing so makes culture into nature (Neale 1980; Schatz 1981) – an ideological operation made explicit in the metaphorical premise of *Altered States*. The move from generic opposition to accommodation is the result, at least in part, of the fact that American companies financed all of Russell's films of this period, but this shift also suggests an attempt by the director to become more acceptable to the mainstream, indicative of Thatcherism's push toward greater prominence in the international marketplace during the 1980s. Yet while some contemporaneous British films, like *Stormy Monday* (1987), critique this policy, economic issues remain virtually absent from these Russell films (although concern is expressed in *Altered States* about maintaining research grants). Rather, they are sublimated as generic conventions that attempt to resolve the cultural anxieties of which Thatcherism itself is in part a symptom.

In this regard Russell's making of *The Rainbow* (1988), an adaptation of D. H. Lawrence's 1915 novel, is significant. Focusing on a bucolic Britain in the days of Empire, *The Rainbow* becomes a heritage drama (Barr 1986: 12), which in its reliance on nostalgia is a particularly conducive genre for the conservatism of Thatcherite ideology: its 'mission,' according to Stuart Hall, was 'to reconstruct social life as a whole around a return to the old values – the philosophies of tradition, Englishness, respectability, patriarchalism, family and nation' (1988: 39). A 'prequel' to *Women in Love*, the film returns Russell to the material which first established his reputation and which, apart from *Tommy* (1975), represents Russell's only unqualified critical and commercial success. Russell emphasises the connection by including cast members Glenda Jackson and Christopher Gable and using cinematographer Billy Williams and production designer Luciana Arrighi – all of whom contributed to *Women in Love*.[3] The casting of Jackson strikes a particularly resonant chord, for her role in the earlier film made her an international star; in *The Rainbow*, she plays, in effect, her own mother. The film thus exists in an aura of personal nostalgia. It suggests that Russell, even as he notes about his own artist characters (Baxter 1973: 134), avoids the present by returning to the past.

At the same time as it invokes an era of past glory for its maker, *The Rainbow* also appeals to cultural nostalgia. Consumed with personal dilemmas of love and desire, Russell's Lawrentian characters recall Roy Armes' description of the good Englishman who, secure in Britain's industrial affluence and international power, 'could pass through life and hardly notice the existence of the state, beyond the post office and the policeman' (1978: 17). The discussions of Britain's presence in India and of democracy and class in *The Rainbow* appear less as explorations of political philosophy, whether about events when the film is set or when it was made, than as weapons in battles of egos. Tellingly, the discussion about democracy and class takes place during a badminton match, a visual metaphor of their petty personal debates. Russell has voiced his discontent with British cinema of the era: 'Most British films these days,' he avers, 'are about people hitting each other over the head with bottles in Brixton' – political nihilism which he thinks is emphasised at the expense of the physical and spiritual beauty of the sceptered isle (Jaehne 1988: 54; Fuller 1989: 2). Russell claims to prefer more nostalgic films, like *Yanks* (1979) and *Hope and Glory* (1987), a movie upon which he lavished rare praise (Jaehne 1988: 54).

The Rainbow is Russell's contribution to the nostalgia cycle, the culmination of the de-emphasis of political themes in his work. Only in *Savage Messiah* (1972) does Russell uncharacteristically set out to depict the artist as 'worker' (Buckley 1972: 14), although *The Devils*, with its examination of the political motives informing the persecution of Urbain Grandier (Oliver Reed), may be Russell's most political film. But even here, the narrative is removed to a distant past. For Russell, the patina of an idyllic past and the story of Ursula Brangwen, 'an aristocrat of the spirit', serve to restore spirituality to the crass materialism of contemporary Thatcherite England (Fuller 1989: 4). Certainly Russell's middle-period films *Tommy*, *Lisztomania* (1975) and *Valentino* (1977) reveal his dislike of contemporary mass culture (Farber 1975: 44), an antipathy not far removed from Thatcherism's view of cultural decline. Like Thatcherite ideology, these films, especially the last of the three, view masscult and the decline of values as largely the result of Americanisation. And, as if in response, Russell's films of the 1980s express an 'aristocratic' fear of cultural levelling, a reaction to the new Britain shown in films like *My Beautiful Laundrette* (1985) and *Sammy and Rosie Get Laid* (1987). For Russell, as for Ursula, the masses are cultural rubes, like the philistine tourists at the beginning and end of *Gothic*, reminiscent of Salomé's description of the Romans in *Salomé's Last Dance* as 'brutal and coarse, with their uncouth jargon'.

However, Russell does not embrace an appropriate corresponding style, an up-lifting aesthetic in the Great Tradition of Leavis. He is satisfied merely for his movies to shock audiences out of complacency (Gow 1970: 8; Baxter 1973: 201). Thus, even as Russell's films of this period work within the constraints of genre, his style remains visually flamboyant, featuring a *mise-en-scène* clearly excessive to the requirements of conventional narrative structures. This characteristic excess appears, for example, in the Eisensteinian montages of Jessup's drug-induced hallucinations in *Altered States*; in the plethora of psychoanalytic signifiers that fill *The Lair of the White Worm*; in the rapid-fire, aphoristic dialogue of *Gothic* and *Crimes of Passion*; and in the latter's over-determined noir visuals, particularly in the depiction of the prostitute China Blue (Kathleen Turner) and the downtown streets she works.

In fact, Russell's excessive style is strikingly similar to that of classic Hollywood melodrama, a connection that, despite its importance for understanding this film-maker's work, seems strangely unexplored. In the Hollywood melodrama, as in *The Rainbow* and Russell's cinema generally, social and political issues become translated into personal terms (Elsaesser 1986: 282). The kinetic energy, rich *mise-en-scène*, and florid music of Hollywood melodrama – those moments of extreme stylisation that break conventional codes of realism – have been explained psychoanalytically by several critics as an excess that reveals an 'hysteria bubbling all the time just below the surface' (Elsaesser 1986: 289), instances of what Freud termed 'conver-sion hysteria' (Nowell-Smith 1977: 117). In this approach, the film text becomes, in a sense, analogous to the physical body, the text's excessive style its symptoma-tology. This description of melodrama also applies to Russell's films, which in fact exhibit an obsessive preoccupation with the body. Indeed, the frequent description of Russell's style as 'hysterical' is more apt than those who use the word negatively to dismiss the director realise.

Robin Wood expresses a common view that Russell's films display a pronounced hatred of the body (1980: 909). Certainly the protagonists of both *Altered States* and *Crimes of Passion* feel trapped by their bodies, although of these films *The Lair of the White Worm* most obviously endorses this view, as it may be read as a horror fable about AIDS: the vampirism of the reptilian *femme fatale*, Lady Sylvia (Amanda Donahoe), is an infectious 'disease' passed through the bloodstream. But, in fact, Russell's films are complex texts that reveal a more ambivalent view of the body, often oscillating between revulsion, desire and guilt. This ambivalence, most frequently articulated alternately as phallic celebration and anxiety about masculine identity, has its most famous instance in *Lisztomania* when Liszt (Roger Daltrey) envisions his phallus as a maypole worshipped by women, abruptly followed by the castration of his 'howitzer-sized penis' (Dempsey 1977/78: 22) by spider-woman Princess Caroline in a guillotine.

Like their predecessors, these Russell films are filled with imagery of ineluctable mortality ('Not damp – decay!' as Shelley shrieks in *Gothic*), of all the natural shocks to which flesh is heir. Also, in *Salomé's Last Dance* Russell makes the age difference

Jessup's (William Hurt) experiments in the isolation tank literalise the Russell protagonist's fear of the body in *Altered States* (1980)

between Herod and Salomé a major element of Wilde's play by casting as Salomé the diminutive and alabaster Imogen Millais-Scott, whose Lolita-like charm strongly contrasts with the flabby, aged skin of Stratford Johns as the Tetrarch. As in the work of Peter Greenaway, Russell's films are obsessed with physical decay and death; but whereas Greenaway's films manage this anxiety through rigorously controlled, almost mathematical aesthetic structures, Russell's films refuse such containment.

If the result, typically, is the perception of aesthetic failure on the director's part – the typical responses that Russell mixes tones unsuccessfully or lacks 'taste' and is 'vulgar' – his 'ill-wrought urns' are significant in that they also reflect contemporary cultural values and tensions no less than did Hollywood melodrama during the Eisenhower period. Regardless of Russell's claim to be himself unaware of his work dealing especially with a 'politics of the body' (Gentry 1983: 9–10), the body is clearly a privileged site of anxiety and struggle in Russell's films. It represents the body politic, especially the fear of cultural pollution and compromise by the inevitable social changes engendered by the post-Empire era and expressed as the political retrenchment and defensive nationalism that characterised Thatcherite ideology. Russell's 'shocking' images of physical decomposition and violence in his 1980s films are, perhaps, the visual equivalent of Britain's excessive show of strength in the Falkland Islands. The frequent artist figures in Russell's work who seek to remain aesthetically 'pure' in the face of cultural 'contamination' express Thatcherism's dismay with Labour's welfare state, which preceded its rise to power.

The site of conflict in the melodrama, usually located within the nuclear family (Nowell-Smith 1977: Kleinhans 1978), reveals a pattern of crisis precipitated by desire and repression. Again, this is also true of Russell's films of the Thatcher era. The woman's appeal as an indiscreet object of desire in *Salomé's Last Dance* casts a wedge between husband and wife ('It is strange that the husband of my mother looks at me like that', Salomé coyly observes). Her dance, like Dorothy Malone's in *Written on the Wind* (1956), is presented as a clear challenge to patriarchal authority. In *Gothic*, the genesis of *Frankenstein* is 'explained' as Mary's response to the loss of her child, while she perceives Byron's philosophy of 'free love' as a threat to her heterosexual coupling with Shelley. In *Crimes of Passion*, the marriage and family life of protagonist Bobby Grady (John Laughlin) is destroyed because of his desire for another woman. After admitting this attraction to his wife, Bobby talks to his young son, the two separated by a chain-link fence, an image of familial separation that is the inevitable result of such a 'fatal attraction'. And toward the end of *The Lair of the White Worm*, one of the Trent sisters discovers her missing mother, but significantly, the fate of the father is never made clear – amid all the sexual anarchy depicted in the film, the patriarch simply vanishes.

Yet if these films display a masculine panic about sexual difference and empowerment, at times they also firmly reinstate patriarchy, as in the end of Oscar Wilde's play *Salomé* (1891), contained within *Salomé's Last Dance*, where a phallic spear by order of Herod summarily kills the threatening woman. In Russell's interpretation of the play, Salomé is a nymphet, a sexual woman who thereby is, in Claire Johnston's words, 'a traumatic presence which must be negated' (1976: 213). Further, Russell uses Wilde himself as a figure that threatens heterosexual monogamy, and like his own Salomé, Wilde is eliminated as a threat to dominant ideology by being arrested at film's end. The paradigm of this hysterical reinstatement of the phallus in these films is the scene in *Crimes of Passion* where Bobby, whose placement as a narrative frame serves to contain the feminine rage of Joanna, mimes 'the human penis' ('direct from the wild untamed jungles of Borneo', according to his friend's introduction) growing erect. Russell punctuates his performance at the backyard barbecue – even the hotdogs are wielded like phalluses – non-diegetically with the opening movement of Strauss's *Also Sprach Zarathustra*, thus giving Bobby's view of the phallus all the monumentality Kubrick earlier associated with this piece of music in *2001: A Space Odyssey* (1968).

In *The Rainbow*, Ursula's desire to desire ('the source of all truth and good', her teacher and lesbian lover, Winifred, tells her) threatens patriarchal tradition in that she wishes to transcend the conventional roles assigned to women. But in her employment as a teacher, Ursula (Sammi Davis) quickly succumbs to phallic control, the part of the film Russell seems most to relish, since it receives particular stylistic emphasis. In short order Ursula changes her approach to teaching from the ideal of appealing to reason in the unruly (male) children to accepting the necessity of thrashing with a cane, which she does to one troublesome lad with such force that it breaks. As the unctuous headmaster bluntly puts it, 'Only my cane rules this school' – and, indeed, in one shot, the cane looms large in the foreground, the composition expressing the inevitability of male power. So even though Russell omits the novel's patriarch Will Brangwen from his adaptation, his power is nonetheless present in Russell's Dickensian treatment of Ursula's teaching experience.

Thatcherism's reification of the family and patriarchy is responsible for the unsatis-fyingly abrupt shift that marks the end of *Altered States*. Throughout the film Jessup is characterised, and his experiments contextualised, in terms of his sexual dread. For example, after imbibing the hallucinogenic mixture offered him by the Mexican indians, Jessup envisions (recalling the fantasia of fleeting fame accompanying *The 1812 Overture* in *The Music Lovers*) himself and his wife, Emily (Blair Brown), as nudes who turn to stone and are then eroded away by a sudden, fierce wind. Even in an impersonal dalliance with a student, he hallucinates a chasm in the floor between them, a space at once the pit of hell and a nightmare of vaginal horror (Bell-Metereau 1982: 174). Intimacy for him is consistently horrifying; his mocking description of family life as 'clutter, clatter and ritual' is nicely conveyed by Russell in, for example, the exceedingly narrow corridors of the Jessups' apartment. So, in terms of the film's sci-fi premise, his initial transformations to primitive man function as an objec-tive correlative of Jessup's unacknowledged 'animal lusts', while his last changes into sheer energy fulfill his fantasy of discorporation, a retreat from the body and the inescapable fact of sexual difference (Sobchack 1986).

But then, in the climax, the film suddenly seeks to erase the hysteria it has expressed in having adopted Jessup's subjective point of view by requiring of the viewer an abrupt and wide leap of faith. Emily reaches into the swirling mass of primal energy that Jessup has become and somehow retrieves him, restoring him to human form. From this experience he learns that 'the ultimate truth of all is that there is no truth'. As if in response to this newly perceived metaphysical absurdity, Jessup suddenly professes love for his estranged wife and family. Later that night he is now able, in turn, to rescue her from primal formlessness. In a final, reposeful moment they embrace. As several commentators have noted (see, for example, Fox 1981; Sobchack 1986), this ending forces an improbable *volte-face* upon the character of Jessup, who suddenly affirms the values of family and platitudes about romantic love. It also redefines Emily as wife and mother rather than professional scientist, a reflection of Thatcherism's regressive view of women (Hall 1990: 21). Thus the film, like many American movies of the time, privileges family and reinstates the power of the Father, an ideological project that may be characteristic not only of Reaganite entertainment but also that of his staunchest ally, Thatcher.

The Lair of the White Worm is also about the struggle of patriarchy and British tradition to retain power. An updating of Bram Stoker's 1911 novel about a prehistoric

Lady Sylvia (Amanda Donohoe) lifts the lid off the id in *The Lair of the White Worm* (1988)

serpent ('wurm') dwelling undetected for centuries in the English Midlands, the film focuses on a battle between patriarchal authority in the figure of Lord D'Ampton (Hugh Grant) and the release of repressed (female) sexual energy, in the form of the reptilian Lady Sylvia, high priestess of the worm cult. Russell represents this conflict with the images of the cross and the snake, respectively. When the virginal Eve (Sammi Davis) touches a crucifix covered with venom expectorated by Lady Sylvia, she has horrifying visions (clearly evoking the more notorious scenes in *The Devils*) of nuns from the nearby ancient convent ('captive virgins praying to an impotent god') being ravaged by Roman soldiers, the Bosch-like scene presided over by the serpent-god. Lady Sylvia's 'monstrous' sexuality threatens the moral fibre of the nation itself. She seduces a young fellow – a boy scout, no less! – and then abruptly reveals her fangs, her head quickly darting below the frame to emasculate him, a horrifying vision of the *vagina dentata*. Her sexuality is a direct challenge to the family, as the Trent sisters' missing mother is discovered under her influence to have become a vampire watching erotic videos; and even the local constable, icon of British law and order, becomes a vampire. Indeed, the nation has become so corrupt that there are few virgins left in Britain to sacrifice, and Lady Sylvia must check Eve on this score before proceeding further.

But ultimately the film is ambivalent about her. Even though she is frightening, she is also witty, lively and refreshingly engaging, certainly a welcome opposite to the stuffiness of the two wooden patriarchal 'heroes'. Russell once noted that 'There's a liberating force in music which ... people can't help responding to, being primitive creatures at heart' (quoted in Baxter 1973: 189) – a liberating lifting of the lid off the id perfectly visualised in the high angle shot of Lady Sylvia emerging from a woven basket and snaking across the floor in a tight lamé dress to the strains of 'exotic' flute music, a direct contrast to the silly traditionalism of Angus's tartans and bagpipes.

The Lair of the White Worm resembles *The Rainbow* in the sense that it too harkens back to the days of traditional British patriarchal hegemony. Significantly, in his adaptation Russell entirely omits the novel's important black character, Oolanga (whom Stoker frequently describes with intense racial hatred), instead simply giving us a white England apparently untroubled by racial difference. Yet the horror figured as sexual difference in the form of Lady Sylvia nevertheless suggests the mythic defense of traditional British culture through the sexual stereotyping typical of colonialism. As Ella Shohat has shown, colonialist discourse intertwines with patriarchal discourse; the colonised land is frequently represented as female, with the result that colonisation is implicitly endorsed by the 'masculinist power of possession ... penetration and knowledge' (1991: 57). (Interestingly, Shohat specifically identifies the figure of Salomé as a particularly clear instance of the colonised Other as a feminised projection of the white European male's colonial/sexual Imaginary (1991: 72).) Thus, Lady Sylvia in *The Lair of the White Worm* is controlled by a recording of 'Turkish charmer' music from D'Ampton's father's 'North African collection' – that is, from a region that Britain no longer 'collects', or, in other words, where it can no longer wield significant colonialist power.

The consistent threat to masculinity in these films suggests 'the profound crisis of national identity' (Hall 1990: 21) to which Thatcherism is a response, the historical erosion of Britain's political power that Thatcherism seeks so strenuously to deny. Russell's films, then, are symptomatic of a nation scaling down from the heady days of Empire and its last moment of greatness as a world power in the 'swinging sixties' to more sobering contemporary political and economic realities. They mark the shift from a restrained national cinema, one dominated by a tasteful 'tradition of quality' (Ellis 1978), to the kind of stylistic indulgence indicative of a nation that, no longer exerting world power, can only turn inward.

Russell's films, filled with stylistic, generic and thematic tensions, express both the values of British tradition and a disdain for them that mirrors the tensions inherent in Thatcherism, itself a bundle of 'contradictory values' (Hall 1988: 53). Russell continues to prefer romantic individuals, usually artists, as his protagonists (Ursula Brangwen,

Byron and the Shelleys, obviously, while Jessup is a kind of 'hunger artist' and China Blue a performance artist), most of whom abandon their idealism toward the end, their very struggle a reflection of Thatcherism's double emphasis on a 'free market and strong state' (Hall 1988: 39). Russell's own appearance in the spy thriller *The Russia House* (1990) as a singular radically-dressed agent amid of sea of nondescript, dark suits who is nonetheless rabidly conservative, not unlike Ed Begley's bellicose fascist General Midwinter in *Billion Dollar Brain*, cleverly employs the director's own persona and his work's characteristic dualities in its casting.

Russell's 1980s films were consistent in their concerns and therefore distinctive in a national cinema that has been characterised by a marked absence of auteurs (Armes 1978: 262). Certainly they reveal that tension between the filmmaker's material and his personality that generates the 'interior meaning' said to be the hallmark of the classic auteur (Sarris 1974: 513). Yet this is not to argue for the 'greatness' of Russell as an individual director; for his films, despite their richness of personal vision, are at the same time revealing cultural expressions. Russell's work, like that of Fellini, Ingmar Bergman and Woody Allen, may suffer from 'boorish megalomania' (Walker 1986: 392) and his films function as 'pretexts for the effluence of his own fantasies' (Wood 1990: 909), but they are not *simply* solipsistic exercises. Given that Russell works more by intuition than by intellect, it is not surprising that his work should have such cultural resonance. His imagination, which his BBC producer and 'industrial *paterfamilias*' Huw Wheldon described as 'like a bird being driven along on a huge gale' (quoted in Baxter 1973: 123), surely rides the winds of social and cultural change. In this sense, then, Russell's cinema, although usually dismissed as marginal within British film, is in fact central. If the 'conventional binary opposition of realist and non-realist' practice in British film needs 'reworking' (Barr 1986: 15), such a re-examination would necessarily move Russell from the margin to the centre.

NOTES

1 *Carry On Dick* might well serve as an epigram for Russell's cinema.
2 Russell emphasises the connection through close-ups of Perkins engaging in sexual voyeurism, as had Hitchcock in the earlier film.
3 In general, Russel's development of a stock company of both actors and crew, the creation of an extended 'family', is at least partially motivated by a desire for comfort and security.

WORKS CITED

Armes, Roy (1978) *A Critical History of the British Cinema*. New York: Oxford University Press.

Barr, Charles (ed.) (1986) *All Our Yesterdays: 90 Years of British Cinema*. London: British Film Institute.

Barthes, Roland (1972) *Mythologies*, ed. and trans. Annette Lavers. New York: Hill and Wang.

Baxter, John (1973) *An Appalling Talent: Ken Russell*. London: Michael Joseph.

Bell-Metereau, Rebecca (1982) '*Altered States* and the Popular Myth of Self-Discovery', *Journal of Popular Film and Television*, 9, 4, 171–9.

Buckley, Peter (1972) 'Savage Saviour', *Films and Filming*, 19, 1, 14–16.

Damico, James (1978) 'Film Noir: A Modest Proposal', *Film Reader*, 3, 48–57.

Dempsey, Michael (1972) 'The World of Ken Russell', *Film Quarterly*, 25, 3, 13–25.

_____ (1977/78) 'Ken Russell, Again', *Film Quarterly*, 31, 2, 1924.

Durgnat, Raymond (1977) 'The Great British Phantasmagoria', *Film Comment*, 13, 3, 48–53.

Ellis, John (1978) 'Art, Culture and Quality: Terms for a Cinema in the Forties and Seventies', *Screen*, 19, 3, 949.

Elsaesser, Thomas (1986 [1972]) 'Tales of Sound and Fury: Observations on the Family Melodrama', in Barry Keith Grant (ed.) *Film Genre Reader*. Austin: University of Texas Press, 278–308.

Farber, Stephen (1975) 'Russellmania', *Film Comment*, 11, 6, 39–46.

Fox, Jordan R. (1981) 'Review of *Altered States*', *Cinefantastique*, 11, 1, 46.

Fuller, Graham (1989) 'Next of Ken', *Film Comment*, 25, 3, 24.

Gentry, Ric (1983) 'Ken Russell: An Interview', *Post Script*, 2, 3, 2–23.

Gomez, Joseph (1976) *Ken Russell: The Adaptor as Creator*. London: Frederick Muller.

Gow, Gordon (1970) 'Shock Treatment', *Films and Filming*, 16, 10, 8–12.

Grant, Barry Keith (ed.) (1986) *Film Genre Reader*. Austin: University of Texas Press.

Hall, Stuart (1988) 'The Toad in the Garden: Thatcherism among the Theorists', in Gary Nelson and Lawrence Grossberg (eds) *Marxism and the Interpretation of Culture*. Urbana and Chicago: University of Illinois Press, 35–57.

_____ (1990) 'The Emergence of Cultural Studies and the Crisis of the Humanities', *October*, 53, 11–23.

Jaehne, Karen (1988) 'Wormomania', *Film Comment*, 24, 6, 52–4.

Johnston, Claire (1976) 'Women's Cinema as Counter Cinema', in Bill Nichols (ed.) *Movies and Methods*. Berkeley: University of California Press, 208–17.

Kleinhans, Chuck (1978) 'Notes on Melodrama and the Family under Capitalism', *Film Reader*, 3, 40–7.

Manvell, Roger (1969) *New Cinema in Britain*. New York: Dutton.

Neale, Stephen (1980) *Genre*. London: British Film Institute.

Nowell-Smith, Geoffrey (1977) 'Minnelli and Melodrama', *Screen*, 18, 2, 113–18.

Sarris, Andrew (1974) 'Notes on the Auteur Theory in 1962', in Gerald Mast and Marshall Cohen (eds) *Film Theory and Criticism*. New York: Oxford University Press, 500–15.

Schatz, Thomas (1981) *Hollywood Genres*. New York: Random House.

Shohat, Ella (1991) 'Gender and Culture of Empire: Toward a Feminist Ethnography of the Cinema', *Quarterly Review of Film and Video*, 13, 13, 45–84.

Sobchack, Vivian (1986) 'Child/Alien/Father: Patriarchal Crisis and Generic Exchange', *Camera Obscura*, 15, 23–4.

Walker, Alexander (1986) *Hollywood, England: The British Film Industry in the Sixties*. London: Harrap.

Wood, Robin (1980) 'Ken Russell', in Richard Roud (ed.) *A Critical Dictionary*, vol. 2. New York: Viking Press, 909–10.

12. 'EVERYONE'S AN AMERICAN NOW': THATCHERITE IDEOLOGY IN THE FILMS OF NICOLAS ROEG

Jim Leach

In Nicolas Roeg's *Eureka* (1983), an American gangster involved in a takeover bid for a Caribbean island is confident that the owner will eventually come to terms because he is 'an American' and thus knows that 'we're all on the same side'. It is the middle of World War Two, a time when national boundaries would seem to have been very clearly defined and when (according to cultural myths skillfully exploited by Margaret Thatcher) Britons discovered a sense of national purpose long since eroded. Yet the gangster declares that 'everyone's an American now' and characterises the war as a conflict between 'Americans who all speak different languages'. He looks forward to a time when even the Japanese will be 'Americans' but does not find it necessary even to mention the British.

The homogenising effect of American cultural power is illustrated by its spokesman: the gangster is named Mayakovsky (after the Russian poet), is of Jewish origin, but works for the Mafia. One of the agencies through which this power has been disseminated is, of course, the cinema. The narrative codes developed in Hollywood prevail in commercial cinema throughout the world, and American companies dominate film production and exhibition in many countries. In this essay I discuss the extent to which Roeg's cinema participates in or resists this process of 'Americanisation' and place Roeg's British perspective on 'American' culture within the context of the ideological project of Thatcherism. Finally, the essay offers an analysis of the cultural and ideological implications in Roeg's films of the 1980s and a brief attempt to define their contribution to recent developments in British cinema.[1]

After starting out as a clapper boy in 1950, Nicolas Roeg became one of Britain's most respected cinematographers before establishing himself as a film director in the 1970s, a time when the 'alternative' cultural movements of the previous decade began to lose their momentum. The new conservatism, signaled in Britain by Margaret Thatcher's rise to power, coincided with the virtual collapse of the British film industry after the brief economic boom in the late 1960s when the Hollywood studios invested heavily in the 'swinging Britain' image. Two aspects of Roeg's films stand out in relation to this social and cinematic context: (i) ignoring the trend toward 'safe' subjects, they continue the formal and sexual 'daring' of 1960s cinema; (ii) they are rarely set in Britain.

In fact, Roeg produced most of his films with American money, the major exception being *The Man Who Fell to Earth* (1976) – the first British-financed film shot entirely in the United States. His career thus seems to confirm Alan Parker's claim that American financing is now required if a British filmmaker wants to make films of any ambition (see Park 1984: 104). Yet unlike Parker and many earlier and more recent British filmmakers, Roeg did not leave to work in Hollywood, although in the 1990s he would make several modestly budgeted films, mainly for cable television, in the United States. His 1980s films exist in a kind of no-man's-land within which he activates and explores the tensions and contradictions in the new order and in the Thatcherite response to it.

During this period, television emerged as an important alternative source of funding for British filmmakers willing to accept budgetary constraints. Roeg did not pursue this option, believing that his vision demanded a large screen (Park 1984: 85). Yet the contemporary experience of television plays a significant role in his films, where the spectator's attention often becomes divided among different elements within the image and on the soundtrack. Roeg likened this strategy to the way 'people watch television and read a magazine at the same time looking from one to the other' (quoted in Waller 1976: 27). Often this kind of viewing involves television screens within the film screen, as with the bank of monitors assembled by Newton in *The Man Who Fell to Earth* or the images and sounds from television sets on (or just off) screen which intrude on the action and dialogue in the opening sequences of *Castaway* (1986) and *Track 29* (1987).

In Britain, commentators often cited the 'distracted' kind of viewing television invites as evidence of the impact of American popular culture. One highly influential attempt to theorise this effect was the concept of 'flow' developed by Raymond Williams after his exposure to commercial television in the United States. Williams claimed that viewers experience little sense of boundaries between programmes and between the different kinds of reality which they represent (1975: 118). Roeg's cinema suggests a parallel between this experience of 'flow' and the erosion of national boundaries by American cultural power.

Televisual flow is built into the structure and imagery of Roeg's films, but the complex patterns it generates require concentrated attention from the spectator in order to grasp their full implications. Roeg uses the habits of television viewing to unsettle the intensity of cinematic viewing and thus to question the dominant assumptions about meanings and pleasure on which the so-called 'information' and 'consumer' society is based. He argued that 'American' culture trains people to demand 'quick opinions' which conceal the disturbing fact that 'we go through life knowing absolutely nothing' (quoted in Combs 1985: 237). The need to generate clear meanings within the flow of television programming (and in much popular cinema) leads to a reliance on formulas and stereotypes that create an illusion of 'mastery', a facade that discourages further enquiry into the 'significance' of experience. Roeg's anticategorical cinema works against this attitude by insisting that, as the Professor puts it in *Insignificance* (1985), 'you cannot understand by making definitions, only by turning over the possibilities'.

In some ways, however, Roeg's resistance to traditional hierarchies and boundaries aligns his work with the 'American' forces in contemporary culture. Like many other British directors, Roeg made television commercials to support himself between film projects, and he argued that commercials often make use of techniques borrowed from films which (like his own) were 'difficult' for their original audiences (Lanza 1989: 35). By incorporating elements of the televisual flow of imagery into his films, while avoiding the illusion of 'easy' consumption that television promotes; he acknowledges that social and cultural contexts must influence the making and viewing of films. All films, therefore, are to some extent complicit with the dominant ideology, but Roeg's films examine this complicity and encourage spectators to reflect on the extent to which that ideology shapes their own responses.

Robert Kolker aptly describes viewing a film by Roeg as an experience that transforms us into 'aliens in a strange land, trying to make sense of our perceptions, and failing' (1977: 84). Because this experience of perceptual failure has proved disturbing for audiences, critics and producers, Roeg's films have been increasingly marginalised, receiving only limited distribution and critical attention. During the 1970s many critics regarded the disruptive narrative structures of Roeg's films as part of an innovative project to create a cinema responsive to the new thinking about sexuality and identity in the 'permissive' society. As Thatcherism tried to turn the tide against these new developments, seeing them as responsible for Britain's political and moral decline, Roeg's later films often seemed willfully obscure and indifferent to the changing ideological climate.

In *Performance* (1970), Roeg's first film as director (in collaboration with Donald Cammell), another gangster, this time a British one, exposes one of the central tensions within Thatcherism, even before Thatcher's rise to power. Harry Flowers admires the efficiency of the 'Yanks' and uses brutal methods to force his competitors to 'merge' with him, but he also claims a strong attachment to the traditional values of family life. Thatcherite ideology offered a similarly ambivalent response to the Americanisation of the postwar world, although *Performance* makes clear that the established British ways of doing things were more sophisticated but hardly less ruthless than the 'American' methods.

On the one hand, Thatcherism presented itself as a return to the values of an earlier period in which Britain possessed the political and cultural power that now belonged to the United States. Thatcher thus exploited and reinforced myths about Britain's decline to the status of a second-class nation and about the negative effects of American popular culture. On the other, Thatcher pointed to the United States (especially after the election of Ronald Reagan in 1980) as exemplifying the success of the 'free enterprise' system over the 'consensus' politics that, she felt, weakened postwar Britain by establishing a noncompetitive 'welfare state'. To Thatcher, 'consensus' was 'the process of abandoning all beliefs, principles, values and policies', and she advocated a return to the clear-cut definitions and boundaries that supposedly made life easier in the past – and in old Hollywood genre films (Derbyshire 1988: 173).

Through its appeal to the past, notably in the comparisons between Thatcher and Churchill during the Falklands War, Thatcherite rhetoric sought to counter the myth of national decline. Thatcher presented herself as a strong leader capable of dealing with Britain's economic woes and with such contemporary problems as terrorism, pornography and racial violence. A confusing bombardment of media images, often seen as the effect of an Americanised cultural environment, tended to magnify the impact of these problems. Thatcher thus blamed the media for spreading the demoralisation she claimed to be fighting, conveniently ignoring the fact that it was the capitalist enterprise of the American media that had largely created the image of 'swinging Britain' in the first place.

In his analysis of Thatcherism, Stuart Hall suggested that it offered a vision based on clearly-defined boundaries and moral categories: 'The language of law and order is sustained by a populist moralism. It is where the great syntax of "good" versus "evil", of civilised and uncivilised standards, of the choice between anarchy and order, constantly divides the world up and classifies it into its appointed stations' (1983: 37–8). Thatcherism thus generates 'quick meanings' that bring about an 'elision between crime and disorder', so that any challenge to the established order can be immediately dismissed as a matter for the police (Kettle 1983: 227). Although Thatcher did not invent this 'language', she synthesised it with the demands of corporate and consumer capitalism. This mythical synthesis was, however, inherently unstable because of the tension between encouraging 'the survival of the fittest' and preaching 'respect for moral absolutes' (Martin 1989: 332).

The 'moral absolutes' in Thatcherism opposed the social explanations for human problems offered by the liberal ideology which shaped the postwar consensus and the welfare state. Thatcher argued that the reliance on social 'safety nets' weakens the individual but also that such social measures are, in any case, too weak to control the disruptive forces at work in a hostile world and in the dark recesses of human nature. Thus, the Thatcherite ideal: a 'self-sufficient' adult whose aggressive individualism can operate successfully in public life but who also needs the security provided by a family structure that offers protection from 'a mean and nasty world' (Segal 1983: 209). The Thatcherite 'adult' is normally a 'father' or perhaps a woman able to demonstrate the 'hardness' and aggression associated with 'masculine' behaviour. Thatcher exploited widespread frustration with a system in which the state seemed to watch over the lives of individuals 'from the cradle to the grave' but whose rules and regulations only added to the muddle and confusion of modern life. She swept away the claims of liberal ideology by insisting that 'there is no such thing as society', her way of saying that 'people had to accept responsibility for their own behaviour because anything else would infantilise us all' (Willetts 1989: 268).

Lindsay Anderson's complaint that Roeg's films lack 'a social element' implies that they share the Thatcherite resistance to social explanations (Hacker & Price 1991: 54). These films certainly ignore the tradition of social realism and explicit social criticism in British cinema and, in fact, Britain itself is conspicuous by its absence. Yet though Roeg himself argued that films should not deal in what he called 'partisan politics', he nevertheless described his own work as an attempt to preserve, in 'reactionary times', the advances made in the 1960s and 1970s (Lanza 1989: 34–5). In confronting a powerful ideology forged from the welding together of traditional moral categories and modern corporate imperatives, Roeg's films do not operate completely outside the domain of this ideology but expose its contradictions by showing its appeal and its limitations. Each film unsettles the spectator by suggesting that meaning is neither absent, as the complexity of contemporary experience often implies, nor absolute, as Thatcherism claims in response to this perceived absence of meaning; Roeg's films suggest rather that meaning is relative, a position that recognises the need for meaning but refuses to allow this need to harden into an acceptance of fixed categories.[2]

Although Roeg's films of the 1980s are clearly not political allegories, they do disturb the secure categories on which Thatcherism depends. While the films (with the partial exception of *Castaway*) make no direct reference to British society and culture, they function as fables that subvert the underlying value system, the way of seeing inherent in Thatcherism. In particular, my analysis concentrates on the way in which the films' treatment of sexuality both appeals to and unsettles the ideological premises which underpin the Thatcherite discourse on the family, as well as on law and order.

The most controversial aspect of *Bad Timing* (1980) is its depiction of the 'crime' whose investigation provides the motivation for the film's complex flashback structure. Alex (Art Garfunkel), an American psychologist working in Vienna, rapes Milena (Theresa Russell), a woman with whom he has been having an affair, while she lies unconscious and apparently dying. Some feminists expressed anger at the way in which the 'camerawork, associative editing and narrative structure compel us in the audience to identify with this assault on the female victim' (Barber 1981: 46). However, Teresa de Lauretis called into question this perception of the film's strategies and argued that it works against the 'visual pleasure' basic to mainstream cinema, which, according to Laura Mulvey's influential theory of spectatorship, privileges the male spectator. De Lauretis suggests that *Bad Timing* creates 'unpleasure' by 'undercutting spectator identification in terms of both vision ... and narrative' (1983: 24).

While Milena's unconscious state does prevent us from identifying with her, it also works against the erotic investment apparently offered through identification with Alex as he cuts the clothes from her body and violates it. The film explicitly raises the issues of voyeurism and spying: Alex shows his students images of 'political voyeurs' and tells them that 'we are all spies'; he does 'top secret' work for NATO. It goes further, however, by inviting spectators to reflect on their complicity with such activities. The rape, in fact, culminates the process by which Alex, fascinated by Milena's 'otherness', nevertheless tries to impose his own sense of order on her 'untidiness'; this process is duplicated in the efforts of the Austrian policeman, Inspector Netusil (Harvey Keitel), to prove that a crime has been committed.

Alex's objections to Milena's 'untidiness' are ostensibly directed at the way she leaves things lying around, but he remains frustrated by her frequent disappearances and by her refusal to commit herself to a permanent relationship. When they take a vacation in Morocco, Alex proposes marriage by offering her a one-way airline ticket to New York. She pleads with him to enjoy 'where we are now'. By learning about her past and by building a future with her in his own 'home' environment, he wants to possess her, and he sees her desire to live only for the present moment as a kind of moral 'untidiness'. But, his encounter with this woman who refuses the terms of his (psycho)analysis leads to the emergence of the 'untidiness' within himself.

When Alex arrives at Milena's apartment to find that she has cleaned and tidied it in order to please him, he responds by demanding that they make love. Her request that they should just talk to each other prompts him to make an excuse to leave. She rushes out after him, offers herself to him like a prostitute, and he takes her brutally on the stairs. Although some (male) critics stress Alex's humiliation, this sequence suggests that he needs her 'untidiness' to justify his own sense of himself as the one who provides order, just as the Inspector needs a 'crime' to define himself as

Milena (Theresa Russell) and Alex (Art Garfunkel) confront each other during the early stages of their affair, in *Bad Timing* (1980)

a man of law (Gow 1980: 29; Pym 1980: 112). Later, after Milena makes her first suicide threat, Alex rushes to her apartment and finds her drunk, garishly made up, and wearing her bra over her blouse, the grotesque mirror reflection of his own repressed desires. When Inspector Netusil searches Milena's apartment for clues, he declares that he shares Alex's contempt for people 'who live in disorder' and thus interfere with 'our will to master reality'. The law, however, fails to impose its shape on 'untidy' experience, since Netusil is unable to extract a confession from Alex before they hear that Milena will survive (which means, apparently, that no 'crime' has been committed).

The sudden cuts from Milena's body as she and Alex make love to that same body being violently worked on in the hospital provide the most obvious instances of how *Bad Timing* both permits erotic viewing and undercuts it. The film never establishes a stable relationship with its spectators. Its flashback structure is sometimes clearly motivated by the consciousness of a character but at other times such motivation is ambiguous or even absent. Roeg presents some flashbacks as Alex's memories during his wait in the hospital corridor, but at least two early flashbacks seem to originate with the unconscious Milena, and it remains possible that Netusil fantasises the entire rape scene. The film constantly threatens to fly apart, suggesting that the spectator's experience incorporates the tension between Alex's sense of time and Milena's, the drive to narrative closure competing with a desire to experience the present moment to the full.

A similar tension operates in *Eureka*, but here the forces of disorder dominate the film's imagery and structure. As Harlan Kennedy has observed, 'Roeg hurls heady visual juxtapositions at us – in a bid to storm the syntactical frontiers between shot and shot, scene and scene, metaphor and reality, parable and paranormal' (1983: 21). These disruptive strategies reflect a tension built into the conception of the film as a treatment of the figure of the self-sufficient individual. Paul Mayersberg, who wrote the screenplay, suggested that the search for gold functions as a metaphor for the human 'desire for self-realisation' (Milne 1982: 282) but, even as Jack (Gene Hackman) insists on the integrity of his own individual will, the film's 'fairy tale' imagery connects his discovery to cosmic forces whose existence shows, as Roeg put it, that 'our actions are connected to everything and everyone around us' (quoted in Kennedy 1983: 21). While the film seems to endorse Jack's Thatcherite desire to take responsibility for his own actions, it simultaneously insists that these actions form part of a complex web of cultural meanings created by past events and representations.

In his discussion of *Bad Timing*, Ian Penman suggests that, for Roeg, 'bliss' can never be expressed 'as an isolated perfection' but only 'as an effect within the interplay of a whole range of problematic discourses' (1980: 109). *Eureka*'s title focuses attention on the 'bliss' of the single moment of discovery, which the film attempts to convey through a battery of visual and musical effects. One of these is a musical quotation from Wagner's *Das Rheingold*, and its effect illustrates the 'problematic' functioning of the discourses in this film. The familiarity of the music denies the uniqueness of the moment, while the allusion to Wagner associates Jack's quest with a cultural tradition taken up by Nazism and thus foreshadows his later isolation from the struggle against fascism during World War Two. The operatic grandeur is, in any case, undercut when Jack's histrionic celebrations only evoke memories of many similar demonstrations by prospectors in other films (including Chaplin's *The Gold Rush*, a poster for which we will see later in the film).

After leaving the vast, frozen spaces of the Yukon, Jack tries to isolate himself from the political turmoil of the outside world in the confined space of his tropical island mansion. Though he found the gold only after he rejected the 'home' offered by Frieda (Helena Kallionites), a brothel owner in the Yukon, he uses his wealth to establish a family within which the tensions take on the archetypal dimensions of Greek tragedy and Freudian psychodrama. His attempts to control his island and his family through the power of his will prove futile in the face of the 'American' invasion, suggesting a Thatcherite view of Britain's plight. However, when Jack is brutally murdered, the film never resolves the uncertainty about whether the killing is a reprisal for his 'un-American' rejection of the takeover bid or whether his son-in-law (Rutger Hauer) has taken revenge for the humiliations suffered in their struggle for control over Jack's daughter (Theresa Russell).

The killing, simultaneously a product of the threat from outside and of the tensions within the family, is carried out in a way that resembles the voodoo rituals practiced on the island. Jack even acquiesces in his own death, recognising that his life after the ecstatic moment of individual triumph has been an anti-climax. Though the film suggests that the forces which destroy Jack are ultimately unknowable, the blown-up photograph of the body exhibited at his son-in-law's trial looks like the well known images of Hiroshima victims (the end of the war is announced during the trial). His desire to isolate himself from a 'mean and nasty world' (from history, politics and society) generates the same outcome produced by the historical forces he tries to escape. The death of the self-sufficient man reveals the complex interconnectedness of things and people which Jack denies in his attempt to 'master' his family and his environment.

Eureka calls into question Jack's claims to self-sufficiency by linking his experiences to images stored in the spectator's cultural memory. This strategy becomes the main source of the unsettling effect in *Insignificance*. The spectator is confronted with actors impersonating four 'stars' of American culture. Known only as the Professor (Michael Emil), the Senator (Tony Curtis), the Actress (Theresa Russell) and the Ballplayer (Gary Busey), they are unmistakably modelled on Albert Einstein, Joseph McCarthy, Marilyn Monroe and Joe DiMaggio. The film thus sets up a gap between the performances in the 'present' and the established star images. By showing these characters grappling with the relationship between their public personae and their private selves, Roeg undermines the supposedly 'fixed' quality of star images. This representational instability parallels the disturbance caused by the Professor's theory of relativity, which challenges traditional belief in the fixed state of the universe and, in turn, the moral absolutism grounded in this belief.

The mythical encounter between these characters takes place in a New York hotel room during the Cold War period, when the 'American' culture celebrated by Mayakovsky in *Eureka* consolidated its dominant position. The Professor, who escaped to the United States from fascism in Europe, remains haunted by an awareness that his ideas helped create the atomic bomb. Despite its practical uses, the theory of relativity generates hostility from those threatened by its scientific complexity. The Senator can respond only by branding the Professor a 'communist', while the Ballplayer suspects any intellectual activity that might raise questions about the American dream. The Actress, however, comes closest to the film's own strategy when she uses toys and other props to act out a playful (and necessarily simplified) version of the Professor's theory.

The Actress's childlike use of 'play' to demonstrate the Professor's theory both reinforces and cuts through the stereotype of the 'dumb blonde', suggesting that the new way of seeing is a threat only to a particular 'adult' view of the world. That this view belongs to the modern 'American' ideology is confirmed by the hotel's elevator operator (Will Sampson). He greets the Professor as a fellow Cherokee, presumably because the theory of relativity supports the belief of 'a true Cherokee' that 'wherever he is, he is at the centre of the universe'. It is hard to sustain this belief in an elevator, and he fears that he is no longer a Cherokee because he watches television; but he later uses the power of imagination to escape from his 'American' environment when he performs a traditional chant on the hotel roof while wolves howl all around him.

The Cherokee belief, suppressed in the course of American history, accords with the Actress's demonstration of relativity which she sums up as showing that 'all measurements of time and space are necessarily made relative to a single observer'. The Ballplayer inadvertently demonstrates her point when he summarises the 'American' view of history by commenting that 'if it wasn't for Columbus, we'd all be Indians'. Traditional belief and modern scientific theory both imply that people should 'take responsibility for their world'; but, according to the Professor, Americans refuse this responsibility and instead establish a 'star' system that invests human beings with absolute values. These fixed points of reference provide the basis for 'quick

The actress (Theresa Russell) uses toys to demonstrate the theory of relativity to the Professor (Michael Emil), in *Insignificance* (1985)

opinions,' thus eliminating the need for people to think through difficult issues for themselves.

The Professor's theory becomes part of a myth, in which $E=MC^2$ functions simply as a sign of the power of science, which the Senator can exploit for his political purposes. Sexuality, too, is subjected to a similar process, as the construction of a 'glamour' image turns the Actress into a projection of male fantasies. This image acts as a screen for repressed sexual feelings liable to emerge in grotesque forms, as Milena demonstrated to Alex in *Bad Timing*. The Actress, first seen on location in the city streets during the filming of a shot in which her skirt is 'blown up around her ears' by a blast of air from the subway (an allusion to the now iconic image of Monroe in *The Seven Year Itch* (1955), later tells the Professor she is glad that he was not there. While the crowd in the street saw 'a star doing glamorous things', she says, he would have seen 'a girl showing her legs to a bunch of jerks'.

The crudity underlying the glamour image also appears in the film's depiction of the Senator. He is seen having sex with a woman who seems to be the Actress but who then pulls off her wig to reveal that she is a prostitute impersonating the star. When he finds the real Actress in the Professor's bed, he mistakes her for a prostitute who looks like the Actress and comments that the Actress 'only got where she is by doing what you're doing'. He rejects her offer of sex in exchange for the safety of the Professor's papers by punching her, causing a miscarriage. His brutality underlines the hypocrisy of an ideology that takes what it cannot 'master' (relativity, sexual desire) and uses it to create a commodity (atomic bomb, glamour image) that then destroys what the ideology claims to protect (peace, family life).

If the central issue in *Insignificance* is the relationship of the 'real' to the cultural imaginary, *Castaway* involves a return to the real through its representation of the cultural reality of contemporary London and the natural reality of the island on which Gerald (Oliver Reed) and Lucy (Amanda Donohoe) are cast away. Yet, as Richard Combs points out, the 'realism' of *Castaway* is deceptive since the film suggests that the 'real' may remain 'inaccessible, even when living naked on a beach' (1986/87: 70). By reducing mastery to a question of survival (as with the children in the Australian outback in Roeg's *Walkabout* (1971)), the situation of the castaways tests the cultural categories within which the real is experienced. Gerald and Lucy find themselves in a transitional world where nature turns much of their cultural backgrounds into nonsense, but where their behaviour remains culturally conditioned; similarly, the film places us in an unstable relationship to the characters in which we both share and remain outside their experience and become aware that the cultural codes from which they are escaping affect the processes of our own spectatorship.

Gerald's desire to escape to a desert island parallels Jack McCann's attempt at self-realisation through the purchase and protection of his island. But, as in *Eureka*, the dream of freedom from cultural constraints gets quickly undermined. The drawings used in the opening credits relate Gerald's desire to memories of Robinson Crusoe, while his advertisement for a 'girl Friday' suggests the combination of cultural and sexual fantasy that underlies his project. When Gerald first sights the island, he calls it their 'home' for the next year. A series of quick cuts confronts us with images of fish in the sea, animals on the island, and the boat seen from the uninhabited island. These shots, which recall the treatment of the animal life of the outback in *Walkabout*, expose the human presumption in Gerald's claim and suggest that the intruders' relationship to each other and to the island will inevitably be shaped by the cultural patterns which they think they have left behind.

The struggle to survive on their desert island takes its toll on Gerald (Oliver Reed) and Lucy (Amanda Donohoe) in *Castaway* (1986)

In the opening sequences, as the film intercuts between Gerald and Lucy acting out their unrewarding personal lives in London, we see, hear or read media reports on such events as a sex-murder trial, a sex-change operation and the shooting of the Pope. Scandal and sensation have driven out any interest in politics, and the basic image is of the cultural and moral decline diagnosed by Thatcherism. The prurience of the British media gives way to the freedom of the desert island on which Lucy proves more ready than Gerald to shed the constraints of clothing. While this leaves the film open to charges of being a 'rather pretentious' treatment of 'what is basically exploitation material' (Cook 1987: 43), it does set up a tension between 'debased' cultural codes within which nudity inevitably becomes 'exploitation' and the 'natural' values that life as a 'noble savage' is supposed to activate.

Although the couple separate at the end of the film, their island experience leads to a tentative sense of renewal that calls into question the culture/nature dichotomy that inspired their adventure. Ironically, Roeg suggests the possibility of renewal through images of 'grotesque' sexuality and 'untidiness' which echo those in *Bad Timing*. After Gerald disappears for days to a neighbouring island, where he works as a mechanic for the native community, Lucy desperately tries to seduce him by painting black stockings on her bare legs. Like Milena, she uses a 'masquerade' to make visible the perverse quality of the sexual demands made on her, but in *Castaway* the result is a passionate episode of lovemaking during a storm that wrecks their 'home'. As a result of Gerald's activities as a mechanic, their pristine desert island has come to resemble a junk yard, but this 'untidiness' also signals a renewal when he decides to stay with the islanders because his mechanical skills give him a valued place in their community.

While *Castaway* calls into question a way of seeing that depends on an absolute opposition between culture and nature, *Track 29* presents a vision of 'American' culture from which nature has almost entirely disappeared. As in *The Man Who Fell to Earth*, this culture is tested by the arrival of a character who is both alien and British. According to the science fiction narrative of the earlier film, Newton comes from another planet, but David Bowie's British origins are evident beneath his alien persona. Martin (Gary Oldman), the equivalent figure in *Track 29*, is ridiculed by the people of the small American town in which the film is set because of his English accent and vocabulary. His status as a character is highly suspect, however, because he first appears as a two-dimensional cut-out and later can only be seen by Linda (Theresa Russell), who thinks he is the child taken from her when she was fifteen and brought up in Britain by foster parents.

Although Martin's arrival can be at least partially explained as a manifestation of Linda's sexual frustration, since she is married to a doctor (Christopher Lloyd) who treats her as a child and refuses to allow her to have a child of her own, Martin's Britishness owes more to the film's British authors than to the fantasies of their character.[3] He also reminds us of the cultural movements of the 1960s, as he traces his birth back to the time of 'flower power' when people believed in 'peace and all that shit'.

Martin is dropped off in town by a truck driver who may be his father since, like the bumper-car attendant with whom Linda had sex on her fifteenth birthday, he has the word 'MOTHER' tattooed across his chest. His powerful and gleaming rig is first seen at the end of a panning shot which begins on Martin and moves across a large American flag. Linda's husband, Dr Henry Henry, is also associated with the American flag, which appears behind him as he delivers the keynote address at 'Trainorama', a convention of model railroad enthusiasts who see their hobby as the basis for a political and moral revival in the United States. Henry describes their models as 'a record of what built this great nation' and thus as a link with a past in which 'we knew who we were, what we were and where we were going'.

According to Roeg, *Track 29* is about 'how we become the person others want us to be although we stay the child that we originally were' (quoted in Hacker & Price 1991: 355). A political platform based on a return to the past becomes highly suspect in a film in which all the characters act out fantasies of regression to childhood. Martin declares that he is 'sick to death at being grown-up' and insists on enjoying the 'American childhood' of which he has been deprived. As a doctor, Henry cares for geriatric patients in their second childhoods, but his own adult world centres on a model railroad. Linda's relationship with Henry is expressed through baby-talk, while her childlike state is attributed to the traumatic effect of being deprived of her child when she was 'a very scared little girl with an overbearing father and a dimwit mother'.

The film's representation of the adult world remains highly ambiguous. It is a world in which speculations about 'the shape of the universe' (like those in which the Professor was engaged) have become material for television cartoons. At the end of the film, a blood stain on the ceiling suggests that Linda has killed Henry but, when she asserts her new independence by leaving the house, she adopts a glamour image like that of the Actress in *Insignificance*.[4] The film also offers the idea of 'play' as an alternative to the fixed images and moral absolutes which govern adult life. If Henry's railroad reveals his desire to construct an alternative world that he can control, the film acknowledges its own (partial) complicity with this project when its own set is confused with Henry's models. Thus, when Henry leads the delegates at 'Trainorama' in a rendition of 'Chattanooga Choo Choo', Roeg intercuts the celebrations with an orgy of destruction in which Martin smashes Henry's model railroad and the truck demolishes Linda's bedroom. The film destroys its own fantasy world as we watch a figure from Linda's imagination destroy the model associated with her husband's fantasy of a return to the American past.

Like all Roeg's films, *Track 29* offers less a reflection of the world as it is than a 'model' that maps out the shape of modern 'American' culture and plays with its own (and our) integration into that culture. These films suggest that the demand for law and order rests on fear and that rigid moral categories generate the very disorder they are intended to control. Law, psychology, science and technology, in Roeg's films, all offer systems of meaning which help define the complexities of human experience but that become dangerous when substituted for that complexity. In its attempt to combine quick opinions, necessary for the process of selling images, with the development of a global culture that challenges the traditional boundaries of local cultures, 'American' culture both promotes and offers the means to contain social unrest. Roeg's films and Thatcherite ideology both remain contradictory, as they simultaneously criticise and comply with the new world order. The films, however, expose the contradictions which Thatcherism tries to conceal through its power as myth.

Any assessment of the contribution of Roeg's films to the cinema of the Thatcherite period must acknowledge the increasing marginalisation of his work. However, these subversive fables do suggest an alternative to the British realist tradition through a formal work (or play) that activates the threat of disorder but also affirms the pleasures of an unsettled spectatorship. Roeg replaces the clear-cut definitions which Thatcherism (and realism) demands with a field of tensions that encourages the spectatorial activity of 'turning over the possibilities'. Although important critiques of Thatcherite ideology lie embedded within the 'realist' films of directors like Stephen Frears, Richard Eyre and David Hare, Roeg's commercial work within an American media environment has cinematic and ideological implications that need further examination, perhaps in relation to the more fantastic and experimental responses to Thatcherism in the films of Peter Greenaway and Derek Jarman. One line of approach is suggested by Lindsay Anderson who argues that Roeg and Ken Russell were the originators of a 'romantic neo-baroque' style, but Anderson feels that the emergence of this style was a sign that British cinema had 'lost its way' (Hacker & Price 1991: 55). The neglect of the complex and contradictory films directed by Nicolas Roeg during the 1980s suggests rather that British film culture may have lost its way.

NOTES

1 I have chosen not to deal with *The Witches* (1989), a film about a boy who is turned into a mouse, because its fantasy functions in a much more conventional manner than in Roeg's earlier films, despite the special effects created by Frank Oz. Roeg also contributed to the compilation film, *Aria* (1987), in which ten directors produced film versions of operatic arias. His resistance to making films for television ended with his adaptation of Tennessee Williams' *Sweet Bird of Youth* (1989) for NBC.

2 Roeg's practice is thus consonant with the emphasis on a 'dispersed' rather than unified subjectivity in psychoanalytic theory based on the ideas of Jacques Lacan, and with Michel Foucault's concept of culture as a site of competing discourses (which both Teresa de Lauretis and Ian Penman invoke in their discussions of *Bad Timing* (1980).

3 The screenplay for *Track 29* was written by Dennis Potter, best known for his television serials such as *Pennies from Heaven* (1978) and *The Singing Detective* (1986), and the film could equally well be analysed in relation to Potter's response to 'American' culture (especially his frequent use of music from the Big Band era). See Barker (1988) for a comparison of Roeg's and Potter's visions.

4 The links between Linda and the Actress are underlined by the fact that both are played by Theresa Russell, the American actress who became a 'star' as a result of her performance in *Bad Timing*, married Roeg, and starred in most of his subsequent films.

WORKS CITED

Barber, Susan (1981) 'Bad Timing – A Sensual Obsession', *Film Quarterly*, Fall, 46–50.

Barker, Adam (1988) 'What the Detective Saw', *Monthly Film Bulletin*, July, 193–5.

Combs, Richard (1985) 'Relatively Speaking', *Monthly Film Bulletin,* August, 237–8.

_____ (1986/87) 'Time Away', *Sight and Sound*, Winter, 70–1.

Cook, Pam (1987) 'Castaway', *Monthly Film Bulletin*, February, 42–3.

de Lauretis, Teresa (1983) 'Now and Nowhere: Roeg's *Bad Timing*', *Discourse*, 5 (Spring), 21–40.

Derbyshire, Ian (1988) *Politics in Britain: From Callaghan to Thatcher*. London: Chambers.

Gow, Gordon (1980) '*Bad Timing*', *Films and Filming*, March, 29–30.

Hacker, Jonathan and David Price (1991) *Take Ten: Contemporary British Directors*. Oxford: Clarendon Press.

Hall, Stuart (1983) 'The Great Moving Right Show', in Stuart Hall and Martin Jacques (eds) *The Politics of Thatcherism*. London: Lawrence and Wishart, 19–39.

Kavanagh, David, and Anthony Selden (eds) (1989) *The Thatcher Effect*. Oxford: Clarendon Press.

Kennedy, Harlan (1983) 'Roeg: Warrior', *Film Comment*, April, 20–3.

Kettle, Martin (1983) 'The Drift to Law and Order', in Stuart Hall and Martin Jacques (eds) *The Politics of Thatcherism*. London: Lawrence and Wishart, 216–34.

Kolker, Robert (1977) 'The Open Texts of Nicolas Roeg', *Sight and Sound*, Spring, 82–4, 113.

Lanza, Joseph (1989) *Fragile Geometry: The Films, Philosophy, and Misadventures of Nicolas Roeg*. New York: PAJ Publications.

Martin, David (1989) 'The Churches: Pink Bishops and the Iron Lady', in David Kavanagh and Anthony Selden (eds) *The Thatcher Effect*. Oxford: Clarendon Press, 330–41.

Milne, Tom (1982) '*Eureka*', *Sight and Sound*, Autumn, 280–5.

Mulvey, Laura (1975) 'Visual Pleasure and Narrative Cinema', *Screen*, 16, 3, 6–18.

Park, James (1984) *Learning to Dream: The New British Cinema*. London: Faber.

Penman, Ian (1980) '*Bad Timing:* A Codifying Love Story', *Screen*, 21, 3, 107–9.

Pym, John (1980) 'Ungratified Desire: Nicolas Roeg's *Bad Timing*', *Sight and Sound*, Spring, 111–12.

Segal, Lynne (1983) 'The Heat in the Kitchen', in *The Politics of Thatcherism,* edited by Stuart Hall and Martin Jacques. London: Lawrence and Wishart, 207–15.

Waller, Nick (1976) 'Nicolas Roeg: A Sense of Wonder', *Film Criticism*, 1, 2, 25–9.

Willetts, David (1989) 'The Family', in David Kavanagh and Anthony Selden (eds) *The Thatcher Effect*. Oxford: Clarendon, 262–73.

Williams, Raymond (1975) *Television: Technology and Cultural Form*. New York: Schocken Books.

13. INSURMOUNTABLE DIFFICULTIES AND MOMENTS OF ECSTASY: CROSSING CLASS, ETHNIC AND SEXUAL BARRIERS IN THE FILMS OF STEPHEN FREARS

Susan Torrey Barber

Stephen Frears was virtually unknown to overseas audiences when he achieved international acclaim as director of the enormously successful *My Beautiful Laundrette* (1985), which featured a community of *nouveau riche* Pakistanis thriving in contemporary South London. This was one of many areas throughout Great Britain to feel the impact of the new economic policies of the Conservative Thatcher regime in the 1980s. According to Frears, *My Beautiful Laundrette* was his and screenwriter Hanif Kureishi's ironic salutation to the entrepreneurial spirit in the 1980s that Margaret Thatcher championed, as her government transformed the postwar socialist state into a 'nation' courting and supported by private capitalistic enterprise.[1]

Sammy and Rosie Get Laid (1987) represented a more acrimonious critique – Frears and Kureishi's 'declaration of war on Thatcher England' – that focused on a broad and diverse cross-section of South London: blacks and whites, in addition to Pakistanis, many of them homeless and unemployed. This blighted area is seen from the viewpoint of a visiting Pakistani politician and former resident of London, one appalled by this new England and longing for the 'civilised' country he fondly remembered two decades ago.

Frears' third film of the decade, *Prick Up Your Ears* (actually made in between *My Beautiful Laundrette* and *Sammy and Rosie Get Laid* and written by Alan Bennett), features the life of gay playwright Joe Orton and does not specifically examine the Thatcher period. Released in 1987, it covers events in the late 1950s and 1960s in Orton's life that can be seen as a comparative historical frame of reference. That is, the class-bound and sexually-repressed society that fuelled Orton's irreverent plays functions as a metaphor for the Thatcher 1980s.

This essay examines these three works as reactions to and critiques of the dynamics of Thatcherism by Frears and Kureishi and Frears and Bennett, specifically with respect to race, class and gender. All three films foreground the seemingly insurmountable difficulties – tempered by moments of ecstasy – that relationships pose when they cross class/ethnic/sexual boundaries, particularly during periods of political changes and economic upheavals. These works also chart Frears' increasing disillusionment with the Thatcher administration. As many historians note, Thatcher's revitalised England valorised capitalistic enterprise and produced a greedier, more intolerant society. Frears readily concurs: 'Thatcher has divided the country between North and South, between the employed and unemployed, between the rich and poor, between the people who've got and the people who haven't' (quoted in Lindsey 1988: 59). In order to understand this social disintegration, we must backtrack and briefly examine Thatcher's agenda for the 1980s.

'See just how far we have fallen', Thatcher said shortly after her victorious entrance to No. 10 in 1979, referring to the 'excesses' of the 1960s and the subsequent economic downturn in the 1970s. As historian Peter Jenkins commented, Thatcher labelled England as sick – morally, socially and economically (1987: 66). She put the blame squarely on the Wilson Labour government for perpetrating a welfare state that created enormous problems for England in the 1970s – inflation, powerful and headstrong labour unions, crippling strikes. All this led to low productivity and no real economic growth. She linked these socialist-induced woes directly to the decline of morality during the permissive 1960s: the breakdown of parental authority as well as of the nuclear family, which led to a generation of irresponsible youths who indulged themselves in too much sexual freedom. According to Jenkins, Thatcher's indictment of the 1960s and 1970s covered just about every aspect of British society: 'crime, especially juvenile crime; violence, personal and political; industrial militancy and public disorder; flouting of the rule of law; loss of parental control, of authority generally; the decline of learning and discipline in the schools; divorce, abortion, illegitimacy, pornographic display, four-letter words on television; the *decline of manners*' (Jenkins 1987: 67–8). She attributed this 'fall from grace' to the Home Office of Roy Jenkins (which liberalised the arts and granted long overdue civil liberties), 'who had presided over the abolition of capital punishment, legalisa-

Omar (Gordon Warnecke) learns from his Uncle Nasser (Saeed Jaffrey) (joined by his mistress Rachel (Shirley Anne Field)) about the privileges capitalistic enterprise brings, in *My Beautiful Laundrette* (1985)

tion of homosexuality and abortion, the liberalisation of divorce, and the abolition of theatre censorship' (Jenkins 1987: 68).

To remedy these 'setbacks,' Thatcher called for a return to Victorian values, harking back to the turn of the century when 'our country became great'. Jenkins adds: 'Her agenda could have been written on a sampler. The individual owed responsibility to self, family, firm, community, country, God in that order. Economic regeneration and moral regeneration [would] go hand in hand' (1987: 67). Thus, a strong national economy would rest upon eager and enterprising individuals, its foundation a strong nuclear (read: heterosexual) family. This context is precisely Frears and Kureishi's focus in *My Beautiful Laundrette*. As if responding to Thatcher's frequent praises of Indian and Asian shopkeepers as the new 'meritocrats' (Ogden 1990: 175), they situate and examine a community of Pakistanis that thrives in this new entrepreneurial age amid an underclass of homeless and unemployed native British, thus comparing the upside and the downside of this new economic order.

Originally immigrating to England in the postwar years and functioning as the servant/service class, Nasser (Saeed Jaffrey) and his extended family, which includes his cousin Salim (Derrick Branche) and nephew and designated heir Omar (Gordon Warnecke), have established a myriad of lucrative businesses, taking every advantage of an atmosphere conducive to private enterprise, including a series of generous tax laws. In her first budget, Thatcher reduced top bracket taxes of 83 per cent on earned income and 98 per cent on unearned income to a uniform 60 per cent. Further, her corporate tax reform dropped the rate for businesses from 52 per cent to 35 per cent (Ogden 1990: 332). All these cuts enabled businessmen such as Nasser and Salim to increase their net profit dramatically from gross earnings.

The Pakistani culture represented a new area of interest for Frears. When Kureishi showed him his screenplay for *My Beautiful Laundrette*, Frears had no idea that this world existed. 'Nobody had ever written from that perspective before. It was astonishing because [Kureishi] got it so right. That someone could be ... so confident about it, make the jokes, be on the inside' (in Friedman 1989: 15). Frears began his career with the 'Angry Young Men' in the late 1950s and the 1960s: dramatists (which included Joe Orton, as well as John Osborne), novelists (Alan Sillitoe, John Braine) and filmmakers (Lindsay Anderson, Tony Richardson, Karel Reisz) obsessed with revolutionising the arts by featuring social realism. They focused on working-class protagonists at odds with the class-bound system and positioned in their own environments: pubs, flats, factories. Frears assisted Reisz on *Morgan: A Suitable Case for Treatment* (1966) and worked under Anderson on *If...* (1969). His first film was a 30-minute short entitled *The Burning* (1967), examining the tensions among black, white and 'coloured' South Africans long before it was fashionable and profitable to do so.

During the 1970s and early 1980s he worked primarily in television,[2] a medium, he has commented, 'that gives an accurate account of what it's like to live in Britain – about men and women who go to work and lead rather desperate lives' (in Friedman 1989: 14). This explains Frears' resistance to the tradition of 'Toryist' cinema when he moved into features, for he has cited *Upstairs, Downstairs* (1970–75), *Brideshead Revisited* (1981) and *The Jewel in the Crown* (1984) as works that 'have perpetrated myths about an England that no longer exists, while failing to illuminate British life as it is' (Lindsey 1988: 59). Frears' attraction to the working and underclasses is consistent with his interest in the Pakistani community – another overlooked and marginalised culture.[3]

As Kureishi and Frears demonstrate in *My Beautiful Laundrette,* the Pakistanis now form part of the privileged class in the 1980s, many holding positions of power in South London. As the new landlords, they reversed the traditional imperial/colonial hierarchy by displacing the native British. Frears dramatically demonstrates this dynamic at the film's beginning when Salim and his henchmen throw out 'squatters' Johnny (Daniel Day Lewis) and Genghis (Richard Graham) from a run-down building Salim has purchased, depriving them of their only home. Salim employs Jamaicans to do his dirty work, which further fuels the hostility and resentment that the young unemployed and homeless males harbour toward both sets of immigrants and reinforces the decades of racial tension between the communities. Living on the streets, sleeping in any available shelter, and stealing to subsist, Johnny, Genghis and their friend Moose (Stephen Marcus) aimlessly roam the streets, their actions emblematic of the expanding underclass of social and economic dropouts in the 1980s, many of them teenagers and young adults without homes. These groups formed 38 per cent of Britain's population during the 1980s, as the unemployment rate skyrocketed, reaching a peak of 3.2 million in 1986 (Ogden 1990: 333).

However, despite their ethnic and class differences (which go back to their days as classmates), Omar and Johnny capitalise on the Thatcher government's endorsement of private enterprise, creating professional and personal bonds by becoming shop partners and lovers. The day their remodelled and refurnished laundrette opens inaugurates a new era in British history – the establishment of private business with the blessings of the government. They call their laundrette Powders, a wry reference to its source of financing – the profits from Salim's illegal drug business. Their situation questions the morality of a government eager to support all business, legal or otherwise, for Salim's business clearly feeds on a subclass of local addicts and pushers.

The laundrette stands as a little oasis in the boarded-up, deserted neighbourhood, its bright neon sign beckoning customers who eagerly flock through its doors. To celebrate, Johnny and Omar make love in the back room, defying the strong heterosexual codes and ethnic boundaries of their respective communities. Their bond, which motivates frequent hostilities from Johnny's abandoned friends, also causes raised eyebrows from members of Nassar's family, who initially look down upon Johnny. Yet they soon welcome him into their midst, providing the family he never had. Though this relationship helps Johnny to become responsible and achieve self-worth, Omar's way of reforming Johnny is to play the boss man, reinforcing the new imperial/colonial order that privileges him. At one point, exasperated with Johnny's bouts of laziness and irresponsibility, Omar comments, 'I'm not going to be beaten down by this country. When we were at school, you and your lot kicked me all round the place. And what are you doing now? Washing my floor, and that's how I like it.'

The most serious flare-up between the two communities – Genghis's and Moose's brutal attack on Salim to avenge his nearly running over Moose – becomes a crucial test for Johnny and Omar, who risk their lives by openly crossing ethnic boundaries: Johnny to save Salim from being beaten to death, Omar to save Johnny from the wrath of his own friends. Their relationship survives, suggesting not only that their bond of mutual love and devotion may bring their two communities together in a spirit of trust and collaboration, but also that they will rebuild their trashed shop and perhaps create a chain of laundrettes. Thus, this 'hybrid' community built on sexual diversity benefits from the Thatcherite vision of private enterprise that serves it (Chari 1989: 21).

Omar's and Johnny's relationship can be compared to that between Joe Orton (Gary Oldman) and Kenneth Halliwell (Alfred Molina) in *Prick Up Your Ears*. They, too, cross class and sexual boundaries to form an initially productive and fulfilling work and love relationship. Just as Omar gives Johnny the family he never had, as well as a job and self-esteem, so Halliwell offers Orton a middle-class lifestyle and literary education. Thus Orton finds a way out of his dreary, unstimulating working-class existence, for Halliwell inspires him to develop his creative potential and achieve a career as a successful writer. However, as Bennett and Frears demonstrate, the homophobic society in the 1950s and 1960s in which Halliwell and Orton live suggests an increasingly conservative, insensitive and narrow-minded establishment in the 1980s, one that frowns on sexual diversity, discriminates against gays and eventually instituted Clause 28 banning homosexual depiction in the arts.[4] As Frears himself commented, *Prick Up Your Ears* and *My Beautiful Laundrette* (and even *Sammy and Rosie Get Laid*, which features a lesbian couple) probably could not have been made after this law was passed.

Boldly challenging the sexually repressive and puritanical 1980s, Frears goes beyond the romantic scenes between Omar and Johnny and prominently features Orton's heady sex life throughout *Prick Up Your Ears*, clearly intending to shake up and shock the establishment. For example, the first time that Orton and Halliwell make love, they begin to undress and kiss passionately while watching the coronation of Queen Elizabeth. Their immense enjoyment is fuelled by their awareness of the watchful eyes of this highest authority in the land, who alludes to another top-ranking female, Margaret Thatcher herself. Further, Frears' creation of highly erotic atmospheres throughout the film plays out the enormous delight Orton derived from his 'subversive' pleasures. (His one-night stands were frequently with men just encountered on the underground and in public toilets). These scenes reflect what Orton's biographer John Lahr labelled his 'restless, ruthless pursuit of sensation' (1986: 14). Frears most dramatically demonstrates this tendency when Joe visits the public toilets after he wins the *Evening Standard* award for 'Loot'. Inside the building exists a shadowy underworld, one washed in blue-green light where figures move slowly and restlessly in and out of the shadows. Orton struts confidently into one of the stalls, casting flirtatious glances at the men. He deftly steps up to unscrew the light-bulbs, throwing the washroom into a murky sensuous darkness illuminated by glowing pools of light. As he urinates, he peeks over the next stall, beckoning the man over. The man drops down to his knees, starting to fellate Orton, who closes his eyes, smiling, as the others slowly gravitate over, their gazes suggesting a highly pleasurable trance.

As the film points out, the failure of Halliwell's and Orton's relationship, due in part to Orton's promiscuity and his intellectual outdistancing of Halliwell, succumbs to the pressures of the times. Ironically, the shunned and embittered Halliwell, who grows to resent and despise Orton, ultimately incorporates the dominant values of the period – monogamy, homophobia – into his psyche, thus appropriating the attitudes

Joe Orton (Gary Oldman) experiences increasing fame at the expense of his relationship with Kenneth Halliwell (Alfred Molina), in *Prick Up Your Ears* (1987)

and mores of the conservative establishment figures who initially disdained Halliwell and Orton for their homosexuality. These included the prison psychiatrist, as well as the librarian who snidely categorised them as 'nancies' and 'shirt-lifters'. The film further suggests that the underlying reason Orton and Halliwell are in jail – ostensibly for defacing library books – is for their homosexuality. Thus, Halliwell functions as an agent of the establishment, ironically killing what he loved and wanted most.

The impossibility of Halliwell's and Orton's relationship in the larger social and political context suggests a fractured, self-destructive and malaised England that contrasts with the close and potentially lasting bond between Omar and Johnny, a healthy union that bridges diverse communities. Because *Prick Up Your Ears* was made after *My Beautiful Laundrette*, this 'regression' characterises Frears' increasing pessimism about the impact of the Thatcher regime on private lives. In this vein, the third film, *Sammy and Rosie Get Laid*, plays out the full-blown, invasive effects of Thatcherism on British society, which breaks down along racial, class and ethnic boundaries in the latter part of the 1980s. As the opening scenes show, the country has become what Frears labelled a 'social disaster' (quoted in Hunter 1988: 30).

The small cadre of homeless youths in *My Beautiful Laundrette* have now increased to a larger, more beleaguered group that transcends race and class. The film's opening shot features waste ground, suggesting the increasing rot in South London (and by implication other urban areas in England). The waste ground, a wide expanse of razed land covered with makeshift camps and abandoned cars and buses, represents the last refuge for the homeless and unemployed, ranging from children to the elderly. This scenario reflects the decline in government funding for public housing, which dropped 60 per cent in the mid-1980s as the number of people living below the poverty line increased to an estimated nine million (Ogden 1990: 333–4).

The waste ground and the surrounding tenements are preyed upon by an increasingly aggressive police force, suggesting a more militaristic state that singles out and persecutes blacks in particular. In South London, even at the beginning of the decade, unemployment among young blacks was already a serious problem. For example, in Brixton (an area in South London with a large underclass of black people), unemployment ran close to 70 per cent in 1981, providing the setting for the worst riot in England's history. When two policemen questioned a black youth, a crowd quickly formed. Soon rocks, bricks and gasoline bombs were flying (Ogden 1990: 173). The ensuing brawl quickly spread to the surrounding neighbourhoods, lasting for three days and nights, involving 1,000 policemen and some 600 black rioters. Over 200 rioters were arrested and 120 buildings damaged, 9 completely destroyed (ibid.).

In the film, a similar racial incident sparks another skirmish, when a policeman mistakes an innocent black woman for her fugitive son and kills her. As the subsequent scenes show, a huge backlash takes place, involving black and white youths who go on a rampage through the neighbourhood, setting cars afire, smashing and looting shops. As Kureishi notes, an openly racist climate still operated during the shooting of *Sammy and Rosie Get Laid*, for throughout the filming of this scene, police randomly stopped blacks who were extras on the set. The production further mirrored ongoing riots in South London that were frequently covered on television.

Danny (Roland Gift), who lives in a caravan on the waste ground with his young son, most dramatically demonstrates the disenfranchisement and alienation of blacks. 'No one knows the shit black people have to go through', he comments in despair and frustration, having watched his friends arrested and attacked. Thus Frears reflects the black community's sense of helplessness, as Danny comments to Rafi (Shashi Kapoor), 'For a long time, right, I've been for nonviolence. Never gone for burning things down. I can see the attraction but not the achievement ... We have a kind of domestic colonialism to deal with here, because they don't allow us to run our own communities. But if a full-scale war ever breaks out, we can only lose.' Throughout the film, Danny is frequently located outside events, for example watching the riots or living in the waste ground on the edge of South London. His positioning suggests the black community's marginalisation in British society. As Danny comments, his only way of centring himself is to ride the trains all day (adopting the name of one of the stations, Victoria, as his alias), as if making contact with various points in the city will centre his identity and re-establish his legal residence.

The strong attraction that Danny and Rosie (Frances Barber) feel for each other, one that cuts across class and racial boundaries, has enormous potential for a mutually beneficial and fulfilling relationship. Both represent persecuted minorities in a system dominated by the white patriarchy, whose agents hover menacingly near their neighbourhood: powerful landowners/developers conspiring with crooked government officials over the fate of the inhabitants of the waste ground and the surrounding area. The official comments, 'You've got to invest in this area – for your sake and ours. You can do whatever you like,' to which the property developer responds, 'I want that open space under the motorway – *then* we can talk.' Danny's and Rosie's mutual victimisation strengthens their friendship; on the evening they passionately make love, Rosie sadly recalls her father's physical and verbal abuse of her, while Danny confides that the woman killed by the police raised him while his own mother was away all day at work.

Yet despite their compatibility, larger events pull them apart. Danny is literally kicked out by developers. The last time Rosie sees him, he is driving his caravan away from the waste ground, which is under siege by a huge devouring bulldozer. The film also suggests that Rosie's role as social worker will consume more and more of her time. As the number of casualties from Thatcher's economic system stack up, the underclass will expand and tax decreasing resources, including housing and welfare, especially for the elderly. For example, after travelling all the way to another part of town, Rosie arrives to find one of her indigent clients dead in his bathtub. Rosie's job suggests her attempts to resurrect Mother England's former role as caretaker welfare state in the 1950s and 1960s, 'picking up the smashed pieces of people's lives,' as she comments to her girlfriends, thus taking to heart the words of Margaret Thatcher heard in voiceover at the beginning of the film – 'We've got a big job to do in the inner cities … No one must slack.'

The demands of Rosie's job have already spilled over into her marriage, which has become less sexual and more maternal, with her husband Sammy (Ayub Khan Din). He frequently regresses into a needy childlike state, which suggests that their relationship has become an extension of her job. 'I can't always mother you, baby', she comments when a clingy Sammy urges her to stay home with him. Unlike Rosie, who dedicates her time and energy into a caretaker role, Sammy's way of dealing with the overwhelming social chaos and economic disintegration around him is to withdraw physically. Often he watches from a safe vantage point (for example, on a corner, away from the riots) muttering platitudes: 'The city is a mass of fascination … Rosie says these revolts are an affirmation of the human spirit.' Other times he just ignores what goes on outside his flat, while indulging himself with all his material comforts. Frears illustrates this when Rosie leaves for an evening to be with her lover, and Sammy becomes all id: trying to eat a hamburger, drink a Coke, snort cocaine and masturbate all at the same time.

His attraction for his latest lover, visiting American Anna (Wendy Gazelle), suggests that she, like Rosie, functions in a maternal role for Sammy. Anna mothers him through his ambiguous feelings about his father, and Sammy even discusses his troubled marriage with her. Sammy desperately seeks to construct the family he never had, for he is estranged from his mother and barely knows his father, who left the country when he was very young. Sammy's degenerate state is initially a turn-on for Anna: she refers to him as a 'couch potato' and enjoys indulging him as he lazes around her apartment. Because of Sammy's proximity to the riots, Anna links him to the excitement of the chaos. She eagerly photographs the police beatings, the burning of cars and the looting of the shops for part of her show, entitled 'Images of a Decaying Europe'. But she eventually tires of his passivity and indolence, literally leaving him behind as she eagerly throws herself into photographing the final destruction of the waste ground.[5]

Ironically, under an administration that extolled and valorised the nuclear family, *Sammy and Rosie Get Laid* suggests the absolute breakdown of this unit under new economic pressures – a situation that was introduced in *My Beautiful Laundrette*. Unlike Omar, who lovingly took care of his sick and depressed father, Sammy humours and indulges Rafi primarily because of the perks he offers him – an expensive new car and luxurious home in the suburbs. Further, Sammy's alienation from his wife and his father suggests the difficulties of maintaining family ties under the pressures of the social disorder that permeates their lives, a direct result of the new economic order.

This dynamic is dramatically demonstrated throughout *My Beautiful Laundrette*, for Nasser's many different business interests preoccupy him and keep him away from his wife and children. In fact, his mistress Rachel (Shirley Anne Field) – *not* his homebound wife Bilquis (Charu Bala Choksi) – is the familiar presence in his garage, Omar's laundrette, or his office (where they frequently make love). Ironically,

Rosie (Frances Barber) and Sammy (Ayub Khan Din), their marriage taxed by the overwhelming social and economic stress in their neighbourhood, become increasingly estranged, in *Sammy and Rosie Get Laid* (1987)

Bilquis's desperate attempt to keep her family together by using black magic to scare Rachel away only further estranges her husband.

Like her mother, Tania (Rita Wolf) also tries to preserve their family unit by taunting and shaming Rachel (on the day the laundrette opens), referring to their affair as 'a pretty disgusting parasitical thing'. Yet Tania soon realises that her father's double standard directly impacts her life, for he intends to marry her off to Omar – the designated heir of his fortune. Disgusted with the patriarchal lineage that capitalism favours and the sham of her home life, she simply leaves her family for a more promising life on her own.

While Nasser has the advantage of economic roots and political connections, which are clearly more important than his family ties, Rafi has neither business nor family links. He remains in exile in Britain, estranged from his native country and on the run from his political enemies, ostensibly having left his second wife behind. By seeking out Alice (Claire Bloom), whom he had admired from afar thirty years ago, he hopes to find a safe haven and precious companionship in the suburbs, far away from his son's scorn and embattled neighbourhood.

Both Rafi and Alice are loners (like Rafi, Alice is alienated from her son), initially drawn together by their memories of a more pleasant, civilised England in the 1950s. Ironically, they romanticise this period, during which strong racial barriers prevented their friendship or marriage. Though they harken from different cultures, their mutual endorsement of establishment ideals that support the status quo solidifies their ties of affection. Both are insensitive to the larger racial/class inequities that the Thatcher administration reinforced. For example, when Rafi refers to the rioters in Sammy's neighbourhood as 'fools and madmen', Alice agrees, commenting 'I hate their ignorant anger and lack of respect for this great land.' Like Margaret Thatcher, Alice remains a product of a provincial town with no ethnic minorities to speak of, having had almost no personal contact with blacks or Asians (Ogden 1990: 174). Rafi is more openly racist. Despite Danny's kind gestures toward him – he functions as a guide, protector and friend – Rafi still displays blatant prejudices. Right in front of Rosie, Rani (Meera Syal), Vivia (Suzette Llewellyn) and several neighbours, Rafi refers to Danny as a 'street rat and bum'.

Rafi's and Alice's racism is duly matched by their homophobia, for they are both openly disdainful of Rosie's lesbian friends Rani and Vivia, whom Alice admittedly finds 'unnatural and odious'. This relationship also throws Rafi into a furious fit when he finds them in Rosie's bed together. Such activities enable him to conclude that the 'West is decadent, sex-mad and diseased', echoing Thatcher's laments of the 'lost virtue' of English society (Jenkins 1987: 67), as well as the anti-gay atmosphere reinforced by her administration in the 1980s, and examined in *Prick Up Your Ears*. As compared with the love affair between Omar and Johnny or Orton and Halliwell, Frears gives the relationship between Rani, who is Pakistani, and Vivia, who is black, a minor role in *Sammy and Rosie Get Laid*, suggesting that same-sex, interracial relationships are increasingly forced to the margins of society.

But ultimately, as with Danny and Rosie, Rosie and Sammy, and Sammy and Anna, the atmosphere of chaos comes between Alice and Rafi. The violence and destruction in Sammy's neighbourhood reminds Rafi of the political disorder in Pakistan when a new regime inaugurated its own reign of terror. This state of affairs, foregrounded by the disfigured ghost of the political prisoner (one of many whom

Rafi (Shashi Kapoor) and Alice (Claire Bloom) in a rare moment of intimacy, in *Sammy and Rosie Get Laid*

Rafi had tortured and/or killed) that constantly hovers around Rafi, distracts him when he is trying to become intimate with Alice. The appearance of the ghost, his face and upper body burned and lacerated, increasingly unsettles Rafi. For example, after an evening of lovemaking when Alice gently tells Rafi she wants him to stay, Rafi is so obsessed with his past as conjured up by the ghost that he declares absentmindedly, 'I want to start writing my memoirs.' The ghost, who initially drives Rafi's cab and follows him through the looted and burning areas, soon looks like the persecuted blacks in the area, thus becoming emblematic of their oppressed status. This explains why Rafi's relationship with Danny remains problematic, for Danny clearly reminds Rafi of his political prisoners, hence his contradictory feelings toward him. Thus, Rafi's few moments of sympathy for Danny remain tainted with distrust and condescension.

Rafi's and Alice's relationship is further strained by Rafi's chauvinism. Such an attitude is perfectly appropriate to his native culture in Pakistan, where he was a 'patriarch and a little king, surrounded by servants' (as Sammy comments). Accordingly, Rafi forced the women 'back into their place' by shutting all the night clubs and casinos. Yet in England, this attitude seems ridiculously callous and inappropriate. This is illustrated before Rafi spends the night with Alice, when he comments: 'There's a good ten years' wear in Alice', after stroking the leg of Anna who sits next to him in Sammy's car. Alice finally comes to realise what a fool she was, waiting thirty years for Rafi, who had promised to send for her. 'All I wanted was a true marriage', she tells him angrily, suggesting her increasing awareness of her need for a mutually respectful relationship and sexual equality. This new perspective functions in the larger context of her raised consciousness, a result of her conversations with Rosie's feminist friends, including Rani and Vivia, who find Rafi's sexism hateful and Alice's attitudes dated. As Vivia chides her, 'You didn't have your own lives. You lived through men.'

Though Rafi's suicide represents one way out of his anguish over his past, and 'closes out' his age of terrorism in Pakistan, the new order there will most likely continue in an equally violent manner. This reign of terror is mirrored in England, dramatically demonstrated on the level of the ongoing racial violence in an atmosphere of class discrimination tacitly endorsed by the state. Whereas Halliwell's suicide following his murder of Orton in *Prick Up Your Ears* suggested a 'disturbed' homophobic and class-bound England lashing out at itself, Rafi's suicide alludes to a more vicious and pervasive cycle, where England not only plays out its internal hostilities, but also directly impacts a postcolonial state. Thus Rafi's comment to Rosie, 'We are still dominated by the West and you reproach us for using the methods you taught us,' suggests that the oppressed only embodies the 'values' and methods of the oppressor.

As *Sammy and Rosie Get Laid* shows, the crushing pressures of Britain's economic and social upheaval render impossible heterosexual relationships that cross ethnic and class boundaries, those that have the potential to create harmony and order. Yet the film applauds a few tattered survivors: a strong group of heterosexual and lesbian females who bond together, as Rosie, Vivia, Rani and their friends do in one of the film's final scenes. These self-appointed guardians take care of England's increasing numbers of underprivileged, while also looking out for political terrorists such as Rafi. While *My Beautiful Laundrette* demonstrated how Omar and Johnny assumed a leadership role as entrepreneurs, bringing two diverse communities together and creating a new hybrid community made stronger by the benefits of their enterprise, in *Sammy and Rosie Get Laid* leaders like Rosie, Rani and Vivia defiantly remain at odds with the businessmen who tragically destroy their communities. This pitched battle is played out when the landowners/developers, under the auspices of the government, raze the waste ground, thus destroying the fragile settlement and creating another group of homeless and alienated people. Though *My Beautiful Laundrette* and *Sammy and Rosie Get Laid* both link sexual diversity to the preservation of communities, *My Beautiful Laundrette*'s optimism that enterprise can build a stronger society shifts to a bleaker message in *Sammy and Rosie Get Laid*: that enterprise is obsessively self-serving.

Sammy and Rosie Get Laid culminates a progressively searing indictment of Thatcher's Britain, aggressively questioning and critiquing the new morality of the 1980s, which is dominated by the profit motive. As Frears commented, the film was intended to fully bring the government down. (It did not, but to Frears' relief, Thatcher was voted out two years later.) Instead of creating a new economic order benefitting all British citizens, the Thatcher establishment wreaked havoc on the working and underclasses, fracturing the country, rupturing families and devastating communities. Only the select few who shared her vision profited and thrived.

After completing *Sammy and Rosie Get Laid,* Frears acknowledged that perhaps having run out of steam, he 'really didn't have anything else to say about England right now' (in Friedman 1989: 30).[6] Nevertheless, Frears, Bennett and Kureishi created a remarkable legacy: a formidable body of work that exposes the enormous shortcomings of an economic system that ravaged England, and boldly challenges Thatcher's era of nation-building.

NOTES

1   *My Beautiful Laundrette*, made on 16mm for approximately £600,000, was completely funded by Channel 4, which was established in 1982 to fund high-quality films for local television viewers and theatre audiences. *Prick Up Your Ears* (1987), financed by Channel 4 and British Zenith Films, was budgeted at £800,000; *Sammy and Rosie Get Laid* (1987) cost £1.5 million and was financed by Channel 4 and the American company Cinecom.

2   Frears also made two features that played with generic conventions: *Gumshoe* (1972), a parody of the gangster and detective genres; and *The Hit* (1984), a psychological thriller mixed with the road picture that takes place in Spain. *Bloody Kids* (1979), a pre-Channel 4 made-for-television feature (later shown in feature-film format in the United States at the Telluride Film Festival in Colorado), focuses on the antics of mischievous youths flirting with crime. *Bloody Kids* is closer to the themes of Frears' television work.

3   The few films in the 1980s to feature Indian characters showcased white actors: for example, Ben Kingsley in Richard Attenborough's *Gandhi* (1982) and Alec Guinness in David Lean's *A Passage to India* (1984).

4   Clause 28 states: 'A local authority shall not … promote homosexuality or publish material for the promotion of homosexuality … [or] give financial or other assistance to any person for either of the purposes referred to above'. Lawrence Driscoll states that 'the aim of the clause is to prevent local authorities from spending their budgets on material which is held by the government to *offer homosexuality as a viable family alternative* (1990: 93; emphasis mine).

5   Frears and Kureishi take a sly glance across the Atlantic at America through the character of Anna, conjuring up the warm bond between Reagan and Thatcher in the 1980s. Anna suggests a power blind to its own decline during the Reagan years, conveniently ignoring and displacing its own domestic problems abroad.

6   Frears subsequently directed *Dangerous Liaisons* (1989) and *Grifters* (1990), both made outside Britain and financed by American companies. These films continue his fascination with power dynamics in various levels of society – the enclave of aristocrats in pre-Revolutionary France and the trio of swindlers in the latter 1950s in Los Angeles.

WORKS CITED

Chari, Hemalatha (1989) 'Decentered on the (a)isle of the post-colonial', *Spectator: University of Southern California Journal of Film and Television Criticism*, Fall, 20–31.

Driscoll, Lawrence (1990) 'Burroughs/Jarman: Anamorphosis, Homosexuality and the_ Metanarratives of Restraint: An Immanent Analysis' *Spectator: University of Southern California Journal of Film and Television Criticism*, Spring, 78–95.

Friedman, Lester (1989) Unpublished interview with Stephen Frears, 7 June. Syracuse University London Centre.

__ (1992) 'Keeping His Own Voice: An Interview With Stephen Frears', *Postscript*, 12–16.

Hunter, Mark (1988) 'Marquise de Merteuil and Comte de Valmont Get Laid', *American Film*, December, 27–31.

Jenkins, Peter (1987) *Mrs Thatcher's Revolution: The Ending of the Socialist Era*. Cambridge: Harvard

University Press.

Lahr, John (1986) *The Orton Diaries*. New York: Harper and Row.

Lindsey, Robert (1988) 'The Dangerous Leap of Stephen Frears', *New York Times*, 18 December.

Ogden, Chris (1990) *Maggie: An Intimate Portrait of a Woman in Power*. New York: Simon and Schuster.

14. NO SUCH THING AS SOCIETY: TELEVISION AND THE APOCALYPSE

Sean O'Sullivan

In 1987 the British Prime Minister gave an interview to *Woman's Own*, a cheery magazine of domestic and sartorial inclinations. The article admiringly details Margaret Thatcher's tea-drinking techniques and aversion to child abuse, and it carefully softens the Iron Lady's notorious glint, while giving her room to exude gravitas on such topics as foreign elections and primary education. The story meanders from subject to subject, until she is asked about a putative 'deterioration in the nation's moral standards', which prompts her to castigate the homeless for asking the government to provide them shelter. And then, without warning, she coined the defining motto of her administration. 'They're casting their problem on society,' she says of those who clamour for the welfare state. 'And, you know, there is no such thing as society. There are individual men and women, and there are families. And no government can do anything except through people, and people must look to themselves first' (in Keay 1987: 10). No formal address, no speech to a party conference, no shard of repartee from the House of Commons would ever come close to eclipsing 'there is no such thing as society' as the phrase by which Thatcher was known, especially by her detractors. When Mark Renton moves to London in Danny Boyle's *Trainspotting* (1995), he describes his enthusiasm for the go-go 1980s of profit, loss, margins and takeovers with these words: 'There was no such thing as society and even if there was, I most certainly had nothing to do with it.' The shibboleth had turned into cliché long before the end of John Major's days in office.

But television had anticipated Margaret Thatcher's vision of atopia, as both a fact of daily life and as a spectre of the future. In the first half of Thatcher's decade in power, two BBC programmes, quite different in scope and subject, had described a country that was no country, a nation defined more by absence than presence. The first of these, Alan Bleasdale's *Boys from the Blackstuff*, snuck up on the public. Unfolding in five episodes on BBC2 over the course of five weeks in October and November of 1982, it traced the lives of a group of jobless men from Liverpool, no longer able to work as layers of road macadam (the 'blackstuff') because of their city's economic devastation. By the end of the series' run, word of mouth had created such a buzz that the BBC took the unusual step of re-running the entire series, on its main channel, only eight weeks later, to allow latecomers the chance to hook onto the zeitgeist.

The series produced its own catch phrases and cult anti-heroes, as the drama's most tragic figure, Yosser Hughes, and his insistent declarations – 'Gissa job' and 'I can do that' – became instant pop culture, even chanted in the Kop of Anfield, the terraces of Liverpool's legendary football team (see, for example, Self 1983: 26 and Smith 1983: 35). *Boys from the Blackstuff*, which was directed by Philip Saville, atomised its city and its characters, exploring in a mosaic of separate stories the diurnal tedium and humiliation of unemployment, the shady snatches of illegal jobs at dangerous work sites, and the gradual erosion of class consciousness and individual worth into bits and pieces. By June of 1983, Bleasdale was being called 'the most famous writer in Britain' and the 1983 general election – the first referendum on the what, rather than the what if, of Thatcherism – was dubbed 'Yosser's Election' (Grant 1983: 15). The series remains a landmark political narrative of its decade. In a 2000 British Film Institute poll, industry insiders and critics named it the best drama series in the history of British television, eclipsing such internationally renowned landmarks as *I, Claudius* (1976) and *The Singing Detective* (1986).

The second programme about the disappearance of society snuck up on no one. When the BBC decided, in 1984, to air *Threads*, a two-hour film about a nuclear attack on Sheffield, newspapers and magazines rushed to prepare the public. In part, *Threads* was seen as an act of atonement, since the BBC had commissioned a 45-minute film in 1965 about a limited nuclear attack on Kent, Peter Watkins' *The War Game*, and then had refused to air the programme.[1] But *The War Game*, which won the Academy Award for Best Documentary Feature in 1967, despite not being in any strict sense of the word a documentary, was in fact more limited than *Threads*, and not simply in the scope of the conflict depicted. *Threads* eschewed the pseudo-*verité* style of its predecessor, its devices of Brechtian alienation, and its focus on the immediate days before and after the attack. Instead, the later film, written by Barry Hines and directed by Mick Jackson, began as a kitchen-sink drama of a young couple who decide to get married after the woman gets pregnant; only piece by piece did *Threads* turn into a story of ballistic holocaust, following and losing its protagonists 13 years beyond the devastation of Sheffield, imagining a world in which imagination itself ceased to exist. The film garnered rave reviews, even from such right-wing outlets as *The Daily Telegraph*, and *Radio Times* was deluged with viewer response (Stringer 1984: 10; Anon. 1984: 96).[2] More newspaper articles were published on *Threads* before the film even aired than were published on *Boys from the Blackstuff* during its entire five-week run. Yet despite the lavish attention and praise it received at the time, *Threads*, as a cultural artefact, has languished in its own nuclear winter.

This essay will address the ways in which these two programmes enacted several problems of Thatcherite Britain, first and foremost the spectre of negation that threatens to replace the presence of community. *Boys from the Blackstuff* and *Threads* are also both about the North, a region defined by its obsessive regionalism, by its sense of local identity and history. By contrast, the South in the 1980s looked like more transient territory – where the Americanisation of British economics was in full swing, where class barriers and neighbourhood identity might seem to matter less than capital and freedom of movement. These dramas participate in the tradition of the Victorian condition-of-England novel of geographic schism, but they leave the South out of the equation, as an off-screen Other. While *Boys from the Blackstuff* concentrated on the particularity of Liverpool, on the specific accents and industries and entertainments of that specific metropolis, *Threads* portrayed Sheffield as a more abstract idea of the North, a territory as important for its strategic intersection of goods and services as for its distinctiveness.[3] Another shared concern of the programmes is the collapse of infrastructure – physical, social and ideological. The road pavers in *Boys from the Blackstuff* are no longer employed to pave roads, and this central crisis speaks to both the tangible and the metaphorical deterioration of the materials that organise the world; likewise, the initial shot of *Threads* of a spider spinning a wispy web illustrates the frailty of social connectedness. This rhetoric of infrastructure dovetails with the less-quoted part of Thatcher's creed, her assertion that 'there are individual men and women, and there are families', by considering these alternative building blocks for a nation-state, or a city, and then dissolving those units of civilisation as well. In *Boys from the Blackstuff*, four separate families collapse, and by the end of *Threads* the very idea of family ceases to have meaning. Individual men and women fare no better, as *Boys from the Blackstuff* unravels what manhood and personhood connote, in portraying the internal entropy of characters like Chrissie Todd and especially Yosser Hughes, who turns into a shambolic synecdoche of his city. *Threads* empties out its characters not only of hope and desire but of psychology itself, interrogating how we begin to define the human in the asocial state.

The five-episode structure of *Boys from the Blackstuff*, at initial glance, seems to fall into an ABBBA pattern, since the first and last stories share a number of common elements, most prominently the death of a member of the Malone family – the middle-aged radical Snowy Malone (Chris Darwin) in the first episode and the revered communal patriarch George Malone (Peter Kerrigan), Snowy's father, in the finale. Furthermore, each of these bracketing stories brings all the main participants together into a shared narrative. The first play, 'Jobs for the Boys', begins by introducing us to each of the central characters as they report to the Department of Employment for their dole money: Chrissie Todd (Michael Angelis), the wry but worn common man; Loggo Lomond (Alan Igbon), the wise-cracking dandy who maintains an emotional distance from his circumstances; Yosser Hughes (Bernard Hill), the violent, maniacal, lost but oddly mesmerising loner; George Malone, the benevolent but ageing historical conscience of the group; and Dixie Dean (Tom Georgeson), the embittered former foreman who wants to stay as far away from his old gang as possible. Soon after, Chrissie, Loggo, Yosser and Snowy (an ideological stand-in for his father) find themselves at a non-unionised job site, earning £14 a day in hard cash for a contractor who cannot or will not make honest men of them. Dixie refuses to go along with this scheme because of the disastrous events related in Bleasdale's earlier single drama, *The Black Stuff* (1978), where these same Scousers travelled together to a paving job in Middlesbrough, tried to make extra money by 'doing a foreigner' (taking on an outside job on company time), lost whatever savings they had, and ended up without jobs. This time the boys are turned into amateurs, since there is no longer an economic need for their real professional skill – laying tarmac. The episode ends in violence when the dole sniffers raid the site, and Snowy, who specialises in spreading plaster and is the one craftsman who actually belongs on this location, falls to his death after trying to escape; he ties a rope to a shoddy banister, a banister he has earlier pointed out as a slapdash addition to a building with much older and better-made features. Bleasdale dispatches Snowy, who wearies his non-ideological mates with socialist harangues, apparently to cleanse the series of partisan agit-prop – although, as has been noted, the fact that he is killed by an object that obviously functions as a symbol of a Thatcherite profit-or-else ethos hardly drains the series of its politics (Millington 1993: 130).

If 'Jobs for the Boys' provides an allegory of a dysfunctional society, the final episode, 'George's Last Ride', works as an elegy, depicting the final days of the old campaigner George Malone, played by an actor who had himself been a dockworker, and who had been banned from the docks for being a Red (Bleasdale 2003). The boys, who are scattered to their separate dramas in the intervening episodes, reconvene to shepherd George through his final days. Despite the neatness of these bookends, I would suggest that in fact 'Jobs for the Boys', 'Moonlighter' and 'Shop Thy Neighbour', the first three episodes, function as a kind of unity, or at least a linked collection of parables, that gets disrupted by the very different style and look of the fourth episode, 'Yosser's Story'. Indeed, as one watches 'Yosser's Story', this feels like a conclusion – as Yosser spirals into a deeper and deeper abyss of isolation and despair – and the episode's closing minutes share an eschatological terror that *Threads* will explore even further. Seen in this light, 'George's Last Ride' will come across as old-fashioned in its storytelling, perhaps pedantic in its oppositional dramas, a postscript that undermines the whirlwind of the preceding episode. This structural unease, this ambivalence about how a series that has dabbled both in the real and the fictional should resolve itself, underscores the fact that the perennial narrative problem of closure is even more vexing when the grim and the escapist have been integrated. What society does a series like this want to return us to?

Perhaps foremost among the instruments that tie together the first three episodes is the use of handheld 'outside broadcast' video equipment, a technology that had heretofore been used either as a minor part of studio-based productions, or for news reporting purposes (Millington & Nelson 1986: 40). The signifying properties of film map out a set of visual associations quite separate from those of video, even at a time when mixed usage of these media was hardly uncommon.[4] Economic and logistical reasons largely drove the choice of video for the first three episodes of *Boys from the Blackstuff*, and the finale. The Pebble Mill studios in Birmingham, which funded the series, were not equipped with the full resources of a sound stage, and almost demanded a mixture of controlled sets and locations. The budget severely restricted the amount of footage that could be done on film, a far more expensive proposition than videotape, and the scripts clearly called for the events to be photographed on the actual streets and empty lots of the city. The decision to use only one medium for each story, and to allot sufficient funds for only one story to be shot on film, may not have been, in its origins, an artistic one. But the caesura this created, with 'Yosser's Story' as the one script to escape videotape, in fact complemented the divide between the more contiguous missions and strategies of the first three episodes and the series' *pièce de résistance*. The rougher, less ambitious feel of the opening triptych would echo the sense of awkwardness that hovers over the episodes, and the society they portray; the seemingly higher art of film would match the unrestrained bravado of cinematic risk in the episode to follow.

After the long view of 'Jobs for the Boys', the two succeeding stories follow the familial troubles of Dixie and Chrissie, respectively. 'Moonlighter' moves back and forth between Dixie's illicit work as a night security guard on the docks and the fraught listlessness of his home life, where his adult children linger with no motivation to seek work and his wife worries about getting caught with her own sideline of dropping leaflets through letterboxes. 'Shop Thy Neighbour' also follows a pattern of parallel editing, juxtaposing Chrissie's fractious marriage with the harried and unsatisfying lives of the dole-office workers, who are employed to catch cheaters but who know that they could be switching places with their targets at any moment. While the individual focus may be different from case to case, each of the first three episodes is organised around the parody or re-consideration of a familiar dramatic genre. 'Jobs for the Boys' satirises the spy movie, from the incompetent sniffers who tail their suspects to the international political intrigue implied by the subtext of Snowy's politics. From the moment that Chrissie spots the contractor's liaison lurking around the Employment office and greets him with a mock code phrase – 'Carnations are red in Albania this winter, comrade' – both the episode's comic energy and its biting reality effect feed off the unlikely intermarriage of the most mundane circumstances and the glamorous intrigue of the genre's structural and verbal language. 'Moonlighter' dips into the vocabulary of film noir, literally in its nighttime setting by the docks but more broadly in its tale of a corrupt social system. Dixie Dean takes bribes to look the other way while thieves ransack the boats he is supposed to be guarding, and he eventually discovers that the man secretly engineering the bribes is his supervisor. When Dixie's wife Freda cowers inside her house, afraid to admit her friends because she knows she is being followed, the friends laugh at her flighty paranoia; but she *is* being followed, and society has turned into a place where shady deals, threats of violence and the fear of homelessness dominate the proceedings. 'Shop Thy Neighbour' presents an updating of the *Upstairs, Downstairs* genre of the melodrama of class, with neither side of the divide aware of the sufferings of the other. The episode begins in the home of a new character, Miss Sutcliffe (Jean Boht), the head of the local Employment office; her living conditions are extravagant by comparison with those of the unemployed whose lives she investigates, but she is unmarried, and her mother has careened into senility. Chrissie also has a troublesome woman at home, but in his case it is his wife, Angie (Julie Walters). In a series with a dearth of fully developed female roles, the prominence of women in this episode also contributes to its status as a 'weepie', a melodrama full of operatic, overwritten dialogue (in Miss Sutcliffe's case) and repeated quarrels over Chrissie's lack of manhood (in the Todd household). The episode concludes with the over-the-top but nonetheless wrenching spectacle of Chrissie, hounded yet again by Angie for not putting food on the table, shooting his pet chickens and geese in a fit of frustration, having reached his limit for being hen-pecked. (That bleak avian pun exactly corresponds to Chrissie's sense of humour.) The moment speaks to the reality of unemployed life in Liverpool; but the psychology and style come from dramatic conventions on which these characters grew up.

The range of allusions, quips and plays on words that festoons the language of virtually all the characters in the series represents the flip side of what is sometimes called Northern miserabilism. Near the end of 'Shop Thy Neighbour', Angie accuses Chrissie of buying into this locally-grown self-ironising affect, the impulse to joke about – and momentarily wish out of existence – the grim facts of existence: 'I've had enough of that.' 'If you don't laugh, you'll cry.' 'I've heard it for years – this stupid soddin' city's full of it. Well, why don't you cry? Why don't you scream? Why don't you fight back, you bastard?' As if in response, the next episode, 'Yosser's Story', will follow exactly such a screamer and fighter, to his extremely dark end. That gives us one clear line of demarcation between 'Yosser's Story' and its predecessors. In the earlier episodes the boys are able to comment on their state, to use the resources of mainstream film and television conventions as a framework, however painful, through which to see their unremarkable lives; like John Milton's Satan, each transforms his brain into a job site where a working definition of the self can be built and rebuilt. Their stories enact the after-effects of collisions between the mind and the body, the imagined self and the unemployed self, and these collisions can be brutal; but the mind always holds out the narcotic illusion of being a refuge, a space outside the real where identity can be sustained. The black stuff of the diurnal – the bleak unavoidable objects of overdue bills, bureaucratic forms, eviction notices and abandoned buildings – always serves as the starting point of the mind's working – the pit that, however miasmic, nonetheless produces the raw material for narratives of the self, and of society.

'Yosser's Story', by contrast, does not start outside the mind but inside it. The episode begins with Yosser taking his children to a park, bringing them fully clothed into a lake, and watching them disappear one by one beneath the water – as Chrissie, Loggo and George drift nonchalantly by in Cantabrigian punts. We discover soon enough that this is a dream sequence, but that full immersion inside the consciousness of a single character signals a sharp break from the materiality of the earlier

'Gissa job', a refrain spoken by the tragic Yosser Hughes (Bernard Hill) in *Boys from the Blackstuff* (1982), became a pop culture catchphrase during the Thatcher years

episodes, not least because the nagging inevitability of family that dominates those stories turns into the gradual annihilation of family this time. In many ways, 'Yosser's Story' will be both more literal and more fantastic than its predecessors, stretching the formula that has sustained the series so far into something much more daunting. Even the soundtrack alerts us to a stark change in cinematic environment: the soulful saxophone that has dominated the series so far gives way to a harpsichord, an instrument that connotes ironically the mathematical order of Baroque music (even as Yosser's life will become more disordered than that of his former mates) and the forceful separation, rather than the piano-like connection, from note to note, imitating Yosser's own sense of alienation from everyone around him. He travels everywhere with his pack of children, as if they were the signifiers without which he would cease to have meaning, even as we are asked to cast doubt on whether these three offspring are in fact his progeny; like everything else in his life, they turn into empty referents. The person who casts the gravest doubt is his estranged wife Maureen, most prominently in an apparent interview with a social services worker – 'apparent' because we never see that worker, in a long take that allows Maureen to spill the secrets of their relationship, as if speaking to a psychiatrist, or more precisely as if speaking to a camera. As the script makes clear, the positioning here is entirely self-conscious: 'The whole delivery is documentary, perhaps almost like World in Action' (Bleasdale 1985: 202). This confusion of styles alerts us to the way that 'Yosser's Story', more than any other episode in the series, will blur the line between documentary and fiction.[5]

Perhaps the most effective blurring arrives a few minutes before Maureen's confession, when Yosser heads to a pub holding a charity event, an event attended by football player Graeme Souness, the famed captain of Liverpool FC. What could be a throwaway cameo in fact underscores the episode's complicated investigation of the social. At the time, Souness was the most prominent player at the best club team in the world, a squad that won a remarkable four European Cups and seven English league championships between 1976 and 1984. Football, as a theme, had peeked into each of the preceding episodes: in 'Jobs for the Boys', Loggo talks about supporting Everton, Liverpool's city rival; in 'Moonlighter', the bedroom of Dixie's sons is festooned with Liverpool posters and photos; and in 'Shop Thy Neighbour', Chrissie discovers an old Liverpool programme while scrounging under his couch for loose change. And the football pitch on a Saturday afternoon would always offer the most prominent rebuttal to Thatcher's denial of society, especially in a working-class context, and especially in the weird situation of a city sitting at once near the bottom of the economic heap and on top of the sporting pile. But the encounter between Souness and Yosser, who thinks he resembles Souness because each has dark hair and a prominent moustache, transforms what had been part of the mise-en-scène of the series into a dialogue between the centre and the periphery, the iconic Souness and the utterly disenfranchised Yosser. Yosser's sidling familiarity slightly unnerves Souness, as this stranger sits next to him, declares 'I'm Yosser Hughes', and asserts 'You look like me.' Yosser's further insistence that they both look like Magnum, P.I., who 'used to be on the television', underscores the series' awareness of television narrative's ability to permeate everyday life. This desire to be 'Yosser Hughes', whatever that might mean, and to be 'somebody' dates back to the end of The Black Stuff, when Yosser erupts in rage at what he sees as Chrissie's milquetoast approach to their troubles, anticipating Angie's critique a few years later: 'I want to be noticed, I want to be somebody, I want to be seen. I'm a human being. I'm alive! I'm here now! Look at me!' As we learned in *The Black Stuff*, Yosser travelled around the world in the 1970s, to such emerging capitalist markets as Saudi Arabia and Nigeria, in search of well-paying jobs that would enable him to secure a big house, and to distinguish him from the other members of his class and his family – a Thatcherite *avant la lettre*. This bifurcation of the individual and the social exactly speaks to the celebrity of Souness, a star in a game that relies on teamwork, on social formations, for success.

Yosser Hughes did become somebody. Soon after 'Yosser's Story' aired, Graeme Souness led his Liverpool team out onto the field at Anfield, and the Kop serenaded him with, 'You look like Yosser Hughes' (Anon. 1983: 16). It is in some ways perverse that the character who rocketed above all the others in popularity and name recognition, out of the array of personalities in *Boys from the Blackstuff*, was a self-deluded, out-of-control misanthrope who crashes through the social net. Of course, perversity is only natural for the Liverpudlian strain of black humour, as Angie has pointed out. This was further illustrated when local discos started playing a novelty tune called 'Yosser's Rap', which pirated Yosser's catch phrases and laid them on top of a music track, yet another irony for the BBC, as the series about people working illegally and trying to scam the system spawned a copyright infringement of the programme's most famous lines (Thornber 1983: 8; Tyler 1983: 4). A romantic would see this wholesale adoption of Yosser as a community's attempt to reintegrate its most alienated member, to see in this schizophrenic personality the city's schizophrenic jumble of past greatness and present failure, of financial woe and sporting conquest – and there may be something to that. But in terms of *Boys from the Blackstuff* as a whole, these spin-offs, whether recreational or commercial, illustrate the way in which 'Yosser's Story' is itself an exception – a dislocation that speaks to the very tension between an enchanting tale of connection and unity ('society') and the tangible pieces of the existence, of the distinct ('individual men and women, and families'). The particular ingredients of 'Yosser's Story' – shooting on film, quoting the methods of documentary, using music that emphasises separation, colliding with actual celebrities, focusing exclusively on a loner – created a narrative that undermined the genre of the drama series itself, establishing a kind of cultural entrepreneur in the figure of this haunted man. One could argue that 'Yosser's Story' is, in narrative terms, the hard Thatcherite episode in the middle of the soft left-wing stories, not because its horror story of psychological collapse in any way endorsed the spirit of radical individualism but because it made the drama of individualism so gripping, so perversely glamorous amidst the inescapable mundanity of barely-viable-but-not-quite-finished houses, families and lives in the other episodes. I am not suggesting a hidden Conservative subtext here – rather, I am pointing out that the attractiveness of heroes or anti-heroes constantly poses a problem to artists who have wanted, since Dziga Vertov and Sergei Eisenstein, to make cinema a collectivist and not a bourgeois medium.

In a lecture delivered in the wake of the series, the renowned theatre director Jonathan Miller compared *Boys from the Blackstuff* to *Ulysses* (Truss 1984: 27), and one is tempted to see Yosser Hughes as an embodiment of both the grim, inward-turning, black-clad Stephen Dedalus and the cuckolded, peripatetic, painfully

Yosser suffers a psychological collapse after losing his wife and children because he cannot find enough work to support his family in *Boys from the Blackstuff*

self-aware Leopold Bloom. Of course, Yosser boasts none of the book learning and intellectual adroitness of those characters, but as a semi-realised amalgam of the insider who wants out and the outsider who wants in, Yosser fits the bill. His erratic and violent ways eventually lead, step by step, to the loss of his wife, his children and his house, but he somehow remains 'Yosser Hughes' – even stopping to deliver another of his trademarked job-hunting phrases, 'I can do that', to the men boarding up the windows of his repossessed house. The last sequence of the episode brings him to Williamson Square, in the centre of the city, in yet another evocation of the documentary particularity of Liverpool, and launches him into a self-destructive finale. Yosser and a Scottish wino whom he had befriended earlier meet again after a soaking rainstorm; the wino mentions his plan to break a shop window, in order to get arrested and secure a dry jail cell for the night. Yosser decides to beat him to the punch, much to the wino's consternation; when the police come to the scene, their initial brief is to arrest just one of the men, and their familiarity with the Scot's modus operandi means that Yosser is in danger of being left on the streets. In order to ensure his apprehension, he responds punningly to the cop's 'don't "but" me' by head-butting him, as he has head-butted many people and objects over the course of the series. As they drive off, the outraged policeman holds a handkerchief to his bloody nose and tells Yosser that 'he's dead'; Yosser responds by taking this metaphorical threat literally, improvising a halting eulogy for his own life, regretting that he never became 'somebody'. On the pretense of needing to vomit, he gets the cops to stop the car near a park; once outside, however, he suddenly exclaims 'I'm Yosser Hughes, and I can't stand it anymore', evoking Peter Finch's cry from *Network* (1976), in yet another addition to the series' fabric of quotations. He tears off across the park and into a lake in order to drown himself, bringing us right back to where the episode began – but the movement here is from the figurative to the literal, as opposed to the shifts of energy from the literal to the figurative that other characters have pursued. The cops reluctantly save him, and as they pump air out of his limp body, he suddenly jerks back to life and cries 'no' repeatedly, as the camera zooms in to a freeze-frame of his bruised left eye. Yosser's 'no' responds to Molly Bloom's 'yes'; if this is to be Liverpool's *Ulysses*, it concludes as an epic of negation, lacking even the *ignus fatuus* of society that Leopold imagines among himself, his wife and his young friend.

Except … except that this is not the end. We still have the fifth episode, 'George's Last Ride', a tale that might seem to be an unnecessary epilogue, a reunion of the gang that may strike us as implausible after the nihilism of 'Yosser's Story'. Oddly enough, we discover that things that we thought were broken have been at least temporarily repaired: Dixie Dean's son Kevin, last seen hitchhiking toward brighter economic climes in the final shot of 'Moonlighter', has inexplicably returned to town; Chrissie and Angie, when glimpsed at George Malone's funeral, seem to have patched things up; even Yosser has come back from the brink of self-immolation, wandering around in a dazed but becalmed state, after ending back home with his mother. Furthermore, the first half of the episode goes through its pedagogical paces, as George in a valedictory moment impugns the weaker new generation (his less-radical sons, or his doctor, who has forsaken his socialist roots for the middle-of-the-road Social Democratic Party) while he still keeps a photo of Marx on his parlour wall. The death of the old lefty leaves the community bereft, but in a more conventional narrative way, at least for series drama, than the relentless modernist fable of 'Yosser's Story'. After the hard edges of the preceding story, Bleasdale opts for lyricism; Chrissie gives the wheelchair-bound George the eponymous last ride, pushing him toward and among the largely abandoned dockside warehouses. The dying man engages in a passionate soliloquy about Saturday afternoons of his youth, boats from Ireland, and the postwar revolution of Clement Attlee and Aneurin Bevan. Inside one of the empty buildings, the camera swirls giddily across the windows as light streams in, clearly suggesting that these structures were George's cathedrals, and establishing a poignant contrast to his rote funeral service, conducted by a tipsy and out-of-touch priest, that we later witness. Religion has been an irrelevance until this point in the series, but here the vain mysteries of Catholicism receive an implied lashing, as yet another veil of community that has ceased to have meaning, and that uses fossilised rituals and language to disguise its passing.

It is not, I would argue, that the episode fails in any particular way; it is just that these requiem gestures and panegyrics to a passing greatest generation feel more predictable than the experimental narrative blends we have seen so far. The episode's climax, however, represents an about-face; we witness a scene of public house chaos as the off-kilter rhythms of something different, a Dadaist state-of-the-nation set-piece that seems to have been co-written by Eugène Ionesco and David Hare. Chrissie and Loggo head inside to find shelter from their grief, and they discover an overpopulated madhouse, fed by a redundancy party of sacked workers looking to blow their severance wages all at one go. The carefully-picked eccentrics include a glass-collector who finishes the customers' drinks before they can start them; Ronny Renaldo, a former waiter who cannot stop whistling 'If I were a blackbird'; Gnasher

Llewellyn, an addled ventriloquist; the whiskey-chugging publican; and the hulking brute Shake-hands, who forces various people into bone-crushing grips and then buys them consolation pints of bitter. The patent constructedness of this scene – the introduction of half-baked Dickensian characters enacting lunatic society in miniature – leaves the world of cause and effect far behind. This has almost become a masque, full of the allegorical, the unlikely, and the spectacular.

But the specific and the local get the last word, as Chrissie and Loggo watch this extravaganza with a sober reserve that they have not mustered until now. When Yosser stumbles out of the bar, Chrissie looks aghast, casts his eyes to the skies, and pleads, 'Beam me up, Scottie.' The eyeline match for this plea to the heavens is not the *Enterprise* but a decaying brick edifice with the legend '1922' at the top – the condemned Tate & Lyle sugar refining plant, bearing the date of the firm's merger. Television as escape (*Star Trek*) meets television as news, in this two-shot distillation of the series' binomial heritage of documentary and drama.[6] Moments earlier, Chrissie had made and then repeated the revelation 'George is dead' to Loggo, and he might have easily have been referring to George V or George VI, the Georges who ruled in the now-hallowed first half of the twentieth century.[7] Chrissie, Yosser and Loggo continue to look to the heavens, as if waiting direction from whatever deity remains, until Yosser looks over at Chrissie and utters the series' final line of dialogue: 'Gissa job – go on, gissa job.' The final images move from a high-angle crane shot, picking the boys out as they wander down a gaping street, to a low-angle shot of the factory and its 'TATE & LYLE' lettering, almost as if to admire this deeply ambiguous structure of capitalism and working-class identity, as it meets the same fate as George. The series closes with a street-level track of the three men scattered across the road, linked only by inference, and then comes to a stop in a freeze-frame, as every other episode has. The past-present push-pull of the freeze frame, which captures a moment in amber, has matched all along the series' swing between nostalgia and reportage, but here we get yet another optical hieroglyph: a lens flare. This device, so radical in 1960s cinema as the putative mistake that becomes central to the image, might have passed into cliché by 1982 – but so, of course, had lines like 'beam me up, Scottie'. Society exists on clichés, on tired gestures that provide a familiar dialect. Indeed, the lens flare's simultaneous indexing of amateurism and sophistication – of the 'error' of the lens flare fused with the 'artistic' intent to make the camera part of the story – allows the programme to straddle the line between the real and the fictional one final time, to leave its options open even as the city seems closed for business for good.

Threads begins with an extreme close-up of a spider unspooling the thinnest of fibres against a black background – the fine line dotted with glistening globs of liquid as the animal industriously lets out its line, its two visible legs working in concert, like a pair of human arms. For a few seconds, before a voiceover intrudes, we might wonder what we are looking at, and why, so detailed is the image; surely this seems to be the start of a nature documentary, and not a drama about nuclear war.[8] In a sequence of eight shots, over the course of half a minute, we move back and forth, through dissolves, from close-ups of the spider at work to nearly abstract images of industrial wires and steam, and generic high-angle long shots of city streets crisscrossed lazily by buses or trucks. Connecting the montage is this voiceover narration:

In an urban society, everything connects. Each person's needs are fed by the skills of many others. Our lives are woven together in a fabric. But the connections that make society strong also make it vulnerable.

The voiceover ends before we reach the ninth shot, which depicts the finished spider web, its white lines stark against the black background – but the spider is gone, and in fact the web seems almost an etching, and not quite real. This shot then slowly zooms out while also going out of focus, turning the web's lines from brown to white, and bringing them vaguely toward us, and finally dissolves into a zooming-in, entering-focus high-angle extreme long shot of a city, its brown buildings distinct enough to differentiate separate structures but not distinct enough to suggest recognisable landmarks. White smoke spews out of the foreground as the title credits are typed onto the image – 'THREADS by Barry Hines' – followed by another typed-out caption – 'Sheffield. Saturday, March 5th'. In sixty seconds, the film has provided us with a lexicon for interpreting not only its cinematic and narrative ambitions but for considering how *Threads* represents the vision of Britain that Margaret Thatcher would endorse three years later. The central dynamic in this prelude, and in the movie as a whole, lies in the tension between the general and the specific.

Thatcher's edict rejects the general ('society') in favour of the specific ('individual men and women, and families'), eschewing collectivism in favour of the personal free enterprise of capitalism. Thatcherism, as a social force, threatened above all other things the notion of class, the category that transcends individuals or families or neighborhoods by allocating identity through larger shared values and histories. Yosser Hughes yearns for specificity, 'to be somebody', because he sees the rubrics of class and society as vortices that consume people like him into types, into symbols. By contrast, *Threads* seems to begin not with the specific, or even the specific wrestling with the general, but with the general first and foremost. Who is this spider? Well, it is not a particular spider; it is the idea of a spider. What are these streets and buses and trucks? Well, they are not particular streets or buses or trucks, they are the idea of streets and buses and trucks. The spider only belongs here because of certain generic conventions – the nature documentary – and the stock shots of the urban environment belong here because of certain generic conventions – the establishing shots of a fiction film.

The voiceover complements this rhetoric of the general, referring twice to that loose word 'society' and invoking 'each person' and 'many others' without bothering to name names, as Bleasdale does in 'Jobs for the Boys'. The web's transformation, by the ninth shot, into something closer to a diagram than to an actual web, confirms the sense that we are operating with concepts or ideas rather than empirical material. And the view of Sheffield clinches this presentation, since perhaps only a local could penetrate the haze of this city-view and identify it readily as the biggest town in South Yorkshire. The smoke, the dull sky and what seems to be a brown filter all work to make this panorama as general as possible, as Northern Industrial City, as idea rather than particular place. Indeed, this composition, especially at the start of a movie, is itself generic, having been adopted quite frequently in New Wave films such as *Saturday Night and Sunday Morning* (1960) and *A Taste of Honey* (1961). Andrew Higson has explored this as the iconography of 'That Long Shot of Our Town from That Hill', and indeed this shot in *Threads* corresponds in its haziness, depth of field and subject-position to those instances of an earlier generation of filmmaking (Higson 1996: 155). The shot is characterised not only by visual indistinctiveness but by narrative conventionality – and indeed we are about to embark on another of those 'kitchen sink' films that Higson associates with 'That Long Shot'. This is the familiarity of genre, and of the generic.

But this is not quite right. There are in fact two very specific gestures that bookend the opening movement of *Threads* – the extreme close-up of the spider and the precise date of Saturday, March 5th. I have argued that the spider is generic, insofar as it has no role to play that any other spider of its species might not play equally as well. And yet any extreme close-up by definition implies specificity, and the striking thing about this shot is that we see the detailed design of a spider's thread in far greater detail than we are likely to have done before, and the image of that glutinous line spinning out of those knitting arms transformed a ponderous and familiar metaphor – the web of society – into something crystallised and almost magical. The date of Saturday, March 5th suggests a superfluity of precision, an odd bit of unnecessary verisimilitude. We will learn eventually that this precise temporal beginning functions at least in part to set a kind of trap for us, for a highly symbolic date in the future of the film, a date that itself synthesises the general and the specific. Finally, these moves prepare us for the three principal competing sources of information that will dominate the film – images, voiceover and captions, each telling its own story about what is happening and what it means. At times, these sources will appear to work in concert, providing complementary glimpses of an event, but at others they will belong to rather different epistemological categories. The voiceover, especially, will veer into the category of the general, not just because of the kind of information it supplies but because the voice is familiar from other documentaries and the generic or class category of BBC English, the accent of authority. The captions, by contrast, will give us nuts-and-bolts information about this city, the attack and the numerical elements and costs of the war – facts that ground themselves in the hard contours of specificity. *Threads* will explore the trauma of the specific gradually getting removed from the general. *Threads* will show us Thatcher's non-society.

Here is the plot of the film. After the opening sequence, we see a car holding two young lovers – Jimmy Kemp and Ruth Becket – parked atop That Hill, overlooking Our Town. Exactly two months later, we discover them again, in a pub, as Ruth tells a perturbed Jimmy that she is pregnant. Against their parents' advice, the two decide to get married, have the child, and set up house on their own. As their plans progress and their families meet, news reports filter in of a growing conflict in the Middle East, as Soviet troops move into northern Iran after a purportedly American-prompted coup; these radio and television broadcasts often occupy the background of a scene, or of a character's attention, rather than the foreground. From 5th May until 26th May, the film unfolds on parallel diegetic and non-diegetic tracks. Diegetically, we gradually get to know the two families, and we discover the growing anxiety in Sheffield as, step by step, the United States and Soviet Union move closer to nuclear conflict. We meet one other family, the late-middle-aged Suttons, and learn that Mr Sutton, as Sheffield's Chief Executive, will have to become wartime controller in the worst-case scenario; as the attack nears, we see him and other officials setting up emergency headquarters in a bomb shelter. Non-diegetically, the information gap between the general and the specific, between voiceover and captions, continues to widen. The voiceover continues to instruct in broad strokes, or through comparisons, referring vaguely to 'an urban district like Sheffield', to headquarters 'like this one' that 'have been hastily improvised up and down the country in the basements of town halls and civic centres', and to the lack of training of 'many of these officers'. The captions, by contrast, are precise, marking off each crucial day from the 5th to the 25th, and spitting out such facts as Sheffield's population and size relative to other British cities; the city's main industries; the proximity of an RAF base; and the step-by-step escalation of the conflict. The spoken words maintain the story at the level of the abstract, or the representative; the printed words insist on the particularity of time and place.

The slightly longer second part of the film, which covers events during and after the detonation of 210 megatons of bombs over the United Kingdom, details not only the horrific effects of the missiles but also the gradual dissolution of the British social structure, and eventually the collapse of human psychology itself. We last see Jimmy running home after the first bomb hits Sheffield, but we never learn his fate. One of the brilliant manoeuvres of the film is to make us feel, eventually, that losing contact with a character no longer means that the character has died; we become more and more aware of the arbitrariness of following any one human life, or any collection of human lives, in a dramatic story. Jimmy's sister, Alison, who has been an earnest yet light-hearted presence in the first part of the film, is not even given a cameo during the attack. Presumably, she has been incinerated. The Kemps discover the body of their younger son, Michael, in the rubble the day after the first strike. Mr Kemp abandons the body of his wife, and he is later seen swigging scotch in a food centre set up in a graveyard; his body is last seen in a collection of photographs of unburied corpses. In the other household, Ruth soon wanders off to look for Jimmy, while her grandmother is left to be covered up with a sheet; later, Ruth returns and notices, without emotion, the bodies of her dead parents. Mr Sutton and the other officers labour incompetently to get things going again from their bunker; four weeks after the attack, their grey and dust-covered bodies are discovered. On her aimless wanderings, Ruth runs into Bob, an old friend of Jimmy's, but she remains emotionally disconnected from him, even as they carve up and eat the raw meat of a sheep. Eventually, Ruth gives birth, without any medical assistance, to a baby girl, in a barn on Christmas day. That delivery becomes one of the last recognisable moments one could call an 'event' in the film, since we begin to drift into the future – one year, three years, ten years on, when an ashen and prematurely wizened Ruth dies. Thirteen years later, Ruth's unnamed daughter herself delivers a child, in a makeshift hospital. The film ends with her wordless horror at she catches of sight of her newborn, wrapped in a bloody blanket.

Throughout this bleak journey, the non-diegetic stream of facts keeps us perpetually shuttling back and forth between the pity and terror of Ruth and the multiple scientific contexts of the events. The voiceover continues to deliver the big picture, informing us of radiation sickness, the massive clouds of debris that shut out the sun and lower the earth's temperature, the disintegration of the Health Service, the meaninglessness of money, the population's shift to the countryside in search of food, the meagre first harvest, the fuel shortages and finally the fatal effect of the first winter. Given the logical absences of diegetic sources of news, the sources that supplied the nuclear narrative in the first part of the film, it is reasonable that the voiceover should have so much more to do after the attack – especially in keeping us aware of the general, as the specifics (particular characters, places, events) become increasingly difficult to locate or interpret. Yet the logic of voiceover becomes difficult to sustain, since this measured, calm voice of polished British enunciation seems a relic in a world now lacking the order and class system that the voice implies. In fact, the last quarter hour of the film, which covers the period from 10 months to 13 years after the war, has no voiceover at all, leaving us dangling without access to the omniscience that has sustained us all along.

The disappearance of voiceover from *Threads* does not necessarily signal the disappearance of the general, of 'society' in Margaret Thatcher's understanding of the word; rather, the general gets horrifically internalised within the diegesis. This slide of the general into the specific is anticipated by the captions, which continue to provide dates, ticking off days, weeks, months and years into the beyond, but which also start to take on the broader tasks that have heretofore been the responsibility of the voiceover. We learn, via captions, about 'likely epidemics', about 'ten to twenty million unburied corpses in the UK', about the shrinking population as 'UK numbers may decline to medieval levels'. This shift can of course be explained as prudent, for a film that lists 26 programme advisors and scientific and social authorities in its final credits, and which relied for its cultural impact on the accuracy of its fiction. But while this kind of circumspection is appropriate on a factual level, the narrative impact tells its own story. This array of educated guesswork drains the film of its specificity, as a story about individual people and individual families in an individual place – the foundation of virtually all moviemaking. The Sheffieldness of Sheffield, compared to the Liverpoolness of Liverpool in Alan Bleasdale's work, had always been marginal, or derived largely from tables and graphs; but even those distinguishing markers and signs are effaced by the end.

If the voiceover and captions push the precious materials of the specific into a wasteland of the general, the images produce their own slippery movement, as the diegetic and non-diegetic visual worlds become hard to distinguish. In the first half of the film, we occasionally see stock footage of buildings, or airports, or overseas battle scenes, images that we understand to provide clarification and context for the human story that we have been following from the moment we saw that car on the hill. These function as identifiable fragments from a documentary library, as mortar that keeps the story together, while never threatening to challenge the greater importance, for the film viewer, of the larger storytelling movements. But in the second half, we start getting black-and-white stills, abstract shots of landscape and vignettes of misery that could either be stock or fresh-made, and these categories of image so dominate the visual story that we cannot always easily segregate what exists as supplementary information and what exists as primary narrative material. Furthermore, as those people whom the narrative had singled out as specifics within the general – as major characters, as opposed to minor characters and extras – gradually disappear, the concept of 'stock footage', namely images of the general, seeps into the central drama of the movie. Ruth remains our nominal contact with traditional storytelling, since presumably her maternal struggle for survival provides the continuing impetus for our engagement as viewers. But with the inevitable erosion of her initial supporting cast, we get more and more scenes of crowds clamouring for food, or of soldiers shooting looters, or of the sick and screaming in hospitals. It is as if the narrative background – the people who exist to provide local colour, or to fill out a pub scene, or to act terrified and run into each other in the chaos of a town square – had been pushed to the foreground, not to take the psychological space of the specific major characters we have lost but to start replacing the very idea of psychological space. *Threads* began as a kitchen-sink drama married to a pseudo-documentary about a nuclear war. By the time we get to the birth of Ruth's baby, we can no longer separate those genres; we no longer know exactly what it is that we are watching.

The birth of that baby leads to the audacious final act of *Threads*, which sketches out a narrative of that child's life. The sequence begins with an extreme long shot, virtually black-and-white, of a silhouetted Ruth struggling against the wind, under a lowering grey sky, and a bare landscape marked only by a bare tree. Given that this bleak picture echoes the bare stage directions of *Waiting for Godot*, it is no surprise that a new Beckett is about to come into the world. Ruth eventually makes her way past a snarling dog, collapses in a barn on a pile of hay, and gives birth in a scene that is particularly graphic, one might say specific, for a television film – as we see Ruth tear off the placenta with her teeth. If there were not already something vaguely familiar about the scene of a birth in a bare building suited for animals, the scene cuts to black, and we are then treated to a tableau of people huddled around a fire, the reddish glow of the image suggesting a night-time nativity of Georges de La Tour. Sure enough, a caption appears to confirm our suspicions by telling us that it is Sunday, 25th December; this affords us a specificity – of day, month and date – that we have not had since mid-June, in the weeks soon after the attack, and it is the last caption of such precision in the film. Barry Hines asks us to accept not only a Christmas birth, but a Sunday Christmas birth, and if we do the math we see that this was in the works all along – a year where 5th March falls on a Saturday, as we learned this year did in the opening sequence, will see 25th December fall on a Sunday. In other words, the apparent innocuous or irrelevant date on which the film began turns out to have been part of a hidden plot to bring all events together into this blatantly symbolic occasion. This vestige of plottedness, in a film that is now tracing a society that has (to use a British expression) lost the plot, seems an odd anachronism, like the lingering voiceover, the voiceover whose last gasp will come at the conclusion of this scene. I would argue that the almost comical obviousness of this painting of the anti-Christ, or a Christ for a world past redemption, serves the shattering purpose of making plot itself look ridiculous, since the events we have witnessed make planning, organising, connecting – all the activities of plot, and of society – completely outdated. *Threads* herein absorbs the central plot of Western civilisation, the plot about a character who stands for both the specific and the general, whose particular resurrection would bring communal resurrection, and turns it into a moment of overly ironic coincidence. Given that none of these people huddled around the fire, including Ruth and her baby girl, is likely to be aware that it is 25th December, we are acutely aware that plot as a structuring device has become an irrelevant mechanism for them, as well.

And what of this anti-Christ, or non-Christ, or person born on a day whose signifying powers are now lost? We have a brief caption, just as Ruth entered the barn for the delivery, that in a pregnancy that has been subjected to radiation the 'foetus carries higher risk of deformity and mental retardation'. But when we see this girl ten years into the future, working alongside Ruth in a barely-fertile field, looking vacantly down at her mother, who has keeled over from exhaustion, it is impossible to determine whether she bears the evidence of any birth defects at all. Physical lassitude and emotional blankness would hardly be distinguishing features in this society, since they apply to virtually everyone we see. Her powers of language and her understanding of how to connect to others may be 'retarded,' as we soon discover, but again a society with the merest shreds of an educational network and no need for traditional discourse would retard all its inhabitants. This girl is in fact one of the most remarkable characters ever put on screen – a person whose psychology it is impossible to fathom, and indeed a person who seems to have no psychological content at all. She is Post-Nuclear Human, an abstract or general idea embodied by an actress, a specific being, and nothing she does from here on out will add any information to what or who she is; Ruth's daughter is a challenge beyond the powers of Henry James. She eludes analysis even on the level of naming, since while she is labelled as 'Jane' in the script and in the final credits, there is absolutely nothing in the film itself that allows us to know this name (Mangan 1990: 232). The meanings that we ascribe to her are purely our own and do not belong to her. This becomes most evident in the scene following Ruth's collapse in the field, when the daughter looms over the bed-ridden Ruth, tugging at her dying mother's arm, instructing her: 'Ruth. Ruth. Work. Work. Up.' Ruth, her hair and eyes both glazed white, looks over at the girl and drops her head back on the pillow, dead. The daughter, unaffected, does the practical thing: she takes her mother's brush, and a spoon, and a scarf, which might have value, and leaves behind her mother's last possession, a book entitled *The Handbook of Foreign Birds*. We know that this book carries a huge and specific mnemonic and psychological value; to Ruth's daughter, it is a generality without meaning.

This is a book that we saw in Jimmy's possession near the beginning of the film, two weeks prior to the attacks, and this book speaks to his particular hobby, namely the careful maintenance of an elaborate aviary in his parents' home. (The book's title resonates ironically with the foreign birds he cannot readily identify – the nuclear missiles – that eventually undo Jimmy, and everyone else.) Ruth, who in the early scenes was more closely associated with her pet cat than her fiancé's birds, had found the book when she had made her way to the Kemp house in the days after the attack and found nothing else but Mrs Kemp's body. We are reminded of the bird theme at other points, such as when Ruth scrambles to retrieve the book from her spilled effects when being chased from a temporary residence, or when she briefly dreams of Jimmy; his face is seen through the wire mesh of a cage, happily ministering to his flock, so that in this point-of-view dream-image, Ruth is the bird. This is the only memory or fantasy shot in all of *Threads*, and its brief glimpse into subjectivity, however striking at the time, becomes all the more powerful when the abandoned bird book provides definitive evidence of the daughter's complete lack of a subjective self. But the abandoned book does not simply illustrate something we might already know, namely that meanings and values are arbitrary; the abandoned book tells us that specificity itself has vanished. The following scene clinches this chilling revelation, as we see Ruth and other children clustered around a barely-oper-ative black-and-white television and video recorder, watching an old educational tape. The topic for the day, as the videotaped host cheerily announces, will be 'words and pictures', modes of representations that are almost fully hollowed out by this point.

Indeed, the illustrations for these concepts will be objects culled from a museum, specifically the skeletons of a cat and a bird. Cat and bird, Ruth and Jimmy's totemic animals, are literally gutted here, and they make no impression whatever on their child. In this skeletal society, the physical insides of things, the general properties that everyone shares, are on display; but the metaphorical insides of things, the specific memories, ideas, associations that we might condense as 'character' or 'the individual' have vanished.

Threads will enact a last stage of this society that is no society, this world of the general divorced from the specific, three years into the future, when Ruth's daughter gives birth to her own child. The scene of conception shows Ruth's daughter being grabbed by a male companion, with whom she has just stolen some food, but the distant long shot of their grunting and crying out makes it difficult to determine whether we can call this a rape or not – yet another event to which we cannot give a specific term. Some months later (we cannot be precise, since the captions have disappeared), she staggers, in the darkness, to a scarcely functional hospital. In this scene of parturition, we see only the daughter's anguished and thrashing face, and not the gore and graphic detail that we saw at the scene of her own birth; the specifics of the event are being denied to us. We cut to a hospital worker wrapping the silent and seemingly still baby in a sheet, and bringing the bloody bundle to Ruth's daughter. She stares at it in confusion for a few moments, lays the child down, and begins to recoil with what seems to be a cry on her lips – and the film ends on this freeze-frame. Is the child dead? Is it hideously deformed? Is having a child itself horrific? Ruth's daughter is jolted into reaction for the first time, but this might as easily be the reaction of a revulsed animal as a human being.

This final image not only prods us to ask a question that has no specific answers; it asks us to wonder what questioning, knowing, making sense of the world, means. The freeze-frame denies us a piece of information that stands as one of the key clauses in the contract of cinema – a reverse-shot. If a shot tells us that something off-screen is important to someone in that shot, and important to the progress of the narrative or psychology of the drama, withholding from us the reverse-shot indicates a fundamental breakdown of the social contract of the art form. By not disclosing the specific source of the off-screen energy of that shot, we are left adrift in the general, unmoored from the community and characters in which the film has tempted us to believe. We lack the ability to care about this general person and her general child, because all the indices of the human on which narrative drama depends have been bombed out of existence. I am arguing that when Margaret Thatcher would say, three years later, that there is no such thing as society, she was unwittingly speaking of this denied reverse-shot, of the society made of no things and only the ghosts of things, of the society of *Threads*.

It should hardly surprise us then that Yosser Hughes lives on as one of the most beloved characters in British television history, since he fulfills the agony of a self separated from the social in a way that television has long made recognisable. The closing freeze-frame 'no' of 'Yosser's Story' makes sense to us, because there is no missing reverse there; the reverse-shot is inside his head, an image of his wife, or his children, or a lost ambition. The despair of that final shot depends on our willingness to believe in an internal, psychological self, no matter how blasted. Society may seem to have fallen apart in *Boys from the Blackstuff*, but our solicited impulse to care about these characters, to pluck their specific torment from the undifferentiated mass of unemployment, itself affirms an idea and a practice of society. Bleasdale's characters tread the narrow boundary between the visible, or the physical or the documentary, and the invisible, or the psychological and the fictional. In *Threads*, all the resources of documentary – voiceover, captions, scientific experts, stock footage – are marshalled to portray the annihilation of the invisible and to shield the visible from our eyes. No wonder Ruth's daughter has disappeared from our cultural memory; to remember her would be to confirm that there is no such thing as society.

NOTES

1 *The War Game* was finally broadcast in 1985, after the perceived watershed of *Threads*.

2 *The Listener* and *City Limits* devoted cover stories to the *Threads* phenomenon.

3 The fact that Jimmy, the film's nominal male lead, is twice associated with Newcastle Brown Ale suggests a broader Northernness at stake in this film.

4 Such mid- to late 1970s situation comedies as *Fawlty Towers* and *To the Manor Born*, which were largely shot in the studio, with a three-camera video set-up, switched to film when the action briefly moved outside domestic spaces; this bifurcation helped signal video's palette as one appropriate for dialogue and character development and film's for geographic context and verisimilitude.

5 Several writers have emphasised what we might call the series' heteroglossia, citing such rhetorics as realism, modernism, humour and surrealism (see, for example, Caughie 2000: 178 and Cooke 2003: 134). By contrast, no critic has addressed what I would consider the more complicated and devastating heteroglossia of *Threads*.

6 The year 1922 also evokes the decade of the first Labour government, and of the general strike, when trade unions and cities like Liverpool provided the country's economic and ideological foundations.

7 I would further suggest that the seemingly unnecessary repetition of 'George is dead', makes us think of a Liverpool echo, of yet another George, and encourages us to substitute 'Paul is dead', in evocation of the city's last gasp of cultural greatness.

8 Compare, for example, *The Day After* (1983), the American counterpart of *Threads*, which begins with a shot of a military plane on a runway in Nebraska. Not much room for confusion there.

WORKS CITED

Anon. (1983) 'Gi us a job', *Listener*, 20 January, 16.

_____ (1984) '*Threads*: More Reaction', *Radio Times, 20* October, 96.

Bleasdale, Alan (1985) *Boys from the Blackstuff*. Cheltenham: Stanley Thornes.

_____ (2003) Audio commentary on DVD of *The Black Stuff*. BBC.

Caughie, John (2000) *Television Drama: Realism, Modernism, and British Culture*. Oxford: Oxford University Press.

Cooke, Lez (2003) *British Television Drama: A History*. London: British Film Institute.

Grant, Steve (1983) 'Yosser's Election', *Time Out*, 3 June, 15–16.

Higson, Andrew (1996) 'Space, Place, Spectacle: Landscape and Townscape in the "Kitchen Sink Film"', in Andrew Higson (ed.) *Dissolving Views: Key Writings on British Cinema*. London: Cassell, 133–56.

Keay, Douglas (1987) 'Aids, Education, and the Year 2000!', *Woman's Own*, 31 October, 8–10.

Mangan, Michael (ed.) (1990) *Threads and other Sheffield Plays*. Sheffield: Sheffield Academic Press.

Millington, Bob (1993) '*Boys from the Blackstuff*', in George W. Brandt (ed.) *British Television Drama in the 1980s*. Cambridge: Cambridge University Press, 119–39.

Millington, Bob and Robin Nelson (1986) *Boys from the Blackstuff: Making a TV Drama*. London: Omedia.

Self, David (1983) 'Black Comedy Stuff', *Times Education Supplement*, 14 January, 26.

Smith, Ruth (1983) '*Boys from the Blackstuff*', *The Leveller*, February, 35.

Stringer, Robin (1984) 'Unthinkable Made Possible', *Daily Telegraph*, 24 September, 10.

Thornber, Robin (1983) 'Beyond the Black Stuff', *Guardian*, 14 January, 8.

Truss, Lynne (1984) 'Message from the Boys', *Times Educational Supplement*, 27 January, 27.

Tyler, Andrew (1983) 'Gis a Break!', *NME*, 15 January, 4–5.

15. THE MASOCHISTIC FIX: GENDER OPPRESSION IN THE FILMS OF TERENCE DAVIES

Tony Williams

In 1983 Andrew Higson criticised a dominant tendency within critical work on British cinema that emphasised realist interpretations at the expense of examining signifying filmic mechanisms. He faulted such readings for failing to advance beyond Christian Metz's model of the cinema as an industrial entity. Higson also condemned these interpretations for remaining solely at the level of 'a sociological desire for neatness and continuity, a desire for the text to be either "progressive" or "reactionary"', as well as refusing 'to pay attention to the permanent and productive tensions, the play of containment and excess, in the film system' (1983: 87). Conversely, Andy Medhurst (1983) reasserted the importance of the social text reflecting a dynamic, but not an unproblematic, historical moment. The work of independent film director Terence Davies, especially *Distant Voices, Still Lives* (1988) represents a body of work that does attempt to unite these critical demands. His films contain non-linear representation, contradictions, tensions and excess, calling on the viewer to engage in an unpleasurable specularity with the narrative in a more masochistic than voyeuristic manner.

However, *Distant Voices, Still Lives* encountered critical misinterpretation. Desperate for another energetic 'New Wave' emerging from a cinematically impoverished culture, British reviewer Derek Malcolm regarded Davies as a 'unique voice' responsible for a 'musical version of *Coronation Street* directed by Robert Bresson, with additional dialogue by Sigmund Freud and Tommy Handley' (1988: 21). Geoff Andrew compared Davies to an Ingmar Bergman who has produced 'the first realist musical' (1988: 16). Thomas Elsaesser associated Davies's cinematic exorcism of male childhood trauma with an upsurge of British films dealing with masculine subjectivity (1988: 291). American reviewer Leonard Quart (1990) noted the film's overt formal composition and its seeming neglect of cultural, historical and psychological explanation.[1]

The film certainly operates on a highly stylistic level, with fragmented memory, tableau-like compositions, meticulously composed photographic shots, and camera movements emphasising the characters' physical and emotional entrapment. With the exception of one brief seaside scene, *Distant Voices, Still Lives* inscribes the spectator within the mental and psychological space of the family domain. Avoiding the distracting spectacular nature of exterior shots, the film allows the spectator no privileged vantage point with which to engage in a pleasurable voyeuristic gaze, thus making the text a non-challenging fetishistic object. Instead Davies implicates the spectator in the pain and pleasure of memory. The audience experiences the present and past effects of a younger generation's traumatic childhood, the logical result of a brutal process of patriarchal gender conditioning. By presenting the viewer with the inner life of a working-class family (rather than from without as in the 1960s British New Wave), Davies avoids the pitfalls of both Hollywood escapism and British cinematic literalism. His work represents an artistic exploration of psychic trauma.

Since his first film, *Children* (1976), Davies has gradually moved away from a 1960s-influenced documentary style toward an achronological, inner world of tormented personal psychobiography. However, even *Children* exhibited particular non-linear memory traits of emotional pain that would develop further in his work. In his initial trilogy, including *Madonna and Child* (1980) and *Death and Transfiguration* (1983), we chart the early years and eventual death of surrogate figure Robert Tucker. Victim of a traumatic family situation, Tucker lives a blighted life under the shadows of family morality and Catholic doctrine. He is unable to accept his gay nature, living an existence of passive misery and emotional torment. Tied too closely to his mother, his dying moments in *Death and Transfiguration* represent an imaginary transcendental union with the maternal realm. It is almost as if he is receiving an imaginary transfiguration into the false angelic costume we saw him wearing while a young boy. Tucker's final moments are ambiguous since we do not share his perceptions, but Davies's trilogy is a bleak, pessimistic work leaving no fragmentary space for any alternatives.

Distant Voices, Still Lives is a more complex work. By identifying himself with the camera instead of a surrogate figure, Davies more acutely explores the familial situation, presenting explanations for its oppressive dominance and suggesting faint possibilities for individual voices to at least briefly contest the living graveyard of 'still lives'. Although set in the recent past, the film eschews the realist devices of earlier decades of British cinema. It instead presents antirealist representations as if recognising the ineffectiveness of traditional British cinematic discourses to combat the historical situation that has resulted in Thatcherism. Like Derek Jarman, Davies recognises that an alternative British cinema must necessarily involve a different set of visual practices.

Funded by the independent sector, Davies must be understood as an entity implicated within that movement's discursive framework. Writing for the British Film Institute Production Board during 1977–78, Pam Cook championed the important concerns of 'personal' filmmakers 'with questions of point of view, memory and fantasy ... the material base of film, and the possibility of creating an alternative language of film' (1981: 276). These features certainly appeared in Davies's trilogy, which received funding from this body. But, unlike the Oedipal norms of most mainstream films, Davies's cinema is one bound up with the pre-Oedipal in an intense relationship with the maternal figure. Also, unlike the sadistic mainstream narratives criticised by Laura Mulvey, Davies's work has significant associations with masochism, particularly the secondary masochism resulting from a traumatic family situation destructive to both male and female. Davies's films represent one answer

Young Robert Tucker's angelic predestination, in *Death and Transfiguration* (1983)

to Mulvey's demand for a cinema based upon unpleasure rather than the typical cinematic mechanism of pleasure.

Although set in the past, *Distant Voices, Still Lives* is by no means irrelevant to the historical context of 1980s Britain. Dealing with the life of a working class thirty years before Thatcher, it is impossible to view it outside her reactionary authoritarianism. This anthology makes abundantly clear that the 1980s were a decade of reaction within British society that witnessed attacks on libertarian values similar to those made in Reagan's United States. One of the chief platforms of Thatcherism was an assault on the 1960s phenomenon of 'the permissive society', especially on one-parent families and gay men and lesbians. This resulted in ideological re-emphasis on the traditional family unit. Despite increasing cuts on welfare and family allowances, Thatcherite discourses led to successful attacks on feminists, gay men and lesbians, minorities and single-parent families, resulting in the increasing isolation of all those outside the family norm. Her 1980s ideological banner of 'Victorian values' disavowed all criticisms of a past imperialistic system that caused considerable damage, both externally and internally, upon the British character. As Leonard Shengold (1988) has shown, several of Charles Dickens' pictures of blighted families reveal more than coincidental links between passivity and masochism that were to contaminate future generations.

As an independent work challenging patriarchal discourses, *Distant Voices, Still Lives* has significant links with feminist concepts in literature and film. Alice Jardine notes that 'struggle' is a crucial component of such texts. 'The *inscription* of struggle … whether written by a man or woman – it was this that was found to be necessary. The *inscription of struggle* – even of *pain*' (1987: 61). Such an inscription characterises *Distant Voices, Still Lives* which, unlike earlier 1960s 'kitchen sink' productions, is a film entirely critical of the masculine ethos behind those earlier representations. Despite its formal nature, Davies's film offers crucial insights into those insidious operations of gender conditioning that would eventually destroy the foundations of the British welfare state and led to Thatcherite hegemony. Such hitherto neglected factors have occupied dominant positions within the British social structure. Susan Pedersen points out that 'the construction of masculine identity as entailing economic rights over women and children was one of the most powerful achievements of the labour movement which understandably guarded it jealously' (1989: 99). Nicky Hart notes that 'gender has never been theorised as a major axiom and stratagem in any of the dominant theoretical approaches to social inequality' (1989: 37). Davies's film provides sufficient internal evidence of gender oppression. One particular scene shows the father exploiting his family by making them chop wood in wartime Britain. While doing this the children nearly die in an air raid. When they face their father in the shelter it is Eileen he hits, not Tony. However, the working-class world of *Distant Voices, Still Lives* is not entirely Hart's 'masculine republic' (1989: 40), since the pub also provides a space where women express solidarity in song and mutual support.[2]

Although it deals with past events, *Distant Voices, Still Lives* is firmly rooted within the historical and cultural context of the 1980s.[3] As a work of fragmented memory, it has undeniable links with artistic recreations of trauma that attempt to re-piece a shattered self by the use of non-linear techniques. The family group that appears at the beginning of *Distant Voices, Still Lives* prior to Eileen's wedding is no mere Bresson imitation. Their frozen demeanor represents a psychic numbing, a particular traumatic symptom due to physical and/or mental abuse usually associated with gender conditioning within a nightmarish family situation. Relevant literature on traumatic phenomena reveals that Davies's cinematic treatment is no banal artistic posturing. Psychic violence has detrimental results. Negative effects usually occur well beyond the period of childhood, often resulting in 'persistent thoughts about the trauma that intrude into everyday affairs; and a general dysphoria, a numbness that takes the meaning out of life and makes it hard to relate to other people. In (some) cases … the symptoms manifest themselves after a latency period of several years or … alternate with apparently asymptomatic periods that on closer inspection, turned out to be periods of denial.'[4]

Whether conscious or not, Davies attempts traumatic depictions using characteristic techniques of memory fragmentation and non-linear representation involving his audience in an unpleasurable realm. By doing this he avoids the nostalgia inherent in any work dealing with the past. Cinematic style reflects a painful content. His re-created family life does not represent cosy memories of 'the good old days'. To counter any deceptive familiarity endemic in other representations of the past (*Upstairs, Downstairs*, *Dr Finlay's Casebook*, *Sherlock Holmes*, Ridley Scott's 1970s Hovis bread television advertisements, and so forth) that often disavow the painful circumstances of people's lives, Davies necessarily resorts to different cinematic strategies. In the opening scenes, we view the family facing us. Although the father is dead, his presence still dominates the group, since his photograph appears prominently on the wall behind them. The family faces the camera with frozen postures. Eileen thinks, 'I wish me Dad were here', denying the torments he had inflicted on the

The traumatised women in the family (Freda Dowie, Angela Walsh and Lorraine Ashbourne) in *Distant Voices, Still Lives* (1988)

family when alive. Maisie refuses such a thought. 'I don't! I don't! He was a bastard and I bleedin' hated him.' The audience then enters her memory of past patriarchal brutality, sharing her pain and humiliation. Illustrating the secretive patterns of co-dependency, the family members never speak of the past. Instead memory haunts them. We often flash back and witness a traumatic family quarrel before returning to the present in the abrupt mode of classic posttraumatic stress disorder symptoms. This occurs in the very opening of the film. We pass from Maisie's voiceover cursing her father to a memory of her brutal maltreatment, before returning to the family tableau. The audience then shares in Tony's memories of a similar past situation. Like Maisie's, they are non-linear and fragmentary and concentrate on moments of pain, whether physical (Tony smashing his fist through a window) or mental (Tony's rejection by his numb father). His memory ends with the military police dragging him into a van and obviously beating him inside closed doors.

The work of Terence Davies thus represents an alternative to that Oedipal law of cinematic articulation formulated by Raymond Bellour. Davies's films depict a masochistic realm of unpleasure rather than pleasure, a situation due to patriarchal oppression.[5] His trilogy and *Distant Voices, Still Lives* illustrate psychic battlegrounds torn between potentially progressive pre-Oedipal worlds and destructive Oedipal prisons. Within his work, the Law of the Father is an entirely negative violent realm psychically punishing both present and future generations. However, the pre-Oedipal arena is not without its problems. Although mother's presence is a comforting one for her children, her inability to oppose Tommy's brutality presents a morbid image of masochistic suffering that will scar her children's lives. Despite her gentle nature, she is a role model whose passivity under patriarchal brutality reveals to her children the negative pattern of suffering in silence. Mother comforts Tony during his scarlet fever, but the next sequence shows her powerless to intervene when Tommy refuses to let him indoors later. He is forced to seek refuge with his grandmother, who Maisie later recognises as being just like her father.

Although the daughters and girlfriends will eventually marry, none of them appear to have an entirely satisfactory relationship with their husbands. All marriages are characterised by traits of physical brutality (mother and father), mental cruelty (Les and Jingles), passive acceptance (Eileen and Dave) and tolerable acquiescence (Maisie and George). All fall into a patriarchal snare, the result of an ideologically harmful romanticism. One sequence makes this clear. Asked why she married, mother replies, 'He was nice. He was a good dancer.' But, as an audience, we immediately remember earlier scenes in the film showing Tommy initially refusing to let Maisie go dancing and forcing her to scrub a rat-infested cellar. The film then flashes back to Tommy beating his wife to the ironic accompaniment of Ella Fitzgerald's 'Taking a Chance on Love'. Successive shots show the battered mother passively polishing furniture, and Eileen shovelling coal in the hated cellar. We later see the daughters weeping at a film performance of one of the most perniciously romantic products of Hollywood cinema – Henry King's *Love Is a Many-Splendored Thing* (1955)!

Mother and children never speak openly of their experiences of traumatic violence. Instead, we remain privy to the truth by memory sequences that reveal the repressed brutality behind supposedly pleasurable memories. One scene pertinently illustrates this. In the pub the predominantly female community sings 'Barefoot Days'. Following a 180-degree panning shot we return to the past. The family prepares wood to sell in the austere wartime era. We then see the children caught in an air raid. They reach shelter just in time. It is clear that Tommy has sent them out to sell wood oblivious of their safety. Seeing his children unharmed, the hypocritically enraged paterfamilias hits Eileen. He then forces her to sing to abate the fear everyone inside feels. The scared people all join in Eileen's plaintive rendition of 'Roll Out the Barrel', a communal British World War Two song. This sequence reveals the buried past pain beneath a seemingly pleasurable present act. The Davies family certainly does not share in the second stanza of the song, '...We'll have a barrel of fun'. These are but two of many sequences showing the inextricable interrelationship of pleasure and pain within patriarchal dominance. Scenes often clash with each other, as they are chosen for their depiction of intense emotional traumatic situations rather than for any smooth, linear, chronological progression.

These masochistic scenarios are reminiscent of the more social interpretations of Wilhelm Reich (1970) and Michel Schneider (1975) rather than Freud's ahistorical, universal concepts. Unlike Freud's later formulations in *Beyond the Pleasure Principle*, masochism is better understood as a secondary rather than a primary process,[6] one caused by the family's role as an agent of social conditioning.[7] Both Reich and Anna Freud notice the rigid armour-plated bodily postures that the ego uses to defend itself against psychic attack in traumatic situations.[8] Indeed, Reich's observations uncannily parallel the opening family 'portrait' in *Distant Voices, Still Lives*: 'All masochistic characters show a specifically *awkward atactic* behaviour in their manners and in their intercourse with others' (1971: 219). However, this scene is not characteristic of others in the film exhibiting tentative opposition toward male dominance. In the pub Eileen and Micky unite in condemning Les's treatment of Jingles. Another scene shows Eileen criticising Dave's table manners at home. Eileen also delivers a solo pub song – Harry Belafonte's 'Brown-Skin Girls' – which ends in a revelation of a wife's murder of her husband, implicitly referring to Dave. Micky is the only female who can manipulate Tommy Davies so that the girls can go off dancing. Tony and Eileen utter separate threats against Father in the course of the film. What we clearly see is a hegemonic situation in which oppressed female subalterns attempt some opposition. However, despite such utopian glimpses, open revolt is clearly impossible within the film's social situation. All characters exist in a complex world of psychic and social entrapment mediated by masochistic mechanisms within the family unit.

Many psychoanalysts such as Bernhard Berliner (1958) now agree that masochism is a fluid term covering many pathologies, not all of them necessarily sexual or perverse. Although Robert Tucker exhibits perverse masochistic practices as a result of his traumatic Catholic conditioning and repressed homosexual desires toward the father, this is not true of the family in *Distant Voices, Still Lives*. Instead we see a more varied depiction where each family member exhibits different tendencies. As the only male who, in father's place, gives away Eileen in the opening sequence, Tony is no Robert Tucker. The only evidence we see of self-inflicted pain is when he thrusts his hand through the window in a vain attempt to reach through to his catatonic father after going 'absent without leave' during his national service. Otherwise, he is more gentle and caring than his father. But he, like Eileen, disavows the traumatic memories of patriarchal oppression. Eileen weeps on his shoulder, crying for her father, before she leaves the family for married life. Tony comforts her, choosing not to contradict her. Both are masochistic victims of childhood trauma, emotionally scarred as a result of their father's dominance during life and beyond death.[9]

As a secondary (non-instinctual) socially mediated process caused by past events, the masochistic fix affecting Davies's characters is an indissoluble result of traumatic conditioning. Jules Glenn has noted that although trauma need not be present in masochism, 'not infrequently it plays a decisive role' (1984: 357). It may also result in obsessive repetitions in later adult life that represent not only attempts at mastery but also masochistic gratification. We need not pause before Freud's repetition-compulsion theory to see a definitive explanation for the cinematic construction of Davies's work. They are masochistic products of traumatic experiences repeated anew within an artistic framework. Torn between the Oedipal imperatives of honouring one's father and keenly aware of his past brutalities, the children are torn by conflicting emotions. Their loving father is a monster. They cannot admit this outside of their home, not even to themselves. Attempting in vain to forget past trauma, the repressed memories return to haunt both them and the audience in fragmented imagery. Davies's work is a form of cinematic moral masochism where fragmentation plays a special role. Writing on the links between masochism and depression, John Gedo comments that moral masochism 'may be viewed as nothing more than active repetition of certain subjective states that the observer would not choose to seek for himself' (1984: 12). Phyllis Greenacre describes infantile traumatic situations that affect later life as being one of 'masked repetition in which the demon [of masochism] is so constantly active that life itself is repeatedly deformed and drawn into a masochistic state of being' (1971: 298). Glenn also points out that as the child gets older and enters later adult life he 'may attempt mastery by repeating or causing repetition of the traumatic event in controlled and modified form, thus causing painful experiences. He may turn his rage and/or sadism toward the perpetrator of the trauma inward and attack himself, or he may turn rage and/or sadism associated with the oral, anal, symbiotic separation experiences inward' (1984: 384).

In the trilogy, Davies uses Robert Tucker as masochistic victim. Since author is completely identified with character, he cannot really step outside the film and view from the outside. That accounts for the trilogy's bleak and pessimistic nature. In *Distant Voices, Still Lives*, there is no surrogate character. Instead, Davies explores through the camera, observing psychic defeats, traumatic incidents and briefly expressed oppositional stances. This explains its more diverse nature. Unlike the trilogy Davies reveals more differential patterns of behaviour, such as close female bonding, family celebration and spontaneous singing, in addition to bleak moments. He now creates a more integrated film that is less negatively overwhelming than its predecessors. Split between several characters rather than merely one, his artistic ego can thus – following the creative axiom of Gilbert J. Rose – communicate a feeling perspective that transcends 'the private dimensions of merely personal trauma' (1987: 61).

Socially-induced masochistic conditioning causes great psychic damage to its victims. Investigating usually neglected areas of environment and class in her psychoanalytic explorations, Eleanor Galenson outlines the damaging nature of aggression in the child's early life that leads to negative results in later Oedipal development. Retreat into passivity has far more serious consequences for boys than girls. Galenson remarks: 'The masochistic development that emerges during the Oedipal phase is then inextricably bound to a basic instability in the sense of masculine identity' (1988: 195). It can also lead to a more malignant type of masochism involving perverse practices. This happens with Robert Tucker. Until Tony leaves home and marries, he is his mother's boy. After his father's death he has a warm emotional bond with her. Since he is not alone and has his sisters, he is not as psychically devastated as Tucker. The women react differently. Eileen curses her father in his presence. Yet she reluctantly returns home like a dutiful daughter when he is dying. She reveres his memory at her own wedding, masochistically repressing past traumatic events. As Galenson notes, 'while the retreat to a passive maternal relationship does not endanger the sense of sexual identity of girls, the more passive nature of their object relations leads toward a permanent masochistic distortion of their relationship to the father and later to all men' (ibid.). Concluding images in the film's first part show Eileen weeping as Dave gloats over her marital entrapment and separation from her girlfriends. All the women are caught within patriarchy in one way or another. If Eileen and Mickey escape Jingles' hellish situation, they cannot freely meet as in the past due to the hindering presence of Dave as 'lord and master'. Ironically, this is despite the fact that Eileen and Dave are living in her grandmother's house.

Distant Voices, Still Lives is thus the work of an artistic ego attempting mastery over a painful past. It is a product of cinematic fragmentary memory depicting the traditional family norm of British society with unpleasurable associations. By virtue of his visual technique, Davies forestalls the spectator's voyeuristic tendencies toward the pleasures of the cinema screen, inserting instead a more unpleasurable masochistic scenario with social consequences. Unlike earlier middle-class British New Wave directors, he depicts working-class life from within rather than without. He thus avoids those distracting external landscapes that Andrew Higson describes as spectacularly creating 'a huge distance between subject and object', situating 'the spectator in a privileged vantage point' (1984: 18). By fragmenting the narrative, the film avoids visual pleasure, the British anthropological Mass Observation tradition, psychological realism and a fetishistic mode prohibiting investigation, in order to challenge the viewer to investigate a social unpleasure still relevant to British life. Excluding any distracting 'objective' historical and geographical reference in all but the most marginal sense, the film can then insert its spectator into a different mode of spectatorship, demanding interrogation rather than captivation.

Like Derek Jarman, Terence Davies as a gay director belongs to the 1980s realm of the 'other.' Jarman highly values Davies's use of an 'autobiographical cinema', recognising his oppositional stance within contemporary independent British cinema (1991: 12). Davies has personally lived in the hell of a family situation. But his films do not engage in an explicit polemic. Instead, like Jarman, Davies works within the vein of an antirealist tradition calling upon the audience to enter into a self-interrogative cinematic world that is by no means irrelevant to a social context. It is thus a mistake to label Davies's technique as solipsistic or narcissistic, since it arises out of a particular historical moment within contemporary British society. Like most of the interesting works of 1980s cinema, it reacts against the attempted imposition of Thatcherite ideological norms both personally and artistically.

Victim of the past but conscious of a contemporary social responsibility, Davies organises his painful masochistic experiences in an artistic autobiographical mode. His method parallels John Gedo and Arnold Goldberg's (1973) observations concerning a hierarchical model of mental functioning involving both conscious and unconscious processes. Gedo also notes that 'it is no longer possible to see the artist primarily as a spinner of fantasies; he must be understood, indeed, as a specially endowed manipulator of varied perceptual elements' (1983: 7). *Distant Voices, Still Lives* is thus a work of the conscious, as well as the unconscious, imagination. Emotively reacting to his past traumatic memories but not allowing himself to become overwhelmed by them, Davies's film organises narrative and visual structures, guiding the spectator to coordinate the various fragmented memories of pleasure and unpleasure into an emotional awareness of a traumatic family situation. It thus represents a much more conscious and developed awareness of a complex situation than does the passive, pessimistic reflective nature of the trilogy.

Distant Voices, Still Lives has also interesting links with D. W. Winnicott's idea of a transitional object or phenomenon.[10] This is an object that the child chooses as a defence against anxiety, coordinating its subjective perceptions to an external world that may (or may not) involve cruel parents and a harsh environment. Winnicott states that this subjective world may be cruel as well as ideal (1965: 145). For our purposes, we may understand it as masochistic, involving fond memories of mother juxtaposed with ugly ones of father traumatically conditioning its recipients as well as future generations. Unlike Freud's themes, Winnicott's transitional objects have social and environmental, as well as cultural, relevance.[11] We may understand a film to be a transitional object, especially one combining subjective memory with a hierarchical mode of translating these experiences into artistic creation. There is no real objection to understanding Winnicott's ideas cinematically.[12] Arnold Modell (1976) and Phillip Weisman (1971) have both applied Winnicott's transitional object toward understanding the mature creations of the adult artist.[13] Following Winnicott and Greenacre, Weisman notes that the transitional object may develop into a fetish object with either positive or negative results.[14] He states that 'the characteristics of a fetish object may prevail over its feature as a created object; conversely ... the qualities of a created object may supersede its fetishistic aspects' (1971: 405). Greenacre also remarks that the artist may have an important capacity to organise sensory impressions with special sensitivity to rhythm and form, particularly in relationship to a 'collective audience' (1971: 482). If we relate these ideas to Davies's films and the period from which they have emerged, we then see some interesting associations between artistic organisation and social context that make his work more than supposedly formalist. The family is, after all, the basic unit of any society, subject to manipulation by forces both inside and outside the home. It generates human personalities equally liable to be developed or stunted by social norms. To understand its psychic operations, an interrogative, non-realist approach is thus essential to raise consciousness.

One scene is especially noteworthy in illustrating Davies's technique in raising audience perceptions in a new materialistic cinematic manner. At the climax of *Distant Voices, Still Lives,* the newly married Tony weeps unseen outside his mother's house. The camera remains static. We sit fixed and immobile, intruding at the spectre of his grief. However, our position in the audience does not make us prurient voyeurs. Instead, we are drawn into his sadness and suffer with him. We remember his placement within a traumatic family situation. Other elements within the scene clarify the nature of his pain. Tony weeps apart from those inside. He has no one to console him as he once consoled Eileen. It is clear that Tony weeps not for his father. He realises his impending departure from his mother, and his transition into the patriarchal realm. The scene opens after a dissolve of mother singing 'For All You Mean To Me'. For Tony it signifies a loss of his original pre-Oedipal closeness. Tony stops weeping after someone puts on a record of 'Oh, My Papa'. Will he permanently leave the pre-Oedipal for the Oedipal realm? We do not know. The scene of his honeymoon car departing morbidly resembles an earlier one of the military police vehicle driving away the imprisoned Tony after the futile confrontation with his father.

This is one of many key scenes in the film that exhibit an acute sense of artistic organisation stressing the miserable implications of submission to patriarchy that creates masochistic victims. Eileen and Tony have suffered traumatically but cannot articulate their pain. After their respective weddings both weep, realising their separation from a lost object. As Edwin and Constance Wood recognise, 'the tearful feeling state is occasioned by the ego temporarily threatened with being inundated by complex memories and affects' (1984: 134). Ironically, Eileen weeps for a lost object that has oppressed both her and her family. She cannot create the necessary psychic space to condemn both the monster and the institution that has violated her individuality. Tony understands the implications of his forthcoming separation from mother. Greenacre notes in her case work: 'Tears come insidiously as part of a change in the individual's attitude toward his modified external reality, usually with a reciprocal change in his self-appreciation and even in his self-image. This *usually involves some degree of renunciation* and the resultant relaxation and the tears express and help along such an internal change' (1971: 251; emphasis mine). As Franco Moretti has pointed out in another context, tears also express powerlessness in the face of an irreversible direction (1983: 162). Tony will now become a husband and future father and may possibly turn into a bastion of the male order. He thus falls victim to his repressed emotions concerning his departure from the maternal realm. All characters within the film are thus past, present and future psychic victims of an oppressive social system.

In *Distant Voices, Still Lives*, Terence Davies positions his audience in an unpleasurable masochistic dimension, uniting cinematically psychoanalytical mechanisms with relevant sociological critique. Unlike the earlier trilogy, *Distant Voices, Still Lives* presents us with a number of characters who represent different masochistic reactions, rather than just one solitary scapegoat such as Robert Tucker. In this way he presents images of possible alternatives (Tony, Eileen, Maisie and Micky) in certain instances rather than just masochistically dwelling on one victim. By creatively splitting his unconscious feelings in the representation of different characters, Davies further explores psychoanalytic mechanisms of masochism among a broader section of the family unit rather than concentrating on one damned soul. His artistic technique is thus akin to those artistic methods used to master trauma noted by Gilbert J. Rose. In referring to both Greenacre and Winnicott, Rose notes the possibility for victims of trauma to use unconscious mechanisms in a creative manner: 'The gifted person, while having the conventional sense of reality, is thus able to hold it in abeyance, in order to explore and concentrate full powers of integration on imaginative possibilities' (1987: 112).

Distant Voices, Still Lives reveals this technique, displaying the creative manipulation of time witnessed in the trilogy. Davies's methodology is also akin to the schizoid personality. The latter and the creative writer share similar traits, as Rose notes:

> They both treat the stuff of time and character as flexible material suitable for being shaped and molded – according to their conscious and creative or unconscious and defensive designs ... The author fashions fictional characters and manipulates the flow of time with flashbacks and fast-forwards according to artistic requirements. In other words, character and time are treated by both author and patient as having the quality of plasticity usually associated with *aesthetic* media. (1987: 108–9)

However, despite its non-didactic quality, the semi-autobiographical work of Terence Davies has undeniable social relevance. It emerged in an era that witnessed increasing attacks on minorities in British society. The work documents the misery that the officially-sanctioned family institution has caused to human potential. Uniting the concerns of traumatic mastery and British cinematic independent film discourses, Davies remains one of the most powerful voices to have emerged from a reactionary decade in British social life.

POSTSCRIPT

The above essay was initially written to apply alternative theories of psychoanalysis, notably those associated with the neglected work of D. W. Winnicott, to the films of Terence Davies. I see no reason to change anything. However, what has changed is the cultural situation of Britain. It has become much worse than the Thatcher era making the type of cinema associated with Davies virtually impossible. Thanks to Tony Blair, Thatcher's economic and spiritual heir, Britain has become more dominated by market forces with violent crime, debased mainstream film and television culture, and binge-drinking among men and women now counterpointing the postwar consensus communal images within Davies's films. The brutal figure of Pete Postelthwaite's father returns with a vengeance reincarnated not only in soccer hooligans but also 'lads' and 'ladettes'.

The Long Day Closes (1992) represents a 'last testament' to the earlier films. Depicting a touching world without a violent father, and populated by a loving mother, warm sisters and caring brothers, the film is another Winnicott 'transitional space' for Davies to recreate a sublimated lost world of family closeness characterised by contemporary British popular culture and utopian images from Hollywood cinema soon to disappear at the climax. Young Bud descends into the cellar receiving his 'comeuppance' like George Minafer for his impossible yearnings concerning a world which will change. The long day closes as the final lyrical audio-visual climax shows. Davies wisely decided to change direction but he did not stray too far away as *The Neon Bible* (1999) shows.

Adapted from the novel by John Kennedy Toole, Davies recreates a rural Southern world of the late 1930s and 1940s inhabited by young Frank, his fragile mother and non-conformist Aunt May. Featuring artistic images of train, rain and Sirkian framing, *The Neon Bible* presents the world of a conformist rural American community characterised by bigotry and violence but also allowing for a brief tender family relationship once the violent father departs. As May (Gena Rowlands) says to her temporary family, 'I never thought I'd be happy here'. But this long day also closes. May departs on another futile search for utopian fulfillment while David leaves on a train for an unknown destination. Though shot in America outside the geographical confines of British cinema, *The Neon Bible* visually and thematic continues Davies's artistic and transcendent concerns.

The same is true of *The House of Mirth* (2001). Like *The Neon Bible*, it is another adaptation. But Edith Wharton's Lily Bart is another of Davies's sensitive and vulnerable victims of a brutal society having much in common with those attempting survival in his earlier films. Davies visually translates Wharton's 'portrait of a lady' to illustrate the traumatic odyssey of another sensitive creature cast adrift in a harsh material world as a scapegoat for its dehumanising codes of class and repression. Beautifully photographed and shot in Glasgow with accomplished professional acting, *The House of Mirth* is no nostalgic 'heritage film'. It has contemporary social relevance showing the dark undertones of Thatcher's espousement of 'Victorian values' leaving its heroine to face either starvation or playing a corrupt social game. She chooses neither path. *The House of Mirth* is a film by one of cinema's great contemporary stylists whose *Sunset Song* project is also eagerly awaited.

NOTES

1   For other critical observations on Davies and his work, see Wyeth (1986); Barker (1988); Floyd (1988); Wrathall (1988); and Williams (1990).

2 For further evidence concerning gender oppression within the British social structure, see the detailed evidence provided by Pedersen (1989) and Hart (1989).

3 See Hall (1988) and (Abse) 1989.

4 Quoted by Tal (1989: 190; see also Frankl (1959: 19–21, 52) and Lifton (1970: 153–4) for descriptions of traumatic apathy and psychic numbing in German concentration camp victims and Hiroshima survivors.

5 For a survey of complex post-Freudian interpretations of masochism, see Loewenstein (1957); Brenner (1959); Glenn (1981); Bernstein (1983); Maleson (1984); Grossman (1986); and Glick & Meyers (1988).

6 In his 1915 essay, 'Instincts and Their Vicissitudes,' Freud originally regarded masochism as a secondary process – a view he changed in his later metapsychological explorations, 'Beyond the Pleasure Principle' (1920) and 'The Economic Problem of Masochism' (1924). Current psycho-analytic interpretation finds many problems with Freud's later work, especially his concepts of the 'Death Instinct' and primary masochism. See, for example, Grunberger (1979: 9). As William I. Grossman notes concerning Freud's formulation, 'the term masochism, however, never did have a precise meaning or one that was generally accepted. It was a controversial term except as a literary designation for any phenomena in which sexual pleasure and physical and mental pain were associated' (1986: 380). Issues of superego formation and object relations, especially in regard to parental figures, are extremely important in current research. Grossman further comments: 'Behaviour that appears self-destructive to an observer may be organised to serve a variety of functions having to do with the regulation of unpleasurable affects, pain and aggression. The term masochism can be most usefully and understandably applied to those activities organised by fantasies involving the obligatory combination of pain and unpleasure, or to the fantasies themselves' (1986: 409). This is especially applicable to the tormented fantasies of Robert Tucker in *Madonna and Child*.

7 Reich refutes Freud's idea of the Death Instinct and regards masochism as a secondary drive rather than an instinct in the biological sense. It is caused by the disastrous effect of social conditioning (1971: 209–18). He also points out that by turning toward the self, sadistic drives become masochistic, since the frustrated person's superego becomes a punishing agent – hence, Tony's self-destructive action in smashing his hand through the window, thus punishing himself for failing to communicate with his father in the film's opening scenes. Reich earlier noted that submission usually follows any rebellion against authority (1970: 37). Isidore Bernstein has relevant comments on female masochism that enable us to understand the social conditioning of the mother and the daughter in the film. He states: 'We must beware ... of underestimating the influence of social customs, which similarly force women into passive positions ... A suppression of women's aggressiveness which is prescribed for them constitutionally and imposed on them socially favours the development of powerful masochistic impulses, which succeed, as we know, in binding erotically the destructive trends which have been diverted inwards. Thus, masochism, as people say, is truly feminine' (1983: 468).

8 Reich (1971: 218–19); Freud (1946: 35).

9 In the child's early life masochistic foundations may occur in a form known as protomasochism preceding the Oedipal phase. Charles A. Sarnoff notes that the parental image may be protosymbolically represented. Through such objects 'aggression aimed at the parent can be turned upon the self' (1988: 205). Eileen's weeping for her father represents such a mechanism. Although she cursed him while he lived she now turns her former aggression against herself. Sarnoff's following observations are extremely important: 'With the development of self-object differentiation, the fused libidinal and aggressive energies of the child can be perceived by the

child as directed outward toward an object. Should the parent withdraw from contact or from view, the child can persist in contact with the parent through an internalised memory of the parent. This internalised image is called the introject. The aggression that had been directed toward the object accompanies the introject. It, too, is directed toward the self of the child. This produces a paradigm for the experience of self-directed aggression, called "secondary" masochism. This becomes the basis for the patterning of relationships in which masochism involves objects. Intensification of the secondary masochistic experience by actual aggression by the parents enhances the masochistic fantasies that will colour the relationships of adult life. As a result, tolerance for such relationships heightens. This permits people to enter similar relationships without challenge, since that which would be extraordinary for the children of parents of ordinary demeanour becomes like home cooking for the children of cruel parents' (1988: 206). The application to the Davies family needs no further comment.

10 See Winnicott (1957: 182–90; 1965: 143–4; 1971: 1–26).

11 See also Winnicott's important essays 'Creativity and Its Origins' and 'The Location of Cultural Experience' in his 1971 collection (65–84; 95–103). In the latter essay, Winnicott notes the role of trauma in a baby's individual development, causing 'a break in life's continuity, so that primitive defences now become organised to defend against a repetition of "unthinkable anxiety" or a return of the acute confusional state that belongs to disintegration of nascent ego structure' (1971: 97). He also understands cultural experience as an extension of the transitional phenomena concept: 'When one speaks of a man one speaks of him *along with* the summation of his cultural experience. The whole forms a unit' (1971: 99). The advantage of Winnicott's ideas result in avoiding Freudian individualism. Cultural experience begins in the potential space between the individual and the environment (originally the object). If creative living is impossible because of a bad family relationship, then mastery of a traumatic situation by means of art would be impossible.

12 For one recent example, see Glass (1990), who also cites Greenacre.

13 See Weisman (1967). For striking parallels of creativity to ego reaction during traumatic neuroses, see Bychowski (1951). He comments that continuous artistic projection 'presupposes a large stock of unconscious material. This is provided not only by repressed id and superego derivatives but by ego states as well. It may be said that the ego of the artist has an unusual ability for splitting off entire constellations reflected in all parts of the mental apparatus' (1951: 596).

14 For Greenacre's observations on the relationship between the transitional object and the fetish, see her essays 'The Fetish and the Transitional Object' and 'The Transitional Object and the Fetish: With Special Reference to the Role of Illusion' (1971: 315–52). Davies's use of voyeuristic and fetish mechanisms is completely opposite to the usual understanding by Mulvey in regard to mainstream cinema. The director avoids the visual pleasure inherent in most forms of spectatorship and spectacle to plunge the audience into an awareness of the tragic nature of the family's emotional wasteland. It is one caused by social conditions.

WORKS CITED

Abse, Leo (1989) *Margaret, Daughter of Beatrice: A Politician's Psycho-Biography of Margaret Thatcher*. London: Jonathan Cape.

Andrew, Geoff (1988) 'Home Truths', *Time Out*, 946, 16.

Barker, Adam (1988) *'Distant Voices, Still Lives'*, *Monthly Film Bulletin*, 55, 657, 293–4.

Berliner, Bernhard (1958) 'The Role of Object Relations in Moral Masochism', *Psychoanalytic Quarterly*, 27, 38–56.

Bernstein, Isidore (1983) 'Masochistic Pathology and Feminine Development', *Journal of the American*

Psychoanalytical Association, 31, 467–86.

Brenner, Charles (1959) 'The Masochistic Character: Genesis and Treatment', *Journal of the American Psychoanalytical Association*, 7, 197–226.

Bychowski, Gustav (1951) 'The Metapsychology of Artistic Creation', *Psychoanalytic Quarterly*, 20, 592–602.

Cook, Pam (1981) 'The Point of Self-Expression in Avant-Garde Film', in John Caughie (ed.) *Theories of Authorship*. London: Routledge and Kegan Paul, 271–81.

Elsaesser, Thomas (1988) 'Games of Love and Death or an Englishman's Guide to the Galaxy', *Monthly Film Bulletin*, 55, 657, 290–3.

Floyd, Nigel (1988) 'A Pebble in the Pool and Ships Like Magic', *Monthly Film Bulletin*, 55, 657, 295–6.

Frankl, Victor E. (1959) *Man's Search for Survival*. Boston: Beacon Press.

Freud, Anna (1946) *The Ego and the Mechanisms of Defense*. trans. New York: International Universities Press.

Freud, Sigmund (1984a [1915]) 'Instincts and Their Vicissitudes', in *On Metapsychology: The Theory of Psychoanalysis*. The Pelican Freud Library, vol. 11. London: Penguin, 105–38

____ (1984b [1920]) 'Beyond the Pleasure Principle', in *On Metapsychology: The Theory of Psychoanalysis*. The Pelican Freud Library, vol. 11. London: Penguin, 269–338.

____ (1984c [1924]) 'The Economic Problem of Masochism', in *On Metapsychology: The Theory of Psychoanalysis*. The Pelican Freud Library, vol. 11. London: Penguin, 409–26.

Galenson, Eleanor (1988) 'The Precursors of Masochism: Protomasochism', in Robert A. Glick and Donald I. Meyers (eds) *Masochism: Current Psychoanalytic Perspectives*. Hilsdale, NJ: Analytic Press, 189–204.

Gedo, John (1983) *Portraits of the Artist: Psychoanalysis of Creativity and Its Vicissitudes*. New York: Guildford Press.

____ (1984) *Psychoanalysis and Its Discontents*. New York: Guildford Press.

Gedo, John and Arnold Goldberg (1973) *Models of the Mind: A Psychoanalytic Theory*. Chicago: University of Chicago Press.

Glass, Fred (1990) 'Totally Recalling Arnold: Sex and Violence in the New Bad Future', *Film Quarterly*, 44, 1, 2–13.

Glenn, Jules (1981) 'Masochism and Narcissism in a Patient Traumatised in Childhood', *Journal of the American Psychoanalytical Association*, 29, 3, 672–80.

____ (1984) 'Psychic Trauma and Masochism', *Journal of the American Psychoanalytical Association*, 32, 2, 357–85.

Glick, Robert A. and Donald I. Meyers (1988) *Masochism: Current Psychoanalytic Perspectives*. Hilsdale, NJ: Analytic Press.

Greenacre, Phyllis (1971) *Emotional Growth: Psychoanalytic Studies of the Gifted and a Great Variety of Other Individuals*. 2 vols. New York: International Universities Press.

Grossman, William I. (1986) 'Notes on Masochism: A Discussion of the History and Development of a Psychoanalytic Concept', *Psychoanalytic Quarterly*, 55, 379–413.

Grunberger, Bela (1979) *Narcissism: Psychoanalytic Essays*, trans. Joyce S. Diamanti. New York: International Universities Press.

Hall, Stuart (1988) *The Hard Road to Renewal: The Crisis of Thatcherism*. London: Verso.

Hart, Nicky (1989) 'Gender and the Rise and Fall of Class Politics', *New Left Review*, 175, 19–47.

Higson, Andrew (1983) 'Critical Theory and British Cinema', *Screen,* 24, 4–5, 80–95.

____ (1984) 'Space, Place, Spectacle', *Screen*, 25, 4/5, 2–21.

Jardine, Alice (1987) 'Men in Feminism: Odor di Uomo or Compagnons de Route', in Alice Jardine and

Paul Smith (eds) *Men in Feminism*. New York: Methuen, 54–61.

Jarman, Derek (1991) 'The Garden of Earthly Delights – Interview', *City Limits*, 483, 12–14.

Lifton, Robert Jay (1970) *History and Human Survival*. New York: Random House.

Loewenstein, Rudolph M. (1957) 'A Contribution to the Psychoanalytic Theory of Masochism', *Journal of the American Psychoanalytical Association*, 5, 197–234.

Malcolm, Derek (1988) 'Voices of Experience', *Guardian*, 13 October, 21.

Maleson, Franklin G. (1984) 'The Multiple Meanings of Masochism', *Journal of the American Psychoanalytical Association*, 32, 2, 325–57.

Medhurst, Andy (1983) '"Victim": Text as Context', *Screen*, 24, 6, 2–21.

Modell, Arnold (1976) 'The Transitional Object and the Creative Act', Psychoanalytic *Quarterly*, 39, 240–50.

Moretti, Franco (1983) *Signs Taken for Wonders*. London: Verso.

Mulvey, Laura (1975) 'Visual Pleasure and Narrative Cinema', *Screen*, 16, 3, 6–18.

Pedersen, Susan (1989) 'The Failure of Feminism in the Making of the British Welfare State', *Radical History Review*, 43, 86–112.

Quart, Leonard (1990) '*Distant Voices, Still Lives*', *Cineaste*, 17, 3, 42–3.

Reich, Wihelm (1970) *The Mass Psychology Fascism*. trans. Vincent R. Carfagno. New York: Farrar, Strauss and Giroux.

____ (1971) *Character Analysis*, third edition, trans. Thomas P. Wolfe. New York: Farrar, Strauss and Giroux.

Rose, Gilbert J. (1987) *Trauma and Mastery in Life and Art*. New Haven: Yale University Press.

Sarnoff, Charles A. (1988) 'Adolescent Masochism', in Robert A. Glick and Donald I. Meyers (eds) *Masochism: Current Psychoanalytic Perspectives*. Hilsdale, NJ: Analytic Press, 205–24.

Schneider, Michel (1975) *Neurosis and Civilisation: A Marxist/Freudian Synthesis*, trans. Michael Roboff. New York: Seabury Press.

Shengold, Leonard (1988) *Soul Murder: The Effects of Childhood Abuse and Deprivation*. New Haven: Yale University Press.

Tal, Kali (1989) 'Feminist Criticism and the Literature of the Vietnam Combat Generation', *Vietnam Generation*, 1, 3/4, 190–201.

Weisman, Phillip (1967) 'Theoretical Considerations of Ego Regression and Ego Functions in Creativity', *Psychoanalytic Quarterly*, 36, 110–23.

____ (1971) 'The Artist and His Objects', *International Journal of Psychoanalysis*, 42, 405.

Williams, Tony (1990) 'Terence Davies Interview', *CineACTION!*, 21/22, 65–9.

Winnicott, D. W. (1957) *Mother and Child: A Primer of First Relationships*. New York: Basic Books.

____ (1965) *The Family and Individual Development*. New York: Basic Books.

____ (1971) *Playing and Reality*. London: Routledge and Kegan Paul.

Wood, Edwin C. and Constance C. Wood (1984) 'Tearfulness: A Psychoanalytic Interpretation', *Journal of the American Psychoanalytical Association*, 32, 1, 117–36.

Wrathall, John (1988) 'Picture This', *City Limits*, 367, 13, 17–18.

Wyeth, Peter (1986) 'Voices from the Past', *Stills*, 25, 36–9.

16. LOCAL FOCUS, GLOBAL FRAME: KEN LOACH AND THE CINEMA OF DISPOSSESSION

James F. English

LOACH, REALISM AND THE DOCUMENTARY TRADITION

It is fitting that the present volume should take its title from a documentary film made more than sixty years ago, for the documentary tradition looms larger in the history of British film than in that of any other national cinema. The documentary film movement of the 1930s and 1940s, spearheaded by John Grierson, established a set of aesthetic and methodological conventions (involving, for example, dramatic re-enactments staged by a historical event's actual participants) and broadly political/ educational aims (such as that of presenting ordinary work as heroic, or that of fomenting collective left-leaning response to some specified national 'crisis') which have continued to structure documentary filmmaking and to secure it a prominent place in national debate down to the present day (see Burton 1994). But these enduring aims and conventions have had an even greater impact outside the genre of the documentary, shaping a substantial portion of the dramatic films on British television and in theatres for nearly half a century, ever since working-class social realism emerged in the late 1950s as the British cinema's most distinctive mode.

The marked influence of documentary practices on some of the most celebrated and enduring strains of British feature filmmaking, especially on films about provincial working-class life, accounts in large measure for the tendency of debates over the politics of cinema in Britain to centre on questions of realism and truth. The most important of these debates, for the discipline of film studies, was that carried out in the pages of *Screen* magazine in the mid-1970s, when that journal was serving as the main vehicle for post-structuralist film theory's explosive arrival onto the British intellectual scene. What came to be called the '*Screen* perspective' on realism was a scorching, neo-Brechtian critique of the realist aesthetic even in its most 'progressive', 'naturalist' or 'working class' guises. Realism was seen as naively in thrall to a nineteenth-century ideology of narrative truth, and thus incapable of handling real contradiction; as Colin MacCabe expressed it, the realist film simply 'articulate[s] a classic relation between narrative and vision in which what we see is true and this truth confirms what we see'.[1]

Unsurprisingly, the filmmaker who landed at the centre of these polemics was Ken Loach, a left-wing director committed to an ideal of authenticity with respect to cinematic representations of working-class experience. Loach had first achieved notoriety by employing documentary devices in the fictional social-issue dramas he made for the BBC *Wednesday Play* series in 1965–66 (notably *Up the Junction* and *Cathy Come Home*), and his 1969 feature film *Kes* had been heralded as the definitive masterpiece of northern working-class realism.[2] At the time of the *Screen* debates, he had just made a highly controversial historical drama for the BBC, *Days of Hope*, about the decisive betrayal of the working class during the General Strike of 1926 by leaders of the trade unions and of the political left. As the key journal in which film studies merged into a broader strain of Continental-inflected anti-empiricism, *Screen* undertook to sever British cinema from certain bad national habits, especially conventional Anglo-Saxon notions about truth, evidence and reality, which were seen as limiting its political as well as its aesthetic potential. Given the sweeping terms of the critique, nearly any British film then in the theatres would have qualified as an instance of naive 'realism'. But *Screen* could not avoid dealing specifically with Loach, for he was both the most outspokenly progressive of Britain's filmmakers and the most unswervingly committed to a realist episteme based in the documentary tradition.

Despite the hammering he received from film theorists in the 1970s, however, Loach's first response to Thatcherism, in the early 1980s, was to abandon even the aesthetically hybrid quality of his earlier work and commit himself for the first time to making 'straight' documentaries concerned with the industrial strikes and the smashing of the trade unions. Unfortunately, far from exerting the kind of immediate political effect he had hoped for, Loach the pure documentarist very nearly disappeared from the field of British cinema altogether. If, from the standpoint of *Screen* and leftist intellectuals generally, Loach was too much a documentarist to be radical, from the standpoint of the television industry and the mainstream press, he was too much a radical, too lacking in balance and objectivity, to be a documentarist. And by the time he began searching for a way back into feature films, he appeared, from the standpoint of potential financial backers, too much of both to be a viable director in the new era of enterprise culture and free-market art which Thatcher had done so much to foster. As the Thatcher decade drew toward its close, there seemed no longer to be a place in British cinema for one of its most influential directors, nor for what had once been among its most distinctive staples: the progressive, documentary-inflected drama about working-class lives.

It is instructive, therefore, to retrace Loach's peculiar career trajectory from this low point in the early 1980s to his astonishing reversal of fortunes in the early to mid-1990s. Loach's vaunted comeback involved a twofold strategy. On the one hand, pushed off the field of British cinema, Loach set out consciously to remake himself as 'a European film director' (in Hill 1997b: 164), and indeed to launch a second career not only supported by the increasingly international system of independent cinematic production, but focused thematically on an increasingly global system of capitalist exploitation. To a certain degree, this involved repressing the very documentary tendencies to which he had given free rein a decade earlier. He worked for the first time with famous professional actors, hewed more closely to the conventions of melodrama, and, at one point, adapted himself to the genre constraints of the political thriller. Though usually retaining a Northern working-class protagonist, he abandoned his accustomed provincial milieus, filming for the first time on location in foreign lands, and using dialogue, in English or other tongues, quite remote from the working-class vernacular of those places. The other part of this twofold strategy, however, called for Loach to capitalise domestically on his rising international prestige and his marketability on the Continent by making a series of relatively low-budget films that remain resolutely local and vernacular, and retain a high degree of continuity with the early documentary dramas. And these, I will argue, are not only the best films he made during the 19-year span of Conservative governance, but the ones that most fully realise his ambition for a political art of international dimensions. What Loach's phoenix-like rise from the ashes of his pure documentary phase suggests is that, far from being a culturally insular, politically backward, commercially hopeless and aesthetically moribund tradition within British cinema, progressive working-class docu-realism has found a second wind, acquiring, in the wake of Thatcherism and neoliberalism generally, a new and more global resonance.

CONTROVERSIAL DOCUDRAMATIST, UNTRANSMITTABLE DOCUMENTARIST

In narrative terms, a typical Ken Loach film follows the downward path of a working-class protagonist who, despite his or her intelligence and resourcefulness, is undone by economic disadvantage articulated through a set of social institutions (family, schools, government services, unions, places of employment) that, however benign the intentions of their individual agents, function to assure the reproduction rather than the transformation of structural inequities. Though conforming with the general pattern of melodrama, Loach's narratives are less melodramatic than 'naturalist' in the sense established by Emile Zola: they are 'experiments' in the social logic of cause and effect, not contrived to maximise our emotive identification, but allowed simply to follow the inexorable course plotted out by the actions of an ordinary, imperfect individual within a fundamentally unjust social system.[3]

From an early point in his career, Loach was using documentary techniques and effects in service of these naturalist narratives. In *Cathy Come Home* (1966), a film credited with forcing Parliament to address the severe housing crisis and attendant problem of homelessness in London, Loach used many devices that would have been familiar to television viewers from instructive social-issue documentaries. There are, for example, anonymous, official-sounding sociological voiceovers reciting dismal housing statistics, as well as ethnographic interview-style voiceovers (again anonymous) describing the actual experience of living in London's overcrowded, squalid and dangerous apartment blocks. Visually, Loach lets the camera wander about through the alleys and into the doorways of buildings, drifting away from the main characters to grab images of the lived environment and its denizens – seemingly more interested, for whole minutes at a time, in documenting what is concretely there than in exploiting it for strict analogues or correlatives to a story about the titular protagonist and her family. Already in these early *Wednesday Plays*, Loach was working with directors of photography (chiefly Tony Imi) whose backgrounds were in documentary. From *Kes* until the 1980s, he collaborated most often with Chris Menges, a former documentary photographer for the ITV's *World in Action*, and since 1989 he has worked with Barry Ackroyd, who has made several documentaries – including the *Roger & Me*-style Thatcher biopic, *Tracking Down Maggie* (1994) – with Nick Broomfield. Loach credits Menges in particular with helping him

An 'aesthetic of authenticity': Carol White (right, as Cathy) with Winifred Dennis (as her mother-in-law) performing domestic chores at a dilapidated housing estate in *Cathy Come Come* (1966)

shed his stage-set perspective, encouraging for example a strong preference for natural lighting, even of interior scenes. By compromising as little as possible the given light of the location, Loach could unclutter the set and free the camera from predetermined angles, allowing it to move more spontaneously with the action – for example, to 'catch up' with the dialogue rather than anticipate it, panning across to 'find' an off-camera speaker rather than sitting in wait for the lines to be delivered. These kinds of camera movements, coupled with a typically shallow depth-of-field and single plane of focus, elaborate what John Caughie has called the 'rhetoric of the "unplanned" or "unpremeditated" shot' that is the most distinctive aspect of the documentary look' in Loach's films (1980: 28).[4]

The 'unplanned' shot is itself in service of a larger aesthetic of spontaneity and authenticity that, in linking Loach to the documentary tradition, underscores his vehement rejection of the stage tradition. The *Wednesday Plays* were thus called because it was normal in Britain in the 1960s to think of television as an extension of the theatre, the 'one-act play subject' being the most 'perfect television material', as John Russell Taylor observed in a 1964 *Listener* review (see Caughie 1980: 16). The documentary look, which puts the camera and the microphone out on the streets, discovering images and sounds that have no place in a prepared script, broke violently with this theatrical paradigm at the BBC. When he began making feature films, Loach extended his anti-theatrical strategy by casting non-professional actors in lead as well as minor roles. Typically these were ordinary people (though they were sometimes experienced, if small-time, performers, accustomed to doing local music or stand-up gigs), chosen on the basis of their similar type and background to the characters they play, and drawn from the actual location of the filming. Rather than drawing on the tremendous resources of the British theatre – as not only the Merchant-Ivory type of filmmakers but the working-class realists themselves, from Tony Richardson to Mike Leigh, have invariably done – Loach has heretically insisted that the nuances of geographic and class difference (what Pierre Bourdieu calls *habitus* and 'bodily *hexis*' (1977: 82–3)) run too deep to be acted: 'You carry your class with you in how you talk, how you behave, how you pick up a fork. You can't really act it, and you can't act a dialect' (quoted in Hattenstone 1994: 10). While the stage may support a certain degree of fudging in this regard, film, according to Loach, is unforgiving: 'A film can see right into your eyes, it can see you think and then it becomes very hard to disguise your class, where you're from, and all those things we do un-self-consciously.'[5]

To heighten the effect of spontaneity and authenticity, Loach encourages the actors to improvise and to adjust their lines as necessary to achieve perfect vernacular pitch. Though he works closely with his writers (and has maintained long-term collaborative relationships with Barry Hines, Jim Allen and Paul Laverty), he famously withholds the full script from his cast, doling it out piecemeal on a need-to-know basis for daily shooting, in story order, so that at certain key moments an actor is caught genuinely unprepared. And, in addition to shooting many takes (with stock ratios as high as 25:1), he sometimes films his actors before or after a shoot, when they 'aren't acting', gathering what might be considered actual documentary footage of them in repose or disarray, and then incorporating that unplanned footage into the film.

For Loach, then, documentary methods enable the filmmaker to eschew theatrical artifice, cinematic conventions and practices drawn from the stage tradition that reduce class to mere surface and place to mere setting. Of course, the documentary look is itself an artifice (as was already well understood by Grierson when he adapted the conventions of Soviet Montage cinema to his first British documentary, *Drifters*, in 1929). But Loach would insist that the resulting effects of spontaneity, at least in his films, lend moral force to fictional narrative precisely because they derive from a genuine ethical commitment to the real, and are not reducible to a mere *effet de réel*. The fictionality itself is perfectly unhidden; as Caughie has described, Loach's films are as dependent on the conventional rhetoric of cinematic drama, which calls the viewer into a position of identification within the narrative through such mechanisms as eye-line match, point of view and shot/reverse-shot formations, as they are on the documentary look. Indeed, it is the integration of these two rhetorics, the dramatic and the documentary, into 'a movement of confirmation ... each function[ing] to support the other rather than to call the other into question', that, according to Caughie's analysis, validates the *Screen* critique: in a Loach film, 'there is no contradiction ... The discourse is ultimately one of unproblematic truth' (1980: 29–31).

That the insufficiently problematised 'truth' at issue here is a politically progressive one meant that Loach's strategic deployment of documentary techniques to heighten the reality-effect of his dramatic films was not only troubling from the Brechtian anti-realist standpoint of 1970s film theory (and other, later variants of the 'modernist' stance), but also from the more widely-shared standpoint of the mainstream press and the programming chiefs at BBC. The latter, under government pressure to rein in the progressive edges of their line-up (such as the designedly 'provocative' and 'pathbreaking' *Wednesday Play* series), issued a pointed policy statement in 1971 expressing concern that excessive experimentation with 'new techniques' of televisual naturalism might 'lead to confusion in the mind of the viewer … [about] whether he is watching a play or a documentary' (Petley 1997a: 38). As Loach and other young innovators at BBC, including his producer Tony Garnett and writer Jim Allen, were quick to point out, this stated concern for formal unity, with its implicit pledge to impose sharper constraints on 'technical' experiment and innovation, was in fact mere camouflage for editorial resistance to certain kinds of political content: 'what the viewer must understand is that this is an argument about content, not about form' (Petley 1997a: 39). The trouble for the BBC, as, in a different way, for *Screen*, was that Loach's films were all too effective in harnessing viewers to a particular political perspective. Had that perspective been an anodyne one, falling within the bounds of the famed consensus of postwar British society, the experiments in naturalist technique could have been welcomed as exciting advances. But it was a perspective from which all the institutions of social reproduction, from the schools to the Welfare State itself, were seen as inimical to the interests of ordinary working-class Britons. Such a perspective, according to the unwritten rules of television, might legitimately structure a left-wing drama; as the political landscape of an imaginative fiction, it fell within the compass of acceptability. But if the landscape were shaded and faceted too much after the fashion of documentary or news programming, replete with those genre's props and devices of truth-telling, controversy would inevitably follow.

Loach thus began the Thatcher decade as already, at age 40, a director of some historical importance and one whose work could be counted on to stir up much controversy – generally a useful trait at the box office. The 'Thatcher revolution' was bound to get his blood up, and one might have expected a period of especial visibility and productivity to ensue. But in fact no major UK film director saw his career undergo such a precipitous decline during the Thatcher years as Loach. From 1980, when he began filming *A Question of Leadership* for Associated Television, until 1987, when he directed Jim Allen's play *Perdition* at the Royal Court Theatre, nearly everything Loach worked on was withheld from its intended audience, editorially censored, shut down during production, strategically delayed until it had lost its topicality or permanently banned. 'Professionally, it was very bad for me', recalls Loach, 'because it seemed everything I touched couldn't be seen' (in Fuller 1998: 75).

What Loach discovered during these years of frustration was that the tactical shift into straight documentary – which he thought would enable him to work faster and produce more topical interventions in the struggle against rampant free-marketism – merely removed all constraints from his would-be censors in the television industry while depriving himself of the limited but adequate protections he had enjoyed as a 'creative' artist directing fictional dramas. Now the controversy was *simply* about certain kinds of political content – no formalist camouflage involved. Or at any rate nothing more than the very thin camouflage of the supposed law of genre governing television documentary, the requirement of 'balance' and 'impartiality'. If Loach's dramas could be accused of flouting the generic obligation to distinguish imaginative fiction from social fact, his documentaries could be accused of flouting that genre's obligation to present a 'balanced' perspective on social reality. The latter is a law much more aggressively enforced, since it protects from serious challenge an assumed political centre (the necessary fulcrum of editorial 'balance') that might otherwise be subject to scrutiny, debate and even perhaps to radical shift. Loach's dramas had been generically deviant in ways that had made them controversial, but his documentaries were generically deviant in ways that made them untransmittable.

Though we should not underestimate the extent to which Thatcher demonised and harassed the media in general and television in particular, nor the degree to which the constant and fierce pressure to celebrate her government's agenda affected internal decision-making at the television channels, it is important to note that it was never the Conservative government or its direct proxies in the programming offices who called for Loach's work to be suppressed. Thatcher, after all, was expressly trying to overthrow the ideals of 'balance' and 'impartiality' at the BBC, replacing them with those of 'patriotism' and 'Britishness'. Her aim was in effect to tabloidise the television. The producers and programmers who censored Loach included such men as Melvyn Bragg of *The South Bank Show*, who commissioned and then rejected Loach's first documentary on the trades unions, *A Question of Leadership*; Nick Elliot, Bragg's superior at London Weekend Television, who blocked Loach's second *South Bank Show* commission, *Which Side Are You On?* (1984); Jeremy Isaacs and Edmund Dell, heads of the start-up Channel 4, who provided a belated venue (with reduced viewership) for both those *South Bank Show* films, but readily acceded to a ban imposed by the Independent Broadcast Authority (IBA) on the much more ambitious, four-part *Questions of Leadership* that they had commissioned in 1983; and Lord Thomson, Chairman of the IBA itself. These were not Thatcherites but centrists of the sort that had fallen out with the Labour Party's socialist wing. (Both Dell and Thomson were among the Labour MPs who had deserted to the Social Democrat Party in 1981.) They were, ideologically, aligned with the neoliberal bloc that would ultimately emerge as the 'New Labour' consensus in the mid-1990s.

But from the vantage of someone like Loach – who viewed even the old Labour Party leadership as 'the enemy in another guise' (in Fuller 1998: 52) – these typical fulcrum-figures of the media were unredeemable 'right-wingers' (1998: 69). Unlike many of the important political films of this period, from the early black British documentaries to such dramas as Stephen Frears' *Sammy and Rosie Get Laid* (1987) and Peter Greenaway's political allegory *The Cook, the Thief, His Wife and Her Lover* (1989), Loach's documentaries cannot be characterised as essentially anti-Thatcherite. Thatcher, for him, was not the heart of the problem, nor was 1979 the critical turning point. The political settlement of the postwar years had involved a fundamental contradiction between the professed commitment to greater social equity and the acceptance of an essentially capitalist mode of production. The turning point had come circa 1968–72, when the inevitable crisis of capitalist overproduction had begun to produce significant social upheaval and to force hard choices on those in power. The leadership of the Labour Party and of the trade unions had shown no more willingness than that of the Conservatives to place the interests of ordinary working people on a par with the interests of capital or with their own interests in holding power. Though Thatcher's government certainly hastened the collapse of organised working-class resistance to market imperatives, the workers, in Loach's view, had been sold out by their ostensible leadership long before she took office. Indeed, the 'extreme' and 'unbalanced' perspective advanced by *Questions of Leadership*, and stated explicitly in voiceover, was that 'in a very real sense the leaders of the trade unions have kept this Conservative government in power'. What was necessary to effect real change, according to the workers whose voices dominate Loach's documentaries, was not obedience to this bankrupt leadership but wildcat initiatives leading to 'mass struggle', the kind of unity in action through which new and more radical political subjects can emerge: 'it's in the course of the fight that you're going to create from the working class the people that can achieve socialism' (quoted in Petley 1997b: 106). Thatcher of course wanted no part of that, but the real bite of the documentaries lay in their insistence that the workers' supposed leaders in the unions and the Labour Party wanted no part of it, either. The Conservatives, the Labour Party, the Unions and of course the media were all locked together in a capitalist worldview that allowed no space for proletarian class-consciousness to develop or for worker rebellion to unfold. Loach's documentaries were intended to break this logjam by exposing, to the enormous audience of working-class viewers still captive to British television in the mid-1980s, the perfidy and cynicism of their most visible leaders.

Loach's foray into documentary was thus frustrated not so much because he was at odds with the Thatcher government, but because his perspective on the Labour Party and the trade unions, represented as inescapable truth within the frame of documentary, positioned him at the farthest left fringe of even the 'alternative' cultural sphere exemplified by Channel 4, which had been created specifically to provide a forum for the kinds of voices and points of view that were under- or unrepresented on BBC and the Independent Television network. Even as Thatcher's hold on the government began to weaken in the late 1980s, therefore, Loach's future as a documentarist looked singularly bleak. But the prospects of resurrecting his career as a director of dramatic features were not much brighter. Having established repeatedly that his politics were beyond the transmittable spectrum, Loach presented a worrying profile to potential financial backers; he seemed simply out of step with the times (which, in financial terms, means being oblivious to the changing preferences of ticket-buyers). His commitment to the documentary aesthetic, especially as it relates to casting decisions and regional accents, had been perceived as a serious obstacle at the box office from the very start – as, for that matter, it had been for Grierson. Even *Kes*, for all its critical success, had hit distribution snags owing to the thick Yorkshire accents of its non-professional cast, many of whom, including the young lead (David Bradley), were actual staff or students at the school in Barnsley that Barry Hines, who wrote the novel and adapted it for the screenplay, had himself attended as a boy. As a *Variety* headline succinctly put it, 'No English Gab Limits "Kes".'

Other filmmakers in the working-class realist tradition, themselves heavily influenced by Loach, were managing to find work in the 1980s: in television, Alan Bleasdale had built a lucrative career on the success of his *Boys from the Blackstuff* series of 1982–83, and Mike Leigh, the director with whom Loach is most frequently compared, had found steady work despite not making a feature film since 1971. By the late 1980s, Leigh made a successful transition back into features with the support of Channel 4's feature production wing, Film on Four, which backed his *High Hopes* (1988) and subsequent films. Film on Four was also sponsoring Stephen Frears (a director who had learned his trade at the knees of Lindsay Anderson and

Karel Reisz) in his highly acclaimed, albeit controversial, collaborations with the writer Hanif Kureishi. But these directors used professional actors and deployed the devices of naturalism much more flexibly and tactically than Loach did; the tripartite structuring of *High Hopes*, for example, allows Leigh to play the claustrophobic realism of a working-class couple's bohemian domestic life off against hilariously cartoonish send-ups of both upper-class and boorishly *arriviste* versions of more 'enterprising' thirty-something couples. This kind of broad satire, which in Leigh's case provided welcome relief from an otherwise irredeemably bleak view of Thatcher's Britain, was never an option for a director of Loach's stringent literalism. But, having reached a point of financial desperation where he was shooting beer commercials for Saatchi & Saatchi (the advertising agency closely associated with Thatcher's political campaigns), Loach well understood the need for some kinds of adjustment and compromise of his method (Ezard 1988).[6]

Those adjustments and compromises are most pronounced in what I will call Loach's international films, which begin with the one, small-budget feature he managed to make before Thatcher left office – *Fatherland* (1986) – and include the Northern Irish political thriller, *Hidden Agenda* (1990), and then continue in the mid-1990s with *Land and Freedom* (1995) and *Carla's Song* (1996), and more recently with *Bread and Roses* (2000). They are much less evident in the series of 'domestic' films Loach made in rapid succession in the early 1990s – *Riff-Raff* (1990), *Raining Stones* (1993) and *Ladybird, Ladybird* (1994) – which has since been extended with *My Name is Joe* (1998), *The Navigators* (2001), *Sweet Sixteen* (2002) and the Cannes Palme d'Or winner *The Wind the Shakes the Barley* (2006). While both sets of films clearly bear the stamp of Loach's late style, and seek to elaborate, from the standpoint of Thatcher-era Britain, his specifically institutional critique of global capitalism, I want in the remaining pages here, focusing on the first two films from each category, to indicate some lines of contrast between them, and to argue that Loach's achievement in this third phase of his career, not only aesthetically but precisely as a political filmmaker of international ambition, lies with the seemingly modest provincial dramas.

LOCATING THE GLOBAL

Loach's first steps toward remaking himself as an international director were *Fatherland* and *Hidden Agenda*. Both were notably international productions, not only in terms of funding but also in terms of story, setting and cast. *Fatherland*, from a script by Trevor Griffiths, was backed by German and French television companies in collaboration with Channel 4, and concerns the persecution of a dissident East German folk singer (Gerulf Pannach) who, forced into exile, emigrates to a no less inhospitable Britain, where he gradually learns of his father's involvement with Stalinist atrocities in Spain, Nazi atrocities in Holland and Cold War espionage work for American intelligence. *Hidden Agenda*, written by Jim Allen and funded by mostly American capital, is a political thriller in the Costa-Gavras tradition, starring Frances McDormand and Brian Cox as truth-seekers who discover, but cannot fully expose, a campaign of 'dirty tricks' orchestrated in the late 1970s by a conspiracy of British Security forces, the CIA, leaders of British industry and right-wing elements of the Conservative shadow cabinet, as well as the continuing conspiracy of these groups through the mid-1980s (the time of the film) to cover up their crimes and maintain British control of Northern Ireland through an undeclared 'shoot to kill' policy.

This turn to the international was motivated not only by the resistance Loach met within the domestic film industry, but by his strong and durable reputation abroad, where his return to feature filmmaking was celebrated with major prizes at Venice (where *Fatherland* won the UNICEF Award) and Cannes (where *Hidden Agenda* won the Special Jury Prize). But it was motivated, as well, by the implicitly international compass of a marxist political outlook, in terms of which the 'working class' is a global rather than a national entity and all individuals are, in the words of Marx and Engels, 'dependent for the satisfaction of their wants on the whole world'. Such a perspective became more urgent in the 1980s, as the imperative to be competitive on world markets was advanced as the chief justification for abandoning the protections of unionisation and the provisions of the welfare state. Loach had become committed to playing out these geographically and culturally broader dimensions of his political vision, and would eventually make films in and about Spain (*Land and Freedom*), Nicaragua (*Carla's Song*) and Los Angeles (*Bread and Roses*).

But as John Hill has argued in a perceptive essay about Loach's struggle to 'find a form' in these years, while *Fatherland* and *Hidden Agenda* clearly represent a new, third phase in Loach's career, they are, in comparison with his earlier work, rather incoherent films both aesthetically and politically. *Fatherland* begins with a documentary-style press conference of a sort very familiar to viewers of Loach's films, characterised by the 'unplanned' camera work of Chris Menges. But much of the film is broodingly 'atmospheric' in a very un-Loachian way, which Hill connects with the 'expressionist' aesthetic of European art cinema (1998: 128–9). There are, for example, extended dream sequences in black-and-white, with the protagonist running through a dark alley to escape snarling police dogs, clawing his way up a nightmarishly precipitous slope, or gazing across an empty white landscape toward his father, who is dressed all in white and seated at a white grand piano, gesturing obscurely toward his son. Whereas in his earlier films, Loach would represent a protagonist's predicament through his or her dealings with a concretely specified set of institutions that owe their existence, and their oppressive effects, to the social contradictions they are designed to 'manage', Klaus Drittemann's predicament in *Fatherland* is mainly conveyed through his generalised sense of anxiety and isolation.

To be sure, Drittemann must deal with several key institutions: the cultural ministry of the GDR, which will not allow him to work there, but will apparently grant him a return visa once his record sales in the West establish him as a reliable source of foreign capital; the progressive wing of the Party, which includes many of his friends and family in the East, who encourage him to modify his dissident stance just enough to remain in the country; the Western press, which wants to promote him as a freedom-fighter and an icon of Western cultural values; the American-dominated recording industry, which hopes to translate his political dissidence into financial profit; the CIA, which subjects him to repeated interviews and debriefings and refuses him entry to the US; and the international Nazi-hunter movement, which wants to use him, even in his ignorance, to track down his father. But Drittemann's posture toward these institutions seems to be one less of political opposition than of aesthetic purity; he is a figure of the lofty and incorruptible artist, alienated from the social, political and commercial spheres alike. And the overall trajectory of the film is toward ever more personal or psychological forms of struggle.

The trouble is that Loach (along with screenwriter Griffiths) so wants to capture the global breadth and complexity of the effects of power that these effects lose their particularity, their ordinary, 'documentable' reality, and become machinations of a shadowy world-conspiracy whose agents are never quite in view. Somehow, the politically oppressive forces that surround Drittemann in Germany seem to follow him into exile, or to relay the task of surveillance to their Western counterparts in Britain and, apparently, in the US, assuring that he will never enjoy the vaunted 'freedom' of our side of the Wall. But, as they display their global reach, these forces appear to have less and less connection with Drittemann's politically dissident art, centring rather on his father's past as an unscrupulous agent of foreign regimes. No very clear system of institutional linkages or parallels between East and West is allowed to emerge, nor is it at all evident why a depressive introvert whose dissidence consists of 'singing the blues in red' (and who has not communicated with his father in over thirty years) would require surveillance and containment on either side of the Iron Curtain. Dritteman himself remains a murky (if also a rather familiar) figure of the artist-in-exile. Cut off from his homeland and obsessed with the disturbing truth of his family history, his rising angst and anger tends to subsume all the other aspects of his personality.

The result is a 'political' film that, despite being directed by a radical artist much of whose work had been aggressively censored and sabotaged, and being centred on a similarly dissident and persecuted artist character (played by Panach, himself a dissident Leipzig folk singer who was deported for political reasons in 1977), achieves few moments of reflexive insight. Whatever material connections there might be between the constraints on Drittemann's artistic freedom and those imposed on Loach during the Thatcher years, between Drittemann's family secrets and British or American covert political operations, between the acts of betrayal committed by the Central Committee and those committed by the contemporary trades union leadership – or, in a more general way, between the unravelling of the Soviet hegemony in the East and the collapse of the welfare-state paradigm in Britain and the West – are mostly left unexplored. In this first European venture, Loach manages neither to reproduce his distinctive brand of realism in a foreign context, nor to bring the political issues of that foreign context 'home' to England.

Hidden Agenda is in many ways a more important Ken Loach picture than *Fatherland*, with a much larger budget, much wider theatrical release and much greater impact on the director's career. While less specifically 'European' than the latter, it is another international venture – not only insofar as its financing came from foreign sources and its stars from Hollywood, but in its attempt to represent the Northern Ireland situation as one of global proportions and implications rather than simply as a matter of domestic UK (and, of course, Irish) politics. Early in the film, Ingrid (Frances McDormand), a researcher with the International League for Civil Liberties, tells her husband Paul Sullivan (Brad Dourif), a senior attorney in the League, that Belfast 'reminds [her] of Chile', where she had first become involved in the civil liberties movement: 'It feels the same ... killings, torture, intrigue.' Sullivan dismisses this analogy as hyperbolic: 'Reality check', he says. 'What happened in

Chile can't happen here.' But within a day, Sullivan will be murdered by a special security unit of the Royal Ulster Constabulary (RUC), on direct orders of Margaret Thatcher's closest advisers, just as, when Ingrid was working in Chile, her lover there (a Chilean documentary filmmaker) was murdered by Pinochet's security forces, acting under the covert auspices of Kissinger and Nixon.

Apart from the nod to Costa-Gavras's *Missing* (1981), the film's aim here is obviously to say, in the first instance, that what happened in Chile (as well as what happened at the Watergate apartment block in Washington) can and has happened in the UK: acts of assassination, torture, burglary, illegal telephone-tapping, 'psychological operations', and so forth, were used systematically to suppress popular resistance in Northern Ireland, and, in Britain, to bring down a democratically-elected government deemed unfriendly to capital. And they had been used, as well, to maintain the new, right-wing government's hold on power both at home and in the territories of its imperial control. But the film wants to go further than this and establish a concrete link between the two sites of violent repression. Aiding and abetting the shadow Conservatives, helping to train the hardcore elements within Britain's Security Service (MI5), Secret Intelligence Service (MI6), and police force of Northern Ireland (the RUC), and indeed applying decisive 'pressure' on the British right to seize power by any available means, was the same nexus of CIA operatives and other proxies of big business that brought down Allende in Chile and contrived to keep Nixon in power in 1972.

The institutional critique is thus more concretely worked out here than in *Fatherland*. But the film suffers from a similar vagueness as regards the sense of place. Screenwriter Jim Allen fashioned his thesis by linking together two fairly well-known conspiracy theories: one, based on allegations by a former MI5 agent named Colin Wallace, involved CIA-inspired dirty tricks to assure Thatcher's successful rise to power; the other concerned a notoriously suppressed 1983 police report by John Stalker, a Deputy Chief Constable from Manchester who was called in to investigate allegations of a shoot-to-kill policy by the RUC in Northern Ireland. The problem with this narrative strategy is not that either theory strains the limits of credulity (Wallace's allegations were largely substantiated in the 2002 BBC documentary series *True Spies*), nor even that, by virtue of its complexity, the grand theory of their interconnection must be presented in singularly undramatic, monologue-driven fashion. (This is the kind of film in which no one keeps his mouth shut for long, and even the Henry Kissingers and Airey Neaves of the world are only too happy to describe their dirty deeds in detail.) The problem is that in using the dirty tricks of the 1970s, with their suggestion of a global fascist network, to enlarge the stakes or implications of the Stalker affair, the film gains its international dimension at the expense of local particulars. Unfolding its thesis about special training programmes at Fort Bragg, secret conversations between MI6 and the CIA, and so forth, the film draws our attention further and further away from the unique social and political problems of Northern Ireland (involving issues of religion, for example).

None of the major characters in the film is Irish; the closest is Chief Constable Brodie (Jim Norton) of the RUC, but he is nothing more than a stereotypical 'perfect bureaucrat' who, like everyone else in the RUC, apparently takes his orders from British intelligence (whose strings, in turn, are pulled by the right-wing cabal led by the Airey Neave character). The real drama is played out among American civil liberties activists, a maverick British intelligence agent with training in America, an 'incorruptible' British police investigator, and right-wing English politicians and businessmen with close ties to Thatcher. It is not just that Loach's documentary-realist aesthetic has given way to a more generic thriller aesthetic; if in *Fatherland* he dabbled with European expressionism, here he adopts the conventions of Hollywood – the revelation of a conspiracy itself being one such convention. More significantly, the central and paradigmatic object of that realist aesthetic has disappeared from view. What can this film tell us about the lives of ordinary people in Belfast, other than that, considered in the broader aspect, their situation is analogous to that of ordinary people in Santiago, Chile, whose fates are similarly manipulated from above by forces beyond their reckoning?

No less than *Fatherland*, *Hidden Agenda* is a film in which 'politics' is located on the level of secret evil agents whose network of power covers the globe. Apart from a few brief scenes, there is no politics of the rank and file in these films, nor any secure grounding in the local, the vernacular.[7] Of course, for socialism, both as critique and as ideal, the place of particular, local, indigenous cultures and forms of struggle in an increasingly international, one-world system (the post-industrial capitalist system of the present, the socialist system of the future) has presented a perennial problem. What we see in these first films of Loach's 'international' period is that he simply has no strategy for addressing the problem; the local just drops away. John Hill notes that the images of England in *Fatherland* are 'curiously unresonant', and that 'while Cambridge may have some validity as a hideout for Drittemann's father, it is also an archetypically "tourist" location' (1997a: 128). The images of Berlin are not much more nuanced, conforming mainly to clichés about the grimy and impoverished East, shot in dimly-lit black-and-white, versus the glitzy and decadent West, in dazzlingly overlit colour, complete with an extended party scene in the luxury apartment of the recording star Rainer (Hans Peter Hallwachs), where lines of cocaine are, of course, snorted from mirrors. The same is true of Belfast in *Hidden Agenda*, which offers the cinematic tourist all the expected images, from Protestant marchers in an Orange Day parade, to Bobby Sands graffiti on bullet-riddled walls, to security-force sentries on rooftops and at roadway checkpoints.

As these kinds of generic or touristic images replace the unplanned and unexpected images of Loach's earlier docu-realism, it is not just the sense of place that is diminished, but the sense of place as constitutive of subjectivity, as inducing the most crucial and, for Loach, 'unactable' elements of class habitus. These are essentially films about outsiders, visitors, interlopers: individuals who lead lives of cosmopolitan mobility, only lightly tethered to any particular city or country. Drittemann's would-be record label in West Germany has been acquired by an American conglomerate, and it is an American producer, Lucy (Cristine Rose), who first takes him in hand when he arrives from the East. His subsequent companion, Emma (Fabienne Babe), is a young French woman whose mother is evidently Dutch, investigating atrocities committed in Holland by a former Nazi now thought to be living in England; she communicates this to Drittemann in halting English. What region of France is Emma from, and what is her class background? Could we venture to say, for example, that politically she is of the French Left? Given that she appears to be a university-educated journalist and/ or activist involved in international causes, how can we explain her poor command of English? The unanswerability of these kinds of question, in both films, points to the fact that the general air of political mystery and ambiguity that Loach conjures up in them depends, among other things, on his abandonment of precisely those points of casting and direction that had comprised the core of his realist aesthetic and of his ethic of cinematic authenticity.

Loach himself has been critical of both these films, particularly *Fatherland*. While they improved his standing in Europe, and the financial success of *Hidden Agenda* was instrumental in enabling him to secure funding for his subsequent projects, he knew that artistically he needed somehow to continue the enlargement of his political perspective, overcoming the little-Englandism with which critics had branded the whole tradition of working-class realism, while effecting a return to his roots in domestic working-class settings and documentary aesthetics. The formation in late 1990 of Parallax Pictures, a small left-leaning film company that teamed Loach with the producer Sally Hibbin, enabled him to achieve this aim. His first two films with Parallax, *Riff-Raff* and *Raining Stones*, both made in part for Film on Four, showed that he could make films less remote from his core aesthetical and political principles without eroding his strong critical and commercial position in Europe, which would continue to be a primary source of both prestige and financing for Loach throughout the 1990s. These films convey the logic of free-market capitalism, as it was now being experienced across Europe and throughout the world, not in terms of far-off conspiracies and cabals but in terms of its local effects, on the ground, in the everyday lives of Britain's struggling and dispossessed majority. They are Loach's first films of what he has termed 'internationalism at the rank and file level' (in Ryan & Porton 1998: 26).

Riff-Raff is a film about the building trade, with a fluid and relaxed, seemingly 'unplanned' narrative centred on a Glaswegian worker, Stevie (Robert Carlyle), as he attempts to settle into a new workplace – a luxury condo project outside of London – and a new domestic situation – squatting in a former council flat with a flaky singer girlfriend named Susie (Emer McCourt). Most of the action takes place on the building site, a historic hospital being renovated and repurposed for the rich by a crew of quintessentially casual labourers, brought together under subcontract for just the one project and enjoying no long-term security or prospects. In this respect, the film continues to elaborate Loach's interest in the increasingly mobile, transient, untethered subjects of the late twentieth century; we are a long way from the 'organic' working-class community of *Kes*. Banter at the worksite is conducted in the accents of Glasgow, Liverpool, Dublin, East London, Barbados and elsewhere. Nevertheless, it is difficult to imagine the characters anywhere else than on a building site in southern England; in the particular complexion of their heterogeneity, the specific form and character of their transience and marginality, their desperate need to follow the paths of the real-estate markets, these labourers unquestionably belong to a particular time and place. The script was written by Bill Jesse, himself a Scot who was working on a London building site when he met Loach and began to pen the project. Loach shot the film at an actual renovation/construction site, and chose his cast almost entirely from men who were working or had previously worked in the building trade. This includes even Carlyle, the star of the film, and Ricky Tomlinson, its great revelation, who had been a plasterer and was one of the workers, known as the 'Shrewsbury Three', whose imprisonment for promoting a walk-out in the early 1970s had made them a *cause célèbre* in the trades unions (see Fuller 1998: 85).

The film explores not just the deterioration of labour conditions during the Thatcher decade, but the disaggregation and dispersal of labour itself, the dissolution of established working-class communities, the emergence of new or more visible lines of division and identity – all of which have greatly narrowed or at any rate complicated opportunities for collective action to resist and reverse the trends toward massive accumulation on the one hand and abject dispossession on the other. With the collapse of the unions, terms of employment are being set unilaterally by employers. A new recruit at the building site is told, for example, not to bother with the legally-mandated P45 tax form; the employer, as is confirmed in a later scene, has his own formulae for calculating withholdings which enable him to extract some extra profit, off the books. The workers – dislocated, transient, unrepresented – must accede to such practices. Any attempt by a member of the crew to organise and mobilise them *as workers* is quickly neutralised by sacking that employee, shunting him along to some other worksite, some other city.

The most politically militant worker is Larry, played brilliantly by Tomlinson, and from him we get the kind of grass-roots political talk that had often functioned as a voice of unequivocal truth in Loach's earlier films. But although Larry serves as central subject of the film's most naturalistic scenes, some welcome complications prevent him from simply functioning as political sage and hero. Much of the time he is represented as a figure of an 'obsolete' politics, an endearingly comical anachronism whose vehement speechifying is punctuated by the other workers' good-natured laughter and eye-rolling. *Riff-Raff* is more humorous than any of Loach's earlier films, but this tonal shift was not, as critics have tended to think, merely a way for Loach to sweeten the bitter pill of his politics for consumption by a mainstream liberal audience. The humour draws Larry, and the director himself, into an ambiguous comic interplay of subjects and objects. In one of the film's best moments of anecdotal whimsy, Larry makes desperate use of a bathroom in the building's luxuriously furbished 'model' flat, and decides once there to have a soak in the oversized tub. In walks the estate agent with a pair of potential buyers, who happen to be young Saudi women. The shot of Tomlinson standing naked, corpulent and bespectacled in the bathtub, facing the veiled women with a hardhat covering his privates, provides the film's most memorably comic image.

The whole sequence is edited in conventional dramatic fashion, with a series of anticipatory cuts beginning with Larry sliding into the bath and a Rolls Royce pulling up to the building's entrance, and culminating in a shot/reverse-shot of exposed male body and astonished female eyes (framed by the black veils). But as soon as Larry has made his escape and returned to the workers' canteen, the 'documentary look', which has dominated the workplace scenes, and especially those of group interaction, is restored. This way of juxtaposing the two aesthetics, characteristic of Loach's late style, here reinforces the structural contrast or high/low contradiction of the whole joke, which is not just between the gilded plumbing and the lower bodily stratum, but between the 'unreal' world of oil millionaires and the hard truths of casual labour. Back in the 'real' world of the makeshift canteen (with its natural lighting and more spontaneous camera movements), Larry is again the speaker, the subject rather than the butt of the joke.

Yet as Larry regales his mates with a rudely embellished version of the episode centring on the supposedly unbridled lust of 'Arab girls' for 'white sausage', it is

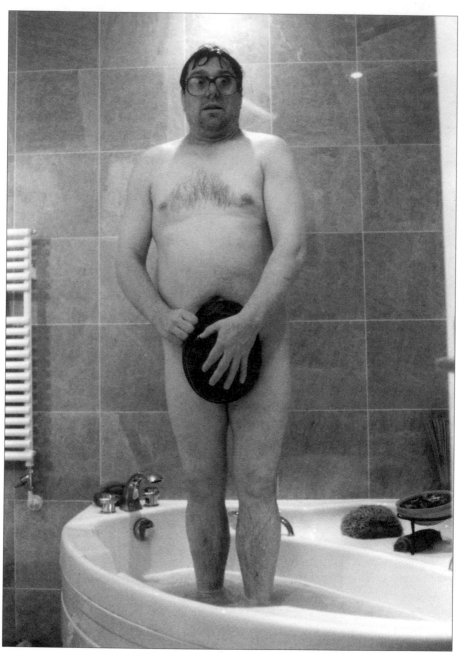

Larry (Ricky Tomlinson), the militant voice of casual labour in *Riff-Raff* (1990), sneaks a quick bath in the building his crew is working on, surprised by an estate agent with two Arab women clients

evident that the joke (in which Loach and his audience are also discomfortingly implicated), depends on displacing the workers' justified resentment of the rich onto their resentment of women and foreigners. Even in this carefully prepared scene of solidary laughter and belonging, Larry's brand of politics, and the view of reality that subtends it, reveals itself as somewhat narrow and out of date. Elsewhere, Loach makes clear that the common interests on which Larry's political rhethoric is predicated do not readily extend across lines of race or sex. Larry is, for example, repeatedly frustrated by an Afro-Caribbean worker on the site (Ade Sapara) who is, more 'enterprising' than the whites, more interested in pursuing opportunities for advancement, and more persuaded of his chances to succeed. And despite a scene in which Larry shames a club audience into bringing Susie back onstage after they have heckled her into the wings, it is never clear how the needs and desires of this aspiring but untalented singer, the only significant female character in the film, connect to a politics of workers' rights. Larry's outlook is too rooted in an all-male unionism of the past even to consider the ways that contemporary sexual (and racial) divisions of labour complicate and impede a politics of class.

The limitations – both ideological and practical – of Larry's position are reflected in his unexpectedly early exit from the film, when management gives him the sack 'for shooting his mouth off'. In tactical terms, his 'straight' political talk from the trenches of the now decimated unions – like Loach's straight documentary work on the unions in the 1980s – is a failure. The film ends with an altogether different sort of worker rebellion – a torching of the building site by two workers which, though more personal than political in its motivations and rather doubtful in its effects (since there is insurance for the owners but not for the workers), seems the most one could hope for: more plausible, certainly, than a rebirth of union fervour in the midst of post-Thatcher disaggregation.

Riff-Raff is a film far more local in aspect than *Fatherland* or *Hidden Agenda*. Its English is heavily accented and dialectic, punctuated with non-portable terms like 'P45' and 'Kango'. (The film's US distributor, Fine Line Pictures, needed to engage the services of an English-to-English subtitling company to translate this vernacular for American ears.) It draws on Loach's documentary aesthetics and his commitment to authenticity of subject and place to convey, more precisely and convincingly than any film of the period, the concrete particulars of working life along the margins of the London metropolis. But the dilemmas its characters face as the increasingly unrestrained interests of capital (symptomatically engaged here in one of the highly speculative industries – real-estate development – whose rise has epitomised and sustained late capitalism) exploit the increasing dislocation and heterogeneity of labour, were, by the early 1990s, readily perceived to be global ones. Indeed, while the film was well received in Britain, its reception was even more favourable abroad – especially in France, where Thatcherism was now seen as the opening wedge of an 'American-style' capitalism aimed at the Continent. At the European Film Awards, *Riff-Raff* was named Film of the Year, and at Cannes it was honoured with the International Critics Award.

If *Riff-Raff* represents the increasingly fractured and transient character of the post-working class, *Raining Stones* is concerned with those (a roughly equal number) who fail to 'adapt' to the demands of casualisation and mobility, remaining embedded in the economically declining, 'unworking' communities of the North – in this case, the Middleton neighbourhood of Northern Manchester.[8] The script is by Jim Allen, himself a lifelong Mancunian, and in its attention to the nuances of class and of religious and institutional affiliation it contrasts sharply with his script for *Hidden Agenda*. In *Raining Stones*, Loach says, Allen was able to treat 'the subject that I think he knows best – the people of the area where he lives' (in Fuller 1998: 91) – much as Barry Hines had done in *Kes*. But it is Loach, too, who finds this ground more familiar and congenial than the world of geopolitical intrigue. He carries the lighter, more whimsical touch he displayed in *Riff-Raff* across to this film, which, despite incorporating elements of melodrama, is the closest thing to a pure comedy Loach has made. It is, however, as Loach himself has observed, 'a comedy about debt' (ibid.), in which the engine of the plot is a jobless family man's increasing desperation in the face of endemic unemployment. And while the comic trajectory assures that the protagonist and his family are saved, just in the nick of time, from their immediate predicament, it leaves them no better off than when the film began.

The film sets out to show, among other things, what hard work it is to be out of work. The hero, Bob (Bruce Jones), and his sidekick, Tommy (Ricky Tomlinson), undertake a series of more or less risky, degrading and ill-executed schemes to bring home a few quid. They steal a sheep from a farm and peddle the mutton to some housewives in their local pub; they participate in an early-morning raid to steal the turf from a Conservative lawn-bowling club; and Bob tries his hand first as a freelance door-to-door drain cleaner (which leaves him literally covered in shit) and then as a bouncer in one of Manchester's thriving Thatcher-era dance clubs (where he gets beaten up and is fired within a few hours). But unlike the hit working-class comedies of a few years later, in which the kind of plucky, enterprising spirits displayed by Bob and Tommy eventually lead to triumphant culminations, *Raining Stones* admits of no easy exit for these kind of men in this kind of place. You could say that *Raining Stones* is to *Brassed Off* (1996) and *The Full Monty* (1997) what

In *Raining Stones* (1993), Bob (Bruce Jones), a chronically unemployed Catholic family man in Northern Manchester, tries his hand at freelance sewer work

Loach's later *Sweet Sixteen* is to *Billy Elliot* (2000). Bob finally gets the money he needs to replace his stolen van and to purchase a communion dress for his daughter, not through exceptional initiative or luck, but from a lending agency linked to the local loan shark, Tansey (Jonathan James), whose collectors we have already seen harassing and assaulting other members of the community. When Tansey moves in for his pound of flesh – taking the engagement ring from Bob's wife's finger and threatening his 'pretty' daughter with injury or mutilation – the comedy of debt shows its dark side.

Debt here operates both as a way to open up the workings of this unworking community – in which barter and credit seem to dominate exchange and practically everyone has his name in Tansey's accounts book – and to situate the community within a larger economic system that demands the impoverishment of the state, the squeezing of maximal profit from the poor, and the foreclosing of the future in the interest of current accounts. The voice of socialist conscience in the film, Bob's father-in-law Jimmy (Mike Fallon, one of the many non-professional actors in the cast), speaks directly to this latter point when he says, of some young kids arguing over a drug deal, that their futures have been 'all mapped out' in advance and hold nothing but 'despair'. Jimmy heads the Tenants' Association of the local estate, and forcefully expresses the views we associate with Loach himself – voicing in particular his disdain for the Labour Party leadership (which does 'fuck all' for its constituency in the housing estates) and the Church (which is not a counterforce to the state or to free-market ideology but is 'part of the problem', pacifying the masses with 'a lot of mumbo jumbo' and preventing them from 'thinking for themselves').

As Jacob Leigh has argued, *Raining Stones* effectively 'embeds' the individual drama of Bob Williams and his family in the larger social context described and critiqued by Jimmy (2002: 151). In both scenes where Bob visits Jimmy at the Association office, the camera is deployed according to Loach's classic documentary method, panning jerkily across the Association bulletin board, with its evidence of diverse projects and initiatives, and turning for long stretches to conversations in which Bob has no part: a woman complaining about insufficient treasury funds to repair flooding damage in her flat – the kind of infrastructural deterioration on which the neoliberal state has simply turned its back; a dispute between this woman's two little girls, who have to come with her to the office since there is no room for government-provided childcare in a privatised economy; a tirade by Jimmy as he threatens the local Labour representative with a rent strike, a form of mass protest which the councilman promises would be severely punished; and the fight between the two young 'smackheads', born into redundancy, not yet fifteen years old and already 'finished'. The 'social framework' into which Loach here 'embeds his narrative structure' (Leigh 2002: 149) is in fact a socialist framework of analysis, the validity of which is supported both by the documentary look of these scenes and by the character, Jimmy, who articulates their meaning for us in terms of class consciousness and mass struggle.

It is significant, though, and characteristic of the less rigid presentation of narrative truth in Loach's late style, that the most prominent posting the camera finds on the Tenants' Association bulletin board reads 'Is Socialism the Answer?' The importance of the question mark is reinforced by Bob's evident and at times slightly comical indifference to Jimmy's socialist rhetoric. Just as Larry's speeches about housing shortages and union-busting never gain any real purchase among the workers in *Riff-Raff*, Jimmy's call for the working class to slough off the propaganda of Church and State and seize the power for change that lies within its own hands is of little use to Bob. While Jimmy attacks religion as the opiate of the masses, the camera fixes on Bob's tired, comically pleading eyes. 'The last thing I need right now', he responds, 'is a lecture.' For all the intensity of Jimmy's discourse, our sympathies here are likely to be with Bob. Though his devotion to the Roman Catholic Church has led to his nearly ruinous financial predicament (since he spent an exorbitant, wasteful sum – £140 – to fit out his daughter in what he deems to be suitably digni-fied fashion for her first Communion), that institution cannot simply be written off as 'part of the problem'. A framework of analysis that affords class an absolute privilege over religion for purposes of situating its objects or mobilising its subjects is simply out of step with the contemporary world, in which religious affiliation increasingly takes precedence on the ground, and the Church is often the most potent site for acts of mass resistance. An anti-capitalist politics that depends on enlisting working-class Roman Catholics (or Evangelicals, or Muslims) in a socialist movement *against* religion is doomed.

At the moment of his greatest need, when he has just killed Tansey, Bob turns not to Jimmy but to his Priest, Father Barry. And the film seems to credit this choice, as the Priest shows himself to be more attuned to the concrete needs of the commu-nity than to the 'mumbo jumbo' of holy writ. The Father tells a rather disconcerted Bob that he should have no regrets or moral qualms about Tansey's death and that he must say nothing to the police. Then he takes Tansey's accounts book – a record both of the community's financial desperation and of the predatory lending practices that exploit and intensify such desperation – and burns it in his heater. At a stroke, the debt is forgiven; Bob finds the salvation he has been seeking.

It is perhaps going too far to see in the local loan shark a figure of the global creditor – RBS, Citibank UK, the World Bank – and thus to read a much broader meaning into the fact that it is here a socially-conscious form of religious faith rather than a doctrinal socialism that succeeds in de-legitimising and unilaterally relieving the debts of the poor. But it is the nature of Loach's later working-class dramas to suggest such extensions of meaning, and to countenance the problems or contradic-tions in working-class politics which thereby emerge. With his first two Parallax films, Loach established what has remained his key place on the field of world cinema. He is the leading anatomist of the 'new' or 'post-' working class in Britain as its circumstances are shaped by local instantiations of late global capitalism. His work in the post-Thatcher period amounts to a series of interestingly varied and modu-lated case studies in what the trailer for his 2001 film *The Navigators* calls 'the new world economy'. He has experimented with different ratios and juxtapositions of the documentary and dramatic 'looks', and with different mixtures of generic conven-tion – comedy and melodrama incorporated to varying degrees into what remains an essentially naturalist narrative paradigm. But among the constants of his work is this recognition of the sheer scale of the forces that are arrayed against ordinary working people – the power of the local loan shark to establish dominance through debt being in a sense derived from that of his global counterparts, just as the power of the subcontractor over his workers is derived from that of multinational real-estate investment firms.

But the fact that Loach has become a director of and for the world cinema does not mean that he is a director truly at home in the world, one who succeeds equally in Berlin, Managua or Los Angeles. Though his projects abroad have helped him and Parallax knit together a valuable set of working relationships and to realise the positive potentialities of the ever more international distribution of independent cinematic labour,[9] his work remains strongest when the particular case under scrutiny is British rather than international. When he leaves Great Britain Loach loses his touch for the ambiguity and unexpectedness on which the convincingly 'authentic' representation must be predicated. He offers us too many touristic images, colourful peasants, noble freedom-fighters. From the vantage afforded us by Loach's own aesthetic achievement, it would seem that these other localities should be left to other directors, who breathe that particular air and speak that particular language. It is enough that Loach survived a desperate decade under Thatcher's government and found a way to adapt his very British sort of political film to the challenges of the global age.

NOTES

1   The original formulation of this critique appears in Colin MacCabe (1974) 'Realism and the Cinema: Notes on Some Brechtian Theses', 10–12, though I take my quotation from MacCabe's later 'Memory, Phantasy, Identity', originally published in 1977, which aims more specifically at Loach's work. The first challenge to MacCabe's argument was offered by McArthur (1975/76) in his review of Loach's *Days of Hope* for *Screen*. The whole sequence of critiques and counter-critiques has been rehearsed many times since; especially valuable is John Caughie's 'Progressive Television and Documentary Drama' from 1980. For a much broader perspective on the realism vs. modernism debates within Western Marxist and post-Marxist thought, Fredric Jameson's classic 1977 essay 'Reflections on the Brecht-Lukács Debate' is an excellent place to start.

2   The high esteem accorded these early Loach films can be gauged by the comments of Alan Parker and Michael Apted in Stephen Frears' *Typically British: A Personal History of British Cinema,* a film Frears made for BFI television in 1995. Discussing the post-New Wave years, Apted says of *Cathy Come Home* that it 'completely cracked everything open' and established a 'fundamental critical turning point' in British filmmaking. It was, he adds, 'the first time I was excited about something that was British and not American'. Parker, in turn, unequivocally declares *Kes* 'the best film made in Britain, since the war'.

3   Zola puts the case in typically extreme terms: 'The naturalist novel ... no longer interests itself in the ingenuity of a well-invented story, developed according to certain rules. Imagination has no longer a place, plot matters little to the novelist, who bothers himself with neither development, mystery, nor dénouement' (1964: 123). This is not, of course, a very accurate description of Zola's own practice; much less so of Loach's, which involves always a blending of (melo)dramatic and documentary elements. A valuable discussion of Loach's place in the history of naturalism is Knight (1977). On the distinction between Loach's work and conventional melodrama, see Hill (1998).

4   On Loach's collaboration with Menges, see Leigh (2002: 59–61).

5   From London Weekend Television, quoted by Nicholls.

6   Even in his commercials, however, Loach elaborated the documentary-realist aesthetic. He pioneered the now common practice of constructing advertisements around ostensibly spontaneous interviews with 'real' people.

7   In *Fatherland*, two brief scenes stand out: the first takes place in the GDR manufacturing shop run by Drittemann's stepfather, and involves a pair of mildly rebellious young workers who scrawl a

joke about Party leaders on a shop wall; the second takes place in England, when a group of would-be picketers are turned away from a strike site by police. In *Hidden Agenda*, what stands out is the pivotal scene of revelation in which the John Stalker character meets the Colin Wallace character. Loach here employs an actual Sinn Fein area representative (Jim McAllister) as the principle Sinn Fein character, Liam Philbin. In its determination to allow an authentic political subject to give voice to unspeakable sentiments (Philbin holds forth, unrebutted, on the moral equivalence of IRA bombers and George Washington), as well as in its use of folk singing to humanise the collective subject of oppositional politics – a strategy that emerges from Loach's work on the documentary *Which Side Are You On?* and is further elaborated in *Land and Freedom* and *Carla's Song* – this scene especially bears the mark of Loach's (still emerging) late realist style.

8   As regards the scale of these neoliberal effects, Will Hutton cites figures showing that by the mid-1990s only 40 per cent of the British labour force could be said to 'enjoy full-time tenured employment; 30 per cent are insecurely self-employed, involuntary part-time or casual workers; and the bottom 30 per cent of society either work for poverty-level wages or are unemployed' (1996: 14).

9   By the time he completed his first three films for Parallax, Loach's producer, Hibbin, was able to secure funding for his next film (*Land and Freedom*) from a combination of British, German, French and Spanish sources, as well as from the regional European Co-Production Fund and Euromarché. By this point, Parallax was establishing repeatable agreements with a set of European distributors to whom each new Loach film could be pre-sold: Road Movies in Germany; Tornasol and Alta in Spain; Diaphana in France; BIM in Italy; and Cinéart in Belgium and Holland. By the end of the decade, Rebecca O'Brien, another co-founder of Parallax, who had first worked with Loach on *Hidden Agenda*, could describe these companies as 'regular partners'.

WORKS CITED

Bourdieu, Pierre (1977) *Outline of a Theory of Practice*. Cambridge: Cambridge University Press.

Burton, Alan (1994) *The People's Cinema: Film and the Co-operative Movement*. London: National Film Theatre.

Caughie, John (1980) 'Progressive Television and Documentary Drama', *Screen*, 21, (Autumn), 9–35.

Ezard, John (1988) 'Radical Film Director Driven to Drink Commercials', *Guardian*, 5 September.

Fuller, Graham (ed.) (1998) *Loach on Loach*. London: Faber and Faber.

Hattenstone, Simon (1994) 'Rock Steady', *Guardian*, 29 September, T10.

Hill, John (1997a) 'Finding a Form: Politics and Aesthetics in *Fatherland, Hidden Agenda*, and *Riff-Raff*', in George McKnight (ed.) *Agent of Challenge and Defiance: The Films of Ken Loach*. Westport, CT: Greenwood Press, 125–43.

____ (1997b) 'Interview with Ken Loach', in George McKnight (ed.) *Agent of Challenge and Defiance: The Films of Ken Loach*. Westport, CT: Greenwood Press, 160–76.

____ (1998) 'Every Fuckin' Choice Stinks', *Sight and Sound*, 8, 11, 18–21.

Hutton, Will (1996) *The State We're In: Why Britain is in Crisis and How to Overcome It*. London: Vintage.

Jameson, Fredric (1988) 'Reflections on the Brecht-Lukács Debate', *The Ideologies of Theory: Essays 1971–1986*, vol. 2. Minnneapolis: University of Minnesota Press, 133–47.

Knight, Deborah (1997) 'Naturalism, Narration, and Critical Perspective: Ken Loach and the Experimental Method', in George McKnight (ed.) *Agent of Challenge and Defiance: The Films of Ken Loach*. Westport, CT: Greenwood Press, 60–81.

Leigh, Jacob (2002) *The Cinema of Ken Loach: Art in the Service of the People*. London: Wallflower

Press.

MacCabe, Colin (1974) 'Realism and the Cinema: Notes on Some Brechtian Theses', *Screen*, 15 (Summer), 7–27.

____ (1976) 'Days of Hope – A Response to Colin MacArther', *Screen* 17 (Spring): 99–101.

____ (1991 [1977]) 'Memory, Phantasy, Identity: *Days of Hope* and the Politics of the Past', in Margaret Dickinson (ed.) *Rogue Reels: Oppositional Film in Britain, 1945–90*. London: British Film Institute, 141–5.

McArthur, Colin (1975/76) 'Review of Ken Loach, *Days of Hope*', *Screen*, 16 (Winter), 139–44.

Nicholls, David (1999) 'Locating Loach Within the History and Theory of the Realist Text', PhD dissertation. Available online at: www.geocities.com/SoHo/Exhibit/5693/locatingloach.htm (accessed January 2004).

Petley, Julian (1997a) 'Factual Fictions and Fictional Fallacies: Ken Loach's Documentary Dramas', in George McKnight (ed.) *Agent of Challenge and Defiance: The Films of Ken Loach*. Westport, CT: Greenwood Press, 28–59.

____ (1997b) 'Ken Loach and Questions of Censorship', in George McKnight (ed.) *Agent of Challenge and Defiance: The Films of Ken Loach*. Westport, CT: Greenwood Press, 99–124.

Ryan, Susan and Richard Porton (1998) 'The Politics of Everyday Life: An Interview with Ken Loach', *Cineaste*, 24, (Winter), 22–7.

Zola, Emile (1964) 'Naturalism on the Stage', *The Experimental Novel and Other Essays*, trans. Belle M. Sherimann. New York: Haskell.

17. ALLEGORIES OF THATCHERISM: PETER GREENAWAY'S FILMS OF THE 1980s

Michael Walsh

Margaret Thatcher became Prime Minister of Britain at the general election of May 1979, was re-elected in both 1983 and 1987, and was deposed by machinations within her own Conservative Party in November 1990. She was replaced as Prime Minister by her protegé, John Major, who was elected to a five-year term in his own right in April 1992. Thus eleven years of Thatcher in office were followed by a further seven years of what some commentators called 'Thatcherism without Thatcher'. On most accounts, the subsequent Labour governments of Tony Blair have made no decisive break with the policies of 1979–97, so that the Thatcherite 'economic settlement of the 1980s' has held sway into the twenty-first century.

Much-theorised during the 1980s, Thatcherism has more recently ceased to inspire much discussion. Yet it remains defining, still forming the horizon of mainstream political possibility in Britain and linking with a worldwide neoliberalism enforced by the International Monetary Fund (IMF) and World Trade Organisation (WTO). So Thatcherism's very inertia, its very taken-for-grantedness, is precisely the reason to continue thinking about it; as a political/cultural sequence that has yet to see its end, the meaning of Thatcherism should not be settled by exhaustion or default.

In Britain, the Thatcher years saw what Terry Eagleton has called 'the most ideo-logically aggressive and explicit régime in living political memory, in a society which traditionally prefers its ruling values to remain implicit' (1991: xi). They also saw one of the most remarkable renewals in the whole history of British cinema. The formal history of the Thatcher years includes the 'second Cold War' with the Soviet Union, the Falklands War with Argentina, a continuing low-intensity war with Irish Republicanism, uprisings in the inner cities, the shutdown of a quarter of British manufacturing, a year-long miners' strike, the systematic stripping of public assets (aka 'privatisation'), booms in money capital, development and consumption, and political battles over left-controlled city councils, gay rights, the poll tax and Europe. As if responding to all of this, the British cinema of the 1980s split between films that remained basically consistent with the principles of realism and films that broke decisively with them. In the first category we can place the work of social realists such as Mike Leigh, Ken Loach, Hanif Kureishi and Stephen Frears, as well as most of the makers of 'heritage cinema'. In the second, we can place the work of such art-cinema directors as Peter Greenaway, Derek Jarman, Sally Potter and Patrick Keiller, as well as Black and Asian collectives like Sankofa and Black Audio, whose members included Isaac Julien, Maureen Blackwood, Reece Auguiste and John Akomfrah. Meanwhile, directors such as Terence Davies and Alan Clarke made films that scrupulously conformed with some codes of realism while flagrantly violating others.

It is certainly not the case that British cinema had never before seen a break with realism; one could cite the films of Powell and Pressburger, the long history of commercial production of melodrama, fantasy and horror, and the films of the Co-op movement from the 1960s on. Yet only the last of these represents the active problematisation of a dominant set of expectations for narrative structure and characterisation, which is what I have in mind when I say that the cinematic keynote of the Thatcher years was a challenge to the hegemony of realism. The term 'challenge' I use advisedly, since no reasonable critic can maintain that realism was seen off in the British cinema of the Thatcher years of 1979–90. Geoff Brown suggests that British cinema of the 1990s represents 'a retreat from the cutting edge' (2000:33). If this is correct, and the Thatcher period in fact constitutes a sort of cinematic interregnum, it is only more important that we continue to think critically about it.

FROM THE AVANT-GARDE TO ART CINEMA

One of the most noticed of British directors whose work of the 1980s offered a direct challenge to the conventions of realism was Peter Greenaway. A filmography annotated by Greenaway for *Film Comment* begins with 1959, but his continuous production of films dates from 1966, and his work until 1989 can be conveniently divided between experimental films and art-house features. The first category includes *H Is For House* (1973), *Windows* (1975), *Water Wrackets* (1975), *Dear Phone* (1977), *A Walk Through H* (1978), *Vertical Features Remake* (1979) and *The Falls* (1980). The second includes *The Draughtsman's Contract* (1982), *A Zed and Two Noughts* (1985), *The Belly of An Architect* (1985), *Drowning By Numbers* (1988) and *The Cook, The Thief, His Wife and Her Lover* (1989).

This division between experimental work and feature films cannot be made hard and fast. We cannot, for example, make the standard distinction between narrative features and non-narrative or anti-narrative experimental work. Greenaway's experimental films play elaborate games with narrative (*Water Wrackets*, for example, develops an entire conquest saga), while narration in the feature films proceeds as much by structural principle as by the traditions of the well-made plot; the most obvious example is *Drowning By Numbers*, whose art-house audiences delight in following the film's sequence of numbers from 1 to 100. Nor can we easily distinguish the two kinds of films in terms of favoured images, themes or conceptual systems: *Water Wrackets* introduces a love of images of the sun criss-crossed by trees and other 'vertical features' which recurs everywhere in Greenaway, a love of the play of light on water which recurs in both *Drowning By Numbers* and *The Cook, The Thief, His Wife and Her Lover*, and a deadpan fascination with the authority of BBC voiceovers which recurs in *A Zed and Two Noughts*. With its patient archaeology of the artificial lakes created by the victorious tribe or clan of Wrackets, this film also anticipates the emphasis throughout Greenaway's work of the 1980s on human transformations of the landscape. This emphasis is peculiarly English; the long obsession of the national culture with the countryside and the country house is the trace of a social history in which an agrarian gentry accumulated the capital for the world's first industrial revolution and then ensured both that Britain would become the first European society to economically minimise agriculture and that industry would remain subordinate to finance capital and empire. Thus, while *H Is For House* seems typical of an entire subgenre of avant-garde films which depict the immediate domestic surroundings of the filmmaker, and *Windows* seems typical of another subgenre which analogises on the materiality of the camera, both films also participate in this peculiarity of the English by anticipating the confinement of *The Draughtsman's Contract* to the interior and grounds of a house in the country and the return of *Drowning By Numbers* to a sun-struck Suffolk.

Also inaugurated in the 1970s films is Greenaway's interest in thoroughgoing rehearsals of the structured materiality of various signifying systems; as its title indicates, *H Is For House* anticipates both *The Draughtsman's Contract* and *A Zed and Two Noughts* by giving pride of place among those systems to the alphabet. Characters too recur from film to film; as Greenaway's own publicity material for *Drowning By Numbers* suggests, Cissie Colpitts is mentioned in *Dear Phone* and *Vertical Features Remake*, becomes three slides of the same woman (right profile, full face, left profile) in *The Falls*, and becomes three women with the same name in *Drowning By Numbers*. Indeed, a whole essay might be written on the avidity with which Greenaway's films recycle and make inter-texts of each other.

However, the fact that many of Greenaway's preoccupations first appear in his work of the 1970s does not make it impossible to distinguish between his artisanal and his commercial films; to paraphrase a remark of John Searle on Derrida, the fact that a distinction is not absolute does not mean that it is not a distinction at all. Most obvious among factors which distinguish the features is the presence of actors, with the concomitant sense of drama, motive and psychology, however stylised. In the experimental films, speech is typically reported; we hear about characters from a tireless, measured, bureaucratic voiceover. The features, by contrast, are populated by highly credentialled actors and often veer comically between the exigencies of structure and those of naturalistic conversation. In other words, the features are based on classically dramatic motives and tensions found only implicitly in the earlier films; *The Draughtsman's Contract* treats a struggle for sexual and social power conditioned by a crisis in symbolic paternity, *Drowning By Numbers* dramatises the impasses of obsessional desire, and *The Cook, The Thief, His Wife and Her Lover* depicts a brutal and adulterous love triangle.

Also more prominent in the features is Greenaway's investment in art history. This is not completely absent from the earlier work, but those films contain nothing like the profusion of paintings found in the features; William E. van Wert (1990/91) discovers more than a dozen direct references to art history in *The Cook, The Thief, His Wife and Her Lover* and feels he has only begun to discuss the topic. Vermeer presides over *A Zed and Two Noughts*, and Brueghel over *Drowning By Numbers*. Meanwhile, various corpses evoke Mantegna's *Dead Christ*, nude departures evoke expulsions of Adam and Eve from Paradise, and feasts evoke both last suppers and Frank Hals' *Banquet of the Officers of the St George Civic Guard* which looms so large in the décor of *The Cook, The Thief, His Wife and Her Lover*. Greenaway's use of large and familiar paintings as backdrops reminds us of Fassbinder's *The Bitter Tears of Petra von Kant* (1973), and his tableaux vivants call to mind Godard's *Passion* (1982), a film full of the logistical comedy involved in trying to render Rembrandt and Delacroix with live actors and animals. This combination of comparisons suggests that Greenaway's meditation on art history places the emphasis on the idea of animation, negotiating between two basics of the film image: the stillness it shares with painting and photography and the motion which decisively distinguishes it from the earlier visual arts.

Noël Burch argues that the passage from the serial photography of Muybridge and Marey to the early cinema is a movement from the scientific analysis of motion to its 'Frankensteinian' synthesis, a formulation which suggests a way of thinking about Greenaway's treatment of art history which passes beyond allusion and reference to link up with other aspects of his style. For example, this perspective makes it less surprising that *A Zed and Two Noughts* should imagine decay as a type of animal locomotion which had not occurred to the apparently exhaustive Muybridge; it also helps us to understand the animate statuary of *The Draughtsman's Contract*, the disturbing amputations with which Alba physically comments on the Venus de Milo in *A Zed and Two Noughts*, and the attraction of Roman statuary for the title character in *The Belly of An Architect*. The wider compass of a relationship between stillness and motion also informs Greenaway's painstakingly assembled still lifes, his delight in sending clouds of mist drifting through his green landscapes, and his occasional freeze-frames, as well as providing a clue as to why all of the paintings, whether directly presented or acted out, are pre-modern; cinema itself stands for and subsumes modernity.

The animate statue (Michael Feast) in *The Draughtsman's Contract* (1982)

ART CINEMA UNDER THATCHER

In order to pass beyond such 'formalist' commentary, 'internal' to the texts, we might notice that Greenaway's passage from the relative deprivation of the avant-garde to the relative luxury of art cinema coincides closely with the beginning of the Thatcher period in 1979. Indeed, if we agree that the first few years of Thatcher were an uncertain transition out of Labourism, marked by the strategic decision to postpone confrontation with the miners and rescued from likely political doom by the godsend of the Falklands, then we can map the story of Greenaway's financing quite exactly onto the historical picture. The independently-funded experimental films gave way during this transitional period to British Film Institute, Arts Council and Channel 4 productions, which in turn gave way, during high Thatcherism, to Greenaway's enviable deal with the Dutch producer Kees Kasander. Such progress from economic strength to strength represents a decisive commentary on Thatcher's Anglocentric ideologemes of self-reliance; Greenaway's state-led transition to capitalist production successfully integrated with Europe reads like a textbook vindication of the 'Gaullist' alternative, presented by Antony Barnett as a strategy more rational than Thatcherism (1982: 63).

Notice also that two of Greenaway's films so far most successful with audiences (*The Draughtsman's Contract* and *The Cook, The Thief, His Wife and Her Lover*) punctually mark the beginning and the end of the Thatcher period. These two films also parenthesise the entire history of the oldest continuously existing bourgeois state in the world, covering the ground from its establishment in the Glorious Revolution of 1688 to the present. Like my earlier remarks on the countryside and the country house, this of course refers to the interpretation of British history first elaborated by Perry Anderson and Tom Nairn in the *New Left Review* of 1964 and later taken up by many writers.

In other words, Greenaway's production of the 1980s is synchronised with a Thatcherism which it parodies and refutes. Greenaway is not obviously or instinctively a political filmmaker, but regularly spoke of *The Cook, The Thief, His Wife and Her Lover* as dealing with Thatcherism. This suggests that we can see him as an allegorist, whose features comment indirectly but decisively on the crisis of post-imperial Britain to which Thatcherism also responds. Anderson, Nairn and Barnett argue that the British crisis should be traced back to the Glorious Revolution; with the consolidation of the first effective challenge to the settlement of 1945, Greenaway made a film about the ancestor-settlement of 1688. A few months before the end of Thatcher, if not of Thatcherism, Greenaway's greatest success to date was widely received as a critique of the consumer/casino economy of the 1980s. If these are coincidences, I will argue that they are informative and telling ones, which may be laid, like historical templates, over films which themselves routinely impose conceptual system upon conceptual system.

Moreover, I would suggest that what Nairn calls the 'political emergency' of Thatcherism (1979: 365) makes for greater urgency in historical and political reading. The crucial question of Thatcherism is whether or not it represents a real departure in British politics, and if the difficulty in answering is largely a matter of historical proximity, it seems reasonable to think that what will prove most helpful is a longer view. In what follows, then, I will work to establish the treatment of the settlement of 1688 in *The Draughtsman's Contract* as a textual and historical base-datum, and will deal with *Drowning By Numbers* and *The Cook, The Thief, His Wife and Her Lover* as different versions of the post-imperial crisis of that settlement. However, the films are not purely and simply historical symptoms, and I will also use psycho-analysis to look at issues of gender. In terms of cultural sociology, I see Greenaway in the context of Perry Anderson's 'culture in contraflow', a vision of middle-class and middle-of-the-road British intellectuals antagonised by Thatcher into moving leftwards while the state has moved to the right. Terry Eagleton re-poses the key question of Thatcherism by following the lines quoted above ('the most ideologically aggressive and explicit regime of living political memory') with a suggestion that this régime may not have decisively transformed the 'vaguely social democratic values' of the British (1991: 33). One evidence of such a contradictory conjuncture is its impact on a filmmaker as natively apolitical as Greenaway.

THE DRAUGHTSMAN'S CONTRACT: A CRISIS IN THE SYMBOLIC ORDER

The opening credits tell us that it is August 1694, and Talmann confirms the date with an enthusiastic comment on William of Orange, whose victory at the Battle of the Boyne helped to secure the settlement of 1689 from potentially resurgent Catholicism and absolutism. This reference to Ireland, along with the suggestion by Sarah Talmann that Neville has 'Scottish sympathies', reminds us that we are in the formative period of both British imperialism and the United Kingdom. Despite the film's emphasis on struggles for social and sexual prestige, Greenaway is therefore dealing with a moment which tends towards political stabilisation; little Augustus will reach maturity in the Augustan age at the beginning of the eighteenth century, and the insistence of Talmann that the boy must have a German tutor points further forward to the Hanoverian succession. The purpose of the tutor is to win Augustus over from his attraction to drawing (in one scene, we see him emulating Neville on a chalkboard) and to teach him mathematics so that he can grow up to join the Royal Society. In Christopher Hill's critical account, the Royal Society indeed emphasised mathematics, along with agricultural improvements and 'gadgetry ... designed to entertain the Fellows', and thus failed 'to contribute to the thinking which underlay the innovations of the Industrial Revolution' (1980: 64). So what is expected of the adult Augustus is a tincture of royalism (but not absolutism) and a genteel, rural amateurism (but not industrial innovation). In other words, the values of the Herbert family central to *The Draughtsman's Contract* conform precisely to those of the agrarian aristocracy which gained the upper hand in 1688 and continued to directly rule Britain deep into the twentieth century. Perry Anderson compares the situation with France and the United States, ruled by lawyers since at least the middle of the nineteenth century (1987: 31).

Augustus will not grow up to become a draughtsman because a profession of any kind is much beneath his aristocratic social status. Indeed, membership in the gentry can make the social distinction which constitutes professionalism difficult to even perceive; for Sarah Talmann, Neville is 'a paid servant contracted to my mother', as if to contract were to wage-labour or even to indenture. The point is underscored early in the film, when the flow of 'ribald gossip' is interrupted by the sociological revelation that thirteen of those present are there because of a 'confidence in one another's money' based on owning 'a fair slice of England', while only one or two others are present on merit. Just before this, we have heard the story of a duke who casually murders his 'water-mechanic', which should already alert us to the possible fate of Neville.

Talmann assumes charge of Augustus after his mother becomes a Catholic, a circumstance which reminds us that the period still thinks its political conflicts in religious terms, and resonates historically with the birth of a male heir to James II in May 1688. According to Hill, this was 'the last straw' for the Glorious Revolutionaries since it threatened a Catholic succession (1961: 199). When Neville mocks Sarah Talmann's suggestion that a boy with a Catholic mother is effectively an orphan, Augustus is further linked with the film's crucial issue. This is not infidelity or murder but inheritance, 'patrimony or the lack of it' as the Talmanns put it. Patrimony, a plainly patriarchal concept, will soon lead us towards the film's treatment of women. At present, however, I use the term to suggest that the dramatic motor of the film is a crisis in symbolic paternity, expressed most obviously as the departure, disappearance and death of Mr Herbert. This crisis does lack the direct historical extension possible in a period emerging from revolution and regicide, restoration and redeposition. Again, however, the film depicts a finally stabilising consensus; the world of Compton Anstey makes reference to Jacobites and colonies, but the film's severe formalities emphasise the more purely symbolic aspect of Mr Herbert's disappearance and the struggles for power which ensue.

Lacan theorises a crisis in symbolic paternity as a failure to properly locate what he calls 'the Name of the Father'. He links this failure with psychosis, in which this key signifier is missing from the Symbolic, and with mourning (at least for a father), in

The severe formalities of *The Draughtsman's Contract*

which it is missing from the Real. Remembering that in mourning a swarm of images seeks to repair the damage to the Real, while in psychosis (for Lacan largely synonymous with paranoia) the signifiers missing from the Symbolic return in the Real, we can gain some insights into *The Draughtsman's Contract*. This is so because the film revolves around the death of Mr Herbert, and the attendant intrigues create a paranoid, conspiratorial maze which suspends cognitive surety. Greenaway presents us with statements which initially mislead us, behaviours whose ambiguity we may initially recognise, actions whose meaning is altered by subsequent events, and events whose layered meanings seem to resist definitive interpretation; it is not surprising to learn that in order to set the tone for cast and crew, Greenaway screened Alain Resnais' *Last Year at Marienbad* (1961).

Chief among the swarm of images which seek to stand in for Mr Herbert are, of course, the drawings, most especially the one in which Neville plans to place his face on the body of the usurper Talmann. With this condensation of images of the two most powerful men in the film, Neville literalises paternity, in marked distinction from the women in the film, for whom paternity is a more purely symbolic principle with which one is obliged (and therefore able) to negotiate. Other signifiers which lead lives of their own are the various fruits, animals and trees, along with Mr Herbert's shirt, coat, boots, cloak and horse, which make a most definite return, both in the fiction's Real and in its Imaginary (the drawings), from the moment that Mrs Herbert lets fall the first clue that her husband may not come home. And when Talmann remarks that Neville has 'the God-like power of emptying the landscape' and that 'It is a wonder the birds still sing', we might be in the imaginative universe of Freud's case of paranoia, the Senätspresident Schreber, who was told by the birds that God had emptied the world of all others in order to repopulate it by procreating with him. As P. Adams Sitney (1990) suggests, such a perspective is more obviously relevant to a film like *The Falls*, which divides its 92 characters between those who believe and those who disbelieve in 'the reponsibility of birds' for the Violent Unknown Event. In *The Draughtsman's Contract*, such lunatic impulses seem more measured, more controlled; nonetheless, Greenaway fills the film with figures who hope, like the paranoiac, to take advantage of the crisis in the symbolic in order to design a universe more in keeping with their own desires. These include Neville with his contract, Mrs Herbert and the two Talmanns with their various 'ingenuities', and Van Hoyten with his landscaping project.

Moreover, Schreber's questions of procreation and subsequent legacy are crucial in the film, resonating not only with specific historical events but also with what Neville calls 'the place of women in English life', an issue which is pointedly addressed at the outset. The first line in the film concerns a Mr Chandos who spends more time with his garden than with his wife. A whole string of related remarks include Mrs Pierpoint's comment that she is 'not properly of the company but a part of its property', Noyes' estimation of her exchange-value as that of 'two parterres and a drive of orange trees', and Sarah Talmann's summary assessment of prevailing values as 'a house, a garden, a horse, a wife, in that order'. Further to this are Mr Herbert's cold instructions to his wife as he leaves, and the sexually abusive treatment she receives at the hands of Neville.

Yet if a wife is not as important as a horse, a house or a garden, she is indispensable in providing the heir who will inherit all three. To the extent that we accept Mrs

Herbert and Mrs Talmann's suggestions that their sexual interest in Neville lies in the hope of conceiving a child, the film's initial proto-feminism seems a stratagem, masking the women's interest in exercising the strictly limited yet pivotal power afforded to them by the way the prevailing social order constructs their biology. The early remarks on sexual politics should not be simply dismissed, since these women do represent an internally oppressed fraction of their class; however, their dedication to producing even an illegitimate heir expresses their ultimate solidarity with that class. Thus we are wrong to imagine much likelihood of Neville gaining the estate by romancing Virginia Herbert; she has already exchanged her father's estate in marriage, but retains a relationship with symbolic paternity so powerful that she is determined to dispatch her husband and, if at all possible, to rewrite the Name of the Father in the shape of an heir. The more purely symbolic aspect of this desire is clear at the end of the film insofar as Mrs Herbert is rid of all the troublesome actual men who might physically support paternity; her father and husband are gone, while her potential son has yet to appear in any shape less symbolic than 'the blood of the newborn' represented by the juice of the pomegranate. That same figure also suggests Mrs Herbert's final rhetorical authority over the various men in the film who have repeatedly equated women's bodies with fruit-trees and fruit.

As a ladies' man, Neville is eager to exploit what he initially takes to be Mrs Herbert's loneliness. In this pursuit, he deploys both the 'innocence and arrogance' perceived by Sarah Talmann, the calculating cruelty depicted in his physical use of Mrs Herbert, and the intellectual conceit conveyed in such virtuoso displays of language as his punning conversational gambit: 'I am permitted to take pleasure without hindrance on her property and enjoy the maturing delights of her country garden.' This last resonates once again with the country estate which is the proprietorial hallmark of the traditional English ruling class, and with the film's particular dramatisations of the body of a woman who can neither inherit nor leave the estate but nonetheless rules it in her husband's absence.

Furthermore, Neville conceives of the sexual contract, and quickly sets about Mrs Herbert with casual and imperious violence; a first reaction shot shows her spitting sperm and vomiting into a basin, a response compounded by her revulsion at his treatment of her and at a sexual act which cannot lead to conception. Neville draws up the first contract with Mrs Herbert in the expectation of sadistic gratification, finds that the second contract with Mrs Talmann has placed him in a position of sexual subordination, but is most completely defeated in his final effort to engage with Mrs Herbert outside the contract. The eager sadist becomes a reluctant masochist, but is fully psychologically exposed only at the dénouement. Conforming with the classical psychoanalytic picture of gender, and challenging us to say whether his conformity underscores the patriarchal or the analytic aspect of that picture, Neville returns at the end of the film to a woman he continues to imagine sadistically – attracted by Mrs Herbert's 'humiliations', he thinks of her as representing loss. Instead, he delivers himself to another contradictory image of femininity, the fatal mother of the masochist.

Significantly, the first-time viewer of the film probably identifies with Neville. Even if he does mistreat women, overestimate his potential social mobility, and strike postures of pride, Neville is certainly more sympathetic than Talmann, Noyes and the Poulencs, whose criticisms of him as 'unconventional', 'impertinent' and 'imprudent and provocative' help to alloy his period professionalism with the traits of a Romantic artist *avant la lettre*. By the end, however, his desire revealed as pathetically Oedipal, hesitant and genuine, he is a more conventional romantic victim, broadly comparable with the Valmont of Stephen Frears' *Dangerous Liasons* (1988). More directly, of course, with his 'I am finished' and his stripped and bleeding body disposed in the frame to evoke a dead Christ, Neville is a social martyr, showing what becomes of 'a tenant farmer's son' who imagines that he can outmanoeuvre his patron.

If any figure in the film seems to offer some relief from the rural but airless enclosure of the 1689 settlement, it is the animate statue, even though Neville at one point thinks of him as a spy or agent of Mrs Herbert. The statue, the most obviously anti-naturalistic device in the film, clarifies the basic comedy of the film's *mise-en-scène*; given the thoroughgoing formality of period manners and costume, it is almost possible to read as naturalistic the dramatic light sources, yellow-lit interiors, framings within framings, strong horizontals, tracking shots back and forth along outdoor banquet tables, and unlikely profusion of obelisks. I have already discussed the broader meaning of Greenaway's interest in animate statuary; here, I would add only that the statue responds exclusively to the artist, his potential apprentice and the servant who shoos him from the gate. Perhaps this romantic conjunction of artist, child and worker suggests a puckish possibility in the English landscape rather different from the geometry favoured by Mr Herbert and the water-mechanics of Van Hoyten.

DROWNING BY NUMBERS: CEREMONIES OF OBSESSION

The historical interval between *The Draughtsman's Contract* and *Drowning By Numbers* is long, but we are still in rural southern England, still in gardens and country houses, and still watching women dispose of disappointing husbands by water while male professionals bond with apprentices and betray their callings. And for all the historical distance of the settlement of 1689, we can still see its traces in the film's presentation of its dreamy, feckless, childish, and yet thoroughly sympathetic representative of the professional and managerial classes. In the Britain of the *New Left Review* analysis, this is the social fraction that never had a chance, that was never allowed to keep its appointment with historical destiny. For Anthony Barnett, restating Perry Anderson's theses of 1964 in a polemical response to Thatcher's war in the Falklands,

> Historically dominated by financial capital located in the south, whose millionaires always outnumbered industrial barons, the British state was animated by those trained in an imperial rather than a domestic role, and in ledgers and in fields rather than in factories. The result has been a marked absence of a recognisable bourgeois political class, in any dominant sense – at once practical, realistic and – yes – businesslike. (1982: 53)

The impasse of British history is reiterated within the analysis itself, in the comedy of a marxism which speaks most forcefully for the bourgeoisie. The point of this for Greenaway is that such lovingly-detailed depictions of the shire gentry as *The Draughtsman's Contract* and of the shire petit-bourgeoisie as *Drowning By Numbers* take on a rather different significance if we think of Britain as a country in which the first of these classes has effectively compromised and subordinated the historical energy of the second.

In point of textual fact, however, that energy seems compromised and subordinated by women. If Virginia Herbert and Sarah Talmann are more interested in the physical than the artistic potency of Neville, the troika of Cissie Colpitts in *Drowning By Numbers* both echoes and outdoes them. Though in legal actuality we probably do not agree with capital punishment for infidelity and sexual indifference, in the dramatic experience of a film we nonetheless sympathise with Cissie Colpitts 1 and 2, who drown Jake and Hardy respectively for such crimes, and perhaps even with Cissie Colpitts 3, who drowns Bellamy for conspiring against her. That third murder is rendered more ritually, and thus we are more likely to notice the echo of *The Draughtsman's Contract*; Cissie 3 has no further use for Bellamy when she is sure she is pregnant, and reveals that she married him only in order to legitimise the child. Yet a film which for a while seems crypto-feminist in a black-comic way turns more troubling when the skipping girl is killed by a car, Smut hangs himself, and the inexorable logic of the Cissies proves determined to do away with Madgett.

Of course Greenaway is intent on a destabilisation of conventional dramatic expectations, and of course he continues to make a symbolic point, perhaps most directly with the game of dead man's catch, in which gender struggle is starkly formalised – all the men lose as the undertakers bear Jake's coffin across the playing field, and they must lie down in the winding sheet as the hearse moves off into the upper-right corner of the frame. Yet as this scene tends to suggest, the more pressing question in *Drowning By Numbers* is to what extent a formal principle can be understood as socially or psychologically over-determined.

In an attempt to answer this question, I will begin with the hardly surprising observation that Greenaway's films tend towards obsessionalism. Yet this issue has not so far been treated systematically, even if we count as symptomatic both the respectful and the reproachful comments of critics on the degree to which intellect animates the films. In what follows, then, I hope to analyse the obsessional aspect of *Drowning By Numbers* without crudely or arbitrarily diagnosing the text. As a first formulation, I would propose that the film makes ceremonials out of obsessional material, that it plays games with obsessional material, that it runs rings around obsessional material. To recognise that psychoanalysis thinks of games and ceremonials themselves as obsessional is an involution, but one appropriate to a film which signals a comic and detailed awareness of its own concerns.

For a first example of that awareness, we might look at two of Smut's waking-ceremonials, his game of 'reverse-strip jump' and the house of cards which may or may not fall before he wakes. Directly comparable with the sleep-ceremonials discussed by Freud in the classic psychoanalysis of obsessional behaviour, these are also quite different, even parodic; rather than a rigid sequence of obligatory observations attached to undressing and going to bed, they form a set of chance outcomes attached to getting up and getting dressed. Similarly, the film's whole catalogue of invented games provide a comic perspective on what Serge Leclaire (1980a) calls 'death in the life of the obsessional'. Games like dead man's catch and hangman's cricket, whose day-long manoeuvres are abruptly terminated when a player designated the loser is delivered to the hangman and the gravedigger, remind us that all games are to some extent obsessional and that familiar games establish a quite effective distance on that fact. Freud's essay on 'Obsessive Actions and Religious Practices' deals directly with the similarities and the differences between private and collective behaviour, an issue which becomes a motif in *Drowning By Numbers* – Hardy walks away from hangman's cricket in disgust that it is not a 'proper' game, Cissie Colpitts 2 remarks that Madgett plays dead man's catch as if it 'meant something', and a local detective construes Madgett's marking of Smut's body with coloured tape for his study of cricketing deaths as child abuse. Amusingly, Madgett himself remains capable of mystification at the obsessional behaviour of others; as the athletes go by, he asks 'What's all this running for?'

Even if it is not revelatory to remark on the obsessional aspect of Greenaway's films, we may still be surprised in reviewing the psychoanalytic literature to discover how much of both the anecdotal evidence and the theoretical elaborations resonate with Greenaway's work. In Leclaire's case of 'Jerome', we hear of the fascination of the obsessional with both the statuary and the photographs which recur in Greenaway, of his vulnerability to sympathetic stomach pains of the kind experienced by Kracklite in *The Belly of An Architect*, and of two symptoms shared by Smut in *Drowning By Numbers* (the fantasy of a 'late circumcision' and the impulse to commit suicide). In Leclaire's theoretical commentary, influenced by Lacan's revision of Freud, we learn that the obsessional devotes his life to death; he expresses the contradictions entailed in an effort to ally himself with death both by believing that he cannot die and by waiting for death, systematically temporising with his rituals and ceremonials, his counting and collecting. According to Freud, the obsessional remains in such a fix because his Oedipal wish for the death of his father so consumes him that he tries, impossibly and yet insistently, to identify with death. Instead of coming to terms with the symbolic otherness of paternity, which would cause him to accept mortality, to defer genital satisfaction and to identify with the father, he identifies with a mortality which he tries to mobilise against the father. For Jacques-Alain Miller, 'while the obsessional can be friends with death, he has trouble with love' (1988: 41).

In *Drowning By Numbers*, our senior male protagonist – a coroner, a professional specialist in death and regular attendant at the funerals of men killed by women – gets nowhere in his numerous romantic pursuits. Moreover, he betrays his calling because his desire is bound up with death. He is serially attracted to the three husband-murdering Cissies and is also suspected of a passion for the corpse; Cissie 2 asks him whether he has ever molested a corpse, and he replies that he once kissed an old lady (a grandmaternal imago), and that he once had trouble bringing himself to close the eyes of a beautiful young woman, that is, trouble in detaching himself from the gaze of life-in-death. His son, the 'little ghoul', is if anything even more identified with mortality, marking the deaths of birds, animals and humans with ceremonials involving numbers, fireworks, paint and Polaroid photographs. While Madgett is exclusively interested in women implicated with death, Smut, remarkably, has no mother either seen or mentioned in the film; thus he cannot answer the question of 'the relation of the mother to the father's word', a phrase from Lacan quoted in another study of the obsessional by Leclaire (1980b: 122). Smut tackles this issue by becoming interested in Rubens' *Samson and Delilah* and in the Bible story of the castrating woman from which it is taken, by interrogating his father on the issue of circumcision, and by attending to the skipping girl's report of her mother's opinion on the same issue. This mother is sexualised insofar as she seems to be a prostitute, and the question of her relation to the father's law is rendered at once quite literally (she is courted by a policeman) and with some subtlety (the police in *Drowning By Numbers* belong to the detective-fiction tradition which banalises quotidian law). At the same time, Smut seals the fate of the skipping girl by challenging the word of the mother, encouraging the girl to skip on the road, and then commits suicide when the police visit him with the news of her death.

According to Freud, obsessional neurosis distinguishes itself by repressing not content but connection, retaining the disturbing material in consciousness while defeating its emotional potential by erasing the logic which binds it together. This seems applicable enough to *Drowning By Numbers*, and yet equally applicable to many intellectually puzzling films. For a more specific answer to our original question of a film so blithe and yet so sombre, we turn to a point made by Charles Melman: the obsessional is not at first or of necessity troubled by his symptoms (1980: 132). Indeed, for the bulk of the film Madgett is a cheerful, avuncular eccentric; only when rejected by the third and final Cissie does he turn to attempted rape, gorging on blackberries, and the doleful declaration that he and his son are eunuchs. This reference to a lost virility suggests the extent to which a film which at first seems to be about vengeful women is actually predicated on the abstract perceptions of the male obsessional; from Madgett's vantage, women (like the three Cissies) are imposing but interchangeable figments, others (like the Bognor brothers) are distant but conspiratorial, and the self is barred from genital achievement by its fixation on mortality. Madgett is friendly with death; putting his shoes away as the rowboat sinks, he is the unemotional obsessional to the end. The framing arithmomania and supporting taxonomies of *Drowning By Numbers* weave through a fictional experience of obsessional desire, suggesting that all of Greenaway's grids, lexicons and encyclopedias are not simply affectless (as critics tend to say) but determinedly distanced from affect.

THE COOK, THE THIEF, HIS WIFE AND HER LOVER: THE SOCIAL CONSTRUCTION OF BODILY FUNCTION

Greenaway's *succès de scandale* is his most direct allegory of Thatcherism, since this is the film he describes to Gavin Smith as dealing with 'my anger and passion about the current British political situation' (1990: 55) and to Kathy Acker as representing the impact of 'an incredible vulgarian hypocrisy which slams anyone who makes radical sexual moves' (1990: 61). Acker enlarges enthusiastically on the idea that the thief Spica represents 'pure vulgarity', 'pure ... evil' (1990: 56), arguing that the figure of a loutish criminal upwardly mobile into restaurant ownership is an effective emblem of Thatcher's Britain. In the interview with Smith, Greenaway adds that Spica is a typical product of the new consumer economy, 'a man who knows the price of everything and the value of nothing' (1990: 55).

My account of *The Cook, The Thief, His Wife and Her Lover* will question this widely accepted view of the film. Noting that Greenaway and his two interviewers imagine politics in terms of the guild-values of artists and writers (Spica's crime is 'vulgarity' or lack of appreciation; Thatcher's is sexual repression), I will suggest that the film is symptomatic as much as analytic of Thatcherism. Thatcherism and Greenaway both respond to the historical impasse of the British middle classes, but

Peter Greenaway and Helen Mirren at work on *The Cook, The Thief, His Wife and Her Lover* (1989)

while Greenaway's earlier films are effectively critical of the situation, the proletarian monster central to *The Cook, The Thief, His Wife and Her Lover* suggests that this film has joined in Thatcher's vengeance on the imagined values of the lower social orders. Thus the film can be usefully compared with the more direct treatments of Thatcherism in British cinema (*My Beautiful Laundrette* (1985), *Sammy and Rosie Get Laid* (1987), *High Hopes* (1988)), and with the different type of allegory found in Dennis Potter's *The Singing Detective* (1986). These comparisons are not meant to twit Greenaway with the realist tradition he scorns, but to make the point that the question of Thatcherism is more likely to be answered by historical analysis than by left or liberal reaction. This point is sharpened by the New Left Review analysis of the whole history of the British state, by the remarks of Terry Eagleton quoted above, and by the various political calculations of Stuart Hall, Paul Hirst and Bob Jessop; it is blunted by Acker, whose progressive good intentions tend to stabilise and to demonise Thatcherism.

I stress Acker's *Village Voice* account of the film because it is a good index of the simultaneously rapturous and scandalised reception of *The Cook, The Thief, His Wife and Her Lover* by an American art-house audience well-versed in imaginary contests between a cultured middle class and a brutish lumpenproletariat, but much less clear that the thief and his wife's lover are not the only possible figures of their respective class-fractions. My point is not that Greenaway should set about producing positive images of the lower social strata, but that for American audiences the issue of Spica's identifying marks of class hardly exists; though the film occasions genuinely horrified reactions and even walkouts, these are prompted typically by the dog-shit smearing, vomiting, van of rotting flesh, and so on. If the film had been set in an allegorised New York, Spica might have been an African American. Such transatlantic class/race analogies are obviously imperfect, so the point may be quite unfair; yet it can still be quite suggestive.

Some might argue that because the figure of Spica is clearly allegorical, we should not imagine that his accent and manners refer directly to British social realities; in this view, Spica becomes a renovated version of the Brechtian idea of the entrepreneur as gangster, and is no more an affront to the working class than the Italian Americans of the *Godfather* films. The problem with this is the exclusively downward mobility of the metaphor; capitalism is identified for dramatic purposes with the gangster, an idea of criminality which is itself capitalist. In one sense, this manoeuvre responds keenly to the contradictions of the system; in another, it makes it only more difficult to think beyond them. At worst, the very excesses of the gangster tend to contain the critique; the fiction serves as a counterphobic or inoculatory device, suggesting not so much that capitalism is criminal but that criminal capitalists spoil things for everyone. Alternatively, one might suggest that the figure of Spica is no more prejudicial than the representatives of the gentry and the petit-bourgeoisie we have already met, that Greenaway's ironic taxonomies have moved with admirably consecutive logic through Britain's social order to arrive at the thief. Yet if Neville is naively arrogant, Mrs Herbert coldly calculating, Madgett obsessional and the Cissies murderous, all have sympathetic traits, in marked distinction from Spica, whose repellent characteristics are a triumph of Greenaway's impulse to catalogue: he is sadistic, bullying, nagging, crude, loud, callous, self-important, sanctimonious, anti-Semitic, racist, misogynist, homophobic, drunken, unlettered and possessed of

The title characters in *The Cook, the Thief, His Wife and Her Lover*

a poor French accent, all of which is only redoubled in the moments of bathos when he mourns his lack of children.

Having complicated the question of political interpretation, I want to introduce some thoughts on the stylistic values of this very striking film, beginning with the remedially exacting simplicities of its colour scheme, camera movement and treatment of space. The first of these has been widely remarked, prompted by Greenaway's own observation that the film is structured into zones corresponding to the sequence of colours in the visible spectrum (blue for the cold exterior of the parking lot, green for the productive interior of the kitchen, red for the central theatre of the restaurant, blinding white for the toilets, yellow for the hospital). Less noticed but equally obtrusive is a treatment of space almost didactic in its limited number of locations, limited number of shots and strong directional cues across cuts. The overall effect of the lateral tracking from one end to the other of the principal enclosure comprised of car park, kitchen, restaurant and bathroom is a modernist bravura, combining with the curtains at the opening and closing of the film and such depth cues as the fan on the rear wall of the kitchen to draw attention both to the theatricality of the pro-filmic space and the flatness of the projected image. However, the effect is more than simply modernist. The film reminds us that we are looking at a studio space temporarily and yet thoroughly made over into a restaurant; this is linked with a 1980s economy of consumption and entertainment in which fashionably transitory restaurants actually did colonise studio-like spaces, often staying in them for a period only slightly longer than the production of a film.

The film makes this link most explicit by beginning with the finishing touch of such a speculative transformation, the installation of the neon sign that will read 'Spica and Boarst'. At the same time, of course, this fairly trumpets the introduction of a whole range of semiotic and symbolic issues. These include the structural imperative (the figures carried in are A and O, the first letter of the alphabet and the zero), the intertext of other Greenaway films (*A Zed and Two Noughts* begins with Z and O and with advertising signs), an ongoing homage to Hollis Frampton (the *Magellan* cycle also begins with a large A), the continuing reference to art history (the thieves staggering along with the huge letters evoke the procession to Calvary), and the constellation of meanings contained in the name Spica; the anagram 'aspic', for example, condenses the film's themes of fine food and boorishness, while its transformation into 'a spic' signals the descent into ethnically stereotyped brutishness. Homophonically, and especially given the film's play with the Cockney tendency to add an 'r' to a final vowel, we may even be reminded of 'Mr Speaker', the bewigged parliamentarian of the British House of Commons, who is comparable with Spica in both the atavism of his dress and his authority over speech.

Similar in elementary elegance is the film's treatment of perspective; screen width predominates in the strong horizontals of the car park, kitchen and dining-room, but is broken up by the confined spaces of assignation between the lovers. Contrasted with this is an occasional strongly marked depth-of-field, as at the book depository. These variations also suggest a psychological distribution of space, with Spica lording it over the banquet table at the film's centre, the lovers cowering in the various enclosures to the right and left, and the book depository with its depth and distance from the restaurant serving as a haven. This distribution, in turn, supports the film's treatment of the social construction of bodily functions. Spica's ravenous vengeance on fine food includes the spoiling of special dishes served to Georgina and Michael, the company of 'associates' who vomit and belch, and a déclassé mother who hopes the restaurant will serve a bottle of Chianti in raffia; it further extends to his terroristic intrusions into bathroom and kitchen, including the symbolic ones which lead him to ask Georgina why she was so long and whether she has washed her hands. The last suggests a sanctimoniousness surprising in someone whose first action is to smear dog-shit and piss on a victim, but Spica is a polymorphous tyrant; he rules dictatorially over the orifices, combining physical savagery ('I'll make you shit through your dick'), physical restraint ('No smoking, Georgina') and physical possession ('that's my property') in the service of his personal authority. However, he remains (like Madgett, another banqueter) barred from genital sexuality. Thus the encounters of the lovers, confined to larders, freezers and toilet stalls, are brutally parodied by Spica in his beating of Georgina in the car and the reported sadism of his bedroom. The figure of symbolic paternity whose absence animates the patrician landscapes of *The Draughtsman's Contract* and whose presence is systematically depreciated in the gardens and meadows of *Drowning By Numbers* returns with shocking vengeance to the vivid interiors of *The Cook, The Thief, His Wife and Her Lover*. This drama of the body was, of course, the aspect of the film which drew the American NC-17 rating, scandalised the more decorous of art-house patrons, and attracted larger audiences than any previous Greenaway film. In closing, I want to suggest that the film's most precise relationship with Thatcherism lies not in the politically questionable class relationships it depicts, but in the fashionable audience it constitutes and discovers; this last (the baby-boom professional and managerial class, arts and media division) was by the end of the 1980s quite familiar with sumptuary restaurants where bookish critics mingled with semi-criminal entrepreneurs, and yet residually uneasy with that very familiarity.

The British context of a capitalism pioneered by a patrician caste complicates the social definition of the middle-classes, who failed to place their own stamp on the polity, instead merging with the gentry during the eighteenth and nineteenth centuries. Thus, *The Draughtsman's Contract*, *Drowning By Numbers* and *The Belly of An Architect* all deal with the dilemmas of a professional stratum which is socially progressive but politically ineffectual. From the point of view of this frustrated segment of society, Albert Spica represents a final insult and inspires a fantasy of revenge. Spica is himself a problem in social definition since he is lumpen and capitalist at once, vividly illustrating the mobility of political signifiers in 'authoritarian populism', Stuart Hall's (1988) term for Thatcherism. In sum, if the social disgust of the film enlarges wildly on the moral culpability of the working-class reactionary, its political acuteness lies in mobilising a middle-class audience which itself spent the 1980s feasting and trying to repress social questions. To be fair, Kathy Acker does recognise this last point as the basis of a liberatory potential in Greenaway. Yet with the replacement of both Thatcher and Reagan by more discreet acolytes, and the media of the 1990s full of superficial breast-beating about the excesses of the 1980s, the reception of the film as a critique of consumerism is another response that seems to be characterised more by ideological fashion than by historical understanding.

I began this essay with a provisional but (I hope) workable distinction between a period of experimental filmmaking and a period of art-house feature making. I want to conclude with a similarly provisional distinction between Greenaway's films of the 1980s and his subsequent work. Of course there are many, many continuities. *The Man in the Bath* (2001) could easily have been made in that wateriest of all Greenaway's watery decades, the 1980s, which saw not only *Drowning By Numbers* but also *The Sea in Their Blood* (1983), *26 Bathrooms* (1985) and *Death in the Seine* (1988). Meanwhile, *Prospero's Books* (1991), *The Pillow Book* (1995) and *8½ Women* (1999) all ring the changes on Greenaway's established fascination with a professional who is led by desire to abandon or betray his calling.

Even so, *The Cook, The Thief, His Wife and Her Lover* writes *finis* to a period in Greenaway's work that does fairly consistently sketch out an alternative cultural history of Britain. *Prospero's Books* and *8½ Women* (especially the former) take us to a more purely imaginary Britain; both are films in which the action struggles to escape from a substantial house which is also a social enclave, yet neither has the bite of the obviously comparable *The Draughtsman's Contract*. *The Cook, The Thief, His Wife and Her Lover* remains Greenaway's last film to date set in a recognisably contemporary urban Britain, which is also to say his last film meaningfully resistant to the understanding of his work in terms of the 'baroque', the 'postmodern' and the 'global'. That reading of course claims the film, as it claims all of Greenaway's films, and it has much of interest to offer. But as must by now be obvious, I have chosen a critical path more informed by social, political and psychoanalytic questions.

Author's note: A review of Greenaway's film and video production since 1989 shows that only four of more than twenty efforts are regular feature films; the profusion of short films, videos and films for television, as well as the giganticism of the current project, *The Tulse Luper Suitcases*, suggests a return to the longer works of his earlier career.

WORKS CITED

Acker, Kathy (1990) 'The Colour of Myth: The World according to Peter Greenaway', *Village Voice*, 17 April, 61–7.

Anderson, Perry (1964) 'Origins of the Present Crisis', *New Left Review*, 23 (January–February).

____ (1987) 'The Figures of Descent', *New Left Review*, 161 (January–February), 20–77.

Barnett, Anthony (1982) 'Iron Britannia', 134 (July–August), 596.

Brown, Geoff (2000) 'Something for Everyone: British Film Culture in the 1980s', in Robert Murphy (ed.) *British Cinema of the 90s*. London: Britiah Film Institute, 27–36.

Burch, Noël (1990) *Life to Those Shadows*. Berkeley: University of California Press.

Eagleton, Terry (1991) *Ideology: An Introduction*. London: Verso.

Freud, Sigmund (1955 [1909]) 'Notes upon a Case of Obsessional Neurosis', in *Standard Edition of the Complete Psychological Works of Sigmund Freud*, vol. 10. London: Hogarth, 153–250.

____ (1958 [1911]) 'Psychoanalytic Notes upon an Autobiographical Account of a Case of Paranoia (Dementia Paranoides)', in *Standard Edition of the Complete Psychological Works of Sigmund Freud*, vol. 12. London: Hogarth, 182.

____ (1959 [1907]) 'Obsessive Actions and Religious Practices', in *Standard Edition of the Complete Psychological Works of Sigmund Freud*, vol. 11. London: Hogarth, 115–28.

Hall, Stuart (1988) *The Hard Road to Renewal: The Crisis of Thatcherism*. London: Verso.

Hill, Christopher (1961) *The Century of Revolution: 1603–1714*. New York: Norton.

____ (1980) *Some Intellectual Consequences of the English Revolution*. Madison: University of Wisconsin Press.

Hirst, Paul (1989) *After Thatcher*. London: Collins.

Jessop, Bob, Kevin Bonnett, Simon Bromley and Tom Ling (1988) *Thatcherism: A Tale of Two Nations*. Cambridge, England: Polity Press.

Leclaire, Serge (1980a) 'Jerome, or Death in the Life of the Obsessional', in Stuart Shneiderman (ed.) *Returning to Freud: Clinical Psychoanalysis in the School of Lacan*. New Haven: Yale University Press, 94–113.

____ (1980b) 'Philo, or the Obsessional and his Desire', in *Returning to Freud: Clinical Psychoanalysis in the School of Lacan*. New Haven: Yale University Press, 114–29.

Melman, Charles (1980) 'On Obsessional Neurosis', in Stuart Shneiderman (ed.) *Returning to Freud: Clinical Psychoanalysis in the School of Lacan*. New Haven: Yale University Press, 130–8.

Miller, Jacques-Alain (1988) 'H20: Suture in Obsessionality', trans. Bruce Fink. Lacan Study Notes 69, 34–44.

Nairn, Tom (1964a) 'The English Working Class', *New Left Review*, 24 (March–April).

____ (1964b) 'The Anatomy of the Labour Party', *New Left Review* 26 (September–October).

____ (1979) *The Break-up of Britain*. London: New Left Books.

Sitney, P. Adams (1979) *Visionary Film*, second edition. Oxford: Oxford University Press.

____ (1990) '*The Falls*', *Persistence of Vision*, 8, 45–51.

Smith, Gavin (1990) 'Food for Thought', *Film Comment*, 26, 3, 54–61.

van Wert, William E. (1990/91) 'Review of *The Cook, The Thief, His Wife and Her Lover*', *Film Quarterly*, 44, 2, 42–50.

18. PRIVATE PRACTICE, PUBLIC HEALTH: THE POLITICS OF SICKNESS AND THE FILMS OF DEREK JARMAN

Chris Lippard and Guy Johnson

There's no place like the HOME-movie.
> – Derek Jarman

Health for me is more than being not-yet-dead. It's not something you patrol; it's something you must forget to patrol or it's not any sort of health at all.
> – Adam Mars-Jones, 'Remission' (1987)

It is vital to underline yet again that art is the spark between private lives and the public.
> – Derek Jarman

The 'private function' that provides both the title and the narrative climax of Malcolm Mowbray's 1984 film set in postwar Yorkshire is ostensibly the pork dinner that Dr Swaby (Denholm Elliot) and his allies in the town's privileged classes will throw to honour Britain's newly married royal couple.[1] The title, however, refers not only to this single event but also to a social practice and an institution just then being converted from a private to a public function. In November 1946 the newly elected Labour government passed an act of Parliament creating Britain's National Health Service (NHS) – a response to, perhaps a reward for, the trauma of the just-won war. It established that medical consultation and treatment should be free to all and that health was a public issue. A Private Function (1984) sets up an opposition between Swaby, the upper-class medical man, and the town chiropodist, Gilbert Chilvers (Michael Palin). We first see Swaby blithely engaged in crossing names off the list of invitees to the private function; in the adjoining room, Chilvers works diagnosing chilblains and scraping at hard skin. His work with feet – and women's feet at that – puts Chilvers on the lowest rung of the medical ladder and makes him the focus of Swaby's contemptuous annoyance: 'Why we need chiropodists, I don't know: something wrong with their feet, people can come to me. They'd always find a sympathetic hearing', he declares petulantly.

But in fact this is just what Swaby does not want to happen. The threat of a new public health system that allows free access to doctors and attempts to abolish the exclusive right of the privileged class to be 'well treated' clearly challenges his prestigious social position. Vexed by the theft of the pig he had been fattening for consumption at the private function, Swaby lets fly at postwar British society: 'Of course, practical socialism, that's what it's going to be like now ... what's mine is yours. What a nasty piss-stained country this is ... It's like this new health service. Do you realise that any little poorly pillock is now going to be able to knock on my door and say I'm ill, treat me. Anybody! Me!'

Arrogant and patronising, Dr Swaby is the villain of the piece, a medical man who boasts of having no feelings and ridicules Chilvers for his qualms about butchering the pig. But such sentiments are not the common British perception of the medical profession. Indeed, what Swaby here predicts developed under the NHS into a system whereby general practitioners (GPs) typically became family doctors dispensing prescriptions and a reliable 'bedside manner'. These doctors were the point at which an ill public first encountered the human face of a state system that gave the poor(ly) an equal chance at the best attention available in the land. Thus in Britain, for a whole generation, the idea of health became firmly linked to a conception of the state as a caring institution that provided for its people's physical well-being.

In the 1980s, however, the notion of private, rather than public, functions took on renewed pertinence, so it remains possible to read the analysis of social class and medical practice found in *A Private Function* as commentary on Margaret Thatcher's radically free-market policies and gradual re-privatisation of many of the industries taken into public ownership at the end of the war. In due course, the National Health Service, too, came up for review. Unlike other postwar nationalisations, however, the Health Service had developed the status of a consensus issue, so when the government published its white paper, 'Working for Patients', at the end of January 1989, both the British Medical Association and most of the British population – the consumers, the prospective patients – reacted adversely.[2] The Queen's speech to Parliament in November 1989 announced that 'a bill will be brought forward to improve the National Health Service and the management of community care'.[3] At the end of June 1990, the NHS and Community Care Bill became law, offering GPs the chance to manage their own budgets and hospitals the opportunity to abandon the NHS in favour of a self-governing status where they might compete for custom by offering patient services more attractive than those of rival institutions. In line with its advocacy of self-reliance, the Thatcher government also sought to put 'the utmost importance on caring for people in their own home' (Anon. 1990: 179). The future of the National Health Service was now up for debate and polls consistently show that access to a reliable NHS remains a key concern of the British electorate today.

Issues of health and illness have long preoccupied British filmmakers. In the 1950s and 1960s, for example, the hospital setting, with its potential for undressing, disturbed bodily functions and hierarchies ripe for toppling, offered the long-running series of *Carry On* films the ideal setting for their sexual innuendo and puncturing of pomposity (Johnson 1983). Jack Gold's film version of Peter Nicholls' *The National Health* plowed the same furrow in 1973. In the Thatcher era, Lindsay Anderson, who previously dissected the British institution of the public school in *If...* (1968),[4] focused his attention on the hospital as an ideal microcosm of a class-riddled, self-serving society. Anderson's *Britannia Hospital* (1982) tells the story of a day in the life of a hospital on the occasion of a royal visit, a series of strikes by the support staff, and the megalomaniac head surgeon's attempted completion of a new Frankenstein-style composite man. Anderson's hospital functions as a clear allegory for a sick, deluded country, one strangled by a useless monarchy, a cruel and insensitive Prime Minister and a work-shy labour force. His film uses the hospital to attach itself to the same stereotypical class markers as, say, the Carry On series. But though it may be as vicious a critique of Thatcherism as any in British film, Britannia Hospital offers little alternative space for either social progress or cinematic practice.[5]

The 1980s, which began with Colin Welland's cry, as he picked up the Oscar for Chariots of Fire (1981), that 'the British are coming',[6] were marked by alternating declamations of British cinema's health or sickness, and in 1985 Alexander Walker applied Anderson's title to his assessment of the state of the film industry in Britain. Walker concludes his survey of the current practices of British film production, National Heroes, with a section 'Renaissance or Remission?' in which he speculates about whether signs of healthy life in the quality of domestic features in the first half of the decade will sufficiently outweigh the difficulties of production in the UK. His final words tend toward the pessimistic: in these years 'Britannia Hospital was still open for business: but that perpetual patient, the British film industry, needed to have a lot of faith in the doctors treating it' (1985: 272).

At the beginning of 1988 the metaphor of contagion resurfaced in the national press when Oxford historian and regular Thatcher adviser Norman Stone took Britain's sick cinema to task in the review section of the archly conservative Sunday Times. Stone contrasts the 'sick scenes from English life' that he finds in the work of a 'worthless and insulting ... farrago of films' (1988: C1–2) with the work of Britain's cinema of quality, past (Lean, Powell, Reed, Saturday Night and Sunday Morning (1960)) and present (A Passage to India (1984), Hope and Glory (1987)). Stone accuses the 'sick', pessimistic films of a 'two-dimensional ideology', lack of plot and no sense of tradition. In passing, he betrays a streak of homophobia, as, surveying the contents of his chosen few, he writes that 'there is much explicit sex, a surprising amount of it homosexual and sadistic'. At the head of the first page of Stone's article rests a still from Derek Jarman's The Last of England (1987): a hooded figure points a machine gun at a few huddled figures gathered on the side of one of London's abandoned docks. Jarman's film exemplifies all the sickness Stone finds in the cinema, and he concludes his section by acknowledging that 'I do not really know what this film is about and fear that its director is all dressed up with nowhere to go.'

In the following week's paper, Jarman responded to Stone, arguing that, as a 46-year-old director, his films were, in fact, a part of British film history and tradition. He points out that two of his six films (The Tempest (1979) and The Angelic Conversation (1985)) have been inspired by Shakespeare;[7] but more important, perhaps, he argues against Stone's view of Britishness – 'all beefeaters and hollyhocks' – in order to defend the decay that permeates The Last of England as an accurate reflection of Thatcher's Britain.[8] In this essay, we choose to retain and reclaim Stone's term for Jarman's cinema: its 'sickness' is a crucial part of its practice. Refusing Stone's and Thatcher's sense of a healthy Britain and a healthy film practice, Jarman attempts to 're-fuse' an active, critical, contaminated cinema of formal experimentation and social critique, one which is both intensely private and wilfully public.

As Thatcher came to power in 1979, another filmic experimenter, Peter Greenaway, was completing The Falls, his three-hour 'medical survey' of a cross section of the 19 million people in Britain suffering from the Violent Unknown Event (VUE). His film details, in 92 segments, the various infections and strangely disturbed bodies of all those in the VUE directory whose names begin with the letters 'F-A-L-L'. Greenaway's project was an elaborate fiction, a postmodern creation of an alternate, parallel world of humans become birds, water, speakers of exotic languages and, indeed, immortals. At the same time in New York and Los Angeles, doctors were noticing the oddity of a series of deaths in the gay population from a skin cancer, Kaposi's sarcoma – the first step toward the identification of a previously unknown and terribly violent disease: the AIDS virus. By the time *The Last of England* was released Jarman had been diagnosed as HIV-positive. The greatest threat to public health in the Thatcher decade had arrived in the body of the anti-Thatcher cinema.[9]

In 1975 Derek Jarman filmed the killing of a pig. In *Sebastiane*, a group of naked Roman soldiers banished to a remote Mediterranean island spear a boar in counterpoint to the delirious ravings of one of their number, Sebastiane. He is pegged out on the sand to suffer the heat of the murderous sun, having refused the seduction of the centurion. In this film the impalement and laceration undergone by the pig points out a larger pattern of meaning, as the film's climax displays Sebastiane half flayed, tied to a pole and shot through with arrows that crucify him. The ecstasy etched onto the facial close-up evokes innumerable classical renditions of Christ's agony, and Jarman's slow-motion effects foreground both the static, pictorial nature of the composition and the filmic medium that depicts it.

Jarman's earliest and least-shown film bears some important motifs and ideas to be reconfigured in his later work. At its heart is the idea of the suffering (male) body, which we see here impaled against a pole, cut and sliced, imagining another, better place. In Jarman's films the recurrence of the body seen in various degrees of suffering is richly significant, and it may be explored in two ways: first, to understand how the suffering body grounds the narratives of the films, such that the stories told in them are never far from bodies in pain; and second, to examine how a filmmaking practice of stories shaped by suffering offers an opportunity to see the larger issues at work in the interplay of health, sexuality and storytelling. It is across these three areas that the condition of AIDS is stretched, and within which Jarman's films articulate a personal understanding of disease.

Suffering male bodies recur in Jarman's work: in *Caravaggio* (1986), the painter (Nigel Terry) is dying and stabs and is stabbed by his lover, Ranuccio (Sean Bean); *The Last of England* echoes with gunfire and shows us the execution of a young man; *War Requiem* (1989) mourns and re-images the slaughter of an entire generation of young men; in *The Garden* (1990), the male lovers are flayed and the filmmaker appears in a hospital bed. Derek Jarman carries the AIDS virus, suffers from its effects, and came close to death during the production of his films. Rather than respect a distance between the filmmaker's private life and his public text, Jarman encourages us to compare the two. 'I feel I have to write this book, coughing and spitting with bloody bronchitis', Jarman writes later of the notes that accompany *The Last of England* (1987: 66).

The idea of production under pressure saturates *Caravaggio*, shot on a strictly-controlled budget within the confines of an old London docklands warehouse. The film is a biography of the Renaissance painter celebrated for his use of a 'cinematic' lighting scheme, the life-story of a gay artist negotiating the patronage of the powerful while always pressed to the margins. It begins and ends in a hospital at Porto Ercole where Caravaggio lays dying. The sickness that seizes him involves the fetching up of his body's fluids, hawked up in spasms that rip the fabric of his still life. From the death-bed, the film builds a biography as a collection of flashbacks diluted from the paintings of Caravaggio's career, and the story flows between these reconstituted scenes as they re-stage the familiar paintings. Incoherence is built into the text, and it is Jarman's accompanying book that provides much-needed 'plot' information. But while the film is a delirious one, driven by the ebbing life-force of the painter, a definite logic governs the narrative that can be traced back to the suffering body at its centre.

Caravaggio is dying, and he endures pain of many colours. Feverish through much of the film, stabbed, afforded no other embrace than those of the people whose deaths he causes, the painter of 'wounded paintings' fades out, dissolving to nothing. He fights the draining of his vital spirit with the ejaculations of remembered desire for his adolescent lover, Pasqualone. The film is pressed out from the concen-trate of the paintings, mixed up from the paste of scenes, governed and grounded by a continual and regular return to the deathbed of the master painter who suffers a series of hallucinations.

A set of dissolves between paintings is also about cuts, or slashes. Thus a partic-ular importance is attached to Caravaggio's knife and to the stabbings in the film, the wounding and daubing of blood on flesh that match the painter's smearing paint onto canvases. This fusion of images occurs particularly at the moments when Ranuccio delivers Caravaggio a stigmata-like wound in a brawl, and in Caravaggio's betrayal of Ranuccio. In the second incident, Caravaggio looks squarely into the face of the one he has painted and loved, and delivers a final, slashing stroke.

Under the sign of suffering, the film text stands in a relation to both realism and to the visual style of Caravaggio's paintings. In reproducing scenes from the painter's canon the film, rather than simply duplicating the originals, gives the sense of an entirely painted world that at certain moments nudges up against the configurations of people and props familiar from the artist's compositions. Yet the visual style is not entirely coherent: regular disturbances destabilise consistency throughout the film. Rather than disrupting a stylistic convention, Ranuccio tending his motorcycle, the Vatican financier tapping a golden calculator and the critic, Baglione, seen at his typewriter become part of a visual pattern marked by instability. The effect is at the core of Jarman's work, promoting a positive sense of incoherence in which the disease of the text becomes linked to the disease (and suffering) of the artist.

This sense of pleasing jarring occurs similarly on the soundtrack in the film, when the hubbub of an antiquated PA system and the distant sound of a steam train do not dissolve the realism of Renaissance Italy but assert a filmic region less tethered in time and space. 'A-sad-reflection-of-our-time' types the critic Baglione, Marat-like in his bath, attacking Caravaggio by identifying a poisonous excess to his paintings, as if the oozings of form and reference might contaminate the body of Rome.[10] Jarman grounds the slippery realism of the film in the confined space of the dying painter: this is the operating theatre of a deteriorating body and mind. The mark of this collapse is felt not only at the visual level but in relation to the narrative thrust of consecutive scenes: the clinical and mental processes of the dying man are linked to the scene-building in the text. Baglione shudders out invective against Caravaggio and throws himself back in blissful relief. This action is cut to Caravaggio in his death

Jerusaleme (Spencer Leigh) watches the knife fight between Caravaggio (Nigel Terry) and Ranuccio (Sean Bean) in *Caravaggio* (1986)

rattle, himself reclined and panting, seeking release in a remembered fantasy of ejaculation with Pasqualone. The sequence ends in the ecstatic transfer of seed and spirit into death and beyond, leaving all exhausted. Jarman's biography foregrounds the body under pressure, its products variously toxic, sexual, written, painted and always vital.

In *The Last of England*, it is the body of England itself that is seen to be sick, and the film attempts a similarly energetic and positive diagnosis of a nation under the malaise of eight years of Thatcher government. 'What proof do you need the world's curling up like an autumn leaf?' asks the narrator. More desperate and bleaker than previous work, *The Last of England* proceeds according to the vague logic of a set of situations or set-pieces, shot mostly in and around the now-derelict parts of London's docklands. It is scored and over-voiced by nonsynchronous sound and the reading of verses that match a sense of destitution caught by the camera. Just as the film takes place in the realm before or after narrative sense, so it refuses the technology of 35mm sound cinema; it is shot, instead, on Super-8, with processed, found and home footage. The result is a wildly 'personal' film that implicates Jarman as a kind of cinematic archaeologist delving into a lost past, someone seeking an irredeemable place amid the shards of contemporary ruin. 'Super-8 is a documentary camera', says Jarman. 'It's very close to the body' (quoted in Charity 1991: 57). Jarman celebrates the endurance and fundamentally nostalgic quality of Super-8 in the film itself by revealing a freshly unearthed skeleton, found peering through the viewfinder of this more intimate camera.

Jarman's resistance to the terms of mainstream cinema sights him as a target for the establishment critic precisely because he declines the stories and the equipment of traditional British cinema. This refusal to work in the mainstream of cinema is crucial in relation to Jarman's situation as a gay/queer artist,[11] one engaged on the one hand in filmic expression and on the other in a sexual practice increasingly associated with disease and under pressure to be silent.[12] Jarman's films, in as much as they centre around suffering and in the light of the filmmaker's own susceptibility to illness, encourage a comparison between the operations and theatres of sickness and those of cinema.

In the absence of exact medical knowledge about the disease, AIDS has long been discussed in terms infected by the fear of and prejudice toward the practices of those infected. In the case of gay men, attention is turned to (sexual) practices rather than to the strictly medical symptoms of the disease, and a false logic of deserved suffering is engaged. Paula Treichler (1988) refers to 'an epidemic of signification', suggesting that the threat of AIDS is as much a narrative issue as a medical one. Simon Watney (1988) describes the logic by which homophobia translates a medical disaster into a political process of identifying and segregating a category of people whose sickness is conceived as punishment. Both writers imply the need to address the terms of the framework that AIDS occupies: the combination of the mystery surrounding the virus and the volatility of feeling towards groups seen as outsiders. In Pratiba Parmar's documentary *Reframing AIDS* (1988), specific count is made of the implicit agendas that underlie the fear and confusion and the film makes it clear how the experience of AIDS delineates the degree of British society's dependence on heterosexuality and, by extension, on the family and the home. Jarman's film, about gay men, for whom all of these options are problematic, made at a time when government urging was to return the responsibility for health 'to the community', is most interesting in its scrutiny of the home, and of those people excluded from this domain.[13]

Frantic and dismembered, *The Last of England* manically tries to recapture and refuse aspects of the past, of homes now rendered redundant and unworkable. Shots of his own childhood, lived in the quasi-prisons of military housing, echo the dereliction of the abandoned housing estates, which themselves point up the destitution of a society where sick people live amid hospital wards vacant for want of funds to staff them.[14] Throughout the film there is a simmering desperation ('the ice in your glass is radioactive') that occasionally ignites into images, as in the depiction of the harassment of the new groups of nomads and dispossesseds that populate Thatcher's Britain. *The Last of England* thus suffers under a political sickness, inscribed on the body of England, on its architecture and landscape, and more directly, onto the bodies of those excluded (from health, from homes, from jobs) under a regime that would make (private) patients of us all. But it is also a beautiful film: Jarman suggests that sickness need not be shackled to images and terms of weakness and stigma, but may empower a different register of social and artistic health.

'After *The Last of England,* someone came up and said, this film tells the story of my life. Well, who was I to say that it didn't?' (Jarman quoted in Romney 1991: 13). Where *Caravaggio* tries to tell a story under pressure, Jarman's next film abandons the attempt. This immediate lack of a clear narrative has been seen as the mark of its sickness. Jarman's remark makes it clear that a lack of coherence provides a certain democratic effect, but it also suggests a questioning of the power relations behind the idea of 'traditional narrative'. The frenetic manner of *The Last of England* marks not only the bodies under pressure that have made and appear in it, but also suggests a similarly diseased, pressurised spectator. Jarman's 'home movie' speaks of a disrupted homeland that repels those who seek order and coherence, but crucially vouchsafes an alternative way of making sense for those who similarly feel themselves to be 'under pressure', uneasy or subjected. The Last of England, then, in its violent, confrontational and disjointed imagery, is not only sick but sickening. Jarman's film, made as he discovered the fragility of his own health, and most graphically describing the political and architectural dereliction of Britain, points up how the idea of sickness is used in a power struggle between the sick and the well, the strong and the excluded, as it suggests the ways in which the term can be redeployed.

Asked why he has not made a film specifically about HIV or AIDS, Jarman responded that such a film would be sentimental and that, in any case, the illness would be impossible to image. 'The best thing is to be talking about it alongside the work', he argues (ibid.) and this he does in many newspaper interviews and as a 'guest' on British radio's 'In the Psychiatrist's Chair' (Jarman 1990).[15] The first film made entirely after his diagnosis, however, needs little displacement to be seen as an imaging of the AIDS crisis. War Requiem, a story of the deaths of some young men and the mourning that accompanies them, is structured by the music of a gay composer and incorporates the verse of a (probably) gay victim of the war. Jarman's film provides a visual accompaniment to Benjamin Britten's War Requiem (first performed in Coventry Cathedral in May 1962). Britten's work embraces many of the poems written at the front by Wilfred Owen during World War One, and Jarman depicts an Owen figure (Nathaniel Parker) together with an unknown British soldier (Owen Teale) and a German (Sean Bean). All die during the film. Their stories are interwoven with those of their mourners, a function largely the province of women: the mothers of Owen and the enemy soldier (Patricia Hayes, Rohan McCullough) and a nurse (Tilda Swinton) who also seems to be Owen's sister.

Perhaps the most daring shot in the film is a nearly seven-minute, almost static, medium shot of the nurse grieving for the dead Owen. She twists and braids her hair, rocks her body back and forth, runs her hands over her face and hugs herself, expressing both despair and rapture as she responds to the mood of the music. The spectator, watching her intently private albeit highly aesthetised mourning, is held up, like the narrative, by the suspended camera. Earlier in the film, we witness Owen's own mourning after he disturbs a snowball fight between the other two soldiers, leading to their deaths in a scene that provides a re-enactment of the knifing of Ranuccio by Caravaggio. In what Jarman refers to as 'the moral climate of clause 28' (1989: 34), War Requiem publicly offers a space for a mourning that, as Simon Watney and Douglas Crimp have argued, is not readily available to gay men in our society (Watney 1987: 7–8; Crimp 1988: 7).[16]

Just as Jarman's camera rests unflinchingly on grief, it also shows us horrific scenes of dismemberment and excruciating pain in the inserted documentary footage from near-contemporary conflicts in Afghanistan and Cambodia. Again, Jarman revives a historical narrative (of the Somme) and contaminates it with current political and social dimensions. That the AIDS virus has created war conditions in Britain is materially expressed by Jarman's filming War Requiem in the newly abandoned hospital at Darenth Park in Kent. Its anonymous winding corridors and ready supply of empty spaces allow Jarman, who had already spun Renaissance Italy out of a Thames-side warehouse, to stage a war in adjoining rooms. Its setting, resonant of a decline in public health facilities, continues the demand for attention to physical suffering that pervades the earlier films.

In contrast with *War Requiem*, critics quickly identified the next film, the one widely expected, as the work of a dying man, to be his last, *The Garden*, as an AIDS allegory.[17] *The Garden* continues Jarman's practice of re-fusing the home movie by setting his work at home: in and around the rocky beach garden he culti-vates behind his cottage at Dungeness on the Kent coast. References to gardens are strewn through Jarman's writings and indeed his films. *Jubilee* (1977) begins in the royal gardens of Elizabeth I, to which a modern-day alternative is later offered when we see Max, a mercenary, in his garden of artificial plants. Max, concerned that all the massive weapons of destruction the world has compiled are going to waste, declares that his 'idea of a perfect garden is a remembrance poppy field'. *The Angelic Conversation* (1984) comes to rest finally in the garden of Montacute House where one of the lovers whom the film tracks discovers a lily pond and 'sees memory in it' (Jarman 1987: 143). In *The Last of England*, the home-movie footage is mostly shot on the lawn. *War Requiem* opens with the old soldier (Laurence Olivier) convalescing in the hospital garden; later, in flashback, his nurse remembers her past happiness sowing seeds in the company of her mother and dead brother. Near the end of his life, Jarman published a lavishly-illustrated collection of writings about the beach-garden, while, as a horticulturalist, he attracted a new audience to come to Dungeness to admire his work.[18]

The space of the garden thus accrues a set of resonances in Jarman's cinema. It is a place for the recovery of both health and memories and in *The Garden* becomes the central metaphor for another dig at British society. For Jarman one of the advan-tages of buying the small house in the lee of one of Britain's oldest and best-known nuclear power plants at Dungeness appears to be the opportunity to create his own strange garden and eventual film set. Jarman's gardening, his filmmaking and his illness are integrated in a film that is also a landscape in the tradition of the nine-teenth-century English painter Turner,[19] another vision of Britain and a place for his own recuperation. Dungeness Beach serves for a new Gethsemane set by the sea in Kent, itself known as the Garden of England. The metaphorically-charged concept of the garden provides fertile ground for contending with the proliferating discourse that surrounds the AIDS epidemic.

In *The Last of England* book Jarman describes the thirty plastic pots that served him as a primitive garden in London. Under constant attack from pigeons, his plants suffer but, he writes, 'it doesn't stop me. Like all true gardeners I'm an optimist' (1987: 151). It is an ill but optimistic filmmaker who sets out to displace our traditional notions of home and garden in his work. Even the hospital is moved onto the beach, as we see Jarman – in scenes of stunning beauty – lying on a metal-framed NHS-like bed set on the damp sands. Water laps at its feet, while flare-carrying men and women circle the patient. It is as if Jarman desires to imitate Caravaggio's seaside death at Porto Ercole in a magical private world totally remote from the decrepit buildings of, say, Darenth Park. *The Garden* remains an intensely personal film; despite the fact that its director's sick body allowed him perhaps less control over the final product than ever before, Jarman is more present than ever. Early on, as he ponders in his garden, we hear a woman's voice call: 'Derek.' He is a gardener and a cameraman, following close

The 'Christ-couple' kissed on the feet, in *The Garden* (1990)

behind his subject with his Super-8; he is a writer slumped at his desk; and he is the bed-ridden, curled up body. With the director unable fully to care for the film, the film elects to care for him.

The Garden, tight with Christian imagery, features two lovers who sometimes stand in for Christ – although there is also a more conventionally-coded Christ figure in robe and beard. The taunting and torture of these figures in the film forges a link between the established Christian church and the homophobia that causes so much suffering. In his *War Requiem* book Jarman writes out what might stand as a dedication to his next film: 'To all those cast out, like myself, from Christendom. To my friends who are dying in a moral climate created by a church with no compassion' (1989: 35). Using the Christian myth as a reference point, *The Garden* tracks the homophobia of British life and lays it bare. The British society that Thatcher has crafted is one that does not care, a garden that has not been tended, a 'piss-stained' country of the small-minded. Denholm Elliot's Swaby would again feel at home in a sick society where films such as Jarman's can only be produced under many pressures. Thus, we witness the turmoil of the film's making more fully here than before: arc lights flare and instructions are shouted as the film begins, and the whirring of the camera motor accompanies the Super-8 footage. Jarman magnifies these records of filmic surveillance by the oft-repeated shot of the revolving arm of the tracking station that overlooks his beach-garden.[20] Its circular motion is picked up early in the film by twelve women, sitting at the table of a last supper, whose fingers circle the rims of their glasses; later these two movements are further elaborated by intercutting images of what looks like a carousel and of Tilda Swinton carrying a ladder in a sweep of dizzying power. Non-narrative film, perhaps, has to circle around the issues because it pursues what *The Garden*'s voiceover calls 'a journey without direction, [of] no certainty'. Near the end of the film, however, we do find a direct expression of both anger and grief. A voiceover laments: 'I walk in this garden holding the hands of dead friends. Old age came quickly for my generation: they died so silently ... I have no words. My shaking hands cannot express my fury. My sadness is all I have.'

But *The Garden also* remains full of fun and hope, a film reflecting the mood of a man who fantasised himself as Thatcher's minister of horticulture, a kind of national gardener in tune with his Prime Minister's thinking because each hates pinks – both flower and colour (Jarman 1987: 151–5). If Jarman cannot ignore the weeds in the garden of England, he was also ready to see the roses. In an interview at the end of 1990 in which he discusses his recent illness and attacks Thatcher's 'starving of the NHS', Jarman continues with this praise for its workers and care-givers:

> One great positive thing in all this has been the care I have received at St Mary's [Hospital] in Paddington. And the way that fortunately, I can say that nobody has stepped out of a room when I entered it, or has not shaken me by the hand. People are better than that, you see. More tolerant and more open than Mrs Thatcher ... would allow. (In Chalmers 1990: 18)

Out of his own suffering, as out of the alternative practice of his films, Jarman conjures both vitriol and sweetness.

He recovered from the illnesses of 1990 sufficiently well, not only to, as he had promised, witness Thatcher's fall from power, but also to conclude his artistic life with a burst of energy quite extraordinary for a man who was in-and-out of hospital. Accompanied by 'ghost' director, Ken Butler, who took charge when Jarman was too sick to come to the set, he completed a queer *Edward II* (1991), stretching Marlowe's words and theme to include such details as a nude rugby scrum and a happy ending in which the homosexual king escapes his bloody fate. Jarman continued his rediscovery/recreation of the lives and loves of his queer heritage – though somewhat less explicitly – in *Wittgenstein* (1993).[21] Just as he cheekily claimed to have 'improved' Marlowe's play, here Jarman substantially adapted an original screenplay by leftist Oxford don, Terry Eagleton, substituting more of the philosopher's biography for his philosophy – deemed a sickness of the mind with which he must be careful not to infect young men – and light-heartedly adding a Martian against whom Wittgenstein tests his theories of language-games. Both these films continue Jarman's aesthetic of spartan sets upon which are staged events bejeweled with surprises – songs, aliens, OutRage demonstrations.[22] While the palate of *Edward II* is restrained, *Wittgenstein* is awash with primary colours. We see these, too, in the rush of paintings of the final years. The last paintings were, like the last few films, created with the substantial aid of assistants whom Jarman instructed in the throwing of paint.

The final film presents just one colour: *Blue* (1993) offers up a monochrome blue screen for the full course of its 75-minute duration. It is accompanied, however, by a complex soundtrack, which features some of Jarman's most frequent collaborators (Tilda Swinton, Nigel Terry), and, as it chronicles his illness – including his failing sight – returns to several of the themes discussed above. Paradoxically, one focus is on the decrepit, visually-depressed conditions of the NHS. Jarman deplores: 'Two light bulbs/Grimly illuminate/The flaking walls/There is a box of dolls/In a corner/ Indescribably grimy/The doctor says/Well of course/The kids don't see them/There are no resources/To brighten the place up' (1993: 22–3).

The influence of Thatcher over Tony Blair's Labour government has clearly been substantial. The health service remains in a tenuous situation, though the last remnants of Clause 28 were finally abandoned in 2003. It is commonplace to see Thatcher's ideologies and policies as having changed the face of Britain. What, however, of Jarman's influence and legacy, ten years after his death? There have been many books;[23] several of his collaborators have flourished;[24] the garden is often visited; and *Jubilee*, *The Tempest* and *The Last of England* are newly out on DVD. Still, it is hard to see a contemporary figure in British cinema who combines Jarman's artistry with his blunt determination to make his point. Without Thatcher, perhaps, the targets for attack are less obvious.[25] Opening the Edinburgh Festival's tribute to Jarman in 2002, Tilda Swinton recalled pointing out that Jarman was in some sense the 'great Thatcherite filmmaker': all his films made money (for someone) within two years (2002: 12). She sees Jarman as the equivalent of a party host who provided the atmosphere that made the filmmaking possible, and she regrets the absence of such a figure today (2004: 76). Still, she has hope for a successor: 'in so many ways you never could disappear, but – it has to be faced – in so many you have. It has snowed since you were here and your tracks are covered. Fortunately, you made them in hard ground' (2002: 12).

Derek Jarman's films, paintings and words display his refusal to accept his sickness as a position of powerlessness. While laying claim to a British tradition in his art, he also revised that tradition as he made his specifically homosexual films of palliation and comfort. Arousing the disquiet, sometimes the fury, of the mainstream, Jarman made films that, beyond suffering and sickness, brought about a fusion of the traditional and the unexamined. He writes: 'Now you project your private world into the public arena and produce the flashpoint: the attrition between the private and public world is the tradition you discover ... When everyone has taken the path we are all art and no audience' (1987: 236). The effect is continually to re-open practices and spaces to the public, to dissolve the boundaries, to seek other homes and gardens in the name of a greater national health.

NOTES

1 Princess Elizabeth, the future Queen, and Philip Mountbatten.
2 A white paper is published by the government and proposes upcoming legislation.
3 The Queen opens each session of Parliament in the UK with a speech that lays down the general tenor of government activity over the period. The Queen is herself purely a mouthpiece for the elected party's policies.
4 In Britain, 'public schools' are of course synonymous with private schools.
5 It would be interesting to see the images that Spider (Malcolm McDowell) is taking with his miniature camera, one so small that it seems as if it might, as in arthroscopic surgery, film *within* the body and is thus more closely connected to it even than the Super-8 camera of Jarman.
6 For an insightful analysis of the state of the British film industry of this time that takes off from Welland's comment see Roddick (1982).
7 *The Angelic Conversation* includes fourteen of the sonnets.

8 Jarman's response to Stone includes the assertion that Michael Powell's *Peeping Tom* (1960) would, in its day, have made Stone's list of sick movies. Powell, who is mentioned by Stone as an example of a British 'tradition of quality', has also been much praised by Jarman at various times.

9 Jarman describes the scene and his feelings on first being told that he was HIV-positive in Jarman (1987), 16–17.

10 Baglione accuses Caravaggio of 'ignorance and depravity' and thus predicts the stand Stone and others later take towards the work of Jarman, Frears and others.

11 Jarman came to prefer the term 'queer', actively using it to re-assert homosexual identity and thus re-orienting its connotations.

12 Clause 28, a part of the 1987 Local Government bill, read: 'a local authority shall not a) promote homosexuality or publish material for the promotion of homosexuality; b) promote the teaching in any maintained school of the acceptability of homosexuality as a pretended family relationship by the publication of such material or otherwise; and c) give financial assistance to any person for either of the purposes referred to in paragraphs a) and b) above.'

13 For a detailed analysis of issues of homelessness in *The Last of England*, see Driscoll (1990).

14 Consider, for example, this report from David Brindle in *The Guardian Weekly* of 30 December 1990: 'With an estimated 3,500 hospital beds closed to save money, the position is likely to deteriorate as health authorities struggle to balance their books in time for the government's NHS changes in April.'

15 'In the Psychiatrist's Chair' was a weekly programme broadcast on the BBC's Radio 4 in which celebrities discuss aspects of their lives with psychiatrist Dr Anthony Clare. Jarman's interview was first heard on 15 August 1990.

16 Mention should be made here of Isaac Julien's narrativeless and lyrical 'This is not an AIDS Advertisement' (1988) about which Julien says: 'There needs to be a space for mourning and this tape is dedicated to those losses.' This video, along with Julien's comment, is included in the package 'Video Against AIDS' put out by Video Data Bank. Their package also includes Pratiba Parmar's *Reframing AIDS*, a project with which Julien was also involved.

17 Jarman was suffering from tuberculosis and toxoplasmosis, before regaining his fragile health sufficiently to embark on the long-cherished *Edward II* (1991) project.

18 In 2004 the Tate Gallery in London organised guided tours of Jarman's garden.

19 Jarman says proudly of *The Garden*: 'When did you see the landscape look like that? It looks like Turner' (quoted in Romney 1991: 13).

20 The revolving arm of the radar reprises Jarman's use of a similar tracking apparatus in *The Angelic Conversation*. In the earlier film, however, the stop-motion effect that Jarman uses throughout breaks up the circling motion into stuttering fragments.

21 This aspect of Jarman's films is the focus of William Pencak's (2002) volume.

22 The OutRage group protested anti-homosexual legislation and outed closeted gays. Jarman saw them as 'the inheritors of Edward's story' (1991: 146).

23 Most important of these volumes is Tony Peake's fine biography from 2000.

24 Tilda Swinton continues to receive acclaim for many challenging films, including *Orlando* (1993), *The War Zone* (1994) and *The Deep End* (2001), as well as occasionally appearing in more commercial fare, such as John Maybury's bio-pic on Francis Bacon, *Love is the Devil* (1998), *The Beach* (2000) and *The Chronicles of Narnia: The Lion, The Witch and the Wardrobe* (2005); Christopher Hobbs has continued to gain prestige as a designer, as has Sandy Powell as a costume designer.

25 Compare *The Who* singer Roger Daltrey: 'The establishment is much more insipid now, like a blancmange. Before it was much more rigid, and you could kick it' (interview on BBC Radio 2, 26 June 2003).

WORKS CITED

Anon. (1990) *Politics Today*. London: Conservative Research Dept., 19 May.

Brindle, David (1990) 'NHS Waiting Lists Rise to Nearly 1 Million', *Guardian Weekly*, 30 December.

Chalmers, Robert (1990) 'Please God, Send Me to Hell', *Sunday Correspondent*, 18 November.

Charity, Tom (1991) 'Avant-gardener', *Time Out*, 3 January.

Crimp, Douglas (ed.) (1988) *AIDS: Cultural Analysis. Cultural Activism*. Cambridge and London: MIT Press.

Driscoll, Lawrence (1990) 'Burroughs/Jarman: Anamorphosis, Homosexuality', *Spectator*, 10, 2, 78–95.

Jarman, Derek (1984) *Dancing Ledge*. London: Quartet.

_____ (1986) *Derek Jarman 's Caravaggio*. London: Thames and Hudson.

_____ (1987) *The Last of England*. London: Constable.

_____ (1988) 'Freedom Fighter for a Vision of the Truth', *Sunday Times*, 17 January.

_____ (1989) *War Requiem: The Film*. London and Boston: Faber and Faber.

_____ (1990) 'Positive Thinking', *Listener*, 16 August.

_____ (1991) *Queer Edward II*. London: BFI.

_____ (1993) *Blue*. London: Channel Four/BBC Radio Three.

_____ (1995) *Derek Jarman's Garden*. London: Thames and Hudson.

Johnson, Marion (1983) 'Carry On ... Follow That Stereotype', in James Curran and Vincent Porter (eds) *British Cinema History*. London: Wiedenfield and Nicholson, 312–27.

Mars-Jones, Adam (1987) 'Remission', *Granta* 22. London: Penguin, 171–93.

Peake, Tony (2000) *Derek Jarman: A Biography*. Woodstock and New York: Overlook.

Pencak, William (2002) *The Films of Derek Jarman*. Jefferson, NC: McFarland.

Roddick, Nick (1982) 'Breathing a Little Harder than Usual', *Sight and Sound*, 51, 3, 159–63.

Romney, Jonathan (1991) 'The Garden of Earthly Delights', *City Limits*, 3 January.

Stone, Norman (1988) 'Through a Lens Darkly', *Sunday Times*, 10 January.

Swinton, Tilda (2002) 'Letter to an Angel', *Guardian*, 17 August.

_____ (2004) 'When the Party's Over', *Sight and Sound*, 14, 3, 76.

Treichler, Paula (1988) 'AIDS, Homophobia and Biomedical Discourse: An Epidemic of Signification', in Douglas Crimp (ed.) *AIDS: Cultural Analysis. Cultural Activism*. Cambridge, MA and London: MIT Press, 31–70.

Walker, Alexander (1985) *National Heroes*. London: Harrap.

Watney, Simon (1987) *Policing Desire*. Minneapolis: University of Minnesota Press.

_____ (1988) 'Policing Desire: Pornography, AIDS and the Media', in Douglas Crimp (ed.) *AIDS: Cultural Analysis. Cultural Activism*. Cambridge, MA and London: MIT Press, 71–86.

19. LOW HOPES: MIKE LEIGH MEETS MARGARET THATCHER

David Sterritt

Life is abrasive for a lot of people, and there's no getting round it. I think the function of art – and the cinema not least – is to confront these things ... I'm absolutely committed as a filmmaker to be entertaining and to amuse; but I am also concerned to confront.

– Mike Leigh (in Sterritt 2000: 43)

The good that came from the Thatcher years was the fight against her.

– Jeremy Hardy (2000)

THE FIGHT

Margaret Thatcher's policies and personality sparked oppositional fights of many shapes, sizes and degrees of intensity. Some of these played out on movie and television screens, where a striking range of filmmakers created works vastly more antagonistic than those usually found in earlier traditions of British cinema. Mike Leigh was an important figure in this energetic set of skirmishes. Albeit in a more oblique manner, his movies of the Thatcher era join the best productions of such filmmakers as Derek Jarman and Stephen Frears by displaying an urgent 'disgust with the current state of British life' and charting 'the inexorably downward spiral of their homeland', in Lester D. Friedman's words (see his introduction to this volume. They remain strongly relevant today, moreover, by virtue of Leigh's ability to see 'far beyond the passing concerns of partisan politics'. In short, Leigh is a gnome-like, bushy-bearded poster boy for those Thatcher-era artists who instinctively knew that their 'alternative vision' need not be 'overtly political' but could accomplish its mission by carefully chronicling its milieu, raising crucial questions, and dredging up discontents glossed over by the myths and mystifications of Thatcherite consensus and conservatism. Like the most gifted of his peers, Leigh thus 'defined a turbulent era, revived the moribund British cinema, and froze a crucial moment in British culture'.

All this would surely have driven Thatcher crazy if she had been paying attention. But she did not do so then and apparently has not done so since, given Leigh's assertion in 1997 that 'Margaret Thatcher is nothing but a philistine. Naturally, she doesn't communicate with artists of any kind. So I've got no letter saying she hates my movies.[1] But she's not sophisticated enough for that anyway' (in Worth 2000:122).

THE FILMS

Leigh produced his first theatrical feature (*Bleak Moments*, 1971) and his first television movie (*Hard Labour*, 1973) not long before Thatcher won the leadership of the Conservative Party in 1975; his comedies *Nuts in May* and *The Kiss of Death* arrived in 1976 and 1977, respectively, and his masterly *Who's Who* had its BBC-television premiere in the year (1979) when her Tory administration took power. From the beginning, his seriousness of purpose was as evident as his belief in humour as a frequent, often grim conceptual tool. *Bleak Moments*, a title as uninviting as it is accurate, tells the mordant tale of a pathologically shy English teacher reaching vainly for romance with a secretary whose companions include a mentally-challenged sister, an insufferably perky office mate, and an ineffectual young activist who rents her garage for his political work. *Hard Labour* chronicles the life and times of a professional cleaning woman whose days are consumed by exactly what the movie's name says – and exactly what it hints at with its implication of underprivileged English life as a virtual prison term. *Nuts in May* comically pits a pair of middle-class holiday-makers, all too pleased with themselves and the solutions they have found to life's problems, against the relatively undisciplined types they cannot help rubbing elbows with at their chosen camping ground. *The Kiss of Death* focuses on an assistant undertaker caught between the stark profundities of death and the equally stark superficialities of working-class life and love. *Who's Who*, discussed at length below, contrasts the private lives of brokerage-firm employees who stand on different rungs of the business-world ladder.

Leigh's subsequent social satires of the Thatcher decade range from *Grown-Ups* (1980) and *Home Sweet Home* (1982) to *High Hopes* (1988) and *Life is Sweet* (1990), with the acerbic *Meantime* (1983) and the equally topical *Four Days in July* (1985) sandwiched in between. After she left 10 Downing Street in 1990, Leigh vented his ongoing sociopolitical anger in the brilliant 1992 short *A Sense of History*, written by and starring his actor-friend Jim Broadbent, and the 1993 feature *Naked*, one of the most ferocious anti-establishment diatribes in memory. *Grown-Ups* and *High Hopes* both take as a starting point the fact that lower-class and middle-class people may find themselves living literally next door to one another in states of mutual bewilderment and incomprehension; in the former film an old woman's state-financed flat somehow persists in an otherwise gentrified neighborhood, while in the latter film a street's arbitrary division into council flats and privately-owned apartments results in a scruffy couple discovering that their former schoolteacher lives just yards away. Sex, seduction and social workers are among the ingredients of everyday experience in *Home Sweet Home*, about a trio of postal-service workers and their families. *Life is Sweet*, a breakthrough Leigh film in terms of international visibility, takes a frequently despairing but ultimately hopeful look at a household whose members include twenty-something twins, one an outwardly well-organised plumber and the other an inwardly disorganised slacker with a snarling expression and an obsessive sex life. (David Thewlis plays her lover, in a superb performance that Leigh had to trim down for the final cut – a move he regretted and decided to compensate for by organising a subsequent movie, *Naked*, entirely around Thewlis's excellent acting.) *Meantime* is another tale of dysfunctional family life, pulling no punches in its squirm-inducing portrait of bratty youths (one of whom imitates a friend by becoming a skinhead, to his own instant embarrassment) and their ill-mannered elders. Set against the backdrop of the Irish 'troubles', *Four Days in July* is at once a topical drama and a characteristically Leigh-like comedy about all-too-ordinary existence in contemporary Ireland.

Leigh then turned to more intimate topics with the family drama *Secrets & Lies* in 1996, the comradely comedy *Career Girls* in 1997, and the brilliant (if uncharacteristic) Gilbert and Sullivan portrait *Topsy-Turvy* in 1999. While some critics saw these projects as retreats into a mellower mode by an ageing and increasingly domesticated filmmaker, Leigh proved them wrong with *All or Nothing*, his compassionate 2002 drama about the miseries of family life in a working-class tenement – which grow all the more miserable when a family member is struck by horrific illness – and the 2004 release *Vera Drake*, about a middle-aged cleaning woman of the 1950s who performs illegal abortions in her spare time – driven not by profit or ideology, but by an intuitive conviction that she is simply providing desperately needed care to desperately needy women.

This catalogue of Leigh's movie work (he has also been active in stage productions) demonstrates his continuing concern with social, cultural and political issues. Although the budgets and production values of his films have spiralled upward since *Naked* and *Secrets & Lies* gained international renown, such movies as *All or Nothing* and *Vera Drake* demonstrate his sustained commitment to acute observation of British society and powerful criticism of its shortcomings.

LEIGH'S LIFE

Leigh's wish to confront has been consistent since he entered the public eye with the unsparing *Bleak Moments*, produced as a play in 1970 and a feature film in 1971. Confrontation is also detectable in his personal manner at times; he has been known to mock an audience member publicly for asking a poorly conceived question in a post-screening discussion, for instance. Psychologically speaking, this trait of Leigh's may stem from a subtly disorienting sense of belonging to more than one socio-cultural world – or conversely, to no socio-cultural world at all – in his early life. Born in 1943 in Salford, a Manchester suburb, he grew up in England's industrial north. His grandfather, Mayer Liebermann, had emigrated from Russia to England in 1902, and his father – a Jewish physician who abbreviated the family name – took pride in being an educated professional who chose to live and work among less fortunate people. This exposed young Mike to an offbeat blend of well-schooled intellectual environs and steady interaction with the working class.

Leigh attended the local Salford school, and by the beginning of his teens he was determined to be a stage or film director. What he later called 'the most important, seminal experience' was his acquisition 'by a fluke' of a scholarship to the Royal Academy of Dramatic Art (RADA), where beginning in 1960 he 'trained as an actor in the most sterile atmosphere' and 'spent two formative years questioning *everything* in that whole procedure' (in Bank 2000: 115). He moved in 1963 to the Camberwell School of Art in London, where he studied drawing and painting; he started night classes at the London School of Film Technique the following year. His first stage work, *The Box Play*, was produced in 1965. Subsequent biographical milestones include the appearance of *Bleak Moments* on stage and screen; his marriage to actress Alison Steadman in 1973; the acceptance of his BBC-television movie *Grown-Ups* by the London Film Festival in 1980; his formation of the production company Thin Man Films with Simon Channing-Williams in 1989; and a pair of Cannes Film Festival triumphs: his best director prize for *Naked* in 1993 (accompanied by David Thewlis's award for best actor) and the Palme d'Or given to *Secrets & Lies* as best film in 1996. The latter also garnered Leigh his first Oscar nomination as best director; the second was for *Vera Drake* in 2004.

It was at RADA in the early 1960s that Leigh began to 'sense other [cultural] things that were happening' and to start exploring them. Influenced by adventurous stage artists like the Living Theatre and Jerzy Grotowski, filmmakers like John Cassavetes and the French New Wave directors, and avant-garde innovations like the Happenings of Allan Kaprow, he hit upon the notion that 'writing, directing, designing, and filmmaking could all be combined on the floor rather than at the desk' (in Bank 115–6). From his newfound strategies and insights came his career-defining practice of developing his projects in tandem with his performers and technicians during long periods of improvisation and rehearsal.[2] Leigh has described this process often, as in the concise account he gave critic Howie Movshovitz in 1994:

> In broad terms, I gather a cast together and we go into rehearsal ... It's a question of creating characters and investigating their relationships, backgrounds and their ideas, and arriving at the premise for the film, and then working from a very simple structural outline ... I then build the film up on location by rehearsing it from an improvisational state into a very tight, very highly disciplined condition, sequence by sequence, and shoot it ... It's the kind of work that is obviously highly creative and collaborative for the actors. But the contributions of designers and cameramen are [also] greater than normal because everybody shares all aspects of the work. So you can get a rock-solid inner truth – textural, social accuracy – and a heightened, distilled cinematic, dramatic [and] even hopefully – although it sounds pretentious – poetic end-product. (In Movshovitz 2000: 52–3)

Leigh's own position is as flexible and open-ended as anyone else's. 'I know a lot and nothing at the start,' he says. 'I'm not an intellectual filmmaker; I'm an intuitive and emotional filmmaker ... I have feelings on the go and conceptions, which are more from the gut than the brain' (in Movshovitz 2000: 53). His function is not so much to craft polished results as to carve galvanising moments from the living rock of living performances. 'At its simplest,' he says, 'things happen in improvisation which I then structure, and that's the end-product. But mostly that's not the case: mostly what I do is to challenge what's happened and thus arrive at a more interesting dramatic essence' (in Carney with Quart 2000: 163).

Between the movie version of *Bleak Moments* in 1971 and the release of *High Hopes* some seventeen years later, Leigh's production funds came from television rather than theatrical-film sources. Some critics therefore divide his film career into TV and theatrical phases. I find such a division close to meaningless, given the consistency of Leigh's concerns and his organic growth as an artist, although of course the aesthetics of such larger-scale works as *Naked* and *Secrets & Lies* are affected by the expectation of big-screen distribution. In any case, while Leigh's definitive turn from TV films to theatrical films in the late 1980s enabled him to broaden his visual scale, he was careful not to let the wide screen interfere with the sense of psychological intimacy and political pungency he had cultivated in his earlier work.

LEIGH'S LEANINGS

It is clear in retrospect that the psychological and political aspects of Leigh's work reached some of their most imposing heights during the 1980s. Going against the grain of mainstream production in Britain and elsewhere, his movies had a distinctive aura that attracted attention from audiences and critics, whether pro or con. More important, they offered an implicit challenge to the set of individualist, materialist and consumerist mindsets that were Thatcher's regrettable gift to the nation that had elected her. The politics of the movies were more often implied than overt, and film scholar Ray Carney has valid reasons for writing that Leigh's pictures do not 'offer [palpable] political alternatives or solutions in the Ken Loach mode' (2000: 6). What needs to be added, though, is that Leigh's cooperative, communal methodology itself served as an implicit critique of the Thatcherite selfishness that the filmmaker so feared and loathed.

Along with Leigh's refusal to be a writer-director in the usual calling-all-the-shots mould has gone a refusal to indulge many of the commonest practices in popular film, including – crucially, in my view – resolving stories with neatly tied-up conclusions, and ladling meanings or messages over the material like so much faux-nutritious sauce that is not nearly as good for you as the chef insists. Leigh has no particular qualms about being called a 'political' artist as long as those using the label understand it the way he does. 'I don't do films that are agenda-driven,' he told me in a 1996 onstage conversation at the Telluride Film Festival during which we discussed his career as a whole. 'I don't do work that is ... propagandist,' he continued. 'But nevertheless, what I do is kind of political, in the sense that my characters are always identifiable, and I instinctively draw them in their social and economic contexts.'

A phrase like 'kind of' seems kind of evasive to Leigh sceptics, of course, and Leigh is very much aware that he has been criticised for not being more politically aggressive. Since his movies have always told straightforward stories with everyday characters, he recalls having an especially 'bad time' during much of the 1970s because this approach was 'unfashionable' in that period. 'People said it was a bit decadent, old-fashioned, square', he told me. 'It didn't look avant-garde, it wasn't abstract or surreal enough ... I said I wasn't concerned with that. The art was there, and I didn't want to advertise it!'

The politics were there too, deeply embedded in his straightforward stories with their everyday characters. Leigh is a subtle enough thinker not merely to pronounce but actually to believe that there is no dividing line between the personal and the political – or at most a dividing line that is as shifting, permeable and blurry as can be. Leigh's definition of 'a political act' is

> just to share with other people things that you feel, in a way that makes them feel in
> some way. What I'm concerned with is the way we live our lives, and what politics should

be concerned with is the way we live our lives, and what our lives are about. It's terribly important there are filmmakers whose films have very direct, specific, political objectives, and it's terribly important that those films work and cause changes to happen ... but I don't make films of that kind ... I make films where I don't leave you clearly able to conclude what I'm asking you to think or feel. I make films that ask a great number of questions but ... don't come up with too many answers. And I hope I make films where you walk away from the [theatre] with work to do, arguments to have, things to worry about, things to care about ... In that sense, I would regard what I do as political. (Sterritt 1996: 13)

Filmmakers as different as Jean-Luc Godard and Spike Lee, who also raise questions whose answers must be found in *real* struggle *outside* the movie theatre, might readily say the same.

An excellent example of Leigh's desire to erase boundaries between the personal and the political is *High Hopes*, the 1988 comedy-drama that marked his return to theatrical filmmaking after some seventeen years of television-funded production. The poles of personal and political are marked from the outset by one of the film's primary settings, a London block where an important character – the creaky Mrs Bender, played by Edna Doré in a sympathetic, empathetic performance – lives in a lone working-class council flat, right next door to one of the gentrified apartments that have taken over the neighbourhood in the years since her son Cyril and his siblings grew up there. She meets her comparatively posh middle-class neighbours – the Boothe-Braines (Lesley Manville and David Bamber) – when she inadvertently locks herself out of her home.

We have already met her son Cyril (Philip Davis), and his wife Shirley (Ruth Sheen), at their own modest home, where the movie began with an unexpected visit from Wayne, a lost young stranger in need of directions. Cyril and Shirley help him out with the wry good humour one might expect from a pair of leftover flower children who have given the name Thatcher (or 'Fatcha', as they pronounce it) to their largest, prickliest living-room cactus. They then pay a visit to Cyril's mum, sneak a peek into the Booth-Braine flat via the front-door letterbox, and get on with their lives, which include Cyril's job as a motorcycle messenger and Shirley's occasional complaints about her unfulfilled desire to have a child. The rest of the movie gives us additional visits with the Boothe-Braines; views of emotional combat between Cyril's self-important sister and her self-satisfied husband; quiet time with Cyril and Shirley – including their long-delayed farewell to Wayne, who finally glides out of their lives on a bus – and, at the climax, a birthday party for Cyril's mother that culminates in a nasty family row, much of which is heard on the soundtrack as Leigh brilliantly holds his camera on a close-up of the old woman's tacitly suffering face.

Described by one account as a 'sometimes bleak satire' about 'the clashes between families and social classes in late twentieth-century London', this remarkable film looks forward to the more acerbic *Naked* in various ways, from its candid political discourse to its ruthless lampoon of middle-class pretension via the Boothe-Braines, who anticipate the solipsistic landlord character (called both Jeremy and Sebastian) in the later film. Numerous reviewers criticised *High Hopes* for exaggerating the fatuity of this middle-class couple, while others defended Leigh by claiming that if he made upwardly-mobile people into less-than-human caricatures, that is only the flip side of how Thatcher treated their working-class counterparts; when I suggested this interpretation to Leigh in 1996, however, he rejected it, asserting that his portrait of the Boothe-Braines was realistic, pure and simple. The more I watch the movie, the more I tend to agree with Leigh's view.

As for Cyril and Shirley, the key moment expressing their politics comes during a visit they make to Karl Marx's grave – a fascinating moment of overt political-philosophical contemplation rare in Leigh's work. 'The philosophers have only interpreted the world in various ways,' Shirley reads from the German philosopher's London memorial stone 'the point, however, is to change it.' Then she wanders over to the grave of a South African communist leader, where her attention quickly turns from deep issues to the sort of flowers people plant on burial sites. This leaves Cyril alone for a moment to ruminate aloud. 'The thing is, change what?' he not-so-rhetorically asks, interrogating Marx even as he gazes at the philosopher's graven head with undisguised awe and reverence. 'It's a different world now, in'it? By the year 2000, there'll be 36 TV stations 24 hours a day, telling you what to think.' Little does he realise that the number of channels (although not their range and variety) will far exceed this in some countries, as what French thinker Guy Debord (1977) calls the 'society of the spectacle' steadily tightens its capital-fuelled grasp. What is important, though, is how accurately Cyril senses the social drift, and how willing he is to criticise as well as venerate Marx's contributions. 'Pissin' in the wind, eh?' he concludes, again pointing toward *Naked* in his mood of mingled melancholy and futility.

JOHNNY'S JEREMIAD

Naked is arguably Leigh's most openly political film. It is also among his most unabashedly angry works, showing the scars he accumulated as an Englishman who clinically observed the results of Thatcher's policies on the people he cares about most: other Brits of the less-than-privileged classes. *Naked* had its world premiere at Cannes in May of 1993, about two-and-a-half years after Thatcher resigned as Prime Minister upon losing her Conservative Party leadership. Technically it is a post-Thatcher production. But discursively it is a compendium of concepts and emotions stirred up in Leigh by her rule – and its aftermath, since a phenomenon as powerful as Thatcherism could obviously not have waned overnight, even if she had not been succeeded in office by John Major, her protégé. 'The only caveat I would sound when people remember the joy of her departure is that her legacy is still with us,' wrote columnist and satirist Jeremy Hardy in *The Guardian*, 'both in the privateering policies of New Labour and in the shape of all those cringing underlings of hers still in circulation' (2000).

Here is a passage (many others would serve equally well) that sums up aspects of England under Thatcher that Leigh and the movie's main character, Johnny, find particularly galling. Asked if he was bored in Manchester before fleeing to London at the beginning of the film, Johnny replies,

I'm never bored. That's the trouble with everybody – you're all so bored. You've 'ad nature explained to you and you're bored with it. You've 'ad the living body explained to you and you're bored with it. You've 'ad the universe explained to you and you're bored with it. So now you just want cheap thrills and like plenty of 'em, and it dun't matter 'ow tawdry or vacuous they are as long as it's new, as long as it's new, as long as it flashes and fuckin' bleeps in forty fuckin' different colours. Well, whatever else you can say about me, I'm not fuckin' bored! (Leigh 1995: 21)

Johnny's jeremiad against boredom amounts to an impassioned indictment of the 'society of the spectacle', a state of affairs wherein once-active tendencies toward meaningful thought and action (introspective in the manner of theory, or extroverted in the manner of practice) are diverted into cynically manipulated pathways at once *unproductive* for socio-political improvement and *productive* of profits for those who control means of production, distribution and above all exhibition, not only of cultural products but of anything that can conceivably be publicised, sold and bought – which, in the era of high-tech 'free market' ideology fostered by Thatcher and her ilk, means anything and everything there is.

Johnny's words struck a strong and disturbing chord among moviegoers, including American ones, among whom I count myself. As an American writing about a British filmmaker, I must stress that nearly everything Leigh explores and conveys in his best movies is as applicable to post-Vietnam culture in the United States as to British society in the Thatcher era. Thatcher inherited power from a Labour administration that had run out of steam, losing its ability to keep up even a credible appearance of progress toward a better country, a more empowered citizenry, a more humane world. She was succeeded by Major, a handpicked heir whose combination of working-class background and upper-class airs would be fine fodder for the barbs of a ferocious Leigh satire; his administration has been followed by the Labour regime of Tony Blair, who speaks of George W. Bush in words as fawning as those accorded to Ronald Reagan by Thatcher, who called herself 'his biggest fan'. In a similar manner, Jimmy Carter's uncertain Democratic administration gave way to two (count 'em) terms of Reagan's feckless rule, one (inexcusably) of George H. W. Bush's bloodthirsty administration, two (against all odds) of Bill Clinton's faux progressivism, and now two (don't get me started) of George W. Bush's escalating cryptofascism. Thatcher's reckless promotion of 'traditional values' at least had the unintended consequence of fostering a cinema of outrage led by figures as various as Isaac Julien, Derek Jarman and Leigh, among others. We still await an equivalent opposition – or even a pale imitation thereof – on the American screen.

All of this helps account for Johnny's resonance with audiences despite the violent failings in his personality and behaviour. Played by Thewlis in one of the most bravura film performances of recent decades, Johnny is an almost literal embodiment of intellectual and emotional anger at what Thatcher and her overseas counterparts have wrought. (Thewlis was a key co-creator of *Naked*, of course, contributing a great deal of the film's verbal and cerebral heft.) To be sure, the movie's many moments of physical and psychological 'shock and awe' have been condemned by some critics as sensationalism, misogyny, misanthropy, or all three. While aspects of Johnny's behaviour undeniably partake of such ugly qualities, this is central to the film's strategy of rubbing our noses in facets of Thatcher-era psychology that have sometimes been difficult for even her critics to face; these centre on the sociological fact that certain particular notions of masculinity have been crucially important for many young, working-class Englishmen to embrace, or at least to think they are embracing – these being sexual potency, freedom of libidinal expression, and feelings of male entitlement and self-sufficiency. The unemployment and sense of diminished (or depleted) usefulness imposed on working-class men during the Thatcher era militated against such values, driving some young men literally crazy with social-psychological frustration. Johnny is among these emotional casualties. But he remains mighty intelligent, and the filmmakers have not lost sight of the finely honed purposes driving Thewlis's character and Leigh's story. Johnny's words and actions have a directly political intent, serving as comments 'about the society we live in – the inequality between the sexes, the races, the classes', as Thewlis told me in 1993, a few months before the film's American debut, going straight to its political heart. Leigh makes the same point in slightly different words. He has described Johnny as 'an idealist who's so frustrated that he turns in on himself and becomes angry with the world [so that] everything he says and everything he expresses ... is a lamentation on the terrible grip of materialism and the terrible lack of values in society'. These resentments, Leigh further notes, 'are things which I share in essence' (in Billington 1999).

Brimming as he is with lamentations and critiques, Leigh has claimed no easy solutions to the social, economic and cultural problems faced by his characters. Nor has he used Thatcherism, or anything else, as a reason to treat those characters more gently than they deserve as individuals who are ultimately responsible for their own existential destinies. Critics who misunderstand this complain that Leigh aims sarcasm and derision at folks too personally addled or culturally deluded to live proper lives. Quite the contrary: he belongs to a brave handful of filmmakers (such as Arturo Ripstein and Luis Buñuel) who refuse to romanticise, patronise or condescend to disadvantaged people. His body of work swells with compassion for individuals who, beneath their motley exteriors, are neither more nor less worthy than you or I of social conditions that encourage the abilities to love, work and feel a sense of inner dignity. Leigh sees no need to convey this in sentimentalised terms, though. Few amiable personality traits are evident in *Meantime*, for instance, a 1983 movie seen as dis-seminating 'a disturbing smog of defeatism' by even so strong a Leigh supporter as Michael Coveney, his biographer (1996: 171). But what this 'smog' chiefly illustrates is Leigh's acute attunement to political realities, since for many people 'defeatism' was a forced option in the Thatcher era. Leigh's aversion to narrative palliatives of 'hope' and 'redemption' is exceeded only by his aversion to romanticising – as opposed to accurately, dispassionately depicting – the awful conditions endured by the people he portrays. Indeed, the genesis of *Meantime* and its smog was simultaneously personal and political for Leigh:

> When I was shooting *Home Sweet Home*, I had this terrible flat ... over a shop in the barren Bedfordshire countryside ... I was in the bath, listening to the radio ... and this story came on about two unemployed kids in Warrington or St Helens or somewhere who had committed suicide. And I thought – I always go through something like this – what we're doing [as filmmakers] is irrelevant. *That's* what we should be doing. Something about unemployment. We were two or three years into Thatcher, it was already an issue, and it lingered at the back of my mind. (In Coveney 1996: 171–2)

It came to the front of his mind before long, generating a film in which Leigh chose 'quite consciously, to say, this is that world where everybody's unemployed, which is the primary condition of what's going on' (1996: 172).

FAMILY VALUES

Meantime is a tragicomic commentary on that world, and also on an institution that faces especially high hurdles therein: the family, in this case the working-class family, challenged at the best of times and besieged at the worst of them. Thatcher sounded off about 'family values' with rhetorical and propagandistic fervour. She took office 'attacking the permissive society and trumpeting traditional bourgeois values like respectability, family and nation,' as film historian Leonard Quart puts it in this volume; yet despite her 'ritualistic deference to the prime significance of the family,' her aggressively promoted economic policies often 'subverted many of those same values'.

In an interesting critical twist, Leigh has been accused of echoing Thatcherite attitudes in portraying the English family. 'In celebrating the virtues of the privatised family as a kind of escape route from political impotence and passivity,' claims critic John Hill with regard to *High Hopes*, 'the film, for all its apparent "socialism", appears to end up reinforcing the very scepticism about more collective (or "socialist") forms of political action that was already such a feature of this era' (quoted in Watson 2004: 91). Noting that *High Hopes* culminates with the decision of a working-class couple to have a child, Hill writes that 'while the film may, in this way, succeed in expressing values of care and responsibility which cut across the prevailing ethos of Thatcherism, it only does so by partly reproducing conservative (and, indeed, Thatcherite) values regarding the family and women' (2004: 92). Hill's argument should interest observers of both British and American society, since members of both have become adept at chirping platitudes about 'family values' while using their own families as veritable wagon trains providing self-obsessed, xenophobic, fiercely intolerant circles of defence against whatever may threaten them, challenge them, or simply call their complacency into question.

This said, I agree with Garry Watson that Leigh does not see 'the privatised family' as an 'escape route' from the need for collective social action. For one thing, Leigh's films reveal an intricately complex attitude toward the family, which he celebrates as haven, home base and familiar terrain – all compatible with the 'escape route' hypothesis – but which he also radically problematises as *huis clos*, inflictor of physical and spiritual claustrophobia, and site of oppressions, rebellions and competitions that inscribe a fiercely critical near-microcosm of Thatcher's nation as a whole.

For another thing, Leigh has had a streak of socialism (without Hill's quotation marks) in his political personality since early life, along with a complementary streak of anarchism and an ingrained scepticism toward all things capitalistic. As noted, he grew up during the 1940s and 1950s in a northern working-class area. 'There was a Labour government which started a national health service,' he said in 1991 to a journalist interested in his Jewish roots, 'that is now being destroyed by the Tories. The first thing my father did was to dispose of his private patients as soon as he could … We weren't Orthodox, but there were a lot of Zionists in the family that went back an unusually long way.' In the 1950s he and fellow members of Zionist youth groups 'shared our money and learned about socialism … It liberated us from the bourgeois, provincial Jewish constraints. We were actually rather anarchic, but we also worked by getting people together in groups and working creatively.' These experiences helped form Leigh's artistic aspiration 'to be sympathetic to everybody and at the same time be tragic and comic' (in Stone 2000: 28–9).

LOST IN SPACE

Leigh sees solid links between English society's increasingly materialistic, acquisitive strain and the fate of the English family. This is illustrated even by *Naked*, which Leigh says is about 'the waste and the unpredictable nature of things' bequeathed to England by Thatcher and her political heirs. While he says he 'didn't want to make a documentary about homelessness' he adds that 'everybody in it, in a manner of speaking, is rootless, or at least displaced ... So the discussion about family continues, but here by default rather than directly' (Carr 2000: 56). Even though family operates in *Naked* as a submerged issue rather than a conspicuous theme, therefore, the film is an affecting sidelong glance at an institution Leigh sees as anything but a ready escape route. If it *were* one, surely the movie's desperate characters would make a stab at escaping through it! Leigh elaborated further on his political views as *Naked* started to reach a wide public:

> The fabric of society is crumbling in England, there are people all around the streets. And while *High Hopes* was on one level a lamentation for socialism being something that maybe has gotten lost somehow, [*Naked*], if I come out of the closet about it, takes more of an anarchist view. I despair that society really will be able to organise itself, ever ... In the end, what [*Naked*] is about is this guy, like a kind of lost communication satellite, floating around the atmosphere, wasted ... I wanted to do a millennium film, and the peculiar thing I felt about a possible pending apocalypse is that it doesn't seem incredibly unfeasible now. (Ibid.)

WHAT'S WHAT

Linking family considerations with the political import of even Leigh's homeliest films, it is revealing that Thatcher's father – who 'shaped her political personality', as Quart observes in this volume – was a 'petit-bourgeois Methodist grocer and self-made man' who 'lived by such values as self-help, moral virtue and public duty'. *Mutatis mutandis*, a wide array of Leigh characters can be described in similar terms.

Alan Dixon in the masterly *Who's Who*, made in 1979 on the very eve of Thatcher's heyday, is a perfect example. Played by Richard Kane, he is as petit a bourgeois as one can imagine, shuttling between his job as mid-level clerk in a London brokerage firm and his home life as householder, hobbiest and husband to a cat fancier (Joolia Cappleman) who clearly cares more about her felines than about her spouse. Perhaps as compensation for his domestic tedium, Alan indulges a sincerely-felt investment in 'moral virtue and public duty' by giving over a substantial portion of their house (and his brain) to a secular shrine celebrating English values of the most conspicuously reactionary kind. His collection comprises royal portraits, impeccably maintained charts of aristocrats and their families, autographs from the rich and famous – or, when the rich and famous refuse to comply, form letters refusing his requests – and other such curios.

Among the many oddities here is that Alan's collecting of lore and mementos has not given him much real knowledge of the aristocratic scene. A cheeky co-worker demonstrates this near the end of the film, feeding Alan a line of bogus information that Alan responds to not honestly – 'I didn't know that' – but with the sorts of uninformed clichés and platitudes that he feels his type of patriotic chap *should* say in these circumstances.

While this aspect of *Who's Who* casts a sardonic light on the petty end of the middle class, another aspect does the same for the *hautes bourgeoises* on the other end. Much of the film chronicles a dinner party given by two upper-level brokers. These scenes are a *tour de force* of satirical analysis, portraying what is essentially a piddling little get-together at which the drinkers and diners work ferociously hard to convince themselves they are having an absolutely fabulous time enjoying the privileges that (in their eyes) people like them automatically deserve. At the end of the evening they are bored, tired and literally fed up in stomach and soul, although nobody present would dream of admitting this. One of Leigh's most perfectly-titled films, *Who's Who* is a superb summary of the fixation on *breeding* that Thatcherism eagerly inherited from a class-obsessed past and turned to its own power-driven purposes. In this movie as in life, manipulative notions of 'moral virtue and public duty' shore up the Thatcherite cultural cluster of neo-Darwinian ideas, 'mythic meritocracy', and prostration before 'traditional bourgeois values like respectability, family and nation' as Leonard Quart describes it.

It is not so much these values that Leigh attacks – although attack them he does, when necessary – as their uncritical embrace by a citizenry that uses them to stave off any temptation to think scrupulously about society and (dare one say it?) to change that society in ways that could make it better for people just like them, not to mention folks even less well off. Leigh deploys seemingly humdrum materials to provoke his audience into recognising the dread liabilities of self-deluding lifestyles and ideas.

Also crucial is Leigh's insistence on addressing political and ideological issues not in theoretical terms (even those of 'against the grain' popular cinema) but rather in terms of the routines and rituals by means of which real, everyday people conduct their real, everyday lives. Carney puts this well when he observes that each of Leigh's figures 'is seized up in an emotional and intellectual "cramp", which manifests itself as a mechanical routine or pattern of thought and feeling' that allows Leigh to play out verbal and visual realisations of his two deepest commitments: 'a rejection of all idealised, abstracted, intellectualised understandings; and a belief in the centrality of social connection and involvement' (2000: 148–9).

CRAMPS AND CONNECTIONS

Such talk of mental cramps and social connectivity helps focus attention on the deeper dimensions of Leigh's more 'entertaining' works, which have often been mistakenly assessed as snobbish lampoons of English mannerisms. It is hard to write about Leigh without citing the late Dennis Potter's famously dismissive *Sunday Times* review of *Abigail's Party*, produced on the London stage in 1977 and aired by the BBC on the popular *Play for Today* programme in a hurriedly-shot film version of regrettably poor technical quality.[3] Writing about its television version, Potter called it an exercise in 'rancid disdain' that amounts to a 'prolonged jeer, twitching with genuine hatred, about the dreadful suburban tastes of the dreadful lower middle classes ... [that sinks] under its own immense condescension. The force of the yelping derision [becomes] a single note of contempt, amplified into a relentless screech' (quoted in Coveney 1996: 120). Nor do particular performances escape Potter's eagle eyes, as when he condemns Steadman's allegedly 'nasty' portrayal 'of the dreadful, blue-lidded Beverly', whose 'every gesture [is] honed into such lethal caricature that it would not [be] too surprising if she ... suddenly changed shape in the manner of the fat, thin or elongated reflections in a fairground mirror' (quoted in Watson 2004: 12). One would hardly guess from this outburst that *Abigail's Party* aims its barbs not at derisory individuals, but rather at the materialism and conformity into which they have been educated, indoctrinated and funnelled by the tenor of modern British society. Evidently the film's deadly serious critiques were too deeply embedded in the story's dark comedy for Potter to appreciate them for what they were.

This has happened more than once in the ongoing dialogue between Leigh's movies and the critics who interpret them. His works have always gone against the grain of mainstream assumptions, offering an implicit challenge to the self-satisfied set of materialist, consumerist attitudes that Leigh has long feared and loathed in Western culture. The key word here – and the approach that has confused Potter and other sceptics – is 'implicit'. Leigh has rarely used the in-your-face tactics of a Ken Loach or a Derek Jarman, whose films throw their cards more aggressively onto the ideological table.

Still and all, how could a writer as generally smart and sensitive as Potter react to *Abigail's Party* with such misjudgement and hostility? I think illumination lies in the extreme fretfulness he expresses over Steadman's performance, with its constant risk of shape-shifting grotesquerie and (one presumes) its threat of psychological disintegration too fractured and disorienting for a defenseless viewer to bear.

TICS AND POLITICS

An important term in Potter's tirade is 'gesture', every one of which in Steadman's portrayal (according to Potter's review) is honed into 'lethal caricature' of angst-producing volatility. Italian philosopher Giorgio Agamben argues that by the end of the nineteenth century the Western world had largely lost the interest in body language, or gesture, that had earlier fascinated many observers. Along with this 'obliteration and loss of gestures' came an inability to understand the 'transfigura-tion [of gestures] into fate', that is, a misapprehension of what the symbolism of gestures can express and reveal about distinctions between 'power and act, natural-ness and manner, contingency and necessity' (2000a: 52). In this climate, the main compensatory mechanism found by artists was 'theatre', by which Agamben means a 'precipitous attempt to recover the lost gestures in extremis' via whatever forms of aesthetic articulation (modern dance, Proustian prose, and so on) lent themselves to so radical an enterprise (2000a: 52–3). Chief among these was silent cinema, then a fledgling art. Agamben asserts that modernists must break the 'paralyzing power' of images as 'immovable and eternal forms', instead liberating them into fragments of mobility and gesture. All of which leads to the conclusion that 'cinema has its centre in the gesture and not in the image', which means film 'belongs essentially to the realm of *ethics* and *politics*', not merely to that of aesthetics (2000a: 54–5; my emphases).

Leigh's films are emphatically about gesture, which means in Agamben's terms that they are emphatically about ethics and politics. Their gestures include the characters' physical movements, of course. They also include Leigh's cinematic moves, such as his frequent habit of cross-cutting between two mutually illuminating scenes and his occasional decision (as in the *Grown-Ups* stairway scene) to record highly mobile action with a largely immobile camera. And they include the dialogue spoken in his stories, which is usually so meagre in informative or interesting content (even to the characters themselves) that it often recalls the anything-but-empty emotional silences in a typical Harold Pinter play. *Naked* aside, Leigh's major characters speak mainly in clichés, platitudes and truisms so trite that we barely need listen to intuit what they are meant to convey – namely, a ritual recognition that somebody else is in one's company and etiquette requires one to acknowledge this by making vocal noises. The speech that ensues may have utilitarian value, as when an employer offers well-meaning advice (such as *The Kiss of Death*) or asks a guest (such as *Who's Who*) how she is planning to get home; or it may carry overtones of caring and affection, as when couples anticipate having a baby (such as *Home Sweet Home*) or siblings open up to each other (such as *Life is Sweet*) in unexpected ways. Most of the time, though, speech among Leigh's characters is more a matter of reflex sound-making than of communication on a richly human scale. Leigh and company use (inarticulate) speech and (ungraceful) movement not as actorly devices to tell and teach us things, but rather as *gestures* meant to be felt and fathomed in purely *expressive* terms that convey revealing clues about ethical and political pressures in the inhibiting, often suffocating culture that Thatcher fostered and encouraged.

And they convey so much! Once again, Agamben cuts to the quick of political modernity when he asserts that the meaningfulness of gesture started to regain its lost recognition when neurologist Oliver Sacks, MD, unexpectedly noticed three apparent cases of Tourette syndrome during a brief stroll down a New York City sidewalk in 1971 – the same year when Leigh was embarking on his major phase with *Bleak Moments*, tellingly enough. Agamben hypothesises that observers lost sight of this (intrusive!) twitchiness for some one hundred years for the very reason that the stresses of modernity made it ubiquitous; that is, 'ataxia, tics, and dystonia [have] become the norm and … at some point everybody [has] lost control of their gestures and [is] walking and gesticulating frantically' (2000a: 51). Leigh's characters are not always frantic, outwardly at least; but deeply dysfunctional things are going on within them, thanks to Thatcherism and other causes. Leigh's self-appointed task is to recover their reality and significance, not just aesthetically but socially, culturally and always already politically.

BAD ACTING

Sadly yet perhaps inevitably, Leigh's cinema of observation is seen by some critics not as an enduring exercise in courageous analysis but as a lazy indulgence in that old bugaboo of cutting-edge cinema, bad acting, abetted in this case by bad improvising and bad screenwriting. This is not the place for a thoroughgoing look at such

Grown-Ups (1980): Mayhem erupts when working-class neighbors bring a family crisis to a schoolteacher's staircase next door

a contentious topic, so I will make only two observations. One is that bad acting unquestionably exists – take it from me, a movie reviewer for almost forty years – and often in films that instantly, lastingly capture the public imagination. The other is that some of modern cinema's most gifted directors have been outrageously dismissed for eliciting performances taken as 'bad acting' for the sole reason that they signal authentic human truths rather than the manufactured Hollywood truths we have been educated (or conditioned; or brainwashed) to regard as realistic. These directors are a diverse lot – the indefatigable Cassavetes and the brilliantly perverse Andy Warhol are textbook specimens of very different types – and while Leigh has certainly made mistakes and miscalculations, he is the equal of those giants in terms of tenacious vision, radical methodology and unstoppable integrity.

The rise, hegemony and legacy of Thatcherism are among the factors that have prodded Leigh into probing the ineffable realities that our all-too-effable exteriors do such a lamentably good job of concealing in historical periods ruled by 'surplus-repression', a phrase from Herbert Marcuse (1955) that distills the essence of the Thatcher era. Leigh's is a cinema where talk is not small, it is microscopic; where gesture is not grand, it is ungainly; where cups of tea are craved and clutched like talismans; where comedy blurs into tragedy not by accident but according to the filmmaker's poignant, precisely calibrated purposes. Above all, it is a cinema of noises, bodies and (to invoke the title of a seminal Cassavetes film) of faces, whose tics, ataxia and dystonia are endlessly revealing symptoms – revealing, that is, if we can overcome our post-Thatcher brands of Thatcherism enough to realise that attention *must* be paid to them. This is why Agamben gets the final word, exquisitely describing goals that Leigh's best artistry invariably strives for:

All living beings are in the open: they manifest themselves and shine in their appearance. But only human beings want to take possession of this opening, to seize hold of their own appearance and of their own being-manifest. Language is this appropriation, which transforms nature into *face*. This is why appearance becomes a problem for human beings: it becomes the location of a struggle for truth ... We may call tragicomedy of appearance the fact that the face uncovers only and precisely inasmuch as it hides, and hides to the extent to which it uncovers ... Be only your face. Go to the threshold. Do not remain the subjects of your properties or faculties, do not stay beneath them: rather, go with them, in them, beyond them. (2000b: 90, 93, 99)

Going with faces, in faces and beyond faces is precisely what Leigh and his most indelible characters manage, often haphazardly and inadvertently, to do. They and their breed are the anti-authoritarian, the anti-culture-industry, the anti-Thatcher itself made cinematic flesh. They are rough beasts, to be sure. But the world has been a more compelling place since they started slouching into Leigh's studios to be born.

NOTES

1   The character called Alan Dixon in *Who's Who* (1979) would have treasured such a letter, as a bolster for his self-esteem rather than (far more appropriately) the opposite! Dixon's devotion to Thatcherite notions in *Who's Who* is discussed later in this essay.

2   The credits of Leigh's earlier films say 'devised and directed by Mike Leigh', while the later ones say 'written and directed by Mike Leigh', indicating the importance he places on his own role as guiding figure during the improvisation process and as collector/collator of the results into a finished screenplay that may then be published under his name. The term 'devised by' has always seemed a bit more accurate and honest to me in Leigh's case than 'written by', but he rarely loses an opportunity to reiterate the core importance of collaboration in his work. He is not the only director to solicit primary contributions (narrative ideas, character traits, dialogue) from his actors, of course; the French auteur Jacques Rivette and American filmmaker Robert Altman are among the others who regularly do so.

3   Supporting my low assessment of the film *qua* film is Leigh himself, who has called it 'really quite a mess' with 'patchy, inconsistent lighting' and occasional glimpses of a carelessly handled microphone swinging into frame (see Coveney 1996: 114).

WORKS CITED

Agamben, Giorgio (2000a [1992]) 'Notes on Gesture', in *Means Without Ends: Notes on Politics*. Minneapolis: University of Minnesota Press, 48–59.

____ (2000b [1995]) 'The Face', in *Means Without Ends: Notes on Politics*. Minneapolis: University of Minnesota Press, 90–9.

Bank, Mirra (2000 [1997]) 'Mike Leigh', in Howie Movshovitz (ed.) *Mike Leigh: Interviews*. Jackson: University Press of Mississippi, 113–21.

Billington, Michael (1999) 'Mike Leigh Interviewed: II – Mike Leigh's Filmic Style', in 'Mike Leigh Interviewed', *Guardian Unlimited*, 11 November. Available online: http://film.guardian.co.uk/Guardian_NFT/interview/0,4479,110594,00.html.

Carney, Ray with Leonard Quart (2000) *The Films of Mike Leigh: Embracing the World*. Cambridge: Cambridge University Press.

Carr, Jay (2000 [1994]) '*Naked*: English Director Mike Leigh Turns His Uncompromising Vision on the Way Things Are', in Howie Movshovitz (ed.) *Mike Leigh: Interviews*. Jackson: University Press of Mississippi, 55–8.

Coveney, Michael (1996) *The World According to Mike Leigh*. London: HarperCollins.

Debord, Guy (1977) *Society of the Spectacle*. Detroit: Black & Red.

Hardy, Jeremy (2000) 'The Bitter End', *Guardian*, 25 November. Available online: www.guardian.co.uk/Thatcher'Story/0,2763,402708,00.html (accessed 25 July 2005).

Leigh, Mike (1995) '*Naked*', in *Naked and Other Screenplays*. London: Faber and Faber, 1–95.

Marcuse, Herbert (1955) *Eros and Civilisation: A Philosophical Inquiry into Freud*. Boston: Beacon Press.

Movshovitz, Howie (2000 [1994]) 'Mike Leigh's Grim Optimism', in Howie Movshovitz (ed.) *Mike Leigh: Interviews*. Jackson: University Press of Mississippi, 51–4.

Sterritt, David (1996) 'Sensitive *Secrets & Lies* Reflects Creative Journey', *The Christian Science Monitor*, 27 September, 13.

____ (2000 [1993]) 'Mike Leigh Calls It as He Sees It', in Howie Movshovitz (ed.) *Mike Leigh: Interviews*. Jackson: University Press of Mississippi, 42-4.

Stone, Judy (2000 [1991]) 'Mike Leigh', in Howie Movshovitz (ed.) *Mike Leigh: Interviews*. Jackson: University Press of Mississippi, 26–9.

Watson, Garry (2004) *The Cinema of Mike Leigh: A Sense of the Real*. London: Wallflower Press.

Worth, Larry (2000) '*Lies* Director Shows True Colors', in Howie Movshovitz (ed.) *Mike Leigh: Interviews*. Jackson: University Press of Mississippi, 122–3.

INDEX